STACK

Date Due

JAN 31 1978

FEB 13 1978

PRINTED IN U.S.A.   CAT. NO. 24 161   BRO DART

P9-DFX-886

Discovery

Discovery

The Autobiography of
Vilhjalmur Stefansson

McGraw-Hill Book Company
New York   Toronto   London

Vilhjalmur Stefansson
1879—1962

ELMWOOD PUBLIC
LIBRARY
PROV.R.I.

Discovery

Copyright © 1964 by Evelyn Stefansson.
All Rights Reserved. Printed in the United
States of America. This book, or parts
thereof, may not be reproduced in any form
without permission of the publishers.

Library of Congress
Catalog Card Number: 64-16477

First Edition

60960

SEP 1 8 1965

B
St322s

To my wife,
Evelyn

c M. V. O.
112677

Contents

One

1 An Ancient Race in a New Land

As I sit in my study under the elms of northern New England beginning to write about the events of my long life, Iceland, Manitoba, Alaska, and the islands of the Canadian Arctic seem a very long way off.

Discovery has been my life. First the discovery, as a boy, of the New World. Then the discovery of the new ideas that were sprouting like prairie wheat in that world. Then the discovery of ancient people and unknown lands, and now, at last, the discovery of what discovery itself has done to my life.

Among the lands that I was fortunate enough to be the first man to find were perhaps the last unknown islands left for the discoverer. If we are to believe the genealogists, the discoverer of the first new lands in North America and of the last, more than nine hundred years later, were members of the same family. After 1920, when historians and geographers began pointing out that I had made the final discoveries of unknown land in North America, the professional cultivators of family trees began offering to trace my descent back to Leif Ericson, who accidentally discovered America, and to his father Erik the Red, who deliberately set out to explore an unknown polar land and thus became the first known planner of a polar expedition.

The story of Scandinavian penetration westward from the time of Erik the Red until the present was made into a modern Icelandic saga in 1927 by the chief librarian of Iceland, Dr. Gudmundur Finnbogason, when he wrote the first book length account of my life.

3

With surprising ease, Dr. Finnbogason traced my ancestry as far back as 1621. In his book he also recorded the birth date of my father, Johann, as January 11, 1830, and that of my mother, Ingibjorg, as September 1, 1842. I have no better records for these two events.

My family's move to North America was the result of a fairly sudden determination to leave the homeland to which their ancestors had come as immigrants nearly a thousand years before. In 1875 my parents were stirred by the talk of a group of north-coast Icelanders who had become passionately eager to settle in Brazil. Icelanders are great coffee drinkers. It was enough for the group to know that in Brazil they could grow their own coffee instead of having to pay cash for it. Soon leaders had recruited enough souls to load a ship and head for South America, by way of Glasgow, Scotland, and Canada.

Coffee or no, not all the emigrants ended up in Brazil. The Governor General of Canada, the Marquess of Dufferin and Ava, had twenty years earlier made a trip to Iceland in his yacht and been very much impressed with the people he met there. In his account of the trip, published in his book *Letters from High Latitudes*, and in speeches he made in Canada, he maintained that Icelanders, knowing how to make their living in a treeless country, would be ideal colonists for the Canadian prairies, then referred to as "the Barren Grounds."

My parents, while aware of Lord Dufferin's desire to attract Icelanders, were signed up for Brazil and fully expected to go there with their children. But for a scapegrace half brother of my mother, I should probably have been born south of the equator.

I never saw my Uncle John Anderson, but I well remember photographs of him, particularly one showing Uncle John in a cutaway coat, with a tall silk hat and a ribboned monocle. The childhood tales I heard of him came naturally to my mind some thirty years later when I read about Get-Rich-Quick Wallingford. It happened that Uncle John had moved to Canada in 1874. In 1876 he started back to Iceland as an agent of the government of Nova Scotia, hoping to see that province get its share of the Icelandic immigration that Lord Dufferin was encouraging as part of his plan for a greater Canada.

When his ship reached Glasgow, Uncle John presumably knew nothing of the Brazilian venture, and he certainly had no thought of my family emigrating to Brazil. When he learned that a shipload of Icelanders was in the harbor, bound for South America, he climbed aboard and began haranguing the group on the folly of sailing to a far-off jungle when their ship would first make port in a land that was especially eager to welcome sturdy Scandinavian settlers. Many of the coffee lovers were won over, my parents among them.

Uncle John was selling Nova Scotia, a land of great forests, not the Governor General's Barren Grounds. The Marquess, however, was considerably more influential than Uncle John, and my family and others found themselves en route for Manitoba and the Hudson's Bay Company post of Fort Garry, which was then just beginning to get used to its new name of Winnipeg.

At Winnipeg, other forces began to exert their influence. The prominent men of the town had been hearing a lot about Dufferin's Icelanders, no doubt visualizing them as Eskimos clad in furs. When the new arrivals turned out to look like ordinary Scandinavians—indeed, much like ordinary Scots or Englishmen—the Canadian government's reception committee suffered an attack of compassion. What a shame it would be to ship these unsuspecting people out to the Barren Grounds. After all, in Manitoba, especially to the north along Lake Winnipeg, there was plenty of forested land available for homesteading. Up there, the Scandinavians could build of logs such cabins as they had been used to in Norway. The Winnipeggers also knew that "all Scandinavians love fish," and there was no lack of fish in Lake Winnipeg. The compassionate Winnipeggers were overlooking one minor point: those particular Scandinavians were Icelanders who had never seen a log cabin, having left forested Norway for treeless Iceland, by their own choice, more than a thousand years before.

Thus were the Governor General's good intentions thwarted by contrary intentions that were equally good. My parents and most of the other immigrants went north into the woods, though some of the party stayed in Winnipeg and took jobs. As far as I know, no Icelanders settled on the prairie at that time, though many did later. As for my parents and others like them, unused to axes, they learned to chop down trees; unused to log cabins, they learned to build them; unused to practically everything that they were expected to do, they nevertheless did the unaccustomed.

For their pains in becoming docile cabin dwellers, my parents, along with several hundred fellow Icelanders, were welcomed on September 13, 1877, by the Governor General, now reconciled to their location. After fifteen hundred words of greeting, some of them mildly cautionary but all of them pleasantly sugar-coated, the Governor General closed with:

> No race has a better right to come among us than yourselves,
> for it is probably to the hardihood of Icelandic navigators that
> the world is indebted for the discovery of this continent . . .
> and remember that in coming among us you will find yourselves
> associated with a race both kindly-hearted and cognate to your
> own; nor need you forget your own time-honored customs, nor the
> picturesque annals of your forefathers. On the contrary, I trust
> that you will continue to cherish for all time the heart-stirring
> literature of your nation. . . .

It might seem, then, that Lord Dufferin wanted the Icelanders to retain their national character, to adhere as steadfastly to their language and culture as had the French settlers in Canada. But other counsel prevailed. Instead of clinging to their own customs and traditions, the Icelanders shed them, rapidly becoming English in language and Scottish in names, Scots then being the most fashionable of nationalities in Manitoba. It seemed desirable for my father to become John Stephenson. My older sister, then about fifteen, happened to have a name that was popular, so she remained Inga. My thirteen-year-old brother changed from Johannes to Joseph, and I grew up to know him as ''Joe.''

These changes took place in 1878, the year after Dufferin had urged the Icelanders to remain forever proud of their customs, their literature, and, presumably, their names. A year later, I was born to parents who had planned to call me Vilhjalmur. In due course I was christened. The name entered in the parish records was William. My father, I feel sure, never called me that, though most others did. Mother, I know, always called me Vilhjalmur, or ''Villi'' for short. To my playmates and schoolmasters I was Willie Stephenson, graduating to ''Bill'' in my teens. Not until I was in my junior year at college did I develop the moral courage to change my name legally to the Old World Vilhjalmur.

2 Growing Up on the Prairie

Thanks to the Icelanders' taste for coffee, my uncle John's taste for power and profit, the dreams of the Marquess of Dufferin and Ava, and the compassion of the Winnipeggers, I was born in a log cabin in the tiny and very little known village of Arnes on the west shore of Lake Winnipeg. The region round about was known, not unnaturally, as New Iceland. Arnes, situated in a forest from which the Indians had not long since departed, was little more than a post office. It lay some twenty miles north of New Iceland's metropolis, Gimli, which means "Heaven," though the word should be interpreted in the Old Norse and pre-Christian sense, as a place agreeable to the Teuton gods. Gimli was a hundred miles or so north of Winnipeg.

I received my first limited view of New Iceland on November 3, 1879. In several respects, 1879 was a memorable year in arctic studies. In Europe, an International Polar Conference was held at Hamburg, the first such conference in history. In the Canadian north, Lieutenant Frederick Schwatka, a brilliant exponent of living off the land, completed one of the great sled journeys of all time. In the course of his search for traces of the long-lost Sir John Franklin expedition, Schwatka helped to develop the technique of sled travel. In the Arctic Ocean, Lieutenant Commander George Washington De Long of the United States Navy, an adventurous explorer but no scientist, contributed without knowing it, through an ill-fated expedition in which he and all but two of his companions lost their lives, scientific evidence that had a profound effect upon the future

7

of exploration in the North Polar basin. Wreckage from De Long's ship, the *Jeannette,* lost off the New Siberian Islands, a hundred-odd miles north of the center of the Soviet Arctic, turned up some years later off the west coast of Greenland, proving what many had previously doubted: the existence of strong and steady currents in the Arctic Ocean.

During 1880, floods in our part of Manitoba destroyed farm buildings, crops, stored hay, and cattle and left many a pioneer family to starve. In that tragedy I lost a brother and a sister. The rest of us, along with many of our neighbors, saved ourselves by the pioneer method of getting up and going elsewhere. In our case, elsewhere was across the United States border into what was then Dakota Territory. First we traveled south along the Red River of the North, passing through Winnipeg at a time when the newly arrived Canadian Pacific Railway was transforming that onetime outpost into a metropolis, and continued by riverboats to the international boundary at Pembina. From there we thumped, creaked, and rattled by ox wagon southwesterly across a fertile prairie that must have seemed, so low and flat was it, scarcely free from danger of inundation by the flood waters of the Red River.

We took up a homestead on somewhat higher and safer, if less fertile, land where there was ample timber for building. Our farm was about two miles west of a place, later a post office, called Mountain. It was so named because from it could be seen what appeared to be a range of hills running north and south. In reality, this was only an escarpment marking the site of the long-vanished glacial Lake Agassiz and dividing the low prairies of the Red River Valley from the higher plains stretching westward to the Missouri River and the Rockies.

Here, in a one-room cabin somewhat grander than most because it had an upstairs loft in which we children slept, I began my life as what most citizens of the United States—in apparent disregard of those other inhabitants of the Americas who live north and south of them—still call an American.

It is not easy at the age of eighty-one to determine what event was the first to become permanently fixed in my memory. In my case, it may have been an eclipse that coincided with my recovery from measles. I clearly remember being in bed with an excruciating headache. I also recall that suddenly everybody rushed outside, leaving the door open and allowing a cloud of chill air to enter the cabin. This must have been in November or later. Excited chatter blew in through the open door, and I, in my white nightshirt, presently found myself standing barefoot in the snow with the others. I looked skyward, as everyone else did, at a darkening edge of the sun. I cannot now swear that it was not the darkening edge of the moon, though I seem to remember a sun about two hours high in the west.

My early childhood memories really begin with the marriage of my sister Inga, who was sixteen years older than I. I confess that I recall this event more in terms of my own discomfort than of her glory. Our cabin was so filled with boisterous people, bulky buffalo-skin overcoats, and plates of food that I had great difficulty finding a place to sleep. I do not know whether or not this early unfavorable impression of a wedding had anything to do with the fact that I myself never went through any such ceremony until I was past sixty.

A background for all my early recollections is reading and being read to. Icelanders are a bookish people, and my first connected memories relate to the alphabet and the Bible, both in Icelandic. Letters and the Bible are linked in my mind through the fortunate circumstance that spelling in Icelandic is phonetic, or more nearly so than that in most European languages, so that a person can begin spelling his way through even the most difficult work as soon as he knows the names and sounds of the letters. I can see the Bible open before me on a table and hear myself reading aloud while my mother did the household chores, half listening, correcting me occasionally or stepping over to have a look at a troublesome word. It was not my mother, however, who taught me to read but an old itinerant teacher who traveled from farm to farm, staying at each place long enough to teach the boys and girls the reading and writing of the alphabet and to show how the letters and their sounds might be combined into written and spoken words. He must have visited our farm sometime in my fifth year, or early in my sixth, for I have my mother's word for it that I read the whole Old Testament to her before I was six.

Reading aloud in the winter evenings was a common custom among Icelanders. In the old country, books had been few and costly. Lights—tallow candles or fish-oil lamps—had been scarce, and there had been much work to do in the long evenings. The practice had grown up that the best reader in a family, man or woman, would sit by the best light and read aloud while the others worked where they could listen. There was no shortage of kerosene lamps in Dakota Territory, but still it was always the reader who was granted the grace of light.

What we read most often were the Icelandic sagas, narratives composed mainly in Iceland and preserved only there. Some of them (especially the prose and poetry called Eddas) had no doubt been written in Norway and perhaps also in Ireland, during the two or three centuries immediately preceding the Scandinavian colonization of Iceland soon after A.D. 850. What we transplanted Icelanders listened to of a winter evening was in effect the history, religious literature, and ancient lore of northwestern Europe, chiefly of Scandinavia but with echoes from Finland, Russia, Germany, Britain, Ireland, and even the Mediterranean countries.

Not only were there the Icelandic sagas to compete with Scripture; there was also a weekly newspaper, one that had been started by another of my mother's half brothers, Friman Arngrimson, who Anglicized his name only in part: to Friman Anderson. The paper was *Heimskringla* (*The Round World*), still published in Winnipeg. Between the sagas and the newspaper, I was weaned away from my early interest in the Bible, though I returned to it later in life.

It was natural for an Icelander to try to learn English by starting with the alphabet and going on from there. Indeed, before they left Iceland, a good many of our people had learned some English that way, and apparently they were able to read and understand the language. Pronunciation, however, was another matter; if they did attempt to speak English at all, it was scarcely recognizable as such. In the early days of New Iceland, I was told, the immigrants often "talked" with their non-Scandinavian neighbors by writing down what they wanted to say and getting written answers.

I do not think I learned any English in this fashion, and even after I started going to school outside of the classroom we spoke mainly Icelandic. As nearly as I can recall, my first lesson in my second tongue was *cat, the cat, my cat*, as found in Appleton's *First Reader*. Now and then I have been asked to feel sorry for myself because the Bible I read aloud to my mother was not the King James Version and my first school reader was not McGuffey's. It seems to me, however, that there is something to be said for knowing the Bible in two languages, even if neither of them be Hebrew or Greek, and for having been able to judge the merits of the McGuffey readers, when first I saw them, in the light shed by a college degree.

Our schooling was always irregular because few of the communities near us had money enough to hire a teacher for more than three or four months a year. I got along by walking several miles in one direction for three or, at most, four months, and then walking as many miles in another direction to catch a last month in another school before it, too, closed.

It seems to me now that I never knew much about my parents. My recollection of my father is of a silent and homely man, unimpressive in appearance. Yet, I know now that the impression that he made in his small circle on those who talked with him, and had a chance to be influenced by his personality, was significant. But it was only some years after he died and after the Boer War began that I first suspected that, under proper circumstances, he might have been a great, or at least a powerful, man. This suspicion might have been the result of his marked resemblance to Paul Kruger, President of the Transvaal. By reading all I could find about Kruger, I came to the conclusion that his personality and gifts were much like my father's, with one exception: Kruger was old-fashioned and orthodox in his religion.

Father was not really irreligious; nor was he against the church. Today he would be called a modernist. He believed in remaining within the Lutheran Church, of which we were members, but he wanted the church to modify and improve its teachings to meet every advance in knowledge. For this view he was looked at askance by most of our neighbors, who were unable to see how there was any room, in our already perfect church, for progress and improvement.

In our community there were a small number of persons called freethinkers who tried to get everyone to read Thomas Paine, Thomas H. Huxley, and Charles Darwin. Unlike most Icelanders, my father was a poor linguist, and the works of those liberal authors were, in our part of the country, available only in English. This handicap may have kept my father from leaving the church and possibly finding greater intellectual companionship among the freethinkers. As it was, his liberality was too much for the orthodox and not enough for the radicals. He really belonged nowhere.

In politics it was the same way. He did not quite fit into the Democratic party, though he always voted their ticket—partly, I think, because he believed in free trade and partly because, by temperament, he always belonged to the minority and Dakota was hopelessly Republican. It was natural that it should be, with its large proportion of Scandinavian and German settlers, who had all been against slavery and bore the Democrats a grudge for having been identified with it in a war that was then no farther back in the past than World War II is today. The Danes, Norwegians, and Swedes were, I believe, solidly Republican in the 1880s. The Icelanders, however, were at least one-third Democrats. Those who believe that blood will tell may attribute this to the fact that Icelanders are, by descent, at least one-third Irish. Grover Cleveland's victory in 1884 must have been a great triumph for my father, but I remember it only vaguely, for I was then only five. I was nine when Cleveland was defeated by Benjamin Harrison, and I remember it as a devastating blow to our whole family. Cleveland's return to power in 1892 was for all of us a rebirth of hope.

That my father read no language other than Icelandic prevented him from keeping abreast of advances in biology and other sciences; however, he was able to read more widely in the fields of politics, sociology, history, and literature, for on these subjects there were available many works, both original and translated, in Icelandic. It is well known that the Icelanders print about twenty times as many books per capita as their nearest literary competitor. My father read many Icelandic books, ancient as well as modern, no more slighting the sagas because of some recent poetic drama than Americans neglect Shakespeare because of the popularity of Robert Frost.

A typical Icelandic intellectual environment had been transplanted without much change from the homeland to the Dakota prairies. A pioneer who read, in translation, Mill's *On Liberty*, Homer's *Iliad*, and Goethe's *Faust*, certainly had some opportunity to form independent opinions of the intellectual world. My father had such opinions and argued them at great length, though perhaps not as frequently as he argued about predestination or free trade, for religion and politics were the chief concern of our community.

If the typical Icelander is by inclination literary in taste—if not especially so in the actual practice of writing prose and verse—there are exceptions, and my mother was one of them. She was said to have been beautiful, and was considered a handsome woman in middle age. My recollection of her extends only from her forty-fifth to her eighty-fifth year. She had very beautiful hair and more than half believed that its beauty and abundance resulted from the practiced rite of combing and trimming it only in the dark of the

The Early
Years

Top — Rosa, Mother, and Inga
Middle — 1887: Age 8, with my
  sister Rosa
Bottom — My mother and father

Above — At age 18
Below — My brother Joe, whose hero is obviously Buffalo Bill

On the steps at Harvard Divinity School

Above — A freshman at North Dakota
Below — My mother's half-brother, Johannas, who brought us to the New World

Lawson's, National Photographic Gallery, Edinburgh

moon. My mother's attitude toward her hair was an indication, I think, of her intellectual status. She believed in such rites, although public ridicule would make her conceal her feelings about them.

My father, on the other hand, was constitutionally unable to believe in such superstitions. No amount of ridicule or social pressure could have induced him to modify either his beliefs or his expression of them. Pressure, in fact, was likely to have the opposite effect. This, as I see it, was not mere contrariness on his part. It was an attribute of his nature, and I perhaps understand it because I, too, possess it in some degree.

My mother seldom read, partly because a pioneer woman's farm work was never done and partly because she lacked the inclination to do so. When she did read it was almost always the Bible—not, I am sure, with any literary motive, as many people read the Bible today. She had two consuming ambitions: to have all of her family get into heaven and, before we got there, to have me, at least, become a clergyman.

As I grew a little older, religion and politics began to impress themselves upon me. I speak of religion because it seemed more important at the time. When we were able to go to church, we had no daytime readings on the Sabbath. If we stayed home, only the Bible was read aloud, and psalms were sung. In church the preaching was always Lutheran, at first the variety brought from Iceland, but later a modification adopted by one or another of the Lutheran synods of the United States, chiefly the Missouri Synod. Sunday evenings we read devotional works and sang more hymns.

The devil was then as real to me as wolves, pigs, or goblins— was indeed a goblin. I remember that I used to crawl up on our square, red-cloth-covered dining table when partly religious and partly folklorish evening discussions were going on, afraid to have my legs dangle over the side lest the devil lurking underneath grab them. Sometime in my seventh or eighth year, I became conscious of an evil trinity: Robert Ingersoll, Darwin, and the devil.

It was not long after that that I began to be worried that my father was growing dangerously liberal. Among the first English expressions I remember learning, possibly during my seventh year, were "liberalism in religion" and, perhaps somewhat later, "higher criticism," suggesting the trend that such matters were taking in our family. Our minister, too, I gathered, was growing dangerously liberal, even more so than my father, for I heard him inveighing against the Missouri Synod of the Lutheran Church. Still and all, I remember no opposition from the minister or from my father when Mother wanted me to be confirmed so, in effect, I swore that I would believe in the teachings of the church. The confirmation came none too soon, I now realize, for I had actually started by then to disbelieve in Santa Claus. Loss of faith in the devil cannot have been far behind.

About this time my center of interest began to shift from religion to politics.

In school and out, my reading and thinking began to change. What seems now to have affected me most was an intellectual change in the social environment. I began to be conscious of a kind of general ferment. The sagas, when they were read aloud, were no longer mere stories. They began to have meaning applicable to my time or to some other period of history. We began to ponder the degree to which they might properly be called historical, the purity of the tradition that they enshrined, their literary merit as compared one with another or with the literature of other peoples, such as Greeks, Romans, Hebrews. It seems to me that for some reason our interest began to shift more and more toward the Old Testament.

Extreme schools developed among those who lived by the Bible. To some, the Scriptures were the literal and perfect writing of God "from the first letter of the first word to the last letter of the last word." This statement I was later told had come from Dwight L. Moody. To others, the Bible was merely the folklore of the Jews, less historical, on the average, than the Icelandic sagas. The Biblical God, along with the gods of other peoples and literatures, was the creation of untutored fancy. Although I do not remember hearing Moody quoted by name on the perfection of the Scripture, everybody knew who it was that had said, "An honest god is the noblest work of man." It was Robert G. Ingersoll, the fiery iconoclast, from whose name we never omitted the "G." Ingersoll was considered by some of our neighbors to be the devil's chief agent. Others regarded him as a deliverer from ignorant superstition.

After politics and religion, an important concern to me was my feeling about the Indian. We had come to Dakota from a land—New Iceland—where furs were the basis of the economy and where the Indian, being the chief supplier of the skins, was more useful alive than dead. In Dakota we were in a region where farm land was the basis of the economy, and it was perhaps not unnatural that, since the Indian had a claim upon the land we needed, we did not need him. In my boyhood the term "Indian lover" signified a man who was a traitor to the race which could afford to feel nothing but scorn for savages. This purely selfish inhumanity gave the Old West its aura of romance which we, forgetting its origin, keep alive today in our Western films and TV programs.

The first ambition I remember with any vividness was the desire to be a cowboy and kill Indians. My parents and a number of those who left Manitoba with them had been fleeing primarily the Red River inundations, but they brought with them also the Canadian-English bitterness of the Riel Rebellion, in which the French-speaking, Indian-blooded Louis Riel made one of the few Canadian attempts to keep Europeans from taking the Indians' land and destroying their way of life. Here we were, perhaps subconsciously feeling guilty because we were occupying the territory of the Indian, fearing Sitting Bull and the Sioux as we had previously feared Riel, his Crees, and the other Indians whom Britain had defeated. Our parents may have felt that we had jumped from the frying pan into the fire by coming to a land where the memory of General Custer's defeat by the Sioux was still vivid.

We did not smile when we said that the only good Indian was a dead one. My favorite book was a life of Buffalo Bill in which a full-page illustration carried the legend "How I Shot My First Indian." It showed the brave scout below a cliff aiming a rifle at an Indian silhouetted against the sky. I confess that I hoped, not without some fear, that there might be an Indian raid on our community, giving me a chance to distinguish myself as Buffalo Bill had done and to save the settlement from the treachery of the red man. Mine was, I feel sure, a state of mind common among our neighborhood children.

When I was in my early teens, my father died of what I now feel certain was appendicitis, though that term was not yet known to us. As families do in such situations, ours closed ranks. My sister Inga, who as Mrs. Bjorn Thorlakson lived in the village of Mountain, now took me in, both to make the burden lighter for Mother and to save me the two-mile winter walk to the village school. Years later I examined the records of that one-room school at Mountain in an attempt to determine the extent of my elementary education.

I am satisfied that up to the time of my entering the Preparatory Department of the University of North Dakota I had spent a total of twenty-seven months in school.

In counting my blessings from that early time, I feel that the greatest of them was that we did not have more than the minimum of anything. No doubt partly because there were so few schools, with such short terms, I always hungered for more schools and longer terms. There were not enough Icelandic sagas and so, when reading aloud in the evening, we had to read some of them over again, and these of course were the best ones. (One of them was the *Saga of Eric the Red,* and when we reread it, Father said he wanted to impress upon us that we ourselves were now living in a western extension of the Wineland that Eric and his descendants discovered.)

The school at Mountain finally acquired a library of about a hundred books in English. I am not sure that this was a wholly good thing, for, had there not been in this collection books like *Scottish Chiefs* and *Fifteen Decisive Battles of the World,* we should have read our textbooks over and over again, remembering them better and gaining more from them. At any rate, there were never enough books in our library. This, I feel sure, was largely what made us yearn for more. Today, with our surfeit of books, all of us, schoolchildren included, are able to be selective in our reading. In the good old nineteenth-century pioneer days, as I remember them, we read everything and, by doing so, kept ourselves from getting any more narrow-minded than it is natural for men to be.

3 Buffalo Bones and Blizzards

In the nineties, my brother Joe, fourteen years my senior, was modeling himself after Buffalo Bill—even to the long hair—and this, no doubt, was one reason why he had little interest in our farm after Father died.

At first there had been a good deal of gardening, dairy farming, and chicken raising in our part of the country, but as time went on the land tended to get plowed into wheat. In this specialization Joe saw not only the chance to live his cowboy life but a business opportunity as well. He mounted his bronco and canvassed the farms for twenty or thirty miles around, proposing to pick up their cattle in the spring and take them some fifty miles southwest, to the southern edge of Cavalier County, and there herd them on government land until autumn. This would free the farm land for wheat growing and at the same time enable the farmers to raise cattle. The first price the farmers agreed to pay Joe was three dollars a head. The tariff rose year by year until he finally collected five dollars a head.

The summer that Father died I became one of Joe's helpers. Our main camp was in the "wild land," as we called the open prairie, beside Semple Lake some miles beyond the last homestead. The Moscrip cattle ranch lay perhaps ten miles south of us, while the nearest farms to the west were probably a hundred miles off, somewhere near the Souris, or, as we called it, the Mouse, River. Had I known more Canadian history at the time, I might have guessed that the lake was named after Robert Semple of the Semple Massacre,

17

which in 1816 climaxed the arsonous and bloody Pemmican War. That struggle, which lasted from 1814 to 1821, nearly ruined both the Hudson's Bay Company and the Northwest Company and eventually brought about their amalgamation.

The buffalo had gone from this country, but their trails were still visible, winding in and out among the rolling hills. Here and there we also saw the trails of wagons and Red River carts. After the autumn fires all these old trails stood out more clearly for a while. There had once been tall grass in the Red River Valley of Dakota. Our oxen had plodded belly-deep through it when my parents brought us to Mountain. However, by the time I was old enough to remember, practically all the tall-grass country had been plowed. Where we herded in 1896 and later, there was only short bunch grass, fetlock-deep, and fires were frequent in dry weather. I witnessed two or three bad grass fires during the summers I herded for Joe. One of these, I remember, rode before a strong wind that carried the flames ahead by leaps and bounds, so that there were many slightly separated fires pursuing each other as they advanced, each in turn catching up to the one ahead of it and becoming part of the larger conflagration. One of our most important jobs in summer was the plowing and burning of firebreaks to protect not only our herd of up to five hundred cattle but our camp houses.

It was after a prairie fire that we would find striking evidence of what a multitude of buffalo there must have once been in this region. When the grass was green in midsummer we would ride for miles, unaware of their hidden skeletons. During the first few days after a prairie fire, however, before the grass had a chance to grow again, the land would be dotted with buffalo skeletons, the white bones showing up sharply against the blackened turf. In some areas they would create a pepper-and-salt effect, especially on the hilltops, with a distinct gray on the slopes and a near-white effect on the level ground and in the hollows.

It was because of my interest in these bones, that I made my first Indian friends. In midsummer of 1897, I was sort of exploring, riding farther afield than usual, when I met an ordinary covered wagon and two young men who seemed not at all unusual in either dress or speech. They said they were about to stop for lunch, and asked if I would join them. I was delighted, both for the company and because I was far from camp and hungry. This pair looked very much like settlers, but their way of doing things seemed a little different. The farmers I knew would have spread their gear and food around on the grass. These travelers laid out a large and spotless tablecloth of a kind that I realized was finer than I had ever seen. Moreover, they had china plates instead of tin ones, as ours would have been, and they had white folded napkins, the first I had ever seen. If we had had napkins at all, they would have been red, with fringe.

As we ate, the younger man told me that they planned to pitch their tent there and start collecting buffalo bones. They hoped to gather a ton or more of bones during that afternoon and the next morning. They would then take them southwest to Devils Lake for sale to a local dealer and eventual shipment, probably to St. Louis. There, as they understood it, the bones were used in some process in the refining of sugar. Did they live at Devils Lake? I asked. No, they lived in the northwest, on the Indian reservation in the Turtle Mountains.

Did they make a regular occupation of gathering bones? No, they did it just during vacations. More often during the summer recess they gathered snakeroot to make some extra money. They were, it seemed, college students from the Indian School at Carlisle, Pennsylvania. Maybe we would meet again, since they thought they would be back later in the season gathering roots. What was snakeroot used for? They did not really know, although they understood that some white men believed that the root made a good Indian medicine.

Early in this conversation it somehow dawned on me that these young men were probably Sioux Indians, members of the very tribe that the Icelandic community so greatly feared. I did not wish to look surprised, and I trust I did not. Yet I cannot recall another time in my life when I made such a quick and thorough readjustment of long-held ideas.

During my second or third summer in the saddle, I took time off from our herding at Semple Lake to learn something about the trade in wild horses.

The chief farm animal of the Red River Valley was originally the ox, hitched to a cart, wagon, or plow. Then horses were used, and grew in favor. In Montana Territory there were thousands of semiwild broncos, or cayuses—small animals weighing from nine hundred to twelve hundred pounds. One of the big Montana ranches, the Diamond G, decided to raise coach horses. Since the grazing was limited, the cayuses had to be killed off or, preferably, sold.

Word went out that anybody who would go into the Montana Rockies and catch his own could have Diamond G ponies for a dollar apiece. With the idea of selling these to the Red River farmers of easternmost North Dakota, an operator named Luke Sweetman organized several groups to capture the horses in Montana and drive them east, where several of us young cowhands would meet them and help to sell the herd.

The group I worked with, like the others, included two "busters," who got approximately double the money the rest of us were paid. Their job was to rope a designated horse, throw him, saddle him, and then ride him until he surrendered, working with him until an ordinary farmer could lead, bridle, saddle, or drive him. Apart from the busters, our outfit had a cook, who drove the chuck wagon and, of course, prepared meals, and a night herder, who kept the horses from straying. In our bunch I was the night herder. The job was simple and I liked it.

My schedule was the reverse of normal. When the other members of the outfit had their supper, I had my breakfast. Then, while the rest relaxed or turned in, I would mount my horse and ride slow circles around our broncos all night. In the morning the breakfast of the others was my supper. It was then up to me how much I loafed or slept during the day.

It might seem that we were in a profitable business, but not so according to our immediate boss, Emmet Currie. For one thing, Sweetman had paid the Diamond G a hundred dollars for the privilege of capturing a hundred cayuses of their brand, but his gangs had succeeded in capturing only seventy. Then there were the wages of the men during the long drive from the Rockies to the Red River, and the loss of horses due to broken legs and other accidents. Furthermore, compensation had to be paid to farmers when our animals trampled their land. The sale price for our "broke" broncos ranged from thirty to fifty dollars, supposedly representing differences in the horses' size and docility. Even at such prices, considered by some purchasers to be exorbitant, Currie maintained that the principals were losing money.

This period of my life seemed at the time highly romantic. Yet, as I look back, the most interesting and profitable part of my experience was what I learned in those years about pioneer diet in the Dakota-Montana region.

In Pembina County, North Dakota, we and most of our farmer-neighbors were, in our eating habits, what I consider typical pioneers. I take my own family as an example. To begin with, we kept cows and earned pin money selling butter; some of our neighbors also sold cheese. Since we wanted our animals to grow up into steers or into milk cows, we rarely butchered our calves. We used milk a good deal, both for drinking and for cooking. We ate a lot of porridge, chiefly oatmeal, with a lot of skimmed or whole milk. We also made *skyr*, a milk product resembling yoghurt, which was served with sugar and cream. Once eaten throughout Europe, it is now, I understand, made only in Iceland and in a formerly Scandinavian section of France.

For fresh meat in summer we had chickens and sheep, and in winter we froze carcasses of beef, chiefly steers or oxen but also elderly cows that had been fattened. Throughout the year, we ate eggs, usually soft-boiled; at first, before we became Americanized, we ate few vegetables and relatively little bread. As far as I can recall, our health was excellent.

One of the reasons my brother Joe went into the business of summer herding was because our non-Icelandic neighbors of the Red River Valley began raising cereal crops. With no pasture left for cows, sheep, and mixed-farming foods, the wheat growers began living on what we Icelanders considered a monotonous diet, consisting mainly of cereal or potatoes and fat pork from the pigsties. The pigs were fed largely on slops, pigweed, and boiled barley. I did not become familiar with this sort of diet until I became a cowboy. At first it startled me, but I soon came to like it and to see the sense of it.

Our meat was largely bacon of the type called sowbelly and some ham, but little other meat except for a fat yearling that we might occasionally kill for the chuck wagon. We liked the bacon best. It was cut in fairly thick chunks, stood on edge in a huge iron bread pan, and fried. All the grease was kept. We poured it hot over our pancakes; we dipped soda biscuits in it; we used it on our fried potatoes. We never got fat and we felt fine.

When my cowboy associates of the 1890s and I were living on a diet so high in fat that it was astonishing to the Icelanders, we were evidently carrying on an old tradition native to North America.

Joe continued to do well with his summer pasturing of our neighbors' cattle. In 1897 it struck me that I might do as well as or even better than Joe with the proper wintering of the farmers'

112677

work horses and oxen. I talked the idea over with several of my contemporaries, and three of us decided to go into partnership. There was still plenty of government land available for squatting, some of it excellent meadow, especially in the neighborhood of Semple Lake. We would build tremendous sod-house barns, buy haying machinery, stack hay close around the barns, hire the necessary number of men to do the feeding, and charge two or three times as much for the wintering as Joe was charging for his summering.

It was an exciting prospect for an eighteen-year-old, and I suppose that, if all had gone well our first year, my dream of establishing a cattle ranch of my own might have come true.

We had no trouble borrowing money for our haying machinery, or indeed for anything else we needed, and farmers tumbled over themselves registering their horses and oxen with us. We contracted to gather them in at the freeze-up, which in the Red River Valley comes in November, and to return them in April. The first barn we built—we expected to build one a year—was larger than planned because the response to our scheme was even greater than we had foreseen. Our establishment was on a camel-back hill, our small house (the one Joe used only in summer) on one hump, our barn on the other, and haystacks all around.

While we expected nothing unusual in the way of storms, we took the precaution of running a wire from the house to the barn, intending to cling to it for guidance should we want to visit our stock during a blizzard. My brother had once been one of a party of twenty young persons who had left their supper food and gear in a farmhouse while they went a hundred yards to a schoolhouse to dance. They were unable to get back to their food until the next morning. That was the sort of storm my partners and I took our routine measures against—but what we got was the Thanksgiving Blizzard of 1897, which is as famous in North Dakota history as the Blizzard of 1888 is in New York. I remember working my way down to the barn by means of the wire, only to find that the door was drifted completely over. Though we worried somewhat about being unable to feed and water our stock, it seemed wise not to try to break into the place during the storm.

The blizzard blew steadily for three days. The morning of the third day dawned clear and beautiful, and we thought that our troubles were over. Not so. When we saddled our own horses and tried to ride them down the hill, we found that the drifts were so deep that we could not get through. We hitched a pair to a sleigh but did no better. Eventually, we reached the barn on skis and began digging our way into it.

Our great plan no longer seemed so promising. In those days there were of course no telephone lines across the prairie. We hoped that our customers, having been through the same blizzard, would assume that we had been snowed in, in our more hilly country, and were not in serious trouble simply because we could not send them word. When midwinter came, and the snow in the deepest sections had settled sufficiently, my two partners left me behind and started out to explain to the owners of the animals what they must already have realized as well as we did: that we could hardly hope to risk the experiment the following year.

I, being the chief villain and originator of the great plan, was given the task of caring for the stock until spring. I took to watering the animals by giving them blocks of snow to gnaw. Finding that this scheme worked, I felt able to leave the place for a while and benefit by some human companionship. I simply stacked in enough hay and snow blocks to keep the animals going for a couple of weeks, turned them loose, and locked the door.

On my skis I covered the ten miles to the Moscrip ranch, which I found in the care of Moscrip's brother-in-law Hanson. He received me joyfully. We had only three things to eat: flour, out of which Hanson made flapjacks; fresh fat pork, which he fried lightly in thick slices; and a sugar-grease combination he made by blending the fat from the fried pork with an equal measure of Karo Syrup. When this mixture cooled, it had the consistency of today's peanut butter, and it was delicious. All our meals were alike, and we ate as much as we liked. I usually drank unsweetened tea. Hanson drank coffee, which he sweetened with Karo.

Here again was the typical cowboy diet, and once again it seemed sensible and satisfying. True, I sometimes overindulged and felt uncomfortable; but when this happened, Hanson advised me to skip a meal. Either I did this or I ate only a small amount of food, and was promptly on an even keel again.

When I returned to the barn at Semple Lake, I found everything there in good shape. After cleaning it and restocking it with hay and snow, I made a trip northeast to stay awhile with the Weirs and the O'Malleys, farmers of that region, helping them with their chores and enjoying their Ontario-style cooking, though no more than I had enjoyed Hanson's.

Thus the winter passed, with visits to distant neighbors breaking up the monotony of my failing business venture. All the animals came through safely, but after delivering them to their owners I went through an informal bankruptcy proceeding. Nobody really seemed to blame me for anything. It was the blizzard rather than human failing that ended my ambition to become a cattle rancher.

In the autumn of 1898, my thoughts directed in a more promising channel, I boarded a railway train for the first time in my life. My destination was Grand Forks, seventy miles away. Notwithstanding my recent occupations, I had always taken it for granted that I would one day go to college. My mother was probably ready to believe that I might do so and still not be eliminated from the ministerial field. The trip to Grand Forks was the first step. I had been accepted in the Preparatory Department of the State University of North Dakota. As I left home I wore a new seven-dollar suit and had in my pocket the substantial sum of fifty-three dollars. I had no doubt about my ability to earn more when that gave out.

4
From Debater
to Delegate

It does not seem to me that the termination of my first railroad journey giving me my first experience with either a city or a college brought any sharp break with the past. The effect might have been more pronounced if I had taken the train all the way to University Station, a flag stop two or three miles past Grand Forks. Instead, having been told that I might be able to find a job there, I got off in Grand Forks and went directly to a boarding-house I knew about on North Fourth Street. The owners, a couple named Johnson, were Icelanders, and they already had about a dozen Icelandic students staying with them, boys ranging scholastically from the lowest preparatory grade, the fourth, to the first year of college. The Johnsons had space for me, and when they offered me room and board for taking care of two or three milk cows and tending their wood-burning kitchen stove, my most immediate problem was solved.

I spent a pleasant first evening with my fellow boarders. We talked of school, but we also talked of Iceland and Icelandic history and of our fellow nationals in the United States and Canada.

The morning after my arrival, I walked with two or three other boys south and then two miles west to the end of University Avenue. Here on the bare prairie stood the two buildings that composed the physical plant of the State University of North Dakota. The chief structure, six stories of red brick, was then known simply as Main. It housed classrooms, laboratories, a library, and a bookstore. It also contained a dormitory for a lucky few, chiefly of college rank. The rest of the student body roomed in town. A few lived with their own families, who had moved to Grand Forks from farm, ranch, or village to be with their boys and girls while they attended college.

The second structure, four stories high and of gray stone, was known as Davis Hall. Among other things, Davis was the residence of President Webster Merrifield and of a few elderly and exalted unmarried professors. On the second floor of Davis was a carpeted social hall equipped with a piano. In the basement were the commons, where the resident girls took their meals and where almost anybody else could arrange to eat, especially at lunch time. With the many boys and a few girls who roomed in town, lunch was a box, pail, or package affair. We ate sitting on benches or chairs in the basement hallways of Main.

The university was a young school, younger than I at first realized. It had been authorized by the legislature of Dakota Territory in 1883, and it opened its doors a year later. President Merrifield, a Yale graduate, told me that he had come to be head of the institution partly because he happened to be on the spot as a young farmer when the legislature started to look around for teachers and administrators. In 1898 the student body, preparatory as well as college, numbered about three hundred.

I found all the faculty considerate and kind, with that hearty openness typical of the frontier. President Merrifield immediately got in touch with me, for it was unusual to have a new boy arrive so late in the fall term. Both he and the registrar assured me that, to judge by the achievements of other Icelandic boys and girls who had attended the university, I would have no trouble catching up in my classes. They suggested that I might even be able to move on from the lowest of the four prep grades by passing with a mark of C or better the special examinations in history and certain other subjects about which Icelanders always seemed to know more than the general run of students.

I have mentioned that in my early thinking the evil trinity of Ingersoll, Darwin, and the devil was very important. In due course, the devil faded and disappeared and Robert Ingersoll acquired normal stature in my consciousness. Darwin, however, became a real hero to me, and I now began to dream of discovering some law of life comparable in importance to the doctrine of evolution. One evening after the Johnsons had gone upstairs, a half-dozen of us boarders sat around the dining table and soon started talking along lines that allowed me to express my own admiration of Darwin and the disapproval of the Missouri Synod that I had inherited from my father. My voice probably grew strident. I had not noticed in the ceiling a register that carried the warmth from the dining room to the inadequately heated upper room to which Mrs. Johnson had retired. It also carried the heat of my discourse. My job and the advantages that went with it terminated next morning. Mrs. Johnson thought highly of her cows and did not want them tended by anyone with views like mine. In addition, she considered me a bad influence on the rest of her boarders and the younger members of her own family.

I had been expecting, during the spring term, to find a job as a schoolteacher, a position to which I was more or less entitled by virtue of my status as "a college man." It was not long after my dismissal from the boardinghouse (and my temporary withdrawal from the university) that I found myself installed in my first teaching job, at I think thirty dollars a month, with about eight of that going for board and room. The community I landed in was Beaulieu, a few miles north of my childhood home. I boarded with the Helgesen family, who were already prominent and later grew more so when Henry T. Helgesen became our state's lone Congressman and—interestingly to me—one of the key figures in the Peary-Cook dispute as to which man, if either, had really discovered the North Pole.

After a few months of teaching, I turned to various other jobs to carry me through the summer. Mostly I "grubbed," that is, dug up tree stumps and bushes preparatory to plowing the land for seeding to wheat. Along with the other grubbers, I slept in haylofts or sheds and made from half a dollar to a dollar a day with meals. When harvest time came, there were better jobs with better pay. With something like two hundred dollars in my pocket, I returned to the University of North Dakota, again several weeks late.

This time I lived on a "batching" arrangement. At the Johnson boardinghouse I had met two brothers of another Johnson family, John and Peter. We had a mutual friend in another student, Gudmundur ("Mundi") Grimson. As I write this, more than sixty years later, Grimson has recently retired after being for some years chief justice of the State Supreme Court of North Dakota. He, John Johnson, and I pooled our resources and spent the winter together.

John and Mundi knew a farmer named Richards who owned a

shanty and a small house on English Coulee. Both were for rent, the shanty at two dollars a month. We took the shanty. Either Richards already had in it or we borrowed or brought a cookstove and a box stove, both wood-burning. Richards sold wood to us at four dollars a cord. After the frost began, the families of John and Mundi sent us meat. We received our first shipment in early November. By protecting it from direct sunlight we were able to keep it fresh-frozen until April. Though meat on the hoof was only three or four cents a pound in those days, it was still a notable saving to get all our beef and mutton free. The fact that we did so goes a long way toward explaining why Justice Grimson and I, the last time we met, were able to agree that our living costs for the season—food, fuel, rent, and laundry—totaled about $1.85 a week.

For light we usually used kerosene lamps. Even cheaper, for they cost us nothing, were candles of mutton tallow sent from home. We found numerous other ways to cut down our expenses. Since the heaviest item was books, we borrowed each other's textbooks or bought used copies from students in grades above ours. The scratch paper we used was the cheapest we could get, and pencils were not discarded until they became unmanageable stubs. Fond memories I have of those years.

As I look back, I find that the ideas and events that made the deepest impressions upon me were those which helped me to free myself of prejudice. Just as my meeting with the Carlisle students helped to rid me of prejudice toward Indians, a similar experience during my second university year cleansed me of my intolerant attitude toward the Irish.

In the old days, Icelanders used to make forays along the coast of Ireland and capture whole families, taking them as slaves. Not unnaturally, the Irish were regarded as an inferior people. In Iceland, an intimation that there might be a trace of Irish in a Norse family was the cause of more than one feud. The Icelanders who came to Canada and the United States began to lose this feeling, but there was a lot of it left in me when I began living in Richards' shanty.

Things came to a head when we discovered that Richards had rented his nearby house to three boys, two of them Icelanders, and one an Irishman, Joe Flanagan. What made the situation difficult for me was that Joe Flanagan was at that time the university's biggest hero. Today, after more than sixty years, his is the name that always comes up first when North Dakota athletes are talked about. But Joe was more than just an athlete. Even if he was not an intellectual giant, he had qualities that convinced us all that he was a bigger and better man than anyone else we knew.

Among his many personal triumphs—of no consequence to him but important to me—was that our friendship completely cured me of looking down upon the Irish, just as my earlier encounter with the two Sioux had changed my mind about Indians. Some years later, and with help from many clear thinkers, I was able to decide that those are wrong, whoever they are, who look down upon any race.

My popularity among the university students greatly increased as a result of a discovery I made while I was in the preparatory department. Originally, I had supposed that scholastic excellence provided the key to popularity with students as well as with faculty, but it gradually dawned upon me that I was wrong as far as the students were concerned. I therefore began to study in secret and loaf in public. As a further refinement, I began to give wrong answers in class even when I knew the correct ones. Immediately I gained new friends. Stories began to circulate to the effect that, although I seldom studied, I never failed to get high marks on my examination papers. One story (I did nothing to discourage it) had it that I attended only the first class of one of my courses and did not appear again until the final examination. I was reported to have been given a mark of 98 and to have claimed that, if I had skipped the first day's class, I might have made a 100.

The year I enrolled as a freshman, I became a real hero by organizing a volunteer corps to help certain of our football players. The faculty had ruled that no player, no matter how good, would be allowed to play against other colleges unless he maintained a scholastic standing of at least *D*. Some of our football stars were not stars intellectually. Even Joe Flanagan, half a football team in himself, was in trouble, for he had made the mistake of enrolling in German, a subject in which he was far from gifted. Two other athletic friends of mine, Fitzmaurice and Jennings, had made the same mistake. My brain-trust plan, as it operated in the German class, called for the services of a good linguist, and I was selected. The scheme worked because our professor, John Macnie, was both nearsighted and absent-minded. It was said that, of the thirty or so members of his German class, Macnie knew by sight only three of the girls and none of the boys. On a typical day Macnie called in alphabetic succession on Fitzmaurice, Flanagan, and Jennings. At their distress signals, I translated for them, varying my voice slightly but not bothering to change my seat, for Macnie never looked at us. I then gilded the lily by saying, when called upon to translate, that I was unprepared. I was scolded and marked *zero*. Such pranks, successful for a long time, eventually contributed to my downfall.

During my freshman year I went out for debating, in part because the university announced two money prizes, one for the best team and one for the best individual debater. Each prize was ten dollars—something like a hundred dollars by today's standard. For me, the contest was to have far-reaching consequences.

That winter, everybody was talking about the struggle in South Africa, and the debate topic chosen by the university was: "Resolved, that the United States ought to sympathize with the British in their war with the Boers." Each contestant chose the side he wished to represent. A series of elimination debates were to reduce the number of finalists to three to a side. The turnout was heavily pro-British: there were more than twenty candidates for the affirmative side, and only two for the negative. These two prevailed on me to join them and fill out the number to the minimum.

All three of us were freshmen. Our opponents, as a result of the elimination, were two seniors and a junior. No doubt largely through the overconfidence of the upper classmen, we freshmen won the debate. Further, it was I who won the prize as the best individual debater. Those were simple pioneer days in our part of the country, and our small triumph was reported in all the weekly newspapers, and in the few dailies, south to Minneapolis and north to Winnipeg.

But for a wholly unforeseen chain of events, my winning of that debate could not have become what I feel it proved to be: one of the turning points of my life. The triggering coincidence was a letter from Boston advising the leaders of the Unitarian Church in Winnipeg that they might no longer expect financial support from the American Unitarian Association. The Winnipeg organization, which for some years had flourished as an accredited mission enterprise, felt that it would be desirable to send a representative to Boston in the hope that the decision might be reconsidered. Through the story in the Winnipeg paper, I, as the young debate winner at the University of North Dakota, was suggested as the delegate. I was invited to Winnipeg, where the plan was put before me by an

Icelandic Unitarian clergyman. There was soon to be an International Conference of Liberal Religions, sponsored by Boston Unitarians. By attending it as a delegate, I might have a chance to persuade influential leaders that this was no time for the Unitarians to abandon their Western mission program.

I pointed out that, even if there was some correlation between making a fairly good fifteen-minute speech and being a good negotiator, it hardly seemed wise to send a schoolboy into a situation that had already been lost by clergymen. Besides, I said, I was not even a Unitarian. The Winnipeg group replied that my father had been known as a liberal Lutheran. If I was my father's son, I was good enough for them. I admitted that I had once lost a job tending cows because I had spoken disrespectfully about the Missouri Synod, and said I guessed I still held approximately the same religious views.

So it was that I was given my first chance to cross the Red River of the North, eastward bound. With a round-trip coach ticket in my pocket, I started for Boston the first week in May, 1900.

At the Hotel Bellevue in Boston, I found myself one of many delegates representing many religions, hearing speech after speech and enjoying much stimulating conversation. Among the speakers who most impressed me were Edward Everett Hale, who spoke emotionally, and President Charles William Eliot of Harvard University, who warned against emotionalism. I learned that Eliot was the father of Dr. Samuel Atkins Eliot, the secretary of the Unitarians, with whom I had expected to negotiate at the Beacon Street headquarters. Instead, I found myself shunted to hotel-room conferences with a young clergyman from Chicago who was said to be an authority on the prospects for Unitarianism in Manitoba and the Dakotas. With what must be a special talent I have for being wrong about people when I meet them, at first I was not much impressed with William Wallace Fenn, though I found him agreeable enough as a person. I had no idea how important he was to be to me and my career.

When I started back to North Dakota from Boston, I had no clear indication of whether I had succeeded or failed in my mission. Later I heard by letter that Unitarians in both Winnipeg and Boston were satisfied with the result.

In my junior year at North Dakota, although some of the escapades of my freshman and sophomore years continued, I was a more serious boy. One evidence of an increasingly thoughtful outlook is that I changed my name. For some years I had been uneasy about what I now thought of as my parents' decision to deprive me of my Icelandic heritage. After a comment by George Thomas, our professor of Greek and Latin, that he considered it a pity that so many immigrants in North America Anglicized or Frenchified their names, I discussed my own case with President Merrifield and several members of the faculty. The opinion seemed to be that I ought to change to the name that would have been mine had my father insisted upon it. Not long afterward I stopped being an imitation Canadian Scot named Stephenson and formally resurrected my Icelandic name.

Another sign of growing seriousness was the abandonment of my plan to become a great poet. During my freshman year I had written verse by the yard, feeling a glow of achievement when samples of it were printed in the university monthly, *The Student*. I had learned by heart Kipling's *Barrack Room Ballads* and his *Departmental Ditties,* not intentionally but as a result of repeatedly reading them aloud to captive audiences. For a time I had a vague idea of becoming Kipling's successor. The dream collapsed the day I discovered in *Scribner's Magazine* a poem, "Gloucester Moors," by a man of whom I had never heard, William Vaughan Moody. After reading that poem, I never wrote another line of verse. It seemed to me that when a man said to be about my own age could write a poem so much better than I could ever hope to, I had better look for a less competitive road to greatness.

Poetry renounced, I next decided to become a great biologist, a second Darwin. But Professor Brannon, of botany and zoology, seemed to regard the use of the microscope as important, and I found that I seldom, if ever, could view the things illustrated in textbooks. I decided to become an anthropologist instead. I do not remember what individual in this field I intended to resemble and probably surpass, but he must have been a great man. In one way or another, the idea of greatness formed part of all my visions.

5 *Iowa and I*

Although there was no doubt in my mind that I would achieve greatness in the field I had chosen, I knew that the achievement would only be realized after several years of graduate work. This was no obstacle, since I loved going to school. But just when my plans were beginning to mature in my mind, I received a severe setback—I was expelled from the University of North Dakota.

In an unhappy conversation with President Merrifield, I heard the technical reason for the action: I had been absent from the university for three weeks without sufficient excuse. Though to my mind this was hardly an important issue, the charge was true enough. A high school principal in Grand Forks had been rushed to the hospital for an emergency operation, and I had been asked to take his place and receive his salary during his absence. The chance to earn some money had been too great to resist. But this reason was only for the record, Merrifield assured me. The real reason was that the faculty felt that the students were getting out of hand and that I was behind the worst, if not all, of the troubles. A majority of the faculty had concluded that my expulsion, regardless of my scholastic standing, would improve things. In Biblical times, Merrifield reminded me, it had been considered right that a chosen man should die for the good of his people. The present action was a minor application of the same principle. Had the morale of the student body been better, Merrifield went on, my absence might have been excused, as had my many previous absences; but under the circumstances the faculty had seen this opportunity for legal punishment as too good to miss.

The official history of the University of North Dakota, published in 1958, does not say that I was expelled but only that I was "suspended for the rest of the period 1902–1903."

When it became known that I had been given three days to remove myself from the campus, there was talk of a student rally protesting my expulsion. I discouraged this, partly because it was good fun to seem magnanimous toward the faculty, partly because I doubted that the rally would call out any large number of students. I was not yet taking the expulsion very seriously, for I felt that I could readily enroll in another university. Thus, I did nothing to discourage the suggestion that a grand mock funeral be conducted. A very popular girl, Mae Hinzie, was my widow, dressed in black, weeping into a handkerchief containing a crushed onion, while to the accompaniment of solemn music I left the campus in a wheelbarrow. A gaily decorated carriage then took my pallbearers and me to the Dacotah, the best hotel in Grand Forks, where we joined the rest of my mourners for a gala wake.

Next morning I received some alarming news. It was happily preceded by two bits of good fortune. First, I was offered the job of city editor (really reporter) on the Grand Forks *Plaindealer,* the Democratic rival of the much more prosperous *Herald.* It appeared that, on the promised pay, I could live sumptuously, for the *Plaindealer* also printed the menus for the Hotel Dacotah in return for what was described to me as the finest room and board in all of Grand Forks. I accepted, planning to keep the job only until I found a university that would admit me for my last year. On top of this, Steve Brynjolfson, chairman of the State Central Committee of the Democratic party, said he would be able to throw my way some plums that would help increase my income.

Then, the bad news. I received it when I called on James M. Cochrane, the best-known lawyer in the state. It was Cochrane who had recommended me to the owner of the *Plaindealer.* First, to cheer me up, Cochrane revealed that he himself had been expelled from the University of Michigan without suffering any permanent ill effect. Then he pointed out that colleges and universities maintained an efficient blacklisting system. Admission to a second university would doubtless be impossible unless I produced a satisfactory record from the first, a procedure that educators defended in part—

according to Cochrane—on the grounds that it discouraged pointless shifting from one institution to another. He felt that the blacklisting would not refer back to my record in the university's preparatory department. I should proceed, Cochrane advised, by entering some institution as a freshman with permission to take immediate examinations for advanced standing. In this way I might get through in a couple of years.

As a first step Cochrane advised that I send a form letter to several universities asking if they would give credit to an entrant on the basis of the knowledge he possessed or only on the basis of what he had studied in an accredited school or college. Most of them replied that they gave credits only on the basis of competence acquired in an accredited institution, some of them explaining that, for instance, a born German would get credits in German language courses only if he had studied German in school.

Six universities on my list replied that they did not make a practice of asking an applicant where or how he had learned anything but only what he knew and how well he knew it. It is a source of lasting regret to me that I have forgotten the names of two of these liberal institutions. The four I do remember were Cornell, Harvard, Iowa, and Yale. I selected the University of Iowa because it was the nearest, because the costs seemed low, and because it offered more courses of the kind I thought I could pass easily.

Cochrane, continuing to act as my unpaid adviser, drafted my letter of application. It explained that I was studying the comparative advantages of various universities, said that I had little money, and made it plain that I wanted to be sure I knew just how liberal Iowa would be in granting special examinations for advanced rating. The Iowa registrar replied with a letter that would serve as my permission to take an examination in any course offered by their catalogue. If I passed with a grade of C or better, I would be granted permission to take the next examination I asked for, and so on indefinitely.

In the midst of my efforts to get into a university from which I could graduate without suffering any great loss of time, I entered —or was drawn into—politics.

In North Dakota the State Superintendent of Public Instruction was legally the head of the state educational system and therefore of the university. There were several people, among them Steve Brynjolfson, who thought it would be a good joke to nominate me for the office. They felt that the humorous element in the situation might bring the Democrats some votes.

As matters developed, I should probably have been nominated even had there been no advance planning. Although Grand Forks was the second largest county in the state, the other counties ganged up on us in the convention, and one after another our candidates were defeated. Finally came the nomination for an office that few cared anything about. At this point a delegate, probably planted by Brynjolfson, arose and decried the folly of antagonizing Grand Forks by rejecting all of its candidates. Let's at least give them this educational job, he said. But who would the candidate be? The county's foremost educators were either Republican or unwilling to serve. Why not nominate Stefansson, who had suffered the iniquity of being expelled by the state university and had many friends who would love to see him vindicated, and who in any case would prove a good campaigner? There was no opposition. I was nominated.

My name on the state ticket gave me temporary membership in the State Central Committee, a status I expected would benefit my position at the University of Iowa. I had planned to reach Iowa City a few weeks before the term began and take special examinations in Latin, Anglo-Saxon, Middle English, Old Norse (Icelandic), Scandinavian literature, German literature, and history. But something happened that threatened to interfere with my plan. The state campaign was in full swing, and partly because of my well-advertised skill in debate, the State Central Committee wanted me to get out on the stump. The Republican candidate for Superintendent of Public Instruction was proving to be one of the best campaigners our opponents had. He was an acquaintance of mine, W. L. Stockwell, a graduate of the University of Minnesota and a really well-qualified educator. His success at campaigning is what saved me. Reminding the Democratic committeemen of what they had been saying about Stockwell's skill as a speaker, I asked them if they would excuse me from making speeches if I could get Stockwell to stop making any. The idea seemed reasonable to them. I therefore wrote Stockwell to suggest that it was really beneath the dignity of contestants for our high educational office to squabble in public. I said that I would leave North Dakota for Iowa immediately on receipt of his agreement to stop campaigning, and take no further part in the contest by letter or otherwise. He lost no time in agreeing. I quit my job on the *Plaindealer* and took the train for Iowa City.

During those weeks, but luckily not before Stockwell made his promise, somebody who had read the constitution of the state of North Dakota checked into the question of my age. I was only twenty-two, three years younger than the required minimum for officeholders. Apparently it had not occurred to Brynjolfson to worry about my age, or perhaps he had decided that it made no real difference, since we were going to lose the election in any case.

When the story broke that, if elected, I would not be able to serve because of my youth, I got my first taste of national publicity. Apparently most of the country's dailies that had wire service carried the story as a human-interest item. This helped to save my academic career. Though he had not mentioned it earlier, the Iowa registrar, whose name was Dorcas, revealed in a last-moment communication that he would expect me to submit a letter of honorable discharge from the University of North Dakota. Accordingly, I approached my first interview with Dorcas in some fear. Beaming, he said he had been reading about my career in politics. Was I really this picturesque character of the newspaper story? On my admitting that I was, he apparently forgot about his request for the letter from North Dakota. Barely glancing at the documents showing my preparatory school records, he handed me the authorization for my first examinations.

There was only one more tense moment: Dorcas pointed out that Iowa granted degrees only to those who had passed creditably a term each of advanced algebra, spherical geometry, and calculus. The only mathematics credits in my record were first-year algebra and plane geometry. Dorcas tut-tutted when I began to stammer excuses. Iowa had, he said, excellent mathematics teachers, particularly an instructor named John Van Etten Westfall. Dr. Westfall was, in fact, such a genius that Dorcas thought it a kindness to warn me against his courses. Westfall, said the registrar, was unable to see any difficulty in mathematics. If a student went to him with a problem, he would simply grab a piece of chalk and scribble on the blackboard the very figures that the student found troublesome. He would then stare at the student and say, "Don't you see?"

When I explained that I had always been weak in mathematics, Dorcas said that it might be advisable for me to hire a tutor, and suggested a man named Paul Dorweiler, reputed to be just as good a teacher as Professor Arthur Smith, head of the Mathematics Department. The plan worked so beautifully that I discovered that my supposed weakness in mathematics had been imaginary.

Being rated a freshman, I was urged by members of that class to join some of their organizations. I declined, pointing out that I would be a sophomore by Thanksgiving. And so I was. Sometime before Christmas, Dean Amos Noyes Currier sent for me. I wondered if my North Dakota expulsion had finally caught up with me, but this was not what was bothering the dean. He opened the interview by complimenting me on my record. I had by now, through my continuing special examinations, practically attained junior rating. Did I plan to do the four years of the Iowa curriculum in one?

This was the sort of interview that Cochrane had foreseen and for which he had briefed me. He had advised me to combine, as best I could, firmness with diffidence. I told Dean Currier that I had planned to ask for examinations only when I felt sure I was ready for them. I also wanted to be sure, I said, that nobody had been making the tests especially easy for me, either by the questions asked or by the way the papers were marked. It seemed to me that the question, if any, was one of contract. On the basis of what I had assumed to be a firm agreement, I had given up consideration of five other universities which had offered to give me credits for whatever I knew, irrespective of how I came to know it. Moreover, I had spent money for travel, for board and room, and for other college expenses. Now I expected the university to live up to its agreement.

Currier admitted that the university had been caught in a situation that no one had foreseen. The upshot was that, if things continued as they had been going, I would probably get my degree in June. And that is just what happened. I received my B.A. from Iowa three days before my former classmates received theirs from North Dakota.

During my last few months at Iowa I had another worry. How was I now going to enter upon my chosen career and become an anthropologist? While there had seemed to be several leads toward fellowships in Eastern universities, I was not in a very good position to seek support from any of the professors who knew me, either at North Dakota or at Iowa. It turned out, however, that I had apparently made more of an impression upon the Eastern Unitarians, especially William Wallace Fenn, than I had realized. Since the spring of 1900, I had received several letters from Fenn, now professor of New England theology at Harvard, and one or more from Dr. Samuel Eliot, now president of the American Unitarian Association. In substance, the letters said that they believed I had the making of a Unitarian clergyman. They were troubled by a dearth of candidates for the ministry, and wanted me to prepare for the Unitarian church by taking a course at the Harvard Divinity School which they would finance.

I did not regard the ministry as a suitable vocation for myself and told them so; but I decided that I had nothing to lose by making a counterproposal. I wrote Fenn that I was determined to go into anthropology. This science has three main subdivisions: somatology or physical anthropology, ethnology, and folklore. To me, I said, religion was folklore; the Harvard Divinity School might therefore be a logical place for the study of religion as a branch of anthropology. Would he and Dr. Eliot be willing to support my study of religion from the folklore point of view? I fully expected to be turned down, but they accepted my plan, Fenn saying he felt sure that, after spending a year in the Divinity School as a folklore student, I would take such a favorable view of the Unitarian ministry that in the second year I would register on a regular Divinity basis.

With all their cards and mine on the table, I was on my way to Cambridge two days after graduation from the University of Iowa. I was to register in June as a student of the Harvard Summer School and then as a Divinity student in September.

6 Entering Harvard Yard

The Harvard commencement of 1903 took place a few days later than Iowa's, and I reached Cambridge in time to be one of the invited guests in Sanders Theatre. There I heard a series of Charles Eliot's famous honorary-degree citations. I remember best what he said to the psychologist and philosopher William James. James had, he said, won his way to one of Harvard's most distinguished chairs without the supposedly necessary advantage of an A.B. or any formal academic distinction except an M.D. I have seen many Harvard commencements since then, but never one that had a master of ceremonies who could compare with Eliot.

Two of the summer-school courses that I attended for six weeks stand out in my memory. In a Greek course I learned that a Greek noun has three numbers, unlike a Latin one, which has only two. Knowing this, I am able to say with confidence that Eskimo, in this respect, resembles Greek more than it does Latin.

In a course dealing with the problem of the divine inspiration of the Bible, I learned from Dr. George Burman Foster, professor of systematic theology in the Divinity School of the University of Chicago, that nobody can prove whether the Bible is inspired or not. I was told that Professor Foster was considered by some to be the foremost of American theologians and that his lectures at the summer school were likely to give a reasonable foretaste of what I would hear after registering in the fall.

It now seems to me that my Divinity year had greater effect upon the future direction of my career than any time spent at North Dakota or Iowa, or at the Harvard Graduate School, which was to come later. Therefore, I feel it appropriate to mention here four teachers who made a deep impression upon me.

Dr. Samuel McChord Crothers was not officially a Divinity professor. He was a university preacher who spoke to us frequently, and I often attended his church. I found him one of the most deeply skeptical of all the skeptics associated with the school. His book *Among Friends* contains a chapter, "The Anglo-American School of Polite Unlearning," the substance of which I heard first as a sermon addressed to Harvard and Radcliffe students. Dr. Crothers' thesis was that, since there are so many schools and colleges teaching us things that are not so, it would be good if we had at least one well-known institution that we could attend to unlearn a few of them. I was destined to attend many schools of unlearning in the course of my career, particularly in the Arctic, and I never graduated from one of them without a grateful recollection of Dr. Crothers.

Ephraim Emerton, formally known as Winn Professor of Ecclesiastical History, was to me the historian who reconciled sacred and profane historical matters. With my heart still set on anthropology and with my special interest in Scandinavian history, I was especially interested in his views on how the second Book of Moses, Deuteronomy, influenced the spread of Christianity northward through Europe.

Emerton considered it an established fact that there had been a split in the young church over the interpretation of the section in Deuteronomy that forbids Jews to eat the flesh of pig or horse. Saint Peter, he told us, was in favor of a rigid observance of all the dietetic rules, while Saint Paul, in the hope of converting non-Jews to Christianity, favored a liberal interpretation. The Christian church, then small and weak, might easily have been split into hostile factions. A compromise was arranged, with Peter giving in to the extent of permitting the eating of pork and Paul agreeing to forbid the eating of horse meat. This seemingly even break between the disputants, said Emerton, was really an important victory for Saint Paul and for the church. The pig was a food source of great importance, being a poor man's animal not only among the Hebrews but also among the Greeks and the Romans. The horse, on the other hand, was of negligible importance as a source of food, for horses were owned by few except soldiers and the wealthy, of whom there were not many among the early converts.

The part of this lecture that impressed me most was his description of what happened as the new religion spread northward. Because the whole European world loved pork, Christianity was not handicapped in popularity, as Judaism was by its arbitrary prohibition. In the Greco-Roman world, horse meat, though eaten, did not have as much appeal as beef and mutton, and there was little objection to the prohibition against it. It was only when the spreaders of Christianity crossed the Alps northward that they began getting into serious trouble. The difficulties increased in Germany and Britain, became really serious only in Sweden and Norway, and were worst of all in Iceland. In Scandinavian lands the midwinter festival, Yule, was comparable to Thanksgiving in the United States, with horse meat the feast dish. In the north the horse had gustatory, sentimental, and religious appeal.

Weaning Norwegians and Swedes from horse meat was merely difficult, said Emerton—weaning Icelanders was impossible. Finally a compromise was arranged. The parliament of the Icelandic republic agreed to national baptism on several conditions, the most important being that nobody should ever be compelled to give up eating horse meat. Thus, for about a century, Iceland was the only country where the Church of Rome did not demand abstinence from horse meat. By the twelfth century, however, according to Emerton, the Icelanders were feeling so sensitive about being the Christian world's only horse-meat eaters that they voluntarily yielded. When Emerton's lecture closed, I was able to contribute the modern footnote that, by 1700, the prejudice against horse-meat eating was stronger in Iceland than in Norway, Sweden, and Denmark. Today, horse meat is fairly popular in all of the Scandinavian countries except Iceland.

George Foot Moore, Frothingham Professor of History of Religion, was in my day looked upon as the most learned member of the Harvard faculty, and my impression was that a large majority of his fellow professors would have voted him the university's greatest man, not merely its greatest scholar.

Moore had a rare wit, and it was his approach to anthropology, physiology, and religion that persuaded me to progress at Harvard by crossing Divinity Avenue to the Peabody Museum, the anthropological wing of the Natural History Museum. I found his views especially valuable when I later began to study and to share the eating and thinking habits of the Eskimos.

In particular, I recall Moore's discussing of what supposed truths might profitably be questioned and what beliefs might be accepted tentatively until they could be tested. He suggested that if a belief was historically ancient and geographically widespread, it was probably wrong. New or fairly recent beliefs, he pointed out, always have to fight their way up against entrenched dogmas and against allegedly well-known and frequently confirmed observations. He mentioned our words "lunacy" and "lunatic," enshrining verbally the belief found in many, if not most, times and places that if the moon has a chance to shine on a person's face while he sleeps he is likely to become insane. This particular belief, we were told, had happily been discredited and was no longer taught in colleges, but beliefs equally absurd were still being taught. For instance, the belief that a man is what he eats. To document this belief, Moore referred us to the literature of the European Middle Ages, where it is often stated or implied that if cowardly meat, such as the flesh of a rabbit, is smuggled into the stew of a brave soldier, he becomes a coward. Similarly, if brave meat, such as that of a lion, is smuggled into the food of a coward, he becomes brave. There is strength in the meat of a strong animal, such as an ox, and a tendency to grow fat develops from eating fat meat. Remember Jack Sprat of nursery-rhyme fame? If you stop to think of it, in order to acquire certain qualities by eating food that contains them, it would seem practically necessary to become a cannibal. The belief in the acquisition of attributes through diet is indeed one of the bases for cannibalism. For instance, if a man wants to gain wisdom, he simply has to eat a wise man.

Though all these and many similar beliefs were formerly taught, or at least not denied, at universities, they have now been discarded—with two notable exceptions. Medical schools still teach that eating fat meat tends to make people fat, and divinity schools insist that eating holy meat tends to eradicate sin. The belief that we are what we eat is the basis of the priest's assurance to a communicant that in the sacrament he is eating the true body of Our Lord and drinking His true blood.

My schooling with George Moore taught me much about such beliefs and practices and gave me a point of view that made understanding easy when, years later, Eskimos explained to me the uniquely effective properties of a murdered man's liver when eaten by the murderer. Though I took only two of Moore's courses, his wisdom remained with me, affecting my views and interpretations.

A marvel to me at the time, and significant to me still, are the things that Moore could get away with without causing a ripple, while his colleague at the Divinity School of the University of Chicago, Dr. Foster, was continually in hot water. I have already mentioned Foster's pronouncement about the divine inspiration of the Bible. When Foster made statements like that in Chicago, head-lines flared across the nation's newspapers. In contrast, I remember that one day, when several of us stayed after class to question Moore, I asked him what he thought of Robert G. Ingersoll. He said that he did not think very highly of him. I asked why. Moore said that he could only feel sorry for a man who wasted so much energy and time in trying to kill things that were already dead. A re-mark like that would have cost Dr. Foster some difficult days.

My fourth teacher was, of course, William Wallace Fenn. As Bussey Professor of Systematic Theology, he gave Divinity students and sociologists of my day what I think was the truest insight then available into the religious thinking of New England from 1620 on, into problems ranging from Salem witchcraft and Cotton Mather, through William Lloyd Garrison and antislavery, to William James, Josiah Royce, and agnosticism. With a creative mind as good as that of any of the recognized philosophers, Fenn gave his time largely to the interpretation of the various philosophies. I never felt I rightly understood what Kant was trying to say until I lis-tened to Fenn on Kant. The same was true for other philosophers, although I did feel that I could understand a few on my own, among these David Hume and William James.

As a student at Harvard, I was one of Fenn's pets. When spring came, he and his wife urged me to spend the Easter vacation with them and Mrs. Fenn's parents at Berkshire, Massachusetts. I learned during that visit that Faith Fenn's mother had painted two paintings, copies of which I had seen in many farm- and ranch houses in Dakota Territory in my youth, "A Yard of Roses" and "A Yard of Pansies"—paintings which usually had for compan-ion pieces on cabin and shanty walls Bonheur's "Horse Fair" and Landseer's "Stag." I understand that the "Pansies" and the "Roses" by Faith Thayer sold so well that they brought her more money than her brother, the famous Abbott Thayer, ever received for any two of his paintings.

The time came when I had to decide whether or not Fenn had

been right about his prediction that after a year's trial I would
want to join the Unitarian ministry. His argument, as he had especially pressed it while I was spending that Easter vacation with
him, was based upon his conviction that I wanted to do what I
could for the good of mankind and that for this purpose the ministry had unexcelled advantages. It had a suitable plant, a priceless store of good will, and would support a minister comfortably,
though perhaps not handsomely, while he did what in any case he
wanted to do.

Fenn agreed with me that there was a good deal wrong with
the churches, but he felt that good institutions were easier to re-
form by work from within than by attack from without. I found
this to be the point of view of most of my fellow students. Many
of them were reluctant to say so, but I came to feel that they thought
Christianity, as then interpreted and practiced, was a good religion
much in need of improvement and not too difficult to improve. The
idea of reforming Christianity from within instead of destroying
it for its sins, as Ingersoll wanted to do, appealed to me strongly
as an argument for joining the Unitarian ministry; but in the end I
decided in favor of anthropology, with the mental reservation that
it was to be a humanistic anthropology. Working against my leaning toward the ministry had been an anthropology course which the
Divinity authorities had permitted me to take as an extra.

First-year anthropology was in 1904 an undergraduate course
handled by the Peabody Museum, but I understood that under the
rules it could be looked upon as a graduate course and counted toward a doctorate. This tentative plan of mine I confided to William
Curtis Farabee, who was interested enough to talk it over with the
head of the Peabody Museum and of the Department of Anthropology, Frederic Ward Putnam. On its becoming clear that the
Divinity School, as well as the American Unitarian Society, had
known all along that I was studying religion as folklore, the museum decided to award me the Phoebe Hearst Fellowship, earmarked for anthropology.

During my first year at the Divinity School I was not, of course,
wholly severed from Icelandic matters or, for that matter, from my
own family, and what I heard from them sometimes brought back
old memories. For instance, when I told my family, through my
sister Inga, that I would be living near Boston when at Harvard,
my mother sent me word that her half brother, the immigration

agent who had switched us from Brazil to Canada, was now living
in Stockbridge, Massachusetts. I was reminded of this one day when
Professor Fenn was lecturing on New England theology. He char-
acterized a proper Bostonian from the religious point of view as
a man who was Unitarian in the Back Bay during winter but in
summer turned Episcopalian in Stockbridge. After class, I mentioned my uncle to Fenn and hinted that I might run up to Stockbridge for a week end and look up the old gentleman and find something interesting to write home about. Fenn said that he had friends
in Stockbridge who lived there all the year round and might know
my relatives.

The next week end I went hopefully to Stockbridge, only to discover that Uncle John Anderson was not nearly so prominent as I
had gathered from the stories about him that I had heard as a
child. Having heard of him as an Episcopalian, I sought out the
sexton of the Stockbridge Episcopal Church. He showed genuine
sadness at my inquiry. All but two of the Anderson family were, it
seemed, buried in the churchyard. There remained only Uncle
John's eldest son William, whose whereabouts the sexton did not
know, and the eldest daughter, a young woman of vivacity and
charm who had become a Navy nurse and was off somewhere on sea
duty. I meant to follow up this lead, but never did. It may have
been she about whom I read some years later when the newspapers
for several days carried front-page stories about a liquor smuggling
ring, the moving spirit of which, though not its financial head, was
a Navy nurse named Mary Anderson.

Harvard, in 1904, had just opened a new hospital, the Stillman
Infirmary. I heard a good deal about it because my roommate,
Thorvaldur Thorvaldson, was a friend of the university's chief physician, a Dr. Bailey. "Valdi" Thorvaldson, who came from Manitoba, was working at Harvard for his B.S. in mathematics and
physics. He and I had become friends two summers earlier, when
we had worked as wheat threshers in North Dakota. One morning
in our Howland Street lodging, Valdi had a fit of vomiting. When
he felt better, he walked over to Dr. Bailey's office in the new
building. There he expected to take his place in a line of ailing boys
and be looked over when his turn came. As ill luck would have it,
Bailey encountered Valdi just as he was about to enter the waiting
room. In order to save Valdi the trouble of standing in line, he

briefly listened to a description of the symptoms, construed them
as indigestion, and prescribed some medicine.

Early the following morning I was awakened by my roommate's violent vomiting. I telephoned Dr. Bailey. By six o'clock
Valdi was on the operating table, but it was too late. His appendix
had burst and peritonitis had set in. Dr. Bailey said later that but
for the unfortunate fact that they were close friends, Valdi would
have had a routine and thorough examination and the operation
would have been performed in time to save his life.

A week later I was on my way to the Icelandic settlement on the
west shore of Lake Winnipeg, taking home for burial one of the
most promising young men I have ever known.

7 *From Anthems to Anthropology*

The transfer across Divinity Avenue to the Peabody Museum once decided upon, I began to discuss with Frederic Putnam what had long been in my mind—a plan to spend the summer of 1904 in Iceland. At the end of our series of conversations, Putnam asked how I apparently knew more than he did about tenth-century relations between Europeans and Eskimos both in Greenland and in Labrador. If that was true, I told him, it might be because I was able to read in both of the main source languages, Icelandic and Latin. Putnam then withdrew what might have been disapproval and supported my plan.

Part of my justification to the Department of Anthropology for visiting my parents' birthplace was that I hoped to distinguish between lore and fact in the accounts of the historic Icelandic diet that I had heard from my parents and other Dakota Icelanders. Putnam had been questioning me on this subject since my transfer to his jurisdiction, and my answers had interested him greatly.

My mother's first knowledge of bread, I had told him, was largely of something called Vienna cookies, which her mother used to bake and store up to give as treats to visiting children. Practically the only cookies my mother herself had had a chance to taste were those offered her on neighbors' farms when she went visiting. Other than this, her only cereal food had been a little oatmeal porridge mixed with *skyr*. In general, her diet, like that of her farm contemporaries on the north coast of Iceland, had been, in descending order, milk and milk products, mutton, beef, and fish. Putnam was struck by the fact that my mother had been in her teens before she ever heard of toothache, and then only as an affliction of people who lived in seaport villages. This, said Putnam, was a matter that should be investigated.

I traveled to Iceland as cheaply as possible on a steamer that had been announced for early retirement by her owners, the Scandinavian-American Line, but it was comfortable enough for a budding anthropologist. We made a stopover in Copenhagen, where I tried to see a cousin of my mother, Dr. Niels R. Finsen, who I learned had been awarded the 1903 Nobel Prize for medicine. Unfortunately, I never had the chance to meet him, for he was already in his last illness when I arrived and he died that September.

On landing in Reykjavik I found, as I had expected, that my Icelandic was rusty. Though I had learned scarcely a word of English before I was five, I had spoken mostly English after my eighth year and practically nothing else since my twelfth. Icelandic came back quickly, however, and my fear that my accent had been corrupted proved groundless. There are dialect differences between Iceland's south and north coasts, though they are not as pronounced as the differences between Vermont and Alabama. In a month the north-coast accent of my parents had come back to me, even though most of my Reykjavik associates spoke the southern variant. After listening to me, those who were language specialists could tell from which counties my parents had come.

Soon after reaching Iceland I began working in the National Library at Reykjavik on the suggested relation of tooth decay to the use of cereal foods. No one in Iceland, I was told, would question the substantial accuracy of my mother's account of the absence both of cereal foods and of tooth decay in her childhood. A thousand years earlier, considerable quantities of bread and porridge, as well as ale and mead, had been consumed in Iceland. But following the so-called ''Viking Age,'' that is from around 1200 to 1800, there had been practically no commerce with Europe, and most Icelanders had undoubtedly lived most of their lives without ever tasting cereals. Then, from roughly the time of the Congress of Vienna, there had been steadily increasing commerce. By the time my mother was in her teens, during the 1850s, village people were getting a substantial amount of cereals and some sugar, which in those days was used mostly as rock candy held in the cheek while one drank hot coffee, the heat of which was suspected as another cause of tooth decay.

These findings pleased me, for I knew that they would whet Putnam's curiosity and better my chances for promoting what I now grandiosely thought of as a Harvard Anthropological Expedition to Iceland in the summer of 1905. But another development proved even more important to my cause, though I did not at first recognize it as grist for my mill. Napier, the chess champion of England, visited Iceland during my stay and matched his skill against that of Bjorn Pallson, a schoolboy who for a year or two had been winning against all comers. His defeat of the Englishman seemed to me a confirmation of what I had always heard : that at the chess board Icelanders scored high. The Pallson-Napier match remained in my mind, and not long after my return to Harvard I mentioned it to Dean Nathaniel Shaler, who had once been a friend of Paul Morphy, the American chess genius. Shaler showed immediate interest. Did I know what Pallson's educational plans were? I did not, but I inquired of a friend in Iceland and learned that Pallson had entered the University at Copenhagen as a freshman in engineering. Did I plan to visit Iceland again? the dean then wanted to know. I replied that it was my hope to do so.

Dean Shaler, who felt that intellectual games such as chess deserved a place in intercollegiate competition no less than athletics, expressed the hope that I would somehow persuade Pallson to transfer his engineering studies from Copenhagen to Cambridge, where he knew he could at least get the boy a scholarship. So, it now seemed to me that I might have support for my Iceland plans from one of Harvard's most influential deans.

During my years at Harvard I joined four clubs, clubs that with the advantage of hindsight I now perceive to have been just those which I should have joined if I were to count on them for help in my career, which at the time was not entirely clear to me.

Joining the Canadian Club was natural for me, since I was born a Canadian. That I also became its secretary was probably because of the fact that the club could find nobody else to do the work. The president, an advanced law student from New Brunswick named Andrew Knox Dysart, was destined to become a leading lawyer of Manitoba. A member well liked but not yet well known was William Lyon Mackenzie King, who became Prime Minister of Canada in 1921 and held that position longer than any other Canadian.

Of the Harvard Folklore Society, I was an eager but inconspicuous member among many who were conspicuous and deserved to be, George Lyman Kittredge being the most notable. My status was the same, without office or distinction, in the Geological and Geographical Society, of which Dean Shaler was the foremost member.

The fourth of the clubs that did their part to spur me on my way—although at the time I still did not perceive the exact direction—was the Scandinavian. Its real name, which I remember though I never understood its meaning, was the Edda Club. Its president, Raymond Hanson Oveson, was that year's most prominent man and also president of the senior class. I do not remember why I was made the Edda Club's secretary except that, as with the Canadian Club, nobody else would do the work. However, there was something in that job that could be made of immediate value to me, for the Edda was frequent host to distinguished scholars, linguists in the Germanic-Nordic-Sanskrit group. It was my job as secretary to correspond with them.

My vaguely planned Harvard Expedition to Iceland ultimately dropped almost fully shaped into my lap from a most unexpected source. There was in the Geology Department a professor better known to the Divinity School than to his geology colleagues, though he was well known to them as a volcanologist. This was Professor Thomas Augustus Jaggar, who was to us Divinity people that incredible thing, a rated scientist who believed—really believed—that the universe had been created during six working days in the year 4004 B.C. When we first heard this we took it for a canard. Professor Jaggar, however, proved to be a Sunday school teacher, and our Divinity spies penetrated his classes again and again without difficulty until we were satisfied that he was really sincere in thinking Bishop Usher's chronology accurate.

Professor Jaggar was as clearly sound in volcanology as he was unsound in cosmic chronology. He knew about the volcanoes of Iceland, and he had heard of me as an authentic Icelander who would like to get up an expedition. We put our heads together and in a few days had developed a plan. With a professor of volcanology as head and me as interpreter, and with my parents' relatives living all over Iceland, we could hardly fail. We were practically assured of funds that more than a dozen Harvard men would contribute to finance Jaggar and me. Putnam also told me that Jack Hastings, a young man of means, was planning to finance a side trip for himself and me, so that while other members of the party, presumably with

Jaggar in command, went off in pursuit of volcanoes, Hastings and I could go off and dig up specimens.

Dean Shaler had not lost sight of his scheme to make Harvard an outstanding chess team by having me bring back from Copenhagen to Iceland, and thence to Boston, the remarkable Bjorn Pallson. I had written Pallson and it was all settled. I was to be a proctor next season in Holyoke, with a sitting room and two bedrooms at my disposal, and Pallson could share my quarters. The dean had arranged the scholarship, and somewhere he had found the cash for a steamer ticket for Pallson.

All this worked out but for one last-minute hitch. I do not now remember, if I ever knew, why Jaggar could not come with us to Iceland, but instead he spent his summer studying the volcanoes of the Hawaiian Islands. About a dozen of us reached Reykjavik in June, 1905. We bought ponies, hired guides, and split up into three parties, the main one crossing Iceland on horseback and the second, a geological party, going to selected places to work. The third, an anthropological party, consisted of Jack Hastings and myself. With two riding horses and a pack horse we anthropologists set out to reach a corner of southwestern Iceland, where there had once been a sandy peninsula jutting out. The eroding waves had cut its neck and converted its tip into an island.

Once there had been a church on the island; now there was only a graveyard, which was being gradually carried away by the ocean. The site was ideal for our purpose, which was to get documentation of the physical characteristics of Icelanders from the eleventh century, when the church had been built, to the thirteenth or fourteenth century, when it was abandoned because the island was growing smaller and the channel between it and the mainland was growing wider. We knew little about the history of the people whose bones we would recover for study, and could only assume that they were ordinary folk whose ancestors had come mainly from Ireland and later from Norway and from Scotland and the lesser isles—the Shetlands, Orkneys, Hebrides, and such.

We were physical anthropologists, concerned primarily with skeletons, but the laws of Iceland did not permit grave robbing, even for the laudable purposes of science. On this small island, however, was a burial site that was being eaten away by the sea, and there were no plans to halt the erosion. We were told by a clergyman that the authorities would certainly permit us to carry away any

skulls that had been disinterred by the sea. Moreover, he thought
that we might venture to dig up two or three of the old graves, especially ones near the edge that looked as if they might soon be
washed away. We went ahead on that basis, and in about two weeks
secured some nearly complete skeletons and a total of eighty-six
skulls, most of which we found rolling around in the surf. Walking
up and down along the beach one day when the tide was low, we
picked up a cupful of loose teeth.

It seemed to us, as we packed up to leave, that the evidence we
had collected would tend to confirm our expectations about the Icelandic diet. The average stature seemed to be less than that of modern
Icelanders. We saw no decayed teeth in any of the skulls; the loose
teeth we found were accounted for by the pounding the skulls took
from the waves. We had not expected to find many articles that had
been buried with the dead and, in fact, we had found none, perhaps
because there had never been finger rings or other jewelry. Or perhaps any that might have existed had been picked up before our
time. This possibility, we thought, might explain the absence of
crucifixes, a few of which we had thought we might find. The bones
were our main concern, and we were quite pleased with them.

Toward autumn the members of the expedition gathered at
Reykjavik; nearly everybody was well satisfied with the summer,
the scenery, and the climate. There had been numerous surprising
discoveries, two of which had pleased the cross-country party: they
had found a marvelous new cheese and also a better way to make
coffee. I could not at first understand what these could be. It turned
out that the "cheese" was unsalted butter that had been deliberately allowed to sour with some of the buttermilk left in it, and that
the especially delicious coffee was the result of the addition of what
the Icelanders call "coffee improver"—chicory. The men who had
been so delighted with the Icelandic cheese lost their taste for it
when they learned that it was butter. It was the same with the
delicious Iceland coffee.

All but two of our party were now through with the Icelandic
journey and were about to separate, some going to Britain or to the
Continent for the autumn, others hurrying back home across the
Atlantic. The exceptions were the geologist Ferguson, who was getting results that pleased him and made him want to continue, and I,
who had to wait for the slow local transport which would bring our
collection of bones from the southwest. This delay pleased me, for it

gave me the chance to ride north across Iceland to visit a brother and sister of my father.

If a man wants to travel fast and far in Iceland, he needs two horses, for the horses are ponies, only some two hundred pounds heavier than a Shetland, and likely to tire when carrying a moderately heavy man. By good fortune I made the two-hundred-mile crossing of Iceland in the company of Professor Finnur Jonsson of the University of Copenhagen, the foremost authority on Greenland during the Middle Ages. For several days Jonsson and I rode side by side. His Icelandic vocabulary and accent had remained perfect, although he had lived in Denmark since his youth and had been back to Iceland only twice. He had been so seriously afflicted with seasickness on his first trip that it had taken him a score of years to make up his mind to make the journey again. He was sure that this visit would be his last.

Jonsson was an expert in Icelandic art and literature, identifying as we passed them the historic sites that were everywhere about us. Among other things, he was able to show me places from which colonists, bound for Greenland in the tenth century, had departed from Iceland. His route branched off from mine before we reached Akureyri, in the neighborhood of which, on different farms, lived my aunt and uncle. My grandfather Stefan had been twice married, and this particular uncle, Stefan Stefansson, was only four years older than I. He had a large farm and agreed to keep both my horses until I came to Iceland again, which I assured him would be in a year or two.

Back in Reykjavik, my chess prodigy awaited me and we traveled together to Edinburgh and by Allan Line from Glasgow to Montreal. During almost the entire trip Pallson was seasick. This was unfortunate for both of us, because there were two chess champions aboard, an Australian, and the Canadian champion, Professor James Mavor from the University of Toronto. These two were constantly at chess in the smoking room and inveigled me into occasional games, most or all of which I lost. I promised them some stiff competition from my friend below decks, but was not able to produce him until after we passed the Strait of Belle Isle, when the Gulf of St. Lawrence became as smooth as a river.

Pallson then made his appearance and won every game. When the older men asked about his ability at blindfold chess, Pallson said that anybody whom he could beat when the board was before him he could also beat without seeing the moves, provided those of his opponent were rightly announced. He was as good as his word in two simultaneous games.

Upon reporting in at the Peabody Museum I discovered that the staff was well pleased with the work that Hastings and I had done during the summer. Jack had reached home ahead of me and had reported to Putnam in a message that gratified the entire museum staff. Since the members of this group became my long-time associates, I shall mention them here.

To begin with, some claimed that Putnam had one eccentricity: he resented the mechanical way in which even at Harvard people were beginning to be rated by the earned degrees they held, the M.A. and Ph.D. labels. His favorite theme was that men like George Lyman Kittredge, an acknowledged authority on Shakespeare and equally eminent in several other fields, had no earned degree beyond an A.B. William James did not even have an A.B. and still had won more honorary degrees than you could shake a stick at. Putnam used to tell how Alexander Agassiz, whose apprentice he himself had been, was accustomed to sneer at men who ground along until they "earned" a Ph.D. It was especially gratifying to me that in Putnam's welcome-home conversation he said that as long as I kept wanting to follow anthropology as a career he hoped I would stop taking examinations. I had an A.B. from a fine Western university and that was enough in his department, where he hoped I would remain.

Putnam thought that I should not aim at becoming solely a classroom worker but should emulate the field study of the men who would be my colleagues, while keeping out of their chosen territories. Roland Burrage Dixon, whose course Anthropology 5 I was taking, had traveled in Siberia and other parts of Asia and so perhaps I ought to keep out of that area. The second in rank was Alfred Marston Tozzer, whom I had not yet met because he was working in the field in southern Mexico. Therefore, that section was already pre-empted. William Curtis Farabee, with whom I had taken Anthropology 1 while I was still in the Divinity School, would perhaps be going to South America. Putnam pointed out that nobody connected with our department had as yet made much of a study of Africa. What would I think of that field?

I thought well of it and Putnam said he was glad. He had friends in the British Museum who might help me to get a berth on an expedition to east central Africa. He would look into this possibility. Meanwhile, he said, I might as well start reading up in my spare time.

Beginning with the fall term of 1905, I was a teaching fellow, looked upon as the Anthropology Department's authority on the polar regions, particularly the Arctic, I suppose because my parents were Icelandic and I had been born "way up north in Canada." Putnam wanted me to write an article for the *American Anthropologist* about how the Icelanders had explored Greenland in the late 900s and how they had then encountered Eskimos in Labrador around 1004. To my objection that all this was an old story in Europe, particularly among Scandinavians, he replied that he simply wanted me to open the topic for Americans, many of whom, he felt sure, were like himself in having few ideas in this field— perhaps some of them wrong. I went ahead with an article that was sent to the *Anthropologist,* then delayed in publication but circulated a bit in its preliminary form.

Dean Shaler's plans and mine for Pallson and the chess club did not turn out to affect the club much but, as it seems to me now, they brought about the second important change of direction in my career, this one turning me from Africa to the Arctic.

The dean's plan for the chess future of Harvard had leaked out—whether through his fault or mine or someone else's I never knew. Probably none of us tried very hard to be secretive. At first, what happened seemed a terrible misfortune. Later, to me at least, it did not seem so. The real chess players of the university, we now learned, did not feel that they needed a ringer from Iceland to guarantee them against disaster in the coming midwinter tournament. They invoked the intercollegiate athletic rules to disqualify Shaler's and my hero. Because Pallson was undeniably a student from Copenhagen who had transferred to Harvard, he was not eligible to play in an intercollegiate match until the following year!

It has been said that this upsetting of our dream broke Pallson's heart, but in fact Dean Shaler and I were the hardest hit. I do not know how it would have affected Pallson if he had not been crushed instead by something else. It seemed an absurdity to me, but it was truly devastating to him. He became obsessed with the idea that he was about to go insane. Just when the rest of us thought he ought to be upset or angry over having some rules keep him out of play, he came to me with the announcement that his mind was breaking down. He had read somewhere that there is a high incidence of mental illness among chess players, that the better the player the greater the danger, and that those in the greatest danger were the chess geniuses who were cursed with an inability to forget their games.

I think the inability to forget affected Pallson most. He had been telling me and others about this very trait in himself. Almost from infancy he remembered every game he had ever played; he could set them up from memory and mentally analyze the mistakes he or his opponent had made. Probably I did not take his case seriously enough when he first presented it to me, for I thought I could laugh him out of it. But a day or two later he disappeared. Fortunately, I did not rush to the police with my first idea, that he might have committed suicide. Shaler, when I consulted him, thought that the truant would turn up in a few days, ashamed of himself.

Some time later a letter came from Winnipeg. A relative of Pallson had found him a job there as a hod carrier. Pallson's thought was that by never playing chess again, and by working himself until he was dead tired and could fall into a dreamless sleep every night, his mind might perhaps be saved. All those who knew him agreed with me that it was best for me to do nothing.

At the University of Toronto, Professor Mavor was disappointed to learn that he could not work out a plan to earn some money for Pallson and increase the boy's fame by a series of exhibition games throughout Canada. While we succeeded in nothing we tried to do for Pallson, our joint failure drew Mavor and me together and eventually made this influential Canadian my chief friend and adviser in the career as an anthropologist which he began to see ahead of me. At the time of the Pallson episode Mavor, I feel sure, had no clear plans for me, nor did I have any for myself.

There is one more thing to tell of Pallson. Frank Marshall, then the chess champion of the United States, had been on a Western tour and was returning East through Canada, stopping for a series of exhibition games in Winnipeg. Someone who knew Pallson suggested that they join the crowd to watch the play. One of the Winnipeg players did not show up. A few of those present who knew Pallson could play chess, but who said later they had no idea he was especially good, practically dragged him up to the vacant board, and the game started in the routine way. After a few moves Marshall seemed puzzled. He complained later that he had not been warned and said this player should have been seated at the head table. Marshall lost that one game of the exhibition, but expressed a desire to meet Pallson later in a return match. Pallson, however, refused to play again, and never played anybody afterward, at least in Winnipeg. His game with Marshall is apparently the only one of those he played west of the Atlantic that has been preserved. It was reprinted from a Winnipeg record by *Lasker's Chess Magazine.*

Pallson remained a year in Canada, gave up his job as a hod carrier, changed his career from engineering to law, and eventually became a lawyer in Iceland. He did not live to see his family's re-entry into the world of chess through his nephew, who for the last three years has been a recognized grand master, playing for Iceland in various international tournaments.

The year 1905—my urge to write poetry having become a thing of the past—marked my first real efforts at prose. Dean Shaler helped me to secure a reporting job on the *Boston Evening Transcript,* partly because he thought that it would be good for me to associate with its editor and staff, some of whom were friends of his. At the dean's suggestion, Frank Basil Tracy, his special friend, got several of his staff to keep a friendly eye on me. On the *Transcript* I had the saddest job ever assigned to me by a boss: I was to keep a death watch on Shaler himself, who was so prominent, and whose coming death was so assuredly forecast by his doctors, that columns of material about him, including headlines, were set up in advance by the *Transcript,* ready to be on the street a few minutes after I telephoned in the news of the professor's death. I remember many things about those preparations, including comment on the dean's most famous course, Geology 4, which I had supplied from my recollections as a student. But I do not recall ever seeing the issue of the *Transcript* that contained Shaler's obituary.

Two years earlier, I had published what I think of as the first of my technical writings. The article attracted wide attention and later happened to catch the eye of Henry Mencken and so was included in the form of fairly extensive quotation in his book *The American Language.* I think of it as a contribution to the theory of grammatical gender. Its title was "English Loan-Nouns Used in the Icelandic Colony of North Dakota," and it appeared first in *Dialect Notes,* 1903. During 1904, I published in the quarterly

Poet Lore two articles, "The Newer Literature of Iceland" and "Present Day Literature of Iceland." During 1905, I wrote two articles which were slow in getting published, as is often the case in technical journals: "Icelandic Beast and Bird Lore" for the *Journal of American Folklore,* and "The Icelandic Colony in Greenland," the paper mentioned earlier that I did at Putnam's suggestion. Though its circulation in galley proof began in 1905, I may have had my first intimation that it was being read attentively when in April, 1906, I received a telegram that turned me from Africa to the Arctic.

The telegram offered to pay my round-trip expenses if I would come to Chicago to discuss taking a job with a polar expedition. At the University of Chicago I met one of the expedition's two commanders, Ernest de Koven Leffingwell, a Ph.D. in geology. A tall, keen man a half-dozen years older than I, Leffingwell had already spent a year in the Arctic as a member of the Baldwin-Ziegler Polar Expedition, and was thus familiar with northerly east Greenland and the Spitsbergen-Franz Josef region. His particular friend on the staff of that expedition had been a Danish naval man, Ejnar Mikkelsen. Things had gone rather badly under their American commander, Evelyn Briggs Baldwin. The staff had come to feel that they could have managed a great deal better than their commander. Upon their return south, they had not felt that they wanted to go north again with William Ziegler's next venture, the Fiala-Ziegler Expedition. They decided instead to promote their own, which might have become known as the Leffingwell-Mikkelsen Expedition but for their choosing another name.

Leffingwell offered me the job of anthropologist with the Anglo-American Polar Expedition. In explaining the plans and the organization of the expedition, he told me that their largest single contributor was the Duchess of Bedford and that their vessel, a schooner without auxiliary power, was accordingly named the *Duchess of Bedford.* A large contributor, too, was his own father, Dr. Charles Wesley Leffingwell. There were many other backers, among them the Royal Geographical Society of London, the American Geographical Society of New York, and *Harper's Magazine.* One of the ideas behind this expedition had been picked up from Sir Clements Markham, president of the Royal Geographical Society, who believed that there probably was an undiscovered continent up in the Arctic Ocean. One reason for his belief was that there were stories of natives who were supposed to have gone back and forth between this land and northeastern Siberia at one time.

Now, said Leffingwell, one of the expedition's substantial backers was a man whose main reason for support was anthropological. The study of these supposed natives of the supposed continent was therefore very important. This man had asked who would be on the expedition to make adequate use of what could be learned from these or other natives. He had been assured that Mikkelsen knew a good deal about Eskimos, having been with a Danish expedition to Greenland in 1900. The prospective donor had not considered this qualification good enough. He expressed full confidence in Mikkelsen as a land traveler and sea navigator, but he wanted a "real" anthropologist to be included in the expedition staff or he would withdraw his support.

With this in mind, Leffingwell and Mikkelsen had cast about for an accredited anthropologist, preferably an ethnologist, and had found most of them already holding down jobs they did not want to relinquish. Finally, they learned about Professor Putnam's perhaps unattached assistant who had recently written a paper on Eskimos. Why not investigate him? The investigation proved satisfactory enough for us to agree that if Putnam advised me to do so I would accept.

Back at Harvard, I found Putnam in favor of my accepting. He was, however, bothered by the fact that the *Duchess of Bedford* lacked auxiliary power. Sailing north from Victoria, British Columbia, through several thousand miles of harborless seas and then proceeding another thousand miles east around the north coasts of Alaska and northwestern arctic Canada under nothing but canvas would be a precarious and time-consuming undertaking. What could an ethnologist do all that time except twiddle his thumbs? Putnam, himself a New Englander and somewhat familiar with Yankee whaling north of Alaska and in the Canadian western Arctic, knew that a sailing vessel might well be detained by ice on the coast of Alaska and never—or at least not in the first year—reach the northwestern Canadian Eskimos, themselves a fascinating study if the sought-for arctic continent were never found.

Putnam's advice was therefore conditional: I should accept, with the understanding that I would join the expedition when it reached the Yankee whaling harbor at Herschel Island, just west of the delta of the Mackenzie River in northwestern arctic Canada. To reach these New England whaling grounds I would go overland by rail from Boston to Edmonton, in Alberta, Canada, and then with the Hudson's Bay Company fur traders northeast along the Athabaska-Slave-Mackenzie river system, studying the little-known Athapaska Indians as I traveled. I would plan to join the Eskimos at the head of the Mackenzie delta and stay with them and the New Bedford whalers if the expedition never got that far. With this program my prospects would be good, Putnam thought. During my leisurely two-thousand-mile journey northwestward with the fur brigades, I would pick up a lot of directly valuable anthropological information and would become gradually initiated into the ways of the north. If the *Duchess* caught up with me at or near Herschel Island, Putnam thought my chances of finding Eskimos who never had met whites might prove good in the Victoria Island region. This would be a help if the hypothetical continent that the water-borne section of the expedition was to seek never materialized.

I told Leffingwell about these conditional plans. I also communicated them to Professor Mavor. Leffingwell was equally conditional in his acceptance. He felt that I should find Harvard money to cover the additional travel expenses that the Harvard plan would entail. Putnam said he would agree to this if the Peabody Museum received any collections I might make on my side trip via the Mackenzie. Mavor was enthusiastic about this revised plan. If Putnam would agree, he said, he would find University of Toronto money on behalf of the Royal Ontario Museum to share the expenses with the Peabody Museum. This three-cornered plan was settled upon.

Putnam sent some message of regret and thanks to the British Museum, which, I understood, had made a tentative arrangement for me, as ethnologist, to accompany a British expedition into east central Africa. In preparation, I did a little hasty Canadian arctic reading, but planned to rely mainly on two things: what I already knew about the northeastern lands and seas and what I could learn from the fur traders with whom I would travel northward along the Mackenzie.

For my northward travel Mavor, being a long-time supporter of Canadian anthropology, was busy making local arrangements, particularly with the three groups whose good will I most needed, the Hudson's Bay Company and missions of the Church of Eng-

land and of the Roman Catholic Church. Mavor was able to get
the funds he had promised for the journey through the Canadian
northwest from Sir Edmund Walker, president of the Canadian
Bank of Commerce, who gave the money to the University of Toronto
earmarked for me.

Everything was now accomplished except the journey itself.

Two

8

My First
Arctic Expedition

The universities of Harvard and Toronto, which where sponsoring my first journey to the North American Arctic, were primarily interested in the Athapaska Indians whom I might encounter on my way from Edmonton to the Mackenzie River. The Eskimos with whom I planned to live after reaching the arctic coast were of secondary importance, and it was left to me to work out with Mikkelsen and Leffingwell a program for studying them.

Putnam of Harvard agreed that Mavor of Toronto could give me the best idea of how to make the most of my time among the Indians. I accordingly headed first for Toronto, learned what I could from Mavor, and met my personal Canadian sponsor, Sir Edmund Walker. There was not much time, for my journey north depended on the breakup of the ice in the northern rivers. I stopped at Winnipeg for a briefing by the men of the Hudson's Bay Company, chiefly by that venerable officer Roderick MacFarlane, who had been to the mouth of the Anderson River as early as 1857 on a mission for the Smithsonian Institution and who had built the company's most northerly trading post in 1861. He knew the region better than any other living man.

In 1906, when I headed for the Arctic for the first time, the Hudson's Bay Company still controlled traffic on the river routes to the north, although it had long since ceased to be the governing body in northern Canada. Travel would have been practically impossible without the cooperation of the company, which Mavor had secured for me. My two most important companions on the trip north were to be John Anderson, chief trader for the company in the Mackenzie District, and Bishop William Day Reeve of the Church of England, who had been carrying on his missionary work in the neighborhood of Great Slave Lake and on the lower river since 1869. His vast knowledge of the Athapaskans gave me an insight into their nature and ways that I could not possibly have acquired by myself in the time at my disposal.

Trader Anderson knew when the ice was likely to go out of the Athabaska River. At what he thought was the right time we went to Edmonton, where we received a confirmation of Anderson's guess. We immediately loaded ourselves and baggage into a demo-crat wagon, an uncovered vehicle with several crosswise seats and room for our equipment behind them.

The trip to Athabaska Landing took two days and, in spite of the roughness of the way and the hardness of the seats, was thoroughly enjoyable. We slept in farmhouses, lying on the floor rolled in our blankets, and ate farm food, to an accompaniment of genial and informative talk that delighted as much as it instructed me.

There were two ways of traveling north on the river from Athabaska Landing: by stern-wheel steamer or by flat-bottomed scow designed for carrying freight. We chose, perhaps for the sake of dignity, the first. We boarded the *Midnight Sun,* and were carried downstream in her for thirteen days. There was never a dull moment, for the little steamer proved to be an expert in stoving in her bottom on hidden rocks and sinking in two or three feet of water. Whenever this happened, she had to be jacked up and her bottom patched. Although the river current ran at from two to four miles an hour, the *Midnight Sun* never averaged that speed. We made only 165 miles in our thirteen days—to Grand Rapids Island, 250 miles north of Edmonton.

In addition to Bishop Reeve, there was on board an Anglican clergyman who was on his way to a missionary post farther north. This cleric suffered so much from the heat and the mosquitoes (his life in mosquitoless England had permitted no building up of im-munity to their stings), and also from his impressions of the Athapaskans he saw along the way, that I believe he would have turned back but for his own pride and Bishop Reeve's encourage-ment. To add to his discomfort he had an encounter, on one of his trips ashore, with an unfamiliar black-and-white creature whose attentions made it necessary for him, when he returned to his un-

appreciative fellow travelers on board, to throw his only clerical
suit overboard.

My first real introduction to the richness of the resources of
the Canadian north came at Pelican Rapids, where the night was
illuminated by a flaming jet of natural gas. Someone, aware of the
seepages of mineral tar along the river, had dug for oil and struck
gas, which had accidentally caught fire and now continued to burn.

Beyond the portage at Grand Rapids we transferred from our
stern-wheeler to scows. We made the run from there to Fort Mc-
Murray, halfway between Athabaska Landing and Athabaska Lake,
in good time despite the sinking of one of the scows and the almost
complete loss of its cargo of sugar and other trade goods. I say
almost complete loss because one item—a bale of various colored
ribbons—was salvaged. Although all the colors had run together
in the dunking, the Hudson's Bay people declared that the Indians
for whom the ribbons were destined would probably much prefer
them multicolored.

I was not discouraged, as the English clergyman was, but there
were things I did not like about this stage of my journey. One
thing was the scourge of mosquitoes, the awfulness of which no one
who has not traveled toward the Arctic Circle could possibly
imagine. The second thing that I could have done without was the
heat. One day after we left Grand Rapids the temperature reached
103° F. in the shade. The third disturbing element in an otherwise
pleasant trip was our constant confrontation with the cruelty of
the Indians and some of the white population toward their dogs.
This was none the less appalling because it was inconsistent. The
Indians loved to keep their animals smart-looking and to deck them
out with bells and all kinds of fancy harness, but they did not
hesitate, before starting on a trip, to beat each member of a team
until he cringed, thereby leaving him and his fellow creatures with
only one desire—to run as fast as they could.

In summer, when the dogs' services were not required, the
Indians often failed to feed them and left them to forage for themselves. The strong ones survived and were rounded up when needed
for winter travel. On our way downstream we were often followed
by packs of stray dogs, some of whose masters were probably members of our crews. They ran along over rocks and windfalls, through
almost impenetrable tangles, trying to keep the scows in sight.
When the channel shifted from one side of the river to another,

these pitiful creatures would plunge into the river, swim across, and take up their hopeless journey on the opposite bank.

At Fort McMurray, eight hundred miles north of Edmonton, we transferred from our scows to another steamer, the *Grahame,* also a stern-wheeler but with less of a tendency to sink than the *Midnight Sun.* We traveled aboard the *Grahame* down the Athabaska and westward across Athabaska Lake to a sixteen-mile rapid at Smith Portage, now known as Fort Fitzgerald. The Smith after whom Smith Portage and Smith's Landing were named was one of Canada's truly great and influential men, later a very influential friend of mine—once plain Donald Smith, then Sir Donald, with a mountain at Banff named after him, and finally Lord Strathcona, with a great number of places named after him.

At the lower end of the rapids we transferred to still another steamer, the *Wrigley,* a miniature oceangoing vessel driven by a propeller instead of a stern paddle wheel. She drew more water than the stern-wheelers and was considered a better risk for the crossing of Great Slave Lake, which is almost as large as, and far more unpredictable than, Lake Erie. The *Wrigley* had inside accommodations for only six passengers. I slept on deck, being more interested in experience than in comfort, and enjoyed it thoroughly. We were out of sight of land for several hours while crossing the lake, and had to take account of many uncharted bars and grounded snags of driftwood. The *Wrigley* had her own way of dealing with these. She normally steamed ahead with a number of two-hundred-pound bags of shot weighting down her bow. If she ran onto a sand bar, both crew and passengers pitched in and moved the bags of shot to the stern, which immediately sank lower into the water. The bow then came up, and the *Wrigley* backed off the bar.

It is difficult to tell where Great Slave Lake ends and the Mackenzie River proper begins. The lake as it narrows toward the northwest, simply commences to flow a little more rapidly. In 1906, trading posts along the Mackenzie were about a hundred miles apart. Each had a luxuriant garden of which fine potatoes were a feature, beneficiaries of the almost constant summer sunlight. I imagine that, except for the few settlements, the river, with its green intervals and dark forests covering the hills, did not in 1906 differ much in appearance from the river that Mackenzie himself saw in 1789.

On this trip I learned that although the Hudson's Bay Company had not had a recognized monopoly in the north since 1809, its servants, as the company's employees are called, had not yet learned to regard the Free Traders, who were not associated with the company, as anything but infiltrating spies and interlopers. John Anderson was compelled by recent company orders to give passage to Free Traders if they asked for it, but when a young man came aboard at arctic Red River to ride with us as far as Fort McPherson, Anderson treated him as if he had the plague.

At the point where the arctic Red River flows into the Mackenzie we were eighteen hundred river miles from Athabaska Landing and almost at the beginning of the Mackenzie delta. At Red River on July 20, 1906, I saw my first Eskimos. They were not at all as my book learning about the north had led me to believe they would be. I had expected them to be short and fat. When I saw them standing among white men on the river bank I was surprised to find them all about the same height. Still under the spell of my book knowledge, I thought it strange that there should be such short white men in the north. When I went ashore, I found, of course, that the men, white and Eskimo alike, were as tall as or taller than I, and I am just under six feet. One thing I noticed about the Eskimos in particular was their graceful, free-swinging walk. This was in distinct contrast to the jerky, almost furtive movements of the forest Indians. I instinctively began to feel that the Eskimos were a superior race.

Along the Mackenzie there was a distinct, though polite, tendency among the Hudson's Bay Company servants to keep the Indian in his place, and this discrimination tended to show its effect in the demeanor of the forest natives. They often had difficult years and were seriously affected by disease and malnutrition. Often they were reduced to eating meat without sufficient fat, and when this happened they sickened and died. The condition from which they suffered was called "rabbit starvation" because rabbits, which are usually plentiful, have very little fat on them, and Indians reduced to a diet of nothing but rabbit were in fact faced with starvation perhaps even more surely than if they had had nothing to eat at all.

On the way north, Bishop Reeve, by sharing his wealth of experience with me, gave me as a running accompaniment to the ever-changing views of forest and river an understanding of the health problems of the people of the north. I learned of the ravages of measles, smallpox, and tuberculosis. I learned also that scurvy and tooth decay had been rare in the north until the white man brought in cereals and sugar and other processed foods. Though it made comparatively little impression on me at the time, Bishop Reeve told me that cancer had once been practically unknown in the north. Bishop Reeve believed, and made me believe, that the tendency of Indians and Eskimos alike to adopt the white man's habits of living and eating was a very serious matter. I have dealt more fully with my development of the ideas that I got from Bishop Reeve in my book *Cancer: Disease of Civilization?*, published in 1960. The planting of the seeds of these ideas made my trip both pleasant and memorable. After my months with the Bishop, I was able to understand what I was seeing.

At Fort McPherson, a few miles up the Peel River from the beginning of the Mackenzie delta, I began in earnest my years of close acquaintance with the Eskimos. Before settling down to live with them, I had to get news of the *Duchess of Bedford* and to confer, if possible, with Mikkelsen and Leffingwell, who had been confident of reaching Herschel Island from the west and had told me that they would be leaving the island by August 10. It was now the end of July, and Herschel was 250 miles away.

John Firth, the company's manager at McPherson, recommended that I go on to Herschel at once with an enterprising Eskimo—by name Memoranna—who was about to take to Herschel Island Constable Walker of the Mounted Police, an Eskimo family, two Indians, and two nuns. I jumped at the chance of joining the party.

On July 30, we started north down the west side of the delta, towing another boat loaded with freight belonging to the police. The westernmost channel of the river ran between banks covered with heavy timber, some spruce standing as high as sixty feet. After something more than a hundred miles the trees quite suddenly disappeared. Here there was nothing but low willows growing on sandy islands. We soon began to feel the presence of the ocean. We could hear the breakers crashing against the outer islands. The sky was leaden and the wind began to shift and rise.

Since we had no power except the whaleboat's sail and had in tow a heavily laden boat, it was obvious that we could do nothing but go ashore, make camp, and wait. We waited for two or three days, but the weather was still far from good. Constable Walker decided to stay in camp with his freight and the two Indians while the rest of us, piloted by Memoranna, went on to Herschel Island, still ninety miles away to the west. It was agreed that we would send back proper help to get Constable Walker and his freight to Herschel.

For a while we made good progress, and I had an opportunity to get acquainted with Oblutok, the Eskimo passenger, and his family as well as with Memoranna. When we ran into a head wind, Memoranna told us that there was ice ahead. Having taken my ideas of arctic ice from books, I thought of it with some dread as a collection of towering bergs grinding against one another, threatening to topple over and engulf our small boat. I soon realized, however, that Memoranna and the other Eskimos were speaking with excited pleasure of the presence of something that books about the Arctic had always presented as a danger.

Memoranna told me that he always felt comfortable when there was ice about. For one thing, he said, its presence always meant that there was fresh water to be had. I found this baffling, the Arctic Ocean being as salt as any other; but I have since learned from experience that the melted water on top of a good-sized old floe is always fresh. Young ice is very salty, but the older it gets, the fresher it becomes.

Memoranna also said that he liked the ice because his little girl was always seasick in open water. In the lee of heavy ice the water was sure to be calm enough to settle her stomach. This turned out to be so. The ice floes were scattered. Few of them were bigger than a city block in area and between them there were half-mile open patches through which we sailed over smooth water in spite of a stiff wind.

This was my first introduction to sea ice. Through many years I gradually became more and more fond of it until I came to regard it as Eskimos do. When I come back to it after an absence, I feel like a forest dweller who comes in sight of trees after a long journey over the prairie.

On August 7 we were still waiting for the wind to change. During this time Memoranna, in his cabin-boy English, gave me an account of the arctic whaling industry, of which I had heard only vaguely. The first whaling ship had arrived at Herschel Island in 1889 at a time when very few of the Eskimos of the Mackenzie delta region had ever seen a white man. From 1889 on, there were always a number of whalers along the coast, sometimes a dozen or more at a time. They brought with them many Alaskan Eskimos who had worked on whaling ships southwest of Point Barrow for many years. These western Eskimos interpreted to the natives around Herschel Island the exciting but confusing and, for Eskimo, usually lethal ways of the white man. The white whalers wanted fresh meat and fish. The Eskimos had these foods in quantity, and it was easy for the whalers to press upon them preserved and processed foods bought cheaply in San Francisco in exchange for items that the white men wanted. It was not long before meat and fish were to a large extent replaced in the Eskimo diet by sugar, bread, canned fruit, bacon, and other things, when such commodities could be had. In my years among the Eskimos I learned how serious this change in diet, and the dependence upon processed foodstuffs, might become in years in which storms or bad ice conditions prevailed.

Just after midnight on August 8, in a kind of rosy twilight, the sun being just below the horizon, we arrived at Herschel Island. Six whalers were in the harbor, but there was no sign of the *Duchess of Bedford*. Nor was there any word of her.

To the whalers, who had been away from home for periods of time up to three years, I was the bearer of bad news. I told them all I knew of the San Francisco earthquake and fire, which had occurred just before I began my journey north. Unfortunately, knowing little about the Western city, I could not identify the parts of it that had been destroyed and so could give the whalers no idea of the possible safety of their homes and families. Their anxiety on this point, together with the fact that the season was growing short, made the captains and crews eager to get away. Ice conditions had made it impossible for them to get home the year before, and their rations were now short. One by one, they pulled up anchor and sailed to the west.

There was another vessel in the harbor, Roald Amundsen's sloop *Gjoa*. Amundsen, having made the first complete traverse of the Northwest Passage by sea, was about to sail west around Alaska. He cordially invited me to be his guest on board the *Gjoa*. I accepted his hospitality and spent many profitable days, waiting for the *Duchess* and gaining much from my conversations with Amundsen and his second-in-command, Godfred Hansen, who explained to me the admirable features of Danish Eskimo policy in Greenland and the lamentable weakness of Canadian and American policy toward the natives. Amundsen and Hansen told me of the happy, healthy, and resourceful Eskimos of King William Island who had not yet been tainted by infiltration of white ideas of diet and way of living. I felt deeply depressed, believing that in the area I had chosen to investigate, where white influence was strong, I would be studying a dying race.

After Amundsen and the *Gjoa* left, my forebodings began to wear off. I found the Eskimo even at civilization-ridden Herschel to be the happiest people I had ever met. If they were on the way to extinction, the prospect worried them no more than the prospect of age and death worries a six- or seven-year-old child.

One of the whaling captains who was not at Herschel at the moment but about whom I heard much was James McKenna, who had once commanded a large fleet of his own, supposedly acquired as a result of selling forbidden liquor to natives along both shores of Bering Sea. The United States government had, however, come very close to putting a stop to rumrunning in the Arctic and, as a result, McKenna's fortunes had suffered a decline. His fleet had, in 1905, been reduced to two small vessels, the *Charles Hanson* and the *Olga*. The year before I arrived at Herschel, he had demoted the commander of the *Olga*, whom he did not trust, and had put in charge of her an amazing character called Charlie Klinkenberg, though his real name was Christian Klengenberg. Charlie, a Dane, had a reputation for enterprise, energy, and fearlessness—but he was also known to be unscrupulous, ruthless, and two-faced. He might have served as a model for the captain in Jack London's *Sea Wolf*. McKenna, who knew all about Charlie's weaknesses, had taken the precaution of removing all but a few supplies from the *Olga*, thinking that the new commander would not be likely to run away with a poorly provisioned ship with the freeze-up coming on.

One day there came one of those heavy fogs that are common in late summer in this part of the Arctic. When the fog lifted, the *Olga*, which had been moored close to the *Charles Hanson*, was nowhere to be seen. She had still not been seen nor heard of when I reached Herschel. Most of the people in the island settlement assumed that the *Olga* would never be seen again.

I came to accept Klinkenberg as a kind of legend in which I only half believed. Then one day a ship was sighted. Since it was coming in from the northeast rather than the west, I felt sure it could not be the *Duchess of Bedford*. It was not. It was the famous *Olga*.

In port, Charlie Klinkenberg did not hesitate to admit that he had stolen the *Olga* the summer before. He had, he said, sailed three hundred miles east to loot a storehouse he knew of, and then had gone still farther east to Victoria Island, where he landed to hunt caribou. While he was ashore, he said, his crew began making alcohol out of the ship's flour and sugar. This caused not only drunkenness but a shortage of supplies. When Charlie reprimanded the chief engineer, the ringleader, the man reached for a gun but was slow on the draw. Charlie shot him dead. That should have left eight white men in the crew, but when the *Olga* reached Herschel there were only five. Charlie maintained that one had died of natural causes and two more had accidentally fallen through thin ice and drowned. The remaining crew members corroborated Charlie's story.

Although Captain McKenna was not at Herschel at the time, several of the whalers who were still there doubted Klinkenberg's story and tried to get the police to arrest him. All the police would do, however, was order Klinkenberg and the *Olga* not to leave the island. The *Olga* obeyed the order, but Charlie did not. He got away in a whaleboat, taking along his Eskimo wife and children.

His departure immediately changed the testimony of his crew. They now claimed that the man who had supposedly died a natural death had really died in chains in the hold, from a combination of freezing and starvation, and that the two sailors said to have gone through the ice had been the only witnesses to the death of the engineer and consequently Klinkenberg had arranged their "accident" for them. According to the new testimony, when the *Olga* had come within sight of Herschel, Klinkenberg had called all hands on deck and said, "Boys, you know the penalty for killing five or six men is no worse than for killing four." I learned all this because I was asked by a United States commissioner who happened to be visiting Herschel to take down the statements of the crew of the *Olga*. While I was fascinated by the felonious aspects of the tale, I was even more interested in what seemed to others incidental information.

This was that Klinkenberg and the men of the *Olga*, while wintering at Victoria Island, had seen a strange people who lived and dressed like Eskimos but who did not look like them. One of the men said that they looked like Europeans; another contended that they looked like Jews; the rest said that the only difference between these people and Eskimos was that some of them had light hair and blue eyes. The whalers at Herschel advised me to pay no attention to this story, and suggested that if I asked the Mackenzie Eskimos who had been on Klinkenberg's ship about it, I would probably get a different and truer version.

Being an anthropologist and concerned with this sort of thing, I did ask the Eskimos and, somewhat to my surprise, got confirmation of the story told by the white members of the crew. I knew the tale of the missing Norse colony in Greenland, and I knew that Sir John Franklin's crew of more than one hundred, lost in the vicinity of King William Island in 1847 or 1848, had never been entirely accounted for. I could not resist trying to connect what I knew of these events with the presence in Victoria Island of Eskimo-like people with light hair and blue eyes. This made me all the more eager for the arrival of the *Duchess of Bedford,* which could, I thought, carry me far enough east to investigate the *Olga* crewmen's story.

While I was still hoping for the arrival of the seaborne part of the expedition, a whaleboat came in from the east carrying the second mate, Markley, of the whaler *Alexander,* which everyone at Herschel believed had passed outside the island and gone directly west. Markley revealed that his ship had been wrecked on a ledge off Cape Parry, three hundred miles to the east. It was not long before other boats began to arrive carrying the *Alexander's* captain and most of her crew. All but one of them took passage on the last of the whalers. When this vessel left, Herschel Island was cut off from the rest of the world until the following year. Inspector Howard of the police then decided that he would prefer to winter at Fort McPherson, up in the spruce forest beyond the delta. His small staff did not discourage his going, for he was a rather severe commander.

Other than the police and myself, there were now only two white men at Herschel. One of these was a Norwegian sailor, Chris Sten, who had been on the *Alexander.* Sten was married to an Eskimo woman who had two wealthy brothers, Ilavinirk and Tutuyak. These three owned a fast schooner, the *Penelope.* Sten, the dominant influence in the trio, told me that the *Alexander* was high and dry on the rocks, easily accessible, and that her master had taken nothing from her but the papers that would enable him to collect her insurance. The ship was still full of silver fox and other skins, and valuable ship's gear, including chronometers.

Sten wanted me to sail with him in the *Penelope* and pick the

Alexander's bones. This would have been exciting, but I was more interested in the unknown Eskimos of Victoria Island and still believed that the *Duchess* might arrive in time to get me to them. I told Sten that if my ship failed to come before the freeze-up I would then go to the wreck with him by sled. He said, however, that he could not risk the wait, since others might try their hands at salvaging the *Alexander's* cargo.

The second white man at Herschel was Alfred Harrison, an Englishman. An amateur explorer with a lot of book knowledge of the Arctic but no real experience, Harrison had been planning a sled journey from Cape Bathurst across the sea ice to Banks Island, and had been trying to buy an outfit from the whalers and to enlist Eskimos to go with him. Everyone thought him crazy and refused to help. When I met him, Harrison had given up hope and had decided to spend the winter exploring the land east of the Mackenzie delta and mapping the region of the Eskimo Lakes. For this scheme, which the natives and whalers did not regard as insane, he had bought a whaleboat and enlisted the Eskimo family of one of Sten's brothers-in-law.

Harrison asked me to go with him. Still hoping for the arrival of the *Duchess,* I agreed to go with him as far as Shingle Point, which is part way between Herschel Island and the delta. I left a note with the police informing Mikkelsen and Leffingwell where I expected to be found.

Harrison and I, after an easy fifty-mile sail, pitched camp on the sand to do a little fishing for winter food. Harrison kept trying to persuade me that the *Duchess* would not come through until the following year and that I should continue on with him. By this time, however, I had made up my mind that if I was going to study the Eskimos I should have to live with the Eskimos and do as they did. One cannot become intimate with a strange race merely through casual visits.

On September 3, Harrison and his group of natives sailed on east from Shingle Point, leaving me to the beginning of my life with the Eskimos.

9

Guest of the Eskimos

Shingle Point, at the bottom of Mackenzie Bay, is just west of the mouth of the Mackenzie River. Almost as large as the Mississippi, the Mackenzie brings down so much fresh water that ships at sea, even out of sight of land, can drop their buckets overboard and bring up water fit to drink.

In 1908, Shingle Point was a place that sometimes could have been called a settlement and sometimes not. At one time there might be more than a dozen tents on the sand behind the beach, at other times only three or four. It depended largely on the number of families who went there to fish, but it also depended on how many footloose Eskimos stopped off on their way east, west, or south. Here I lived with Memoranna, the Eskimo who had taken me to Herschel Island. Becoming in effect a member of his family, I had misgivings at first, since I had been brought up to believe that I could not eat sea food. I must have thought this peculiarity very interesting, for ever since I could remember I had never lost an opportunity to tell anybody who was willing to listen about the curious fact that, while most people could eat fish, it was quite impossible for me to do so. Back home, I had always rather welcomed a chance, when a fish course was served, to entertain the table with the story of my strange peculiarity. Now I was face to face with a series of dinners and breakfasts and lunches and suppers at which the only course would be fish. Under the circumstances my appetite at first was not good.

Ordinarily, the Shingle Point people would have had some canned goods, flour, and sugar, but the whalers had not been able to spare much of these in the summer of 1906. We therefore had to concentrate on fishing.

The commonest catch at Shingle Point was what the whalers called "whitefish," although it was no relative of our commercial lake whitefish. It was the Great Bear Lake herring, which the Eskimos know as *kaktat*. These were caught at night in nets some three feet wide and thirty feet long, manipulated from the beach by long booms of split driftwood logs lashed end to end. These nets were set out two or three at a time, and the fishermen were kept busy hurrying from one to another, pulling the fish out of the meshes in which their gills had caught and tossing them into piles on the beach. We must often have netted as many as a thousand pound-and-a-half fish in a single night.

In the morning the women, with half-moon-shaped knives sharp as razors, came to the beach to split the fish, clean them, and remove the backbone. If the catch was so large that there was no time to remove the spines, the women merely cleaned the fish and threw them into cribs of driftwood, which, when full, were roofed over with logs for protection against dogs and foxes.

These piles of fish sometimes became a little high, although it is never really hot at Shingle Point, but the Eskimos do not consider slight putrefaction a defect—as many white people do not object to overripe cheese or game. I myself eventually learned to like gamy fish, especially when it had been frozen and then thawed to about the consistency of firm ice cream.

In the midst of our fishing, considerable excitement was aroused by the sight of a schooner coming from the west. I supposed at first that it was the missing *Duchess of Bedford*, looking for me, but it soon turned out that she was Chris Sten's *Penelope*, on her way at last to loot the wreck of the *Alexander*. Sten came ashore with his two Eskimo brothers-in-law and was given the boisterous welcome that encamped Eskimos always accord travelers.

After the entertainment, Sten discovered that his Eskimos had decided that Fritz Wolki, a hunter-trader living not far from the wreck, would by this time undoubtedly have taken everything worth salvaging. Sten denied the possibility of this, but his Eskimos remained firm. Instead of heading for the *Alexander*, Sten then persuaded his men to run east for fifteen miles or so and dismantle and pick up a cabin he had built the year before, in which he had left much valuable property.

At Sten's invitation I went along. We tore down the cabin, loaded lumber, tools, ropes, and such stuff on board, and in less than a week were back at Shingle Point, building Sten a house out of the salvaged materials. Chris asked me to share the cabin with him but I refused, as I had earlier refused to accept Harrison's hospitality. I intended to live with the Eskimos and visit with my white neighbors instead of doing the opposite.

Not long after the freeze-up, Memoranna renovated an old Eskimo house for his family and me to live in. The house was built of sod and earth heaped against and over a frame of driftwood. It was heated, not in the old Eskimo fashion by seal- or whale-oil lamps, but by a much less tractable, though powerful, sheet-iron stove. The house was on a sandspit extending out from a high bluff, with the sea on three sides of it. Behind the bluff the rolling prairie stretched away, gradually rising toward the mountains some thirty miles in from the coast.

My stay with Memoranna was again interrupted by news of the arrival of a whaler, the *Narwhal,* which had brought messages from the *Duchess of Bedford.* Because the messages were extremely confused, I decided to go to Herschel Island to learn for myself what had happened to the missing section of my expedition. A visit to the island would also enable me to pick up a few extra supplies, which, in my present state of skepticism about fish as a complete diet, I thought I needed.

Memoranna and his partner Oblutok decided to go with me. We found the *Narwhal* in port. I got a warm welcome from her captain, George Leavitt, but little in the way of provisions. Leavitt told me that the *Duchess of Bedford* had been ahead of the *Narwhal* at Point Barrow but that somewhere between there and Herschel he had passed her without seeing her, either because the smaller vessel was following inshore leads and was hidden by the ice or because of blanketing fog. Leavitt advised me to return to Shingle Point and remain there. He pointed out that after the freeze-up there would be much travel along the coast and that I would be sure to get news of the *Duchess.* I took his advice and sailed east again to await the coming of winter while learning what I could from the Shingle Point people.

The winter brought an opportunity to study the hunting habits of the Eskimos. We were visited by a party of Eskimos who had cold-weather homes on the other side of the mountains, where they spent the winter hunting caribou. What these people had to say about their hunting success interested Memoranna. It interested me, too, for I had discovered, on returning to Shingle Point, that the few groceries I had been able to get from Captain Leavitt would not constitute a personal stock for me to feed on during the winter, since anything brought into an Eskimo house is supposed to be shared with everyone in it. Caribou sounded good to me. So did this opportunity for inland travel with the people I had come to study.

Memoranna and I, each with a dog team, set out for the mountains. We traveled slowly and usually sat up until after midnight, telling and listening to stories and then sleeping until noon. There were no more than four or five hours of traveling light.

The snow was light, and the sled runners often scraped the bare earth as we traveled up and down the ridges that lay across our path. When we could, we followed river valleys, in which there were willows to use for fuel. Finally, we had to cross the higher slopes of the mountains on which there were no willows. On the downward slopes of the south side, however, we soon found willows as high as our heads. It was among these that our hunting Eskimos had their settlement.

Their houses were made of woven willows stuffed with moss, with a canvas covering thrown over the frame. Over the covering a few inches of soft snow was sifted. After we arrived, two of the houses were heated by the sheet-iron stoves we had brought with us, these replacing the central fireplace surrounded by stones. The houses were comfortably warm most of the time, and uncomfortably warm when the fire was built up for cooking.

When a fireplace was used, it was built in the center of the house under a skylight covered by a parchment of deerskin which let in light. Just before the fire was lighted, the deerskin was removed and a great pile of resinous twigs and sticks heaped on the hearth. When this was ignited, the strong updraft carried all the smoke and cinders through the hole in the roof. This practice kept the house reasonably free of smoke. Air to feed the fire came in through a small opening under the door. When the cooking was done and the fire had been allowed to subside, the superheated stones surrounding the hearth acted as radiators.

On our way over the mountains, Memoranna and I had talked about spending a week or two at the caribou camp, but the weather continued bad for hunting. The period of midwinter darkness, when hunting even in good weather is difficult, was approaching. The meat in camp was therefore precious. Memoranna and I had fifteen dogs. On the coast, where fish was piled up by the ton, this would not have mattered. Here on the mountain we saw the supply of caribou meat and fat and seal fat growing steadily smaller. We could see that, if our hosts were to live through the winter, they would not have enough meat to take care of guests. Accordingly, we loaded our sledges with what meat we had been able to secure and headed back toward Shingle Point.

We traveled in the river valley, with Memoranna leading. Every few yards he poked a long staff with a sharpened file in the end of it down through the snow to test the ice. With snow or river ice, it is impossible to tell by sight alone where the ice is thick and where it is thin.

We were in more danger of getting our feet wet than of drowning. Sometimes, when a river runs over a shallow bar, it may freeze to the bottom. When this happens, the back-up water can flow only on top of the ice, where the traveler has to walk unless he wishes to keep scrambling up the icy slopes of the hills between which the stream flows. I learned from Memoranna that if, immediately after getting our feet wet, we jumped into a powdery snowbank, the snow would act as a blotter and absorb the water before it soaked through our footgear. Eskimo boots of sealskin are waterproof but cold, and are used only in summer. On this trip I wore deerskin boots and socks and, because I was inexpert, got them soaking wet. The result was that I suffered a slightly frozen heel. This was the only time in ten winters in the north that my feet were even touched by frost.

Although Memoranna and his family continued to be very helpful, I felt a need to experience the real Eskimo way of life. I had heard that an Eskimo named Ovayuak, who lived at Tuktoyaktuk (the Caribou Place), a hundred miles to the east, was still living as Eskimos had done before Memoranna was born, before whalers had begun to bring in white influence. Memoranna assured me that I would find what I was looking for at Tuktoyaktuk. Ovoyuak's family would outfit me with the proper Eskimo clothes, with which I had not yet completely replaced the business suit in which I had arrived.

Memoranna and I and an Eskimo named Sitsak set out across

the delta on October 1. During this trip I learned several things. One of them was that, despite James Fenimore Cooper's confidence in the skill of the noble native, Eskimos can get lost. When we were about three days out, Memoranna and Sitsak got themselves and me quite lost, so much so that for two days we wandered about only to end up at the camp we had left forty-eight hours before.

I also learned that Eskimos do not always build snowhouses, even in winter. Memoranna carried with him a large square of canvas with a stovepipe ring in it, and this he stretched across a snow wall when we camped. Before we were many days out, this canvas was so perforated by sparks that it could not keep out more than what Artemus Ward once called "the coarsest of the cold." I could watch stars through the holes while the cold outside was coming through them and lowering the inside temperature to something like −20° F.

Although this was the time when the sun began to stay below the horizon, we still had six or seven hours of light by which one could read fairly large print and by which it was easy and pleasant to travel. It got dark shortly after noon, and on cloudy days the light was not good enough for traveling after eleven in the morning.

Memoranna in his attitude toward his dogs was quite unlike the Athapaska Indians. If the dogs grew tired, he would hitch on to the sled and pull it himself. He never whipped the animals, because he knew it would lower his standing in the community to do so. This considerate attitude toward their beasts of burden had, I am sorry to say, almost died out among the Eskimos by the time of my final expedition.

Our dogs were worn out when we were still some fifteen miles from Tuktoyaktuk, but they immediately perked up when we struck the first local sled tracks. They began to pull so hard that we were able to unhitch ourselves and simply walk behind them. There was soon an uproar of barking dogs and shouting people, in the midst of whom, grave and distinguished but full of effusive welcome, was Ovayuak, the man regarded as the "Chief" of the settlement.

My experience at Tuktoyaktuk dispelled two more superstitions I had about living in the Arctic. One of these was my belief that I needed salt to make my fish diet more palatable. The other was that during the weeks when the arctic darkness is most nearly complete, I would inevitably become depressed and irritable.

I got over the salt notion simply by being deprived of that

commodity. Ovayuak had none and we had brought none with us. An Eskimo family who later came to Tuktoyaktuk presented me with half a baking-powder tin of salt, but I absent-mindedly forgot that I had it when the next meal came around. When I remembered it, I realized that I had not really craved it at all. From then on I liked fish as fish.

As for the presumed effects of arctic darkness, as soon as the stars became the only source of light, I began to realize that the Eskimos regarded this period as their vacation time. They showed no signs of mental depression, and neither did I. As a matter of fact, when the sun reappeared for the first time, I happened to be visiting Alfred Harrison near the Eskimo Lakes. I remember climbing a hill to have a look at the sun, but do not remember being especially impressed or delighted by it.

Ovayuak's house at Tuktoyaktuk was a typical Eskimo dwelling of the time. It had a driftwood frame and driftwood roof supports sloping up to a six-foot-square level place in the center. The walls were of earth, five or six feet thick at the base and somewhat thinner at the top. Four to six inches of earth were piled on the roof timbers. At the center the roof was about nine feet above the ground. The walls were about five feet high. In the center of the roof was an opening, about three feet square, with a cover made by sewing together translucent strips of polar bear intestines. On a clear day in midwinter, this ''window'' provided enough light so that all the seal- or whale-oil lamps could perfectly well have been extinguished for as much as four hours except for reading or sewing.

Actually, the lamps were never extinguished. We needed them for heat. Usually there were three or four lamps, one in each corner of the house; they were large, half-moon-shaped bowls carved out of blocks of soapstone. The wick was a ridge of powder lying along the twelve- or eighteen-inch straight edge of the lamp. This powder was sometimes hardwood sawdust, sometimes a dust made by scraping or sawing walrus ivory, and sometimes dried moss that had been rubbed into powder between the hands. Occasionally, if other materials gave out, the Eskimos would take small pieces of manila rope which had been secured from the whalers and hack the fibers into lengths of one-twentieth of an inch or less, thus virtually converting the fibers into powder. Sometimes Ovayuak's household tried to use ordinary commercial lamp wicks, but they were much more difficult to keep burning properly, and Eskimo women are particular that the lamp shall never smoke. No duty of a house-keeper is more important than to keep the lamp well trimmed.

For ideal burning, the two- or three-inch-deep bowl of the lamp must be nearly but never quite full of oil. This requirement was met in a simple but ingenious way. A slab of polar-bear or seal blubber was hung above the flame. (A bacon slab could be used if it contained no lean.) As the oil in the lamp became lower, more of the wick was exposed and the flame became higher. The increasing heat of the flame melted the fat hanging over the lamp; as the oil trickled down more, it gradually raised the level of the oil in the bowl, until it flooded part of the wick and in that way decreased the volume of the flame. The air above the lamp soon became cooler and the slab of blubber stopped dripping. Once properly prepared in this way, a lamp will burn, with fluctuations, for six to eight hours at a time. Lamps that were properly trimmed when the Eskimos went to bed would still be burning brightly when they awoke. Occasionally, one of the women would forget to put quite enough blubber on the hook above the lamp and it would begin to smoke during the night. I do not think that Eskimos have keener ears or eyes than other peoples, but they certainly have a more acute sense of smell. The least bit of smoke in a house would rouse a sleeper, who would warn the offending guardian to look after her lamp.

Because the walls and roof of Ovayuak's house were so thick, scarcely any cold came through them. The only chill came from an opening by which the house was ventilated. The floor of the dwelling was level with the ground outside. The entrance was a kind of tunnel about thirty feet long, covered by a shed. The tunnel or ditch was probably four feet deep where it came in under the house wall, so that a person had to stoop low to enter. Once inside the wall, he could stand up in the end of the ditch, with his shoulders above floor level. I speak of this entrance as the door, but it was really only a hole in the floor about four feet square. There was a lid available with which to cover the opening but I never saw it used, except to keep puppies out or to prevent a child from tumbling through. The temperature in the alleyway was about as low as outdoors, but our house was so full of warm air that the cold air in the alleyway could not enter. Cold air, being heavier, will of course not rise into any space occupied by warm air.

Even with a ventilator about four inches in diameter, in the roof the even flame of the lamps kept the temperature of the house day and night between 70° and 80° F. We were modern enough to have a stove, but this was used only for cooking, usually for two or three hours in the afternoon. At that time the temperature in the house rose to about 100° F. The warm air of the house went out through the ventilator with the force of a strong wind, as I determined by climbing onto the roof and testing with my hand. On a clear and cold day, from a distance, the column of warm, damp air rising through the ventilator looked like chimney smoke.

Before going to live with the Eskimos I had heard much about the bad smell of their houses, and at first it seemed to me that they did smell bad. I soon came to realize, however, that this was only the smell of the food they ate, corresponding to the odor of coffee, bacon, or garlic in our own homes. If you are fond of bacon or coffee, you do not dislike the smell. Similarly, I found that, as I gradually became used to the Eskimo food and eventually fond of it, smells changed from odors to fragrances.

In the center of our house was an open space about twelve feet square. In three directions from this ran three alcoves, so that the ground plan of the house was not very different from the club pip on a playing card. In each one of the alcoves was a sleeping platform about a foot higher than the floor. From one alcove a door led to a separate house occupied by an uncle of Ovayuak and his wife and family. In our big house and in this little connected house twenty-three people lived, not counting visitors—and there were visitors nearly every night. There was just enough room on the bed-platforms for all the family to sleep. After all the others had gone to bed, I used to spread my blankets on the floor near the trap door so that I could get some of the cool air.

There was little furniture in the house. Eskimos of Ovayuak's generation quite sensibly got along with as little as possible. Ordinarily, there is in the alleyway leading out from an Eskimo house a side chamber where frequently used articles of furniture are kept. Whenever a piece is needed, somebody brings it in. Other things, less frequently used, are kept on an elevated platform outdoors. Here are also kept reserves of food for men and dogs, and any property seldom needed.

It is customary to keep in the house the cooking gear and low movable tables upon which meals are prepared and eaten. These articles took up some floor space in Ovayuak's house, and so did the sheet-iron stove that was used for cooking. When visitors were numerous, the tables were moved out into the alleyway. Occasionally, the stove also had to be moved out, or hoisted up and suspended from the ceiling, in order to provide more sleeping space. If there was still not enough room, the visitors had to make a camp of their own outside, coming into the house to visit and join us at meals and in singing and storytelling.

There was no regular time for getting up in the morning. Most of the Eskimos were great smokers, and I used to be wakened by the crackling of a match at perhaps four or five o'clock. Commonly, these early smokers took a few puffs at their pipes and then went to sleep again. If it was as late as five or six o'clock, the smokers would not go to sleep but would begin talking with one another. The bed-platforms were wider toward the center of the house than they were toward the walls. All the occupants slept with their heads toward the center. This made it easy for a man or a woman to rise on one elbow and talk across the floor.

After half an hour or so of conversation, in which more and more people joined, somebody would finally say that it was time for breakfast. This would give rise to a discussion among the women as to which of them would go out and fetch the fish. It was all amiable and accompanied by a great deal of laughter. The two or three women who were chosen generally had a race to see who could dress the fastest. Putting on clothes is about as simple a matter for an Eskimo as it is for a fireman. There are no buckles, everything slips on easily, and the only things to be fastened are belts and drawstrings.

I never actually timed these breakfast getters, but I feel sure that it took them less than a minute to dress. After the last string was tied, they would run out and presently return with arms full of frozen fish, which they carried somewhat as a farmer carries a load of firewood. The fish were thrown upon the floor with a clatter. While they were thawing, conversation was gay and general. When the fish reached the proper consistency, the women would take their half-moon-shaped knives and cut off the heads and tails, to be saved for later cooking as delicacies for the children. Then they would cut straight along the back and the belly of each fish, take one edge of the skin between their teeth, and strip it off sideways. Large fish were cut into segments, but if they weighed no more than a pound or two apiece, they were left whole. The entrails were not removed. These were fresh fish, most of them weighing from one to three pounds, which had been frozen solid within a few minutes of being caught. We gnawed at them as if we were eating corn on the cob. We would bite as close to the entrails as we wished, setting the core of entrails and bones aside as one would discard the cob after finishing an ear of corn. We ate only as much as we liked of any piece, but there was never any waste, since all the leavings would be given to the dogs.

In a big family like ours, the fish were put on several platters so that no one had too far to reach. Before the platters were distributed, Ovayuak's wife used to look them over and pick out the best pieces for the children. It is an Eskimo custom to favor children in all things even more scrupulously than the most influential member of the family or the most respected visitor. In a family where only one fish tray was served, the visitors were given their choice after the children. In a big family, visitors took their chances with the others. In our house there was always a separate tray for each platform. Visitors shared the fish with those members of the family who slept on the platform nearest to them.

In an Eskimo household like Ovayuak's, the first activity after breakfast was fishing. Ovayuak himself was always the first to go out to the fishing grounds on the river ice half a mile away. Members of his family always followed. It was optional with visitors whether or not they helped with the fishing. All of them did, however, unless they had something else to do. Had someone abstained entirely from all work, I do not think that our host would have taken any action, nor would have the rest of the community. What keeps any Eskimo guest at work is not the fear that he may be turned out of the house, but rather the dread of getting a low rating in the community. From my own experience I would say that the stimulating and wholesome all-flesh diet, combined with the brisk climate and the social pressure, are important factors in making Eskimos mutually cooperative.

Ovayuak necessarily fished every day and I usually went with him.

Our house was on one of the branches of the Mackenzie delta, and the river ice was at that time about three feet thick. In those days I did not use an ice chisel very well. At first it took me nearly half an hour to make a hole ten inches in diameter through three feet of ice. Ovayuak could do it in a few minutes. For a fishing rod we each had a stick about two feet long with a slender line of braided caribou sinew about four or five feet long attached to it. On the end of this line hung a little fish, about two inches in length, carved out of walrus ivory. A hole had been bored in the head of the fish and a shingle nail stuck through, bent, and sharpened. This sort of tackle is bait and hook in one. When a fish bites, you must not give it any slack. If you do, it can slip the hook, for there is no barb to hold it. There are two tricks to this type of fishing. One is to keep jiggling the hook so that the ivory fish squirms around in the water much as a live minnow would. The other is to pull the minute you feel a strike and to keep pulling until your catch is on the ice.

Ovayuak and I used to get several kinds of fish. The largest of these was called by the Eskimos *si* (pronounced approximately *shee*) and by the Hudson's Bay traders *connie*. The Eskimo name is merely plain Eskimo, but the white man's name is said to come from the French *l'inconnu*, "the unknown" fish. It is a scaly fish with white flesh. I have seen them more than three feet in length, weighing over forty pounds, and have heard that they sometimes reach seventy pounds. At Tuktoyaktuk we seldom got any weighing more than thirty pounds, and most were eight-pounders.

In six or seven hours of work on a good day we would catch from four to eight fish of various sorts—approximately ten to forty pounds per man. There were seldom more than five or six of us fishing, although, counting visitors, we had, on an average, more than thirty people to feed and about fifty or sixty dogs. The people ate about five pounds each and the dogs two or three pounds each per day. This meant that, although we were catching fish in considerable quantity, our store was getting smaller every day. Although several tons had been accumulated in the fall, Ovayuak said he thought that we would do well if we did not come to the end of our reserves before the last of March. I did a little estimating and assured him that the fish would last longer than that. He replied that they would if our family did not increase in size. He expected, however, that a shortage of food would soon be felt in various neighboring communities and that those affected by it would gradually gather at Tuktoyaktuk.

Ovayuak explained to me how he had happened to become a chief. The concept of "chief" was purely a Hudson's Bay Company's idea, at first incomprehensible to the Eskimos. The traders were used to dealing with Indian chiefs in Canada. Most Indian chiefs have real legal power over their tribes, the power having been either inherited or granted as a result of a formal election. When the Hudson's Bay men penetrated north to the Arctic Ocean, they always asked the Eskimos who their chiefs were, taking it for granted that there would be leaders here too. When the Eskimos were unable to name any, such an idea being strange to them, the traders picked out the most active and influential men, called them "chiefs," and that was that. Ovayuak's uncle had been a man of good judgment and great energy and therefore influential with his people. The Hudson's Bay people had decided that he was the local chief and had accordingly made him their representative. This trust on the part of the company increased his influence even further, so that eventually he came to have more power than any Eskimo had had before him. His position was not comparable to the authority of an elected official in our society, but was rather the prestige of a naturally successful man. When the uncle died, the Hudson's Bay Company found that Ovayuak himself was the next most influential man in the community, so they made him chief. As far as the Eskimos were concerned, Ovayuak was a man of influence not because the white men called him chief but because he had good judgment and had kept to the ways of his fathers more closely than most.

While others spent nearly all of each summer in repeated journeys to Fort McPherson and Herschel Island for purposes of trading, Ovayuak made only one quick journey to McPherson, returning immediately to the fishing grounds. The best run of fish ordinarily came while the main body of Eskimos were still engaged in selling their furs either to the Hudson's Bay Company or to the whalers. When the fur sellers returned to the fishing grounds with their silks, phonographs, chewing gum, and whatever else they had bought from the traders, Ovayuak would already have accumulated tons of fish.

When the trading season was over, each Eskimo would fish energetically in the location he had picked for that year. Yet no matter how diligent they might be, few of these late-starting fishermen secured even half as much fish as they needed. Ovayuak told me how proud it made him that in midwinter or toward spring, when the prodigals came to the end of their own food supply, they would say, "Let us go to Ovayuak. He will have food if anybody has."

It would never have occurred to Ovayuak to refuse food to anyone. In fact, it seemed to him that they had as much right to his fish as he had himself. Ovayuak never said to anyone, "You must take orders from me if I am to give you food." He never issued orders. If, however, it was known that he wanted anything done, everyone was eager to do it for him. Though he had no formal or legal power, he had the respect and good will of everyone so fully that it amounted to natural power.

Ovayuak's fishing hole and mine were only a few feet apart. Each morning as we began our fishing he would build a semicircular wall of snow about five feet high as a wind shelter. We then sat in comfort and talked. Since my knowledge of the language was still limited, I insisted that Ovayuak speak nothing but Eskimo. He was very patient, first speaking to me in plain Eskimo and then explaining it in the jargon which I had already learned. I know now that I misunderstood many things when he first explained them. No doubt there were many that I did not understand at all.

We used to fish until about four in the afternoon. At about noon the people at home would have a lunch of frozen fish similar to our breakfast. We fishermen missed this meal. About an hour before the rest of us were ready to quit work, Ovayuak's wife, who usually fished with us, would leave for home to start the cooking. Although nearly every one of my Eskimo friends carried a watch, our quitting time in the afternoon depended not on the clock but on the daylight. And the daylight depended on the cloud cover. When we got home we usually found that dinner was not quite ready. However, by the time we had taken off our outdoor garments and were sitting around, dressed in short, lightweight indoor trunks, naked above the waist and below the knee, huge platters of steaming boiled fish would be ready for us. It was now my fifth month among the Eskimos, and I enjoyed the boiled fish as much as any of them.

After dinner no formal work was done, although everybody was always busy at something—carving ivory, cleaning rifles, or even taking a watch apart to repair it. Most Eskimos are clever with their hands, and they were particularly good at watch repair. I was usually asleep before my companions finished tinkering. Sometimes I lay awake thinking over what I had seen and heard. At the end of each day I felt that I was closer to an understanding of these companionable people.

10 A Race against Bad News

My stay with Ovayuak at Tuktoyaktuk was unbroken by anything more than occasional visits from traveling Eskimos. During the winter I wondered more than once if I should not go looking for my expedition, but each time I concluded that my anthropological work would be better served by my remaining with Ovayuak and learning more about these primitive people.

About the first of March, 1907, just as I was about to return to Herschel Island, a traveling Mackenzie Eskimo brought news that the *Duchess of Bedford* was wintering between the mainland and Flaxman Island, about halfway between Shingle Point and Point Barrow, Alaska.

I reached Herschel early in March. There, Captain Leavitt of the *Narwhal* handed me a letter that Leffingwell and Mikkelsen had left for me several months earlier, urging me to join the expedition at Flaxman Island. With a dog team and a hired companion—an Eskimo from that part of the Bering coast known as Cape York— I set out on April 7. It was still winter, and the trip was simple enough over the smooth shore ice with typical snow-covered prairie between us and the Endicott Mountains to the south. After some two hundred miles we came to a small earth-and-timber house, the first habitation we had seen since leaving Herschel. The Eskimos living there reported that the *Duchess of Bedford* was held fast in six or seven feet of ice, but had sprung a leak that was bound to sink her when the ice went out. Her hold was already full of water and she was uninhabitable. Her superstructure had been broken up

91

and used in building a house ashore. If this report was true, it could well mean an end to my hope of visiting Victoria Island in the spring. What was more serious, however, was the report that Leffingwell, Mikkelsen, and Storker Storkerson, the first mate of the *Duchess,* had gone north over the sea ice looking for land. This venture, I was told, had been undertaken against all local advice, Eskimo and otherwise. The explorers had tried to get some Eskimos to go with them, but the Eskimos had refused, being certain that there was no land to be found and equally certain that travel over sea ice was suicidal. While Eskimos never traveled over sea ice if they could avoid doing so, they could, if put to it, make a living at sea by hunting. This the white men could not do—or such, at least, was the Eskimo belief. Since all the men engaged in the present northward journey were white men, it followed that they must be dead, the only survivor being one of the expedition's dogs which had come ashore sometime after the ice party had set out.

I hurried on to Flaxman Island, where I found the expedition's surgeon, George Plummer Howe, in charge of the camp of three white men and a number of hired Eskimos. Ned Arey, a Cape Codder who owned a large house near the Eskimo house we had passed, was staying in the camp with his Eskimo wife and family. Dr. Howe was not worried. He said that the party was equipped for two months' travel. Ned Arey was doubtful. He did not believe that sea-ice travel was impossible, but he seemed to feel that, if all had gone well, the party would have been back by this time. I knew from my reading of polar books that travel over sea ice was perfectly possible although it had its dangers. I shared Dr. Howe's feeling that the men would return safely.

We settled down to talk about our future plans. I was of course disappointed that, once the *Duchess* had gone to the bottom, we should have no opportunity of visiting Victoria Island. Howe, an anthropologist as well as a physician, agreed, when I told him of Charlie Klinkenberg's story, that it would be extremely interesting to visit Victoria and look for the Eskimos who seemed to resemble white men. He felt, however, and I was bound to admit, that the best plan would be for us to go home and organize a new expedition for that purpose. He felt that we should go out by whaling ship at the first opportunity. Later, we talked about Eskimo diet and disease, and especially about Captain Leavitt's belief that cancer had been unknown among the Eskimos before they adopted our civilized habits of eating and living.

I enjoyed my stay at Flaxman Island, although it was comparatively uneventful. There were a lot of books in the camp, brought ashore from the doomed *Duchess,* and I had plenty of time for reading and for writing down my thoughts about my experiences of the past months. I got restless, however, and to work off energy made a trip back to Herschel Island.

During my absence, Leffingwell, Mikkelsen, and Storkerson returned safely. They had traveled north one hundred miles from land, taking soundings as they went. Although they had imagined that the sea north of the Alaskan coast would prove to be shallow and dotted with islands, they were astonished to find, only thirty miles from shore, that their two-thousand-foot wire could no longer touch the sea floor. They had turned back after running into a gale because the rapidly moving ice had threatened to carry them westward beyond Point Barrow.

As a result of this journey, it was plain to all of us that the idea of unknown land existing not far from the Alaskan shoreline was untenable. It was equally plain that sea-ice travel north of Alaska was not impossible. Although I was much impressed by what I learned from the ice party, at the time I could think of little but the mysterious Victoria Island people I was so eager to meet. Had I known then that seven years later I was to be a traveler over that same ice, I would have been even more deeply interested in the expedition's achievements.

The Anglo-American Polar Expedition was breaking up. Leffingwell planned to stay on the coast for at least another year studying the geology of the mountains to the south, but Mikkelsen, after considering a trip eastward in a small boat, gave up the idea and decided to go home as soon as possible.

I remained at Flaxman Island, waiting for summer. I had enjoyed the winter—in fact, once I was properly dressed by the Eskimos, I found that the arctic winter seemed more pleasant than winter in North Dakota. Summer, however, seemed a long time coming. April was like a bad January in Iowa or Massachusetts. May was worse. It rained on the sixth day of that month, and the mosquitoes grew more bothersome every day. Although I speak with some lack of charity of the mosquitoes, Flaxman Island was comparatively free of them, since it was narrow, swept by breezes, and separated from the mainland breeding places of the pest. Moreover, our living quarters were equipped with screens, and we all were provided with head nets. Almost as numerous as the mosquitoes, but far more pleasant were the birds—land birds from sparrows to cranes and waterfowl from teal to swans. There were thousands of each species, pouring in from the south.

In July, Mikkelsen, Dr. Howe, Storkerson, several of the other men, and I started west along the coast in an Eskimo umiak and a small boat salvaged from the *Duchess of Bedford*. Although Point Barrow was our tentative destination, we were in no great hurry to reach it, for no ships would be likely to arrive here until later. We stopped occasionally to hunt geese and ducks but saw no caribou. After we had gone about a hundred miles Storkerson accidentally shot himself through the foot. Dr. Howe, fearing that the wound might become serious, insisted on returning with him to Flaxman Island, where he had left all his medical equipment except a first-aid kit. Mikkelsen went with them, leaving me with an Eskimo companion and one of the crew of the *Duchess* to do some archaeological work in the Jones Islands, where there had been in prehistoric times a large Eskimo settlement.

The contour of these islands is constantly changing as a result of the work of wind and water and a gradual sinking of the Alaskan shoreline. As long as the sea ice remains, in winter or spring, nothing happens to reduce the size of the islands. When the ice goes away, however, as it does nearly every summer, and when gales come in from the open sea, the waves undermine the mud and ice cliffs of the islands and the coastline sometimes recedes as much as a hundred yards in a single summer. Where there had been early settlements, traces of them were often carried away by the sea.

We camped near the ruins of an old Jones Island village, half of which had already been washed away. I found several carvings of bone and ivory and many weapons of bone and wood. From these and from the nature of the ruined houses, now reduced to mere mounds, I concluded that the settlement had been inhabited as recently as the seventeenth or eighteenth century. I enjoyed this work and the island's freedom from mosquitoes, and was therefore disappointed when the appearance of the first whaler bound east provided us with an opportunity to return to Flaxman. This ship was the *Belvedere,* of San Francisco, commanded by Captain Stephen Cottle of Martha's Vineyard, Massachusetts. The *Belvedere* took us to Flaxman Island, where we picked up Mikkelsen. Our plans were now changed. We no longer considered a small-boat journey to Barrow to meet the revenue cutter, which would have taken us out, but would go west by whaler from Herschel Island.

At Flaxman Island we heard disquieting news. On my last trip to Herschel, I had mentioned that Leffingwell, Mikkelsen, and Storkerson were out on the sea ice, unreported, and thought by Eskimos and others to be dead. It now appeared that although Captain Leavitt had believed that the ice party would return safely, the notion that they would not had been more widely accepted. Consequently, a party that had left Herschel to catch the steamer *Wrigley* at Fort McPherson had planned to announce the loss of the ice party to the world as soon as they reached the first telegraph office, at Athabaska Landing.

Dissemination of this shocking and false story was a bad enough prospect. But I felt all the worse because it would be spread on the strength of information that I had provided. Mikkelsen's mother was ailing, and he was worried that word of his death might kill her. Since he had an obligation to return to Flaxman Island to wind up the affairs of the expedition, he asked me to do what I could, in his stead, to correct the situation. There was a chance that a quick trip across the mountains to the Yukon and down to the United States government wireless station at Eagle City, Alaska, would enable me to make the truth known before the false story could be put on the wires at Athabaska Landing.

The police lent me a whaleboat with a crew of three Indians. We got away in a couple of hours. At McPherson, with the help of Hudson's Bay Factor, John Firth, I arranged for two Indians to go with me over the mountains to the Bell River, which runs first into the Porcupine and then into the Yukon.

The two Indians, William and Joseph, were about seventeen and twenty. They had very firm ideas about what should be carried on such a trip. Factor John Firth had made it clear to me that an employer should never carry as much as his Indians. Each of the boys packed about eighty pounds to my forty. Soon after we started out, I discovered that William was suffering from tuberculosis and could not possibly carry his full load. Joseph and I jointly relieved him of some twenty pounds—and I got my first experience in carrying a heavy back load.

In three days we struggled up out of the spruces, crossed the first bare mountains, descended again into the trees, and camped by a small river that flowed westward in the direction of the larger Bell River. I planned to build a raft when we reached the Bell and float downstream to Eagle City. In order to do this we would have to find a place along that river where the trees were large enough to be used as raft timber.

During the next lap of the journey the two Indians evidently did some thinking, and both became sulky. When we reached the Bell they sat down as if they never intended to rise again. It seemed that what was troubling them was their arithmetic. Since the gold-rush days, native packers had always received four dollars a day. Before we left Fort McPherson it had been agreed that I would pay each boy thirty-five dollars for six days. Their thinking along the way had convinced them that thirty-five dollars for six days was not as good as four dollars a day. We argued about this for more than an hour. I was unable to make them believe that they were not being cheated. I had arranged with Firth at Mc-Pherson to give the boys a letter saying that they had served me properly, on receipt of which he would give each one the sum agreed upon. Finally, I wrote a letter to Firth saying that William and Joseph were not satisfied with thirty-five dollars and wanted to have four dollars a day. I left it up to Firth to pay whichever amount he thought best. I read this letter to Joseph, who nodded, smiled, put it in his pocket, and immediately got up and began chopping down trees for my raft.

It took all day to cut and bind the logs with the rope we had brought. Since most of the timber was green and heavy, it was not an ideal raft, but it was twenty feet long and ten feet wide and had a stone fireplace in its center for cooking. I did not intend to leave it until I reached Eagle City.

On August 19, William and Joseph started back and I set out alone down the slow-moving and wandering Bell. I knew that I had to reach the telegraph office by the first of September in order to accomplish my purpose, but I was unable to go faster than the current would carry me. This form of frustration took some of the pleasure out of what could have been a very pleasant trip. The wooded river, with vistas of mountains, snowless but bare, was calmly beautiful. Sometimes a moose would stand and look at me from a distance of only a boat length, but show no signs of fright. Once a large bull, evidently thinking my raft was merely a cluster of drifting spruce, swam toward me until he got my scent, then turned and, swimming back to shore, quickly disappeared in the trees. In addition to my concern over being unable to hurry, I was troubled by lack of a map and an inability to remember exactly what Firth had told me about the route. I had supposed that when I reached the Porcupine it would be on my right. The only river that could have been the Porcupine came in on my left. Shortly after entering the river I saw an Indian food cache on the bank. Since my food was getting low, I went ashore and, although no Indians were present, exchanged a silk handkerchief for a bundle of dried moose meat.

My raft had now begun to get waterlogged and was riding so low in the water that the deck was always awash. I had to throw the fireplace overboard and make a nest of dry willows to sleep on. This, too, soon got wet, and I was glad to see a deserted Indian village come into view. I landed and spent the night under a roof and the next morning built a bonfire to dry myself out. While standing before the fire I heard a voice behind me. It belonged to the owner of the house, an old Indian whom I had met at McPherson the year before. We were delighted to see each other, I perhaps more than he, for his presence meant that there might be a better form of transportation near at hand.

There was. The old fellow guided me to his village where, after receiving a splendid welcome, I managed to persuade him to paddle me in his canoe at least part way to the trading post at Rampart House on the Porcupine near the Alaskan border. A few miles above Rampart we met a white man, Archie Linklater, who took me the rest of the way to the trading post on his raft. As soon as arrangements could be made, he took me in a post rowboat from Rampart to Fort Yukon, which we reached on September 3. From there, the only way of covering the remaining two hundred miles up the Yukon to Eagle City was by river steamer, which was not due at Fort Yukon until the next day. When the steamer *Hanna* arrived, she was so heavily loaded that shortly after we set out she had to pull up alongside the river bank to unload some of her cargo before passing through a shallow stretch. Some of the passengers worked with the crew for twelve hours unloading six hundred tons of oats. We did not reach Eagle City until September 7, and I was thirty-six hours too late with my news. The supposed tragedy on the arctic ice had been made known to the world, and my announcement from Eagle City could not spare those who had read or heard the bad news a period of grief. Had I not made my trip over the mountains, their unnecessary suffering would have lasted for two months, until the whaling ships carrying out the rest of the Anglo-American Polar Expedition reached the telegraph office at Nome.

11 Time and Matches on the Arctic Coast

My trip over the mountains and up the Yukon had been planned as a race against an unseen adversary, a race in which I had no control over my own speed. Although my progress was slow and steady, like that of the tortoise, I did not win. Saddened by my inability to prevent the suffering of the families and friends of Mikkelsen, Leffingwell, and Storkerson, I set out from the telegraph office at Eagle on another race against time. I could not spare a moment if I was to get to New York soon enough to enlist support for my next expedition, on which I wished to set out by the middle of the following season.

Here again I could not control my speed. After a year of almost no kind of transportation but my own feet, it was frustrating to have to depend on engines and wheels guided by others. However, the trip up the Yukon and over the White Pass to Skagway, by steamer to Vancouver and Seattle, and then by train to Chicago and New York, did give me a chance to write letters and consolidate my notes. I was carrying to the American Geographical Society in New York City the expedition's scientific reports and a presumably popular account of our work for *Harper's Magazine*.

In Seattle, I learned for the first time about Dr. Frederick A. Cook, who had recently claimed credit for having been the first man to climb Mount McKinley. Although some people believed Dr. Cook, there were many who did not and regarded with misgiving his rumored plan to beat his former commander, Robert E. Peary, to the North Pole. A number of Seattle doubters who knew that I

was on my way to New York suggested that it would be a good
idea for me to warn Peary, who had been trying for twenty years
to reach that coveted spot.

New York was almost as strange to me as Alaska and the
Arctic had been a year before. I learned from the newspapers that
Peary's headquarters were in the Grand Union Hotel, near Grand
Central Station. With the idea of calling on Peary and telling
him what I had heard about Cook, I checked in at the Grand Union.
I did not find Peary there—he was away at the time—so I went
about my own business, beginning with *Harper's*. Editor Henry
Mills Alden turned me over to Henry E. Rood, the man who was
to work on Mikkelsen's story. During the course of my work with
Rood, I visited the American Geographical Society, then opposite
the American Museum of Natural History.

I told both Rood and Cyrus Adams, editor of the Geographical
Society's publications, of my original ambition to write poetry. I
explained my presence in the anthropological field by telling them
how William Vaughn Moody's "Gloucester Moors" had put an
end to my career as a poet. Adams mentioned the fact that Moody,
until royalties from his hit play *The Great Divide* made it possible
for him to live a more gilded life elsewhere, had stayed in an inexpensive hotel on the south side of Washington Square. I looked
into it and ended up in the Judson Annex. This was the beginning
of a lifelong association with what might be called greater Greenwich Village.

The people at *Harper's* decided that, since Mikkelsen's material
was more suited to book publication, they wanted me to write some
articles for them about the Anglo-American Polar Expedition.
In between my sessions with them, I slipped back into the world
of poetry from which I had resigned some years before. Through
the Judson dining room and its patrons I met Olivia Dunbar and
Ridgely Torrence, poets both and later man and wife, and Edwin
Arlington Robinson. Olivia and Ridgely became my close friends,
but I never really got very close to Robinson. I had the feeling
that he admired himself so much that he had little room in his
pantheon for Moody, whom I worshiped, as did Olivia and Ridgely.
Although at the time I was not destined to be in New York long
enough to become a real Greenwich Villager, I did, so to speak,
take out first papers and later became a full-fledged citizen of that
remarkable community.

The Geographical Society gave me a desk but no money, and pressed me to write scientific articles as a background for enlisting interest in my planned expedition to Victoria Island. I wrote not only for the society's *Bulletin* but also for the *American Anthropologist,* the *Journal of American Folklore,* and the *Summary Report of the Geological Survey of Canada.* Time was passing, however, and I still had no sponsor for my new venture.

It was Cyrus Adams who sent me to the Natural History Museum, where, after being handed from Clark Wissler, curator of anthropology, to Herman C. Bumpus, the museum's director, I finally reached the institution's president, Henry Fairfield Osborn. Osborn, who had obviously been thoroughly briefed by his lieutenants on my plan, was, it turned out, more impressed by my personality than by my ideas on the financing of an arctic expedition. I said that I would probably need between two and three thousand dollars. Osborn felt that I would need many times what I asked. He decided, however, to take a chance and back me.

At this point, I had a letter from an old Iowa State classmate, Rudolph Martin Anderson, saying that he had heard of my plans and wanted to go north with me. This was a stroke of luck for the museum and for me. Anderson was a Phi Beta Kappa, a Sigma Xi, an all-American athlete, a Ph.D. in ornithology, and the author of *The Birds of Iowa.* He was skilled in geology and botany as well as zoology, and had had considerable experience in field collection. The museum officials snapped him up as soon as they learned of his qualifications, and told him that when the expedition was over they would give him a permanent post in their Department of Zoology.

My experience with my first expedition made me feel that, as our field of operation was to be almost entirely in Canada, we would do well to have some Canadian backing. The museum agreed, and, calling again on the helpful James Mavor, we secured the partnership of the Ottawa Geological Survey, which, under the leadership of Dr. Reginald W. Brock, was responsible for official Canadian anthropological work. We also undertook to establish some weather stations along our route for the Canadian weather service.

It is interesting to record—as Professor Osborn did in his preface to *My Life with the Eskimo,* my account of the expedition published in 1913—that the Natural History Museum ultimately spent far more than the two or three thousand dollars I had asked for, though it was through no fault of mine. The museum's administrators sent two thousand dollars' worth of supplies to me on the arctic coast, but I did not receive any of them. Since Anderson and I were then living off the land, there was no way of communicating with us, and it was assumed that we were lost or at least starving. Under this assumption, the museum spent something like fourteen thousand dollars trying to locate us. Meanwhile, we were doing well with no expenditure of anything but ammunition.

Six months after my arrival in New York, Anderson and I were ready to go. We met in Toronto and started north before the first of May, 1908, taking the same route through Winnipeg, Edmonton, and Athabaska Landing that I had made two years before. The principal change was a new stern-wheeler, the *Mackenzie River,* built out of native lumber cut in a sawmill that came into the region at the same time I did in 1906. We made the trip partly in this relatively luxurious vessel and partly by scow and whaleboat, arriving at Fort McPherson early in July.

In the two years that had elapsed since I first visited the Mackenzie, an astonishing change had come over the delta and north-coast Eskimos. My first awareness of this came with the realization that the Eskimos who met the *Mackenzie River* when it reached McPherson a few days after I did were less interested in seeing the steamer than in meeting the new missionary. Christianity and its exponents, which had aroused very little interest in 1906, now appeared to be the Eskimos' chief concern. This was the result not of increased missionary pressure but of contact with other Christianized Eskimos. Religion had become fashionable—very inconveniently, it turned out, for Anderson and me.

It was our plan to head for Herschel Island, pick up what we needed there, chiefly matches, and then set out on our search for the Victoria Island people. At McPherson we managed to persuade a friend of my Shingle Point days, Ilavinirk, and his wife Mamayauk and daughter Noashak to go with us to Herschel and at least as far east as Tuktoyaktuk. I hoped that they could be persuaded to go all the way with us. It happened that we were stormbound at Shingle Point, and the first good weather that would have permitted us to get away arrived on Sunday. Anderson and I were prepared to take advantage of it. Not so the Eskimos. They were now Christians, and knew what happened to Christians who broke the Sabbath. They said that if we could find any not-very-Christian Eskimos at the Point who might be willing to start off they would be glad to follow, but punishment would fall on them if they took the lead in wrongdoing. We would not have got off at all that day had not a police whale-boat put in. When the sergeant in charge learned of our predicament, he kindly offered, after a meal with us, to draw the lightning upon himself by leading the way out to sea. Not only our own party but every Eskimo at the Point was then glad to load up and follow. Unfortunately, we started at sundown, after the wind had died down, and this meant rowing through most of the night. In the morning we ran into head winds and had to tack against them. We reached Herschel many days later than planned, unaware of the far greater delays that lay ahead of us.

The whaling industry, formerly the mainstay of Herschel Island, was on its last legs. The few whalers who touched at the island in 1908 were short of supplies and could spare little. The Eskimos had become so indoctrinated with the belief that they needed white man's food that they felt they could no longer live off the land, though the land—and the sea—still offered a good living. It was plain to the whalers and the police that the Eskimos of the north coast were in for a bad winter. I still believed that they could get along as Anderson and I planned to do. My plans for going east toward Victoria Island depended, however, on my ability to obtain one all-important item—matches. I had not brought any with me because on my earlier journey I had had no difficulty getting all I needed from whalers, traders, police, and even the Eskimos themselves.

I went to the Mounted Police and asked for enough matches to last me through the winter. Sergeant Francis J. Fitzgerald, in command of the police post, was a man with a great sense of responsibility. He now added my party to his responsibilities. He was certain that if we went east and tried to live off the land, we would either become a charge upon such already starving Eskimos as we might meet or would ourselves starve before we met any. The sergeant's only means of preventing this tragedy, other than shipping us back home as men without visible means of support, lay in his ability to refuse us matches, without which we could not travel. This he did, quite firmly.

He said that if we would discharge the Eskimos we had hired and stay in a small house near the police barracks he would give us food and matches for the winter. Since we had not come north to study the habits of the police at Herschel Island, we decided, with the sergeant's blessing, to head for Point Barrow, more than four hundred miles to the west, where we knew we could get matches— and where Fitzgerald believed we would settle down to enjoy the comparative comfort of that well-equipped trading post.

We knew that it would take what was left of the summer for us to reach Barrow and that we would have to winter somewhere along the coast, with no chance of starting east before the spring of 1909. I therefore tried to shorten our match hunt when we passed Flaxman Island on our way to Barrow by asking Leffingwell, who was still there surveying the coast, to let me have some. He said that he only had enough for the Eskimos, who depended on him, and could spare none. We had to go on, making up for the loss of time by doing what scientific work we could. I planned to do ethnological, anthropological, and archaeological work among the Eskimos we were sure to meet, and Anderson expected to take side trips into the mountains to collect zoological specimens.

It was during this period that I formed a tie with Natkusiak, a Port Clarence (Bering Sea) Eskimo who turned out to be the best traveling companion I have ever had of any race. He had the added attraction of being a student of Eskimo dialects, and since I was at this time strengthening my knowledge of Eskimo, Natkusiak's knowledge of dialects was a great help. At Point Barrow, during a necessary waiting period, I copied down, with the help of Annie Koodlalook, an Eskimo who had studied at the Carlisle Indian School, a nine-thousand-word Eskimo vocabulary, and wrote out a hundred thousand words of Eskimo folklore that Annie had translated into English. After this task was completed, I had such a command of the Eskimo language that I was able to set down folklore directly in Eskimo in the narrator's own dialect. If our long journey in quest of matches had diverted us from our main purpose—that of reaching the people of Victoria Island—the time spent was not entirely wasted, though it took far longer than either Anderson or I had expected it would. It was past the middle of August, 1909, before I was again back at Herschel Island.

Shortly after my arrival there the whaler *Karluk*, under Captain Stephen Cottle, arrived on her way to a brief whaling trip toward Banks Island, the great island just west of Victoria. Captain Cottle agreed to take me as far as Cape Bathurst, on the mainland a little to the southwest of Banks Island. Although Anderson, who had been left behind west of Herschel, had not yet arrived, I felt that the opportunity to get a lift as far as Bathurst was too good to miss. I boarded the *Karluk* with Natkusiak and a widowed Eskimo woman, Pannigabluk, who came from Natkusiak's part of Alaska. She was an excellent seamstress, something no party wintering on the arctic coast can afford to be without.

When we reached the Baillie Islands, which are separated from the tip of Cape Bathurst by a narrow and difficult channel, the weather was so bad that Captain Cottle would not risk entering. My companions and I were forced to take a short whaling cruise toward Banks Island, a luxury which would have been wasted time but for the fact that it gave us a chance to see the capture of a bowhead whale. This was something that no later arctic traveler would be likely to see, the invention of an inexpensive substitute for whalebone having made the taking of that type of whale unprofitable.

Two days later the *Karluk* put up at the Baillie Islands, where we transferred to Captain Fritz Wolki's *Rosie H.* Wolki was on his way to the old wreck of the *Alexander* at Cape Parry, hoping to find some coal in her hold.

On August 29, the *Rosie H.* put us and our gear ashore at Cape Parry. Sixteen months out of New York, I was just beginning the real work of the expedition: the push eastward toward the hopefully exceptional Eskimos of Victoria Island.

We were on the edge of a region about whose inhabitants— if indeed there were any—nothing was known. Coronation Gulf, which, with Dolphin and Union Strait and Dease Strait separated Victoria Island from the mainland, was three hundred miles east of us—barely three-quarters of the distance from Herschel Island to Point Barrow, but as far away in time as the Stone Age.

12 We Find a Strange People

With our destination so near, it may seem strange that we did not simply hitch up our dogs and head for Victoria Island. There were a number of reasons for not doing this. Dr. Anderson, with his part of the expedition's personnel and equipment, was not likely to catch up with us for some time. Winter was approaching and it would be necessary for us to accumulate food by hunting and fishing and to make depots large enough to supply a party as big as ours would be when we were joined by Anderson and his six Eskimos. Moreover, our dogs were inadequate.

The most important element in my decision to spend the winter of 1909–1910 in the Cape Parry region, however, was the fact that the region between the cape and Dolphin and Union Strait was almost unknown and badly thought of by the then current generation of western Eskimos.

What was known of this area had been learned largely from Sir John Richardson's accounts of his two voyages, in 1826 and 1848. Richardson, however, had viewed the territory between Coronation Gulf and Cape Parry only from boats traveling some distance off-shore. It is not strange that he decided that the coast was uninhabited. Although I did not agree with his conclusion, I had to consider the effect on my plans if his judgment should prove to be correct. I was trying to perfect my system of arctic travel, which depended for success on the presence of game wherever I went. If there were no Eskimos living along the southeastern shore of what is now Amundsen Gulf and the southwestern coast of

Dolphin and Union Strait, it might be because there was no game there to support them. Most of the western Eskimos were sure that this was so.

It therefore seemed advisable to establish a base in the neighborhood of Langton Bay, which is a triangular opening at the western base of Cape Parry. The cape itself is high and rocky, deeply penetrated by fjords. It is not good hunting ground. With some difficulty caused by bad weather we got our part of the expedition's supplies, including a large quantity of blubber from the bowhead whale Captain Cottle had killed, ashore at Parry and stored in an old house that had been built near the wreck of the *Alexander*.

We then made our way south to Langton Bay and established a supply base in an old hut which had been built by the last whalers to visit that locality. Caribou were not plentiful here, but we found bear and wolf fairly common. The bear and wolf were fat and provided us with good food, but we needed caribou for skins out of which to make winter clothing. Leaving the woman Pannigabluk, who did not seem to mind being alone, to make the camp comfortable, Natkusiak and I started south in the hope of finding caribou. Natkusiak went southeast and I southwest, each of us climbing the thousand-foot Melville Mountains by a separate ravine. Although several miles apart, we could see each other. I soon saw that Natkusiak had spotted game. He was an expert hunter, and I knew that he needed no help.

I tramped twenty miles over soggy tundra without seeing anything but scenery. Since dusk was approaching and hunting would soon be impossible, I turned back toward camp. As I started down the mountain toward the sea I saw in the distance what I at first took to be the flutter of a raven. As I watched, I thought I saw four ravens. Turning my field glasses on them, I saw to my surprise and delight that what I had taken for ravens were the four paws of a Barren Ground grizzly (*Ursus arctos richardsoni*), the rarest of all North American land carnivora. Although an old male, this specimen was lying on his back, pawing the air like a puppy, unaware of my presence.

This was good luck for the American Museum of Natural History but bad luck for the bear and, in a sense, for me, for after I had shot him I had to skin him, leaving the head and paws attached, and then carry the pelt back to camp. It was the heaviest back load I ever carried, weighing, as it did soaking wet, at least two hundred pounds. I could not even attempt to carry any of the meat, which was extremely fat.

Natkusiak, however, had secured three fairly fat caribou. We therefore had enough meat for three weeks, enough skins for at least one suit of clothes, and enough oil to feed our lamps for a month. We returned to our Langton Bay base, cached the bearskin and the few caribou we had left there, and then moved camp inland about ten miles in order to be nearer the caribou that Natkusiak had seen from the mountain.

The next day I found a small valley through which flowed an unnamed stream that ran into the Horton River. This, in turn, flows into Franklin Bay some distance west of Langton. I have seldom been more delighted by anything than I was by what I saw in that ravine. Below me, growing upward from the edge of the stream, there was a wedge of small spruces, the most northerly I had yet found. This was truly a heartening experience, for we had been using for our fires tiny willow twigs, which sometimes seemed to be almost fireproof. I carried a green branch back to camp, and had no difficulty persuading my companions to move camp to the evergreen gully. The next night we were camped by a blazing fire in a sheltered spruce grove near the unnamed stream. We took up hunting again the following day with some success, aided by a fall of snow that prompted us to go back to Langton Bay for the sled we had left there. Dragging this behind us, we headed southeast up the Horton River.

My Eskimos were beginning to be concerned over Anderson's absence. They argued that since western Eskimos all believed that there was no game in the Parry region, the Eskimos in Anderson's party would probably insist on staying where they were. Since Anderson could not travel without them, he would be stuck. They were probably still at the Baillie Islands, only 150 miles away. My Eskimos pointed out that if we were to go west to the islands we could assure Anderson's people that we were finding food and they would therefore return with us.

I agreed, quite unnecessarily as it turned out, to follow their suggestion. It was a mistake, the first of many. The season of poor light (sometimes referred to by those who should know better as the "blackness of the long polar night") was approaching, and we should have used the good light while we had it to build up a stock-

pile of meat and skins. It was not long before I had occasion to regret my decision. Leaving Pannigabluk to take care of the camp and
keep the wolverines away from our meat caches, Natkusiak and I
headed west, only to meet Anderson on his way to join us. It was
a happy reunion, but it created new problems.

At our Horton River camp we were short of three things: ammunition, which we all knew was a necessity, and tea and tobacco,
which the Eskimos believed were necessities. When we reached the
mouth of the Horton on our way back to camp, we divided our
party in two. Anderson, with Natkusiak and Pikaluk, a new man
who had volunteered to come east with them, was to go to Cape
Parry for the things we needed. I took the rest of Anderson's party
with me and headed upriver. My companions were Ilavinirk, his
wife Mamayauk and daughter Noashak, an eighteen-year-old boy
named Polaiyak, and a supercargo in the form of Kunaslik, Pikaluk's decrepit father.

Our troubles began. It took us thirteen days to get to camp.
We were delayed by blizzards, and found the hunting poor along
the way. There was not enough food for the six of us. We ate
what we could get, including the tongue of a beached bowhead
whale. Four years dead, the carcass would have been hidden in the
snow except that foxes had been digging into it. When fresh, a
whale's tongue is rich in fat. The pieces we ate were more like
rubber than flesh. After ten days we robbed our own natural-history
cache of its valuable specimens, including the head and paws of
the Barren Ground grizzly. There was not enough food for the
dogs, and we ourselves, weakened by our inadequate diet, often had
to pull on the sleds. At the end of the trip we were reduced to eating
strips of skin dipped in oil. These will keep a man alive, but they
give him little energy.

We reached camp in bad shape, but believing that our troubles
were over. For the next four or five weeks we kept looking for caribou to the south, but I was the only one of the party not ailing in
one way or another as a result of recent hardships which better
judgment on my part might have avoided. Caribou were no longer
plentiful near our camp, and I learned during these difficult weeks
that if you do not know the habits of game in the region in which
you are looking for it, there are bound to be many delays and
disappointments.

By mid-January, 1910, I was alarmed by Anderson's failure to return from Cape Parry. Since my party was beginning to return to normal health and it had been increased by three Eskimos who had come to visit us—my old friend Memoranna, Okuk, and a Mackenzie boy named Tannaumirk—I decided to go looking for Anderson. On January 21, Tannaumirk, the boy Polaiyak, and I reached the cabin by the wreck of the *Alexander* and found Anderson and Pikaluk seriously ill with pneumonia but recovering. Natkusiak, who had not been stricken, had been supplying the sick men with food. Since I knew that Anderson and Pikaluk would be unable to travel for at least a month, I sent Natkusiak and Polaiyak back to the Horton River camp with a load of things that were needed there. I took care of the sick men as best I could through a dismal and trying February. I was not at all cheered at the end of it by the arrival of the entire Horton River contingent, who had decided that the upriver hunting was not good enough.

Since there were not enough bear or seal at Parry either for such a large party, we had to move to Okat (The Tomcod Place), where fish of that name were plentiful. I was particularly discouraged, however, by the Eskimos' insistence that if game were scarce here, it was sure to be even scarcer farther east. Most of the group with me also insisted that there were no people living between Parry and Cape Krusenstern, two hundred miles east.

Anderson, now fully recovered, decided to go west to the Mackenzie delta for mail and for the supplies that we were sure the Natural History Museum had sent. In spite of the forebodings of my Eskimos, I told him before he left on March 14 that I would be going east and would probably be gone at least nine months. I had learned many lessons the previous winter and was sure that I could do what I wanted to do, which was to find the Victoria Island Eskimos. We were now two years out of New York, and these mysterious people seemed as far away as ever. I knew that unless I took definite action they would remain far away.

By April 21, I had persuaded Natkusiak, Pannigabluk, and Tannaumirk to accompany me and had sent Ilavinirk and his family to camp at Langton Bay and look over our stores there. On that day, with a sledgeload of two weeks' supplies and a brainload of theory about living off the land, we set out along the supposedly uninhabited eastern coast. On the twenty-seventh, at Cape Lyon, we left behind the farthest point of the mainland upon which any American whalers were known to have landed.

From the start we found game, though not at first plentiful. It was not long before we found traces of human habitation as well, remains of whaling villages like those existing in Alaska and the Mackenzie delta. Though it was plain that these villages had not been inhabited recently, I was encouraged to believe that if Eskimos had once found the region habitable they might do so still. My Eskimos were not greatly impressed by this reasoning. Each time we shot a caribou they insisted that it was probably only a straggler and that there would be no more. They were gloomy even while gorging themselves on huge quantities of seal meat. For this reason I once shot three caribou when I knew that we could only use one. This conspicuous waste was psychologically helpful, however unsound it may have been from the point of view of conservation.

On May 9, nineteen days from the Parry peninsula, we had a surprise that made me feel a little like Robinson Crusoe. It occurred at a place called Point Wise, where the open sea begins to narrow into Dolphin and Union Strait, across which lies the mountainous southern shore of Victoria Island, a land larger than England. Here we came upon a beach strewn with driftwood. There was nothing unusual in that, but there was in what I saw when I stopped to examine the first piece. The wood had been hacked at with a dull adz-like tool. This could only mean that men who were unknown to the western Eskimos, whalers, and explorers had been here looking for sledge-making material.

My Eskimos were immediately alarmed. Young Tannaumirk had been regaling us all the way from Langton Bay with wild tales of the "People of the Caribou Antler" who captured their brides with a crook of horn, often killing them in the act, and who reputedly "killed all strangers." What else could account for the tool marks on the driftwood? Excitement grew the following day when we found footprints and sled tracks not more than three months old. That evening we found a deserted village of more than fifty snowhouses, an astonishing number. Tannaumirk, the Mackenzie boy, had never seen a village among his own people of more than twelve or fifteen houses. The occupants of the houses had apparently moved on during the midwinter. Their broad trail led out across the ice of Dolphin and Union Strait, in the direction of Victoria Island.

Although I had intended to go all the way to Coronation Gulf before making a northward crossing of the ice, I now decided that

I would try to locate the people who had made this trail. I left Pannigabluk in charge of our camp and told Tannaumirk, who had scared himself into a sweat with his own stories, that he might stay with her if he wished. When he realized that the Caribou Antler people might just as easily descend on our base camp as on us while we crossed the ice, he decided that Natkusiak and I would be better protectors than Pannigabluk.

On May 13 the three of us set out across the ice, coming, in a few hours, to another large deserted village. From the roof of one of its snowhouses I could see, a long way off, a scattering of men sitting at seal holes, watching. Our dogs became suddenly alert; the Eskimos looked at each other somewhat doubtfully as we drove toward the distant figures. As we drew nearer, apparently unseen, we singled out one still figure and approached cautiously, Tannaumirk, fascinated though terrified, leading the way.

The strange Eskimo did not move until Tannaumirk was within five paces of him. Suddenly, realizing our presence, he jumped to his feet and stood in a threatening position brandishing a long knife, the blade of which was certainly metal. Tannaumirk cringed a little and began talking wildly. The frightened sealer began a monotonous, staccato intonation that seemed to be merely sound without words. I later learned that this was a defense against being struck dumb, since a man confronted by a spirit will never speak again if he fails to make a sound with every breath he draws.

For several minutes Tannaumirk's talk and the sealer's weird noise continued. Finally, the strange Eskimo recovered himself enough to notice our dogs and their harness, which seemed to convince him that we were no evil spirits. Tannaumirk, too, got hold of himself and began to explain that he was unarmed and meant no harm. The sealer came slowly forward and touched Tannaumirk's arm. Convinced that it was a human arm, the stranger said that he would take us to his village. Tannaumirk followed him, and Natkusiak and I decided to remain a little behind until the villagers had been convinced that they could safely accept us. We soon were left in no doubt about our welcome.

From all about on the white ice, dark figures now converged upon us, crowding about and scaring Tannaumirk all over again. Women and children and old men came from their houses in the distance. When convinced that we were men and not spirits, they ran toward us, shouting, "I am So-and-So. I am well disposed. See

—no knife! Who are you?" We introduced ourselves while the women went back to their houses to cook for us. We had become very important persons.

The men asked where we would like to camp. I pointed out a spot a little way from their village, explaining that I did not want our dogs to have any chance to fight with theirs. Children rushed back into the houses to fetch their fathers' snow knives and building mittens. We were not allowed to do anything but watch the rapid construction of our house and its furnishing with skins and lamps. We were told that it was ours to occupy until all the food in the village was used up. The next day was to be a holiday, with no hunting or fishing but with plenty of opportunity for each of us to learn about the others' ways.

13 Life in the Stone Age

I have since looked back to that day with the warmest and most vivid of memories. It marked my introduction to men and women of a bygone age. Mark Twain's Connecticut Yankee went to sleep in the nineteenth century and woke up in King Arthur's time. I, without going to sleep at all, had walked out of the twentieth century into the intellectual and cultural world of men and women of an age far earlier than Arthur's.

These Eskimos were more nearly like the hunting tribes of Britain and Gaul during the Ice Age. Their existence in 1910 on the same continent with our populous cities was an anachronism representing a time lapse of more than ten thousand years. These people gathered their food with the weapons of the Stone Age, in their case made of copper, which is so characteristic of them that they are known as the Copper Eskimos. While archaeological remains can tell a fascinating story to the trained scientist whose imagination can piece it together and fill in the gaps, I had to imagine nothing. I had merely to look and listen, for here were not remains of the Stone Age but the Stone Age itself, its men and women welcoming us to their homes.

The dialect that the easterners spoke differed so little from Mackenzie River speech, which I had acquired in three years of living in the houses and traveling camps of the western Eskimos, that we could make ourselves understood from the first. It cannot have happened often in the history of the world that the first explorer to visit a primitive people was one who spoke their language.

There was no doubt that, like our distant European ancestors, these American Stone Age people feared strangers. Our first meeting had been somewhat taut and dramatic because they supposed us to be spirits. Once they were convinced that we were human, they had no fear of us since, in spite of our strangeness, they greatly outnumbered us. Besides, they told us, the freedom and frankness with which we came among them showed that we could harbor no guile. A man who plots treachery, they said, never turns his back on those whom he intends to stab from behind.

Before the house they were building for us was quite ready, children came running from the village to announce that their mothers had dinner cooked. The houses were so small that it was not convenient to invite all three of us into the same one. Moreover, it was not etiquette to do so, as we learned. Each of us was therefore taken to a different place. My host was the seal hunter whom we had first approached on the ice. His house would, he said, be a fitting one in which to offer me my first meal among them. It happened that his wife had been born farther west on the mainland coast than anyone else in their village, and it was even said that her ancestors had not belonged originally to the Copper people but were migrants from the westward. She would therefore like to ask me questions.

It turned out that his wife was not a talkative or inquisitive person. She was motherly, kindly, and hospitable. Her first questions were not about the land from which I came but about my footgear. Were my feet not just a little damp? Might she not pull my boots off for me and dry them over the lamp? Would I not put on a pair of her husband's dry socks? Was there no little hole in my mittens or my coat that she could mend for me? She had boiled some lean seal meat for me, but she had not boiled any fat, for she thought I might prefer it raw. They always cut the fat in small pieces and ate it raw themselves. The pot still hung over the lamp, and anything she put into it would be cooked in a moment.

When I told her that my taste in seal fat coincided with theirs —as indeed it did—she was delighted. People were much alike, then, after all, though they came from a great distance. She would accordingly treat me as if I were one of their own people come to visit them from afar—and, in fact, I was one of their own people, for she had heard that the wicked forest people to the south spoke a language no man could understand and I spoke with only a slight touch of strangeness.

When we entered the house the boiled pieces of seal meat had already been taken out of the pot and lay steaming on a wooden side table. On being assured that my tastes were not likely to differ from theirs, my hostess picked out for me the lower joint of a seal's foreleg, squeezed it firmly between her hands to make sure that nothing would later drip from it, and handed it to me, along with her own copper-bladed knife. The next most desirable piece was similarly squeezed and handed to her husband and other pieces given in turn to the rest of the family.

When this had been done, one extra piece was set aside in case I should want a second helping. The rest of the boiled meat was divided into four portions, with the explanation that there were four families in the village who had no fresh meat. The little adopted daughter of the house, a girl of seven or eight, had not begun to eat with the rest of us. It was her assignment to take a wooden platter and carry the four pieces of meat to the families who had none of their own.

I thought to myself that the pieces sent out were smaller than the portions we were eating and that the recipients would not get a square meal. I learned later that night from my two companions that similar presents had been sent out from each of the houses in which they visited. I know now that every house in the village in which any cooking was done had likewise sent four portions, so that the aggregate must have been a good deal more than the recipients could eat at one time.

During our meal, presents of food were also brought from other houses. Each housewife apparently knew what the others would be eating. Those who had any variety to offer would send some of it to others, so that every few minutes a child messenger appeared at our door with a platter of contributions to our meal. Some of the gifts were designated for me—mother had said that, however they divided the rest of what she was sending, the boiled kidney was for me. Or mother had sent this small piece of boiled seal flipper to me with the message that if I would take breakfast at ther house tomorrow I would have a whole flipper. It happened that one of my companions was at their house now and had told them that I considered the flipper the best part of a seal.

As we ate we sat on the front edge of the bed-platform, each holding his piece of meat in the left hand and a knife in the right. This was my first experience with a knife of native copper. I found it sharp and serviceable. The piece of copper from which the blade had been hammered out had been found on Victoria Island, to the north, in the territory of another group from whom it had been traded for some mainland driftwood.

My hostess sat on my right in front of the cooking lamp, her husband on my left. As the house was an ordinary oval snow dome, about seven by nine feet, there was room only for the three of us on the front edge of the two-foot-high snow platform, over which reindeer, bear, and musk-ox skins had been spread to make the bed. The children, therefore, ate standing in the bit of open floor space to the left of the door. The lamp and cooking gear and frames for clothing over the lamp took up the space to the right.

In the inverted horseshoe-shaped three-foot-high doorway stood the family's three dogs, side by side, waiting for someone to finish the picking of a bone. As each of us in turn finished a bone, it was tossed to one of the dogs. Each dog retired to the alleyway to eat, returning to his position in line as soon as he had finished. The animals behaved well, each taking its turn. When the meal was over, they went unbidden to curl up and sleep in the alleyway or outside.

Our meal consisted of two courses—the first, lean and fat meat; the second, soup. Soup was made by chopping frozen seal blood into the boiling broth immediately after the cooked meat had been taken out of the pot. The pot was then stirred briskly until the whole came nearly, but never quite, to a second boil. This made a soup of a thickness comparable to our pea soup. If the pot had been allowed to come to a boil, the blood would have coagulated and settled to the bottom. When the pot was within a few degrees of boiling, the cooking lamp was extinguished and a few handfuls of snow stirred into the soup to cool it to drinking temperature. With a dipper the housewife then filled large musk-ox-horn drinking cups and gave one to each person.

After I had eaten my fill of fresh seal and drunk two cupfuls of blood soup, my host and I moved farther back on the bed-platform, where we could sit comfortably propped up against bundles of soft caribou skins while we talked. He and his wife asked few questions, none of which could be considered intrusive, according to either their standards or mine. They understood, they said, why we had left behind the woman of our party when we came upon their trail, for it is always safest to assume that strangers are going to prove hostile. Now that we had found them to be harmless and friendly, would we not allow them to send a sledge in the morning to bring her to the village?

They had often heard that their ancestors had occasional contact with people from the west. Now it was their good fortune to have with them some men from that region. They would like to see a western woman too. It could be a very long way to the land from which we came. Were we not tired of traveling, and did we not think of spending the summer with them? Of course, all of the eastern groups would treat us well, unless we went too far to the east and fell in with the treacherous Netsilik people of King William Island. Still farther east, they had heard, lived the white men (Kablunat), of whom, no doubt, seeing that we came from the west, we had never heard.

The white men, they told me, live farthest to the east of all people. They were said to have various physical deformities and to be of a strangely eccentric disposition. Sometimes when they gave valuable things to an Eskimo they would take no pay for them. At other times they wanted exorbitant prices for useless articles or mere curiosities. White people would not eat good, ordinary food, but subsisted on various things that a normal person could not think of forcing himself to swallow except in case of starvation. The strange thing was that the white men could have had better things to eat if they wanted to. Seals, whales, fish, and even caribou abound in their country.

These and a great many other things I was told with friendly readiness. I had only to give a hint of what interested me to be told whatever they knew. In the telling, they differentiated between what was considered certain, merely probable, or possibly unreliable. They showed delicacy in asking questions. Were they not interested, I asked them, to know why I had come and where I was going? Yes, they were interested, but they knew that if I wanted them to know I would tell them. Asking many questions of strangers was not their custom. They considered that I asked many because to do so was no doubt good manners among my people. It was to be expected that men coming from so great a distance would have customs different from theirs.

We sat and talked perhaps an hour, until a messenger came (it was always the children who carried messages) to say that my companions had gone to the house that had been built for us and that the people hoped I could come there too. It was a big house, and many could sit in it at once and talk with us.

On arriving at the house I found that although several had already arrived there was still plenty of room within doors for the four or five who had come along to see me home. The floor of the inner half of the house had been raised into the usual two-foot-high snow sleeping platform, covered with skins, partly ours and partly contributed by various households. A seal-oil lamp for heating and lighting had been installed. It was a cozy place, heated by the lamp to 50° F. Our guests stayed only a few minutes. Someone suggested that we were no doubt tired and sleepy and would like to be left alone. In the morning, they said, we would have plenty of time for talking.

When they were all gone, however, we did not go to sleep, but sat up half the night discussing the strange things we had seen and heard. My companions were quite as excited as I. It was, they said, as if we were living through a story such as old people tell in the assembly house when the sun is away during the winter. What kindly, inoffensive-looking people these were! No doubt, however, they were powerful and dangerous magicians, such as the stories tell about, and such as my companions' fathers had known in their youth.

Tannaumirk had heard something that seemed to bear this out. He had been guest in the house of a man who last winter had dropped his knife into a seal hole through the ice where the sea was very deep. So powerful was the spell the hunter pronounced that when he reached down into the sea the water came only to his elbow, yet he picked the knife right off the ocean bottom! This, Tannaumirk commented, was where the ice alone was at least a fathom thick, and the water beneath the ice so deep that a stone dropped into it would take a long time to sink to the bottom.

I asked my companions if they believed such stories. I knew what the answer would be. Of course they did. Why should I ask? Had they not often told me that their own people were able to do such things until a few years ago, when they abjured their familiar spirits on learning from missionaries that no one can attain salvation who employs spirits to do his bidding? It was too bad that salvation and the practice of magic were incompatible. Not that such a trivial thing as the recovery of lost articles was very important.

In the cure of sickness, however, and in control of the weather, prayers seemed much less efficient than the old charms.

Still, of course, they did not really regret the loss of the old power. For did they not have the inestimable prospect of salvation, the very possibility of which had been unknown to their forefathers, who lived before the missionaries arrived in their country? It was mere shortsightedness to regret having renounced the miraculous ability to cure diseases. God certainly knew best how and when one should die. To him who prayed faithfully and never worked on Sunday, death was but the entrance to a happier life. In this vein we talked and moralized until we finally grew drowsy.

The next morning, when we woke up and began to stir about within doors, we were unaware that someone had been listening outside our snowhouse for a long time, waiting for signs that we were awake. From familiarity with their customs I now know that it was a signal from this watcher that brought us our earliest visitor of the morning, the hunter whom we had first encountered. He came from the village, walking slowly and singing at the top of his voice so that we might have ample warning of his approach. When he came to the outer door of our twenty-foot alleyway he stopped and announced himself: "I am So-and-So; my intentions are friendly; I have no knife. May I come in?" This was the formula in dealing with us. Among themselves they would merely announce as they were about to enter the house, "I am So-and-So; I am coming in."

The talk that morning turned on various things. Who were their neighbors to the east and to the north? Had they ever come in contact with the forest Indians to the south? Had they ever heard of white men visiting their country? I considered it possible, though not likely, that some survivors of Franklin's ships, wrecked more than half a century ago near the east coast of Victoria Island, might have lived for a time among these people.

Although they were doubtless as curious concerning us as I was about them, they continued to ask very few questions, even after I had given them an opening. Their reticence and good breeding made me feel more nearly ashamed of my calling than I had ever been before. An ethnologist has to make constant and often impertinent inquiries. Our hosts answered me with the greatest good humor.

They had never seen white men, they told me. Nor had they ever seen the woodland Indians. They had, however, discovered traces of these people on the mainland to the south, and they knew by hearsay from the Coppermine River Eskimos that the Indians were treacherous, bloodthirsty people, wicked and great magicians. No greater magicians, perhaps, than the white men but quicker to use their power for evil purposes. To the east lived various Eskimo groups (of whom they named over a dozen), and beyond those the white men, the Kablunat. To the north, on Victoria Island, lived their nearest neighbors and best friends, the Haneragmiut, People-of-the-Shoreline.

And what did they think of me—to what people did they suppose I belonged? Oh, but they did not have to guess; they knew. Tannaumirk had told them that he belonged to the Kupagmiut, of whom they had heard many stories from their fathers. My accent made it plain that I belonged to the Kupagmiut also, and not to that more distant people to whom my other companion, Natkusiak, belonged, and whose language was more strange—a people whose name they had never even heard of until we came.

But, I asked, did they not consider the color of my blue-gray eyes and of my light brown beard unusual? Did not these things incline them to believe that I must belong to a different people? They replied, "We never felt that you belonged to a different people. Your speech differs from ours only a little more than does that of some people with whom we trade every year. As for your eyes and beard, they are much like those of some of our neighbors to the north, whom you must visit. They will never cease being sorry if you pass on to the east without seeing them." So it was arranged that on the following day we should visit the Haneragmiut.

Meanwhile, what should we do today? Was there not some way in which the western people customarily celebrated the arrival of visitors? We replied that, usually, all the village gathered in a great dance. That was just their way, our hosts told us. Seeing that our customs coincided, they immediately planned to make a large dance house. We should see how they danced, and possibly we might dance for them too.

A dozen young men ran off to don their house-building coats and mittens and get their snow knives. By midafternoon the dance house was finished, a snow dome at least nine feet high. Since a snowhouse is half a sphere, this meant a floor eighteen feet in diameter. It was large enough to accommodate forty people standing in a circle around a five-foot dancing space in the center.

We were told that conditions of life among the Copper Eskimos had been hard for many years, and that, while their ancestors had danced often and had owned many drums (the only musical instrument of the Eskimos), they themselves had of late years danced but seldom, and there was only one drum left among them.

While the men were putting the finishing touches on the dance house, someone fetched the drum and a young woman sang for us to its accompaniment. She handled it like a tambourine and played it in a manner quite different from that of the western Eskimos. The songs were different too. She sang them charmingly. One song had a rhythm that seemed to me to resemble that of the ancient Norse scaldic poems. The girl who sang it was very fair for an Eskimo and had the long-fingered hands I have seen only among half-bloods in Alaska.

The festival continued all through the afternoon. None of the dances were identical with any known to my companions from Alaska or the Mackenzie, but there was a general similarity. The manner of the performers was quite varied. Many of the dances were performed without moving the feet at all, merely by swaying the body and gesticulating with the arms. In some cases the performer sang, recited, or uttered a series of exclamations. In others he was silent.

At this time of year—the middle of May—there was no darkness at midnight. Nevertheless, the people ate three meals a day with fair regularity. When our dance ended, about eight o'clock in the evening, the women announced supper. After supper I sat awhile and talked with my host and hostess and one or two visitors. When I got up to go, all of them walked home with me. Some others were already there, as they had been on the evening before. They stayed only a short while. By eleven o'clock the last visitors had said good night and our first whole day among the Stone Age people had come to its end.

14 Copper Knives and Blond Men

Now that we had established the reality of the Eskimos reported by Klinkenberg and Mogg during my first expedition, I wanted to travel and live with these people, to learn their ways and their folklore, and to find out if among them there were any who might remember contact with early white explorers. I learned that many—perhaps hundreds—of the Victoria Island people went south at about this time of year to the region between the northeast corner of Great Bear Lake and the Coppermine River. There, they obtained wood for bows, sled parts, spears, shovels, and tool handles.

Accordingly, Natkusiak, Tannaumirk, Pannigabluk, and I set out along the southern shore of Dolphin and Union Strait, visiting the villages we encountered on the way, and then turning south toward the Coppermine River. We followed the east side of the river, not because we wished to, but because we had started on the eastern shore and it turned out to be impossible to cross until we reached the tributary Kendall River, which flows from the Dismal Lakes into the Coppermine. At that point we built a raft and, after being carried some distance downstream, got across.

It was frightfully hot and the mosquitoes were terrible when we reached the Dismal Lakes, so called no doubt because of the lack of trees and the monotonous expanse of scrub willow that surrounds them. Here we found a group of Rae River Eskimos, among whom I had been told there was a man who remembered Dr. John Richardson's crossing of their river in 1848. Unfortunately, the old man was away at the time.

Between the Dismal Lakes and Great Bear Lake there were, and had been for many years, numerous Eskimo camps. It seemed strange to me that their annual presence in that region was at that time unknown either to the Athapaskan Indians of Bear Lake or to the local Hudson's Bay Company's people.

In late autumn the Eskimos started for the sea coast, where they hunted seals. The kind of seal hunting with which Anderson, Natkusiak, and I had had some experience was entirely strange to the Copper Eskimos of Dolphin and Union Strait. It is simply a matter of stalking seals on the ice when, in spring, they lie basking in the sun. This method of taking seals was supposed to be something of a mystery, many early explorers having declared that no white man could ever master it. As a matter of fact, once a man has acquired a slight familiarity with the psychology of seals, it is quite easy.

Anderson and I had noticed one day that a seal on the ice will sleep for anywhere from half a minute to two minutes and then stay awake, raising its head and looking about for a few seconds. All a hunter has to do is to realize that he cannot keep the seal from seeing him. He has to make the seal believe that he is another seal by lying still, flat on his belly, while the seal is awake and looking at him, and crawling toward it on all fours while the seal is asleep. In this way, a man can get within two hundred yards of his quarry. To get nearer, he must snake along, lying flat, through slush and pools of water, not forgetting that he is supposed to be another seal. No seal would believe in a seal that did not alternately sleep and rise to look about.

When the hunter is within a hundred to seventy-five yards, the seal will stay awake and stare at him. At this time it is vitally important to do only what a seal would do and to keep the body sideways to the seal's view. The hunter, at this point, has to keep alternately raising and lowering his head. If he does this for ten or fifteen minutes, the seal's doubts are satisfied. It knows that it is looking at another seal. Then it is easy for the hunter to shoot the trusting creature, necessarily through the spine or the brain, and run forward to catch it by a flipper before the body begins to slide into the water. Some Eskimo hunters even crawl close enough to a seal to grab it by a flipper and drag it away from its hole while it is still alive.

The Copper Eskimos take seals by watching at their blowholes and harpooning them as they come up for air. We had never tried this method and did not feel that we could trust ourselves to be successful enough at it to keep from being a burden to the Eskimos.

Rather than impose upon the Eskimos, I decided to spend the winter of 1910–1911 in the forest region of the Dease River, where there were plenty of caribou and a number of accessible fishing lakes. It occurred to me that Anderson, whom I had left at Langton Bay to carry on his zoological work, might have begun to wonder what had become of me. Before settling down, therefore, I decided to make the three-hundred-mile journey across unknown country from the Dease River to Langton Bay. Leaving Tannaumirk and Pannigabluk to care for the Dease River camp, Natkusiak and I and Johnny, a Slavey Indian we had picked up who said he knew at least part of the way, set out through the forest. It soon became clear, however, that Johnny did not know the way, and his information about the abundance of caribou along the route turned out to be wrong. In fact, he was in every way a trial to Natkusiak and me.

We eventually managed to reach the Horton River and follow its uncharted course until we hit the part of it that we had visited the year before. We then left the river and crossed to Langton Bay, descending from the high plateau in the face of a terrific gale. We found Anderson and his party safe and comfortable, with plenty of food, thanks to a whale that had drifted inshore just before the freeze-up.

We rested in camp from our arduous twenty-six-day journey and after two weeks packed up for the return trip to the Dease River. It was slow going, for the light was now poor and the temperature hovered around −50° F. We were on short rations before we found caribou in the woods. They were easy to find, for in the intense cold they left trails of steam as they passed among the trees.

The next six weeks were spent piling up stores of caribou meat and preparing for our northward journey across Coronation Gulf to visit the Eskimo villages.

On March 22, 1911, Anderson, Natkusiak, Tannaumirk, and I set out toward Coronation Gulf. On this trip occurred one of those near-disasters that even in the Arctic are sure to be the result of careless or foolhardy action, and it almost ended our explorations. We came upon an abandoned snowhouse and decided to spend the night in it. The four of us entered and made it snug, pulling the snow-block door tightly shut. I was the cook that night. While my three companions sat on the snow platform, talking and joking, I lighted the primus stove, which we were then using instead of blubber lamps.

It was not long before Tannaumirk, who had been telling a funny story with characteristic gestures, suddenly fell back on the bed-platform and gurgled strangely. Nobody paid much attention, supposing that this unusual behavior would turn out to be part of Tannaumirk's pantomime. The man lay still for so long, however, that I suggested that Anderson find out what was the matter with him. Anderson turned to look at Tannaumirk and promptly fell face forward across the Eskimo's body. I knew then what was happening. I told Natkusiak to break a hole in the wall. To do so he had to get up to reach for his knife. He was unable to rise. This frightened him so that he threw himself backward against the snow-block door and broke it through. He dragged himself out and I followed him. I had already extinguished the primus stove. I stretched out beside Natkusiak. When I thought I could move, I tried to get to the door in order to drag out Anderson and Tannaumirk. I was unable to make it. Although the temperature was something like −45° F. and we were lightly dressed, Natkusiak and I simply lay on the ground until Anderson, and later Tannaumirk, revived by the fresh air from the opened door, were able to join us. This narrow escape from carbon-monoxide poisoning, caused by civilized stupidity and civilized equipment, was the closest brush with death we had on that expedition.

We were, in spite of this misadventure, able to move on the following day. During the evening we came to a village of Eskimos who were in the habit of hunting in Victoria Island in summer and who were now on their way to the hunting grounds. We traded with them for ethnological specimens, largely stone lamps, stone pots, bows and arrows, and copper-tipped spears and harpoons. From these people we learned the source of the soapstone that is used all along the artic coast for lamps and pots. They told us that there was a place called Utkusiksalik, meaning "the place where there is material for pots." This spot was visible from the village as a V-shaped gap in the hills of the mainland to the south. There were other quarries in the vicinity, and apparently all the pots and lamps from Coronation Gulf to Siberia were made of Utkusiksalik steatite. I was able to purchase a soapstone lamp, forty-three inches long and weighing about fifty pounds, which is now in the American Museum of Natural History in New York.

We were surprised to have these Coronation Gulf Eskimos tell us that a ship manned by white men and strange Eskimos was wintering not far from their village. I was not pleased to hear this, for I had hoped that the Copper Eskimos might remain untouched by civilization for a long time. We decided, however, that since the ship was there we had better pay her a visit.

That visit changed all our plans. The ship was the thirteen-ton gasoline schooner *Teddy Bear*, Captain Joseph Bernard master. She had been on her way to hunt and trade along the south coast of Victoria Island. Having heard at Cape Bathurst that we were in the vicinity, Captain Bernard had decided to look for us. By the time we reached the *Teddy Bear*, Bernard had almost given us up. He now agreed to take on board our heavy load of ethnological and other specimens, which we had intended to freight overland from the Dease River to Franklin Bay. He would land them at the mouth of the Dease River and arrange to have them carried from there by boat by way of Great Bear Lake to Fort Norman on the Mackenzie, where the Hudson's Bay Company would take them for shipment to New York.

We decided that Anderson, with Tannaumirk and Pannigabluk, would remain in Coronation Gulf and continue adding to his zoological collections. Natkusiak and I would cross that part of Victoria Island once known as Wollaston Land, now the Wollaston Peninsula, to Prince Albert Sound, and then go on to Banks Island to visit the Eskimos I believed lived there. Captain Bernard and his *Teddy Bear* would pick us up at the southeastern corner of Banks Island in the autumn.

It was on April 30 that Natkusiak and I started north with a single sledge pulled by six dogs. The ice was smooth and dangerously thin, but by following caribou tracks we made the traverse of Dolphin and Union Strait successfully. On May 7 we began the crossing of the Wollaston Peninsula to Prince Albert Sound, where we had been told that the Copper Eskimos gathered for a spring trading festival. Our crossing of the Wollaston Peninsula was the first in which a white man had participated, but I was not especially interested in being first. We chose the route simply because it was the best way to get to where we wanted to go, but during the course of the trip we did do some surveying, which helped to fill in some blank spaces on the map.

Among the groups gathered at Prince Albert Sound would be the Kanghiryaugmiut, the People-of-the-Great-Gulf whom Klinkenberg and Mogg had seen in 1906 and 1908. Every group of Copper Eskimos we met told us that these people looked very much as I did, having reddish beards and, some of them, blue eyes.

In five days we crossed the peninsula and from a height at the edge of the sound saw through our glasses that the Eskimo festivities were still going on far out on the ice. As we approached, we were met by several seal hunters who were at first puzzled by our arrival from the south. They had supposed that they knew everyone who lived in that direction, but we were strange both in appearance and in the manner of arranging our dogs, which were hitched tandem. A Copper Eskimo sledge would have been pulled by a single dog, or at most three, hitched fanwise.

The seal hunters understood readily who we were as soon as we explained that we really belonged to the southwest and were now coming from the southeast merely because we had been visiting the Haneragmiut. We added that we belonged to the same people who, we understood, had visited them some years ago in ships. We described the *Olga* to them. They had liked the *Olga's* people and, when they recognized our description of them, their welcome became enthusiastic.

After we had made it plain that Natkusiak was a real western Eskimo and I a white man who had learned Eskimo speech, we continued toward the village. When less than a mile from it, our ambassadors began to introduce us by means of a kind of sign language. A local person, if he wants to vouch for approaching visitors, will run a few yards to one side, then an equal distance to the other, shouting his own name. When our hosts did this, everybody came running toward us, children as well as grown men and women. All talked loudly and even shouted as they ran, their arms above their heads. They kept opening and closing their hands to show that they carried no weapons. Over and over again they said, ''You need not be afraid of us, we have no weapons, we are as we seem, we are glad you came to see us.''

We had been halted farther from the village than I liked. During a momentary lull in the welcoming racket I pointed this out. One of our hosts then jumped on top of our load and shouted that the crowd must let us pass on to a spot where he and others could make camp for us. The mob then yielded with shouts of good will, but our dogs were so excited and confused that they would not pull. Hereupon it was suggested that we unhitch our dogs and that the villagers take their places, hauling the sledge by their own power to whatever spot we chose. We agreed, but our dogs used their freedom to get into fights with the local animals, so that growls and snarls were added to the cheering. Through this uproar our load was hauled to the place we had chosen, and the local campmakers took over.

When quiet was restored, we heard something that changed our plans for the summer. We had intended to cross Prince of Wales Strait over to Banks Island, where we had planned to spend the summer, hunting caribou and molting geese, and learning about the people of the locality by associating with them while we waited for Bernard's *Teddy Bear* to come along and pick us up for the journey to Langton Bay. Now we were told that there would be no people on Banks Island that summer. Our informants had themselves spent the winter there, but they were the only people who had. They had left Banks in what we understood to be the last part of March and were now headed east. The majority intended to ascend the Kagloryuak River, which flows from the center of Victoria Island into the east end of Prince Albert Sound.

These people were, as we had been told, the most widely traveled of all the Copper Eskimos. They certainly were the most unusual in appearance. Natkusiak and I agreed that among them there was a greater percentage of individuals who looked like Europeans than we had found elsewhere. They told us that every year they visited a river called Akilinik on the Atlantic side of northern Canada, where they met Eskimos who were in close contact with Europeans. I got so much information and folklore from these people that in addition to my diary notes I later wrote a small book called *Prehistoric and Present Commerce Among the Arctic Coast Eskimos,* which was published by the Canadian Geological Survey.

Primitive as the people of Prince Albert Sound were, they were the most prosperous Eskimos I have ever seen and the best informed about the region in which they lived.

In view of their report that there would be no Eskimos at Banks that summer, we decided to head south and make our way toward our base at Langton Bay. Our sled was again heavily loaded with ethnological and geological specimens. Since we could not carry much meat, we had to stop and hunt whenever we saw a seal.

The seventy-mile crossing of the eastern end of what is now called Amundsen Gulf taught me a great deal about travel over moving ice that was of much value later on. As I now see it, the significant thing about this crossing was that every day I lost a little more of my fear of drifting sea ice in arctic waters. Here we were crossing a strait by a course longer than any we would have followed had we been attempting to cross from Asia to North America. The sea was covered, or not quite covered, by floes that Natkusiak assured me behaved in much the same way as did those in his home region of Bering Sea and Bering Strait.

For years I had been hearing Eskimos talk of walking, during the winter, from northeastern Siberia to northwestern America somewhat as a New Yorker might speak of crossing Fifth Avenue. Until the time about which I am now writing, such casual remarks had failed to sink in. They gradually took on significance as I compared Natkusiak's and my present experiences crossing an arctic strait to my past experiences in crossing city streets. Nobody claims that it is perfectly safe to jaywalk Fifth Avenue. Many of us do it, however. If a taxi misses us by five inches, we forget about the incident in a few minutes.

After some difficulty caused by the arrival of spring on the mainland, which made onshore sledging impossible and poured warm water from the rivers against the sea ice, we arrived at Langton Bay minus our load of specimens. These we had had to leave at the southwest corner of Darnley Bay because the sea ice had become impossible for heavy sledging and there was no snow on the land. When we got within a few miles of our camp, cutting across the uncertain bay ice, we came to open water and could go no farther. Fortunately, Ilavinirk and his wife, who were watching for seals through field glasses, saw me waving my coat. The moment of danger passed as they paddled across in their kayaks and ferried us home.

I spent the summer doing archaeological work between Langton Bay and Cape Parry, writing up notes and gathering in the specimens that we had had to leave behind. The archaeological work gave me great pleasure, for its chief feature was the settling of a controversy that had for a long time divided scientific circles.

It was the contention of Dr. Franz Boas, of Columbia University, a somewhat intransigent theorist who was nevertheless considered the leading Eskimo authority of the day, that the Eskimos had no pottery of their own other than vessels of hollowed-out soapstone. While I was busy in Victoria Island, Ilavinirk had found a spot at Point Stivens that was full of broken potsherds. I told him about Boas' theory, and it baffled him. He had often, when a boy at Kotzebue Sound, helped his mother to make pottery and bake it in driftwood fires, and he had heard the old people telling how Eskimos used clay pottery before they learned to use soapstone. It was a surprise to him, therefore, that scientists believed that Eskimos used only imported pottery. Ilavinirk offered to show me the place where he had found the shards. He did, and there I received another lesson in unlearning. There was no question about the pottery or its age. In addition to the ceramic fragments, the site at Point Stivens produced many articles of whalebone, antler, and ivory and, perhaps most interesting of all, proof through the absence of nets and their accessories that the Eskimos of this region had not originally used nets for fishing.

The box of shards that I shipped to the American Museum plainly marked "POTTERY" seemed to annoy Dr. Boas very much. He told the museum staff before it arrived that the shipment would undoubtedly turn out to be soapstone, implying that I was so ignorant that I would not know the difference between pottery and stone. Pliny Goddard, a friend of mine in the museum's Anthropology Department, invited Boas to be present when the box was opened, and offered to eat the contents if it turned out to be soapstone if Boas would agree to eat any pottery that turned up in the shipment. Boas evidently did not consider this very funny. I was told later that he did not turn up for the opening.

When winter came and further archaeological work was impossible, I spent most of my time either hunting or improving my knowledge of the Eskimo language and the lore it provided. We wintered on the lower part of Horton River, living entirely as the Eskimos did and, for my part, speaking Eskimo to all but one of the party. Anderson, who had rejoined us after doing much valuable work, was the exception. I could never get him interested in the Eskimo language.

During that winter at Horton River, Anderson and I talked over plans for a new expedition, he serving as a devil's advocate, presenting all sorts of difficult questions to which I had to find answers. It was Anderson's contention that if I could convince him

I would have no difficulty in convincing those who would have to put financial backing behind my plans, which called for a further demonstration of the practicability of living off the land in the Arctic and thus widening the scope of exploration.

In the spring of 1912, both Anderson and I considered that we had done what we had undertaken to do. As soon as travel was possible, I set out on the nine-hundred-mile trip to Point Barrow, where I planned to do more archaeological and ethnological work while awaiting transportation to Nome. I reached Barrow in June and spent the next two months continuing my Eskimo studies and digging at Birnik, a site near Cape Smythe. On August 13, I sailed for Nome on the revenue cutter *Bear*. After a week in that romantic gold town I took a passenger liner for the States, unaware of what was awaiting me in Seattle. It was the somewhat questionable beginning of a new phase of my career.

15 The Press Complicates My Life

The passenger steamer on which I came south from Nome in the fall of 1912 was met at the Seattle pier by a newspaper reporter named John J. Underwood. Underwood was an authority on Alaska. He was well known to Alaskans as the man who made news of their goings and comings. Memories of the gold rush were still fresh in Seattle, and the arrival of the Nome steamer was always news. The fact that I was one of the passengers was not in itself newsworthy, but Underwood made it so by using his ingenuity and imagination. I woke up the next morning to find myself famous, or rather, notorious. On September 9, 1912, the *Seattle Daily Times* printed a story which was picked up by the news services and distributed by them to the ends of the earth. I read the headline with consternation: AMERICAN EXPLORER DISCOVERS LOST TRIBE OF WHITES, DESCENDANTS OF LIEF ERIKSSON.

> Ranking next in importance from an ethnological standpoint to the discovery of the lost tribes of Israel [Underwood wrote] is the discovery made by Prof. Vilhjalmur Stefansson of the American Museum of Natural History of a lost tribe of 1,000 white people, who are believed to be direct descendants from the followers of Leif Eriksson who came to Greenland from Iceland about the year 1000 and a few years later discovered the north coast of America. . . .
>
> The tribe of white people, which Stefansson declares are purely of Norwegian origin, never had seen other persons of their own color. Their number is about 1,000, and more than half of them have rusty-red hair, blue eyes, fair skins and two-colored

eyebrows and beards. They live on both shores of Coronation Gulf, on the mainland of North America and Victoria Island, which formerly was known as Prince Edward Island.

It was for these people that Roald Amundsen, discoverer of the South Pole, searched while making his celebrated trip through the Northwest Passage. Amundsen, it will be remembered, stated that natives had told him of a race of white people living to the northward, but he was unable to find them. Amundsen sent an expedition along the shore of the island, but saw nothing of the tribe, nor did they see anything of him. . . .

Professor Stefansson accounts for their existence by the fact that in the year 982, Greenland was discovered and settled by 5,000 Icelandic Norsemen. One thousand of these people sailed from Norway and missed Greenland but landed on the coast of Newfoundland, where they established a colony, built fourteen churches, two monasteries, a nunnery and other structures, the ruins of which are still in existence. . . .

The Norsemen settled in two colonies, one on the north and one on the south side of Newfoundland. In the fourteenth century Eskimos came from the North and exterminated the people at the northern settlement.

Their record was complete till 1418, when the black plague scourged Europe, and for two centuries communication between Newfoundland and the old country was cut off. When communication was restored, the people of the second settlement were missing. Their graveyards, buildings and other adjuncts of their semicivilization were found, and the theory was formed that the people had drifted to a settlement further to the west, across the narrow straits that divided them from the Arctic archipelago, where they intermingled with Eskimos, whom they took along with them to the islands on which their descendants now live. . . .

Not unnaturally, Underwood's story drew a chorus of ridicule from local Seattle readers who reprimanded me by telephone, and from foreign authorities who cabled their views through the news services.

Although what I had said to acquaintances aboard ship on the way to Seattle, and to Underwood on shore, was merely that I had found Eskimos in and about Victoria Island, some of whom were in physiognomy and coloring quite unlike other Eskimos, most of whom had never seen a white man or a rifle, and all of whom used Stone Age implements, a storm broke over my head. My sponsor, the American Museum of Natural History, was showered with telephone calls, telegrams, and letters from thousands of members

demanding that I be fired, or at the very least that a public statement be issued disowning me and explaining that no one had suspected the sort of charlatan I would turn out to be. For several days
the staff was busy smoothing down the ruffled feathers of members
who discovered that the museum, in view of dispatches I had been
sending in to them for years, thought that I must have been mis-
quoted but that, if I were now being rightly quoted, there must be
substantial truth behind the press reports.

About the Seattle story and its echoes throughout the world,
I felt I had better not do anything for the time being. It was a
hodgepodge of facts, half-truths, nonmalicious fiction, and sheer
nonsense. I did suggest to the reporters, who now swarmed around
me, that they check with the backers of my former and current
expeditions to find out what I had really been reporting to them and
what they thought about my reports and me.

Opportunity for me to get wide circulation for a straightforward review of the case came when I received a telegram from the
New York Sun offering me a fee if I would give them an exclusive
statement of any desired length which they might first syndicate to
all their affiliates and then make available elsewhere. On the *Sun's*
further agreeing to interview the American Museum and as many of
my other backers as they could conveniently and quickly reach, and
then to print their replies, I signed up.

Except for some unintended wrong impressions conveyed by
headline writers, mainly in the subheads, the long telegram I sent
to the *Sun* was printed unaltered on September 15. It occupied more
than a full page, with pictures and a map supplied by the American
Museum. The debate to which the telegram was my first contribution
is still continuing in 1961, unresolved after forty-nine years. The
facts, as stated in this book, speak for themselves and should have
done so in 1912.

While the *Sun* printed my side of the story, it ran at the same
time terse statements cabled in from all over the world branding
what I was supposed to have said as everything from childish and
harmless nonsense to malicious and arrant falsehood. Personal
friends were not always on my side, although those of them who were
not with me usually deprecated the suggestion of intended deception
and simply thought me deluded. Only a few commentators were
impartial. A cartoonist for the Hearst papers appeared to think the
confusion over my story an excuse for ridiculing Theodore Roose-

velt's Bull Moose campaign, then in full swing, by pretending that
Teddy was campaigning not in the humdrum United States but in
the exotic land of the "Blond Eskimos." This, intended to ridicule
both Roosevelt and me, did so without other than political malice
directed at him, and is a good sample of publicity that worked in
favor of the plans for my next expedition by keeping my name
before the public.

The heaviest blow against me was struck by the greatest of
northern historians and most famous of European polar explorers,
Fridtjof Nansen, whose opinion of my alleged report, cabled to
New York, was indicated by his suggestion that the United States
must have produced another Dr. Cook. However, Nansen withdrew
from the side of my critics when it occurred to him that as an Icelander I could hardly be as ignorant of Greenlandic and Scandinavian history as the Seattle dispatches made me out to be.

Another equally famous Norwegian explorer did not withdraw
but instead intensified the personal attacks that had been reported
by the press. This was Roald Amundsen, who was then at the height
of his fame as the first man to navigate the Northwest Passage from
the Atlantic to the Pacific, and who was additionally prominent in
that he favored Cook against Peary in the North Pole dispute and that
he was, or had been, planning an expedition of his own to the North
Pole.

Amundsen and I were both members of the Explorers Club of
New York. He was one of the club's first honorary members and
medalists. I was later recipient of both these honors, though at the
time when the dispute was bitterest I had not achieved such distinction. Since Amundsen attacked me in a book, I am able to quote him
accurately. True, the book—his autobiography—was not published
until 1927, but it contained the substance of the attacks upon me
which he began making in 1912.

The Explorers Club did not want to take sides officially in this
row between two of its own members, but was troubled by the fact
that the attacks on me were not available in English. The reason
for this is interesting. Under United States law and custom, such
remarks as those in question are considered by newspaper publishers
perfectly safe to print. They are not so regarded by book publishers.
Here the case in point is that neither the British nor the United
States publishers of Amundsen's autobiography had considered his
remarks about me safely translatable from Norwegian into English.

Accordingly, what the Explorers Club did toward bringing the dispute into the open was to hire a translator from the *New York Times* and print his rendering verbatim in a symposium, *Explorers Club Tales.*

Introducing the contribution, the Explorers Club says:

> In publishing this article, in the belief that it is the first ade-quate literal translation of a portion of Amundsen's *Mit Lif Som Polarforsker,* in the chapter "Om Stefansson og Andre" ["About Stefansson and Others"], the editors have acted without desire to promote any controversy and only in the interests of polar re-search. . . . The square disagreements and contradictions on facts between men of such standing is a material issue for science, and especially for geography. It is serious for exploration. . . . It is more than possible Amundsen was misled since Stefansson never made many of the statements attributed to him . . . it has seemed to the Publication Committee a fitting thing to do to clear the rec-ord, without rancor or recrimination, solely in the cause of scientific exploration.

In the following extracts from the chapter "On Stefansson and Others," Amundsen is attacking me in general but particularly on two counts. First, my account of and views on the Europeanlike character of the Copper Eskimos, and, second, my opinion that, without undue risk, one may depend upon hunting seals while exploring the drifting arctic sea ice far from land. I deal here only with the first count. Amundsen says:

> I always characterize the first of Vilhjalmur Stefansson's two famous "discoveries" as about the most palpable nonsense that ever came from the North. . . . It is, of course, not beyond the limits of possibility that one or another little Eskimo tribe may have escaped up to now being found by white men; but to say that this is probable is to stretch the limits of possibility further than one can agree to, and really to have any faith in it would be impossible unless the discovery were supported by irrefutable proof. Stefans-son has never produced any such proof.
>
> The probable explanation of "blond Eskimos" is quite obvious. The Arctic regions have for four hundred years been the favorite field of the explorer. Expedition after expedition of white men has gone into these regions, and most of them have wintered there. Besides these discoveries, innumerable fur traders have journeyed to the North, generation after generation. In all these enterprises the British and the Scandinavians have been in the majority. The man who is married to a native woman is a phenomenon constantly met with here. . . .

> Blond Eskimos are almost certainly halfbreed children of half-
> breed Eskimo mothers and light-haired, blue-eyed white fathers
> from the northern lands. . . . Stefansson's tale of a special race
> of blond Eskimos merits no more serious consideration than a sen-
> sational news item in the boulevard press. Stefansson's *Blond
> Eskimos* is merely an amusing figment of the imagination. . . .

I never saw Amundsen after the time in 1906 when I was his
guest at Herschel Island. He seems never to have changed his opinion of me or of my opinions. For some years the reports from the
Canadian north were at least partly on his side. The most pronounced verdict against me, of those I know about, appeared in
Hearst's *New York American* of June 24, 1936, under the headline
NO BLOND ESKIMOS:

> Amundsen's statement that there are no blond Eskimos in the
> Arctic Circle has been verified by officers of the Royal Canadian
> Mounted Police.
> One mounted officer, who made a hazardous journey into the
> Melbourne peninsula to bring out an Eskimo murderer, says he has
> traveled from the Arctic through Hudson Straits and Fury and
> Hecla Straits as far as Coronation Gulf, and knows every tribe of
> Eskimos for hundreds of miles from every direction from the
> straits and islands. Yet he maintains he never saw one of the
> natives with light hair.
> Thus another popular legend of the writers of Northern
> thrillers is punctured by cold facts.

This newspaper confirmation of "Amundsen's statement that
there are no blond Eskimos" may have been the last. If so, it was
the last of many. For such confirmations were a decided journalistic
fashion from the day after Amundsen and Nansen issued their pro-
nouncements in opposition to what the *Seattle Daily Times* said I
had said.

The real beginning of the rehabilitation of my reputation began
with an article entitled "A Tribe of White Eskimos," by David
MacRitchie, in the London scientific journal *Nature* for October 3,
1912. MacRitchie pointed out that De Poincy's *Histoire naturelle &
morale des Iles Antilles de l'Amérique,* published in Rotterdam in
1658, had included a very full description by Nicholas Tunes, captain of a Flushing vessel that had visited Davis Strait, of natives
living on its shores. It said:

As regards the inhabitants, our travelers report having seen two kinds, who live together on the most friendly terms. Of these one kind is described as very tall, well-built, of rather fair complexion, and very swift of foot. The others are very much smaller, of an olive complexion, and tolerably well-proportioned except that their legs are short and thick. The former delight in hunting, for which they are suited by their agility and natural disposition, whereas the latter occupy themselves in fishing.

Others who favored my side of the "Blond Eskimo" dispute were later to point out that three Portuguese navigators, the Corte-real brothers, just after 1500 saw natives in Labrador who looked to them fairer and more Europeanlike than the ordinary inhabitants of the Americas.

Following the appearance of the MacRitchie article, my critics began to cast me in dual and contradictory roles. One contingent had it that, if there really were any blond Eskimos in the Arctic, surely other explorers would have reported them long before me. The other claimed that, although I could have seen blond Eskimos in the Arctic, I could not claim to have discovered them because they had so often been reported. For a long time nobody paid any attention to my denial that I had ever made any discovery claims for myself. I never said anything but that the first I ever heard of blond Eskimos was during the summer of 1906, when Klinkenberg returned from wintering in southwestern Victoria Island. It was he who reported having found a hundred or more Eskimos, some of whom looked like mixed-bloods, who told him that only a few of their oldest people had ever seen white men (obviously Captain R. Collinson and Dr. John Rae) and declared that their own skin color had nothing to do with white men.

When I joined Professor Putnam's staff at Harvard, I knew little about Eskimos beyond what is told in the Icelandic sagas. From the sagas I knew, however, that the Scandinavians used to mix with the Eskimos in Labrador and in Greenland from the eleventh to the fourteenth centuries. This information is repeated by Nansen in his *In Northern Mists,* a book that his countryman Amundsen seemingly never read. It was my ignorance of Sir John Franklin's own work, *Narrative of a Second Expedition to the Shores of the Polar Sea in 1824–27,* and of the Franklin Search in the 1850s that made Klinkenberg's news such a surprise to me.

Other people disturbed by the newspaper squabble centering on Amundsen and me were less ignorant than he and I were. One of these was the prominent student of polar history Major General Adolphus W. Greely.

Shortly after seeing the Underwood story, General Greely undertook a survey of the entire mass of arctic literature in the hope of finding references to previous discoveries of exceptionally lightskinned natives by the early voyagers. His familiarity with the printed sources, and his personal possession of rare manuscript documents, enabled him to bring together many things that had previously escaped notice and now established a fairly complete historical chain of references to "Blond Eskimos" from the time of John Davis, who explored Greenland in 1585, to the present. The first, and perhaps the most interesting, reference is to Nicolas Tunes, which had been located by MacRitchie. Coming to more recent times and to more westerly districts, Greely found (on what he considered a road that any migrating people must have traveled between Greenland and Victoria Island) numerous references by explorers at various times to people whom they did not consider typical Eskimos.

Comparing what Greely had to say with my own knowledge, I concluded, as I wrote at the time, that "there is no reason for insisting now or ever that the 'Blond Eskimos' of Victoria Island are descended from the Scandinavian colonists of Greenland, but looking at it historically or geographically there is no reason why they might not be." We have seen that the Scandinavians flourished for centuries on the west coast of Greenland. We know that at the time when communications between Europe and Greenland were cut off, there were still large numbers of them living in Greenland in proximity to the Eskimos. We know that the habits of the Eskimos are such, as exemplified in their relations with the forest Indians and the white man in recent times, that they are, and probably always have been, inclined to mix with any race with which they come in contact.

Greenland may readily be reached from Victoria Island. If there were any reason for doing so, I could in less than two years go by sled from the southwest corner of Victoria Island, where I saw the most Europeanlike Eskimos, by way of Smith Sound, to the districts of Greenland that the Scandinavians inhabited. The Eskimos who now winter on the ice west of Victoria Island set out in

March every year, and by August are trading with the Eskimos of Hudson Bay, just above Chesterfield Inlet. There is, then, no more reason geographically than there is historically to imagine the existence of any barrier that could have kept the Scandinavians from moving west to Victoria Island had they wanted to.

In 1824, Franklin found among these people the same blond traits that I found in 1910. However, the contact was so slight, from Franklin himself to and including those who participated in the Franklin Search, that no physical change of whole tribes could have been produced. Had Franklin's entire ship's company of 129 men survived in Victoria Island, and had they all married among and lived among the Eskimos, their descendants could not have been numerous enough to produce the condition that Klinkenberg, Mogg, and I found between 1905 and 1911. Moreover, we have records of the actual death of more than half of Franklin's men, and it is fairly certain that they had all perished before the year 1860 at the latest.

It is now over two hundred years since the Eskimos of Alaska began to have contact with the Russians. For over a century they have been in contact with whalers and other male Americans numbering at times as many as a thousand. A good many of these Americans married Eskimo women and settled in the country. Yet, all this mixing of races has produced in northern Alaska no such proportion of individuals with light complexion as observers from Rae, in 1850, to me, in 1910, found in Victoria Island. There were known to be in northern Alaska and the Mackenzie district perhaps a hundred individuals of mixed white and Eskimo descent around 1900. If this hundred had been gathered together in one place, it would have appeared that many of them could not have been distinguished from full-blooded Eskimos. The group as a whole would by no means have presented as north European an appearance as the southwest Victoria Eskimos did to those of us who saw them between 1905 and 1911.

It is to be noted also that if a recent admixture of European blood had been the cause of the light complexions that we reported from the Victoria Island Eskimos, one would have expected to find more blondness the farther east one went, because the European contact would have had to come from the direction of Hudson Bay. The fact is that the most numerous light types were reported farthest west. To the eastward, they gradually faded.

I have not myself ever seen the Eskimos of Hudson Bay, who

have for more than a century been in contact with Scottish and American whalers. Captain George Comer, of East Haddam, Connecticut, however, who had dealings with them continuously for more than a quarter of a century, wrote me, when the "Blond Eskimo" storm blew up, saying that such Europeanlike appearance as I described, and as my photographs showed, was quite beyond anything he ever saw, even among those groups whom he knew to have most heavily intermarried with the whalers.

In 1912, when I wrote out the substance of this as part of my comments on the dispute with Amundsen, I was not familiar with much beyond what General Greely had either cited or suggested. Later that year, as told hereinafter in connection with my first appearance before the Royal Geographical Society of London, I learned that my view of the Eskimos and their country had been anticipated more than half a century before by Dr. John Rae. This induced me to look up writings that were scattered through British journals during the decades after the Franklin Search. When I got deeply into Rae's work I found that he both noticed and theorized about the blond Eskimos!

I learned about Dr. Rae and his observations on the Victoria Island Eskimos too late to use him in my part of the "Blond Eskimo" dispute. Yet, it is not too late for this retrospective mention of it. My excuses for being so late are in a way a justification. Rae's work was almost ignored in his time. It was partly my rediscovery of him that made the Hudson's Bay Company, his former employers, begin to take pride in him.

Preceded only by Franklin in 1824 and by Thomas Simpson in 1837, Rae saw during the Franklin Search the ancestors of the Eskimos seen by Klinkenberg, Mogg, and me. Rae had become the Hudson's Bay Company's chief physician in 1833 and had seen nearly all the Eskimos of the western shore of Hudson Bay as far north as what is now the Rae Isthmus. He also knew the people of Victoria Island's south coast as far as its southwest corner, and it was his belief that the Eskimos of the Coppermine River mouth and those of the southwest corner of Victoria Island differed most from what he considered typical Eskimo appearance.

In the heat of the row that was precipitated by Underwood's alleged quotations from me, some of Klinkenberg's and Mogg's friends pointed out that I was said to have discovered the blond Eskimos. This information induced them to charge me not merely with robbing them of credit but also with being inaccurate in what I said about the Copper Eskimos, particularly as to their comparatively light complexions. Naturally, people told me about their comments and showed me newspaper cuttings quoting them. I was busy organizing a new expedition, however, and sailed before I had a chance to arrange for the three of us to get together, with witnesses. I felt sure that at such a meeting we would find little on which to disagree, since, as I have already made clear, I never claimed to have "discovered" the blond Eskimos. Later on, we did meet and agreed on a signed statement.

As I review the debacle that followed the Underwood news story, I must try to explain its crushing effect on me. I think Underwood really meant it a few years afterward when he said that I ought to be grateful to him because it had been his interview that made me famous. The "interview" and the start of the dispute took place forty-nine years ago, and thirty-three years have passed since Amundsen died. There surely has been time for clarifying thought, but I still feel bewildered. I had been a great admirer of Amundsen and had shared with him the heartbreak he also must have felt over what we both knew was happening to the people of the Stone Age. And here we were squabbling over theories we held about them!

In my mind I saw him as a failure and myself as no better. We had nailed to the mast of a sinking ship a banner upon which was inscribed his Eskimo slogan: "My sincerest wish is that civilization may *never* reach them." He, no less than I, must have known we were failing to save them from being crushed by civilization's juggernaut, that we were vainly trying to protect them from a civilization against which they did not want to be protected.

I felt so badly about this that, through the new expedition I was planning, I hoped to create such a world-wide understanding of how admirable Stone Age man used to be that everyone would agree to preserve and keep unspoiled forever the Eskimos and their country. As a sort of beginning, I intended to eliminate the unexplored region north of Alaska. I planned to do this on a large and convincing scale by returning to the Arctic and adopting the Eskimo way of being healthy, long-lived, and comfortable in the center of an icy world into which even Eskimos had not penetrated.

I reminded myself that converting my notoriety into fame was my immediate job and that I must go to work. I set about counting my blessings. My frequent reports back from the field had saved me from the accusation that I had made up on the spur of the moment things that I had long been observing. The civilization to which I belonged was interested in discovering new lands. I told myself that I knew how to discover those lands, if they existed. I thought it would be just to say to the civilized: My accomplishments are Stone Age accomplishments. It is only by studying the ways of our undervalued primitive northern neighbors that I have been enabled to accomplish what I have in the Arctic.

16 *The Birth of a New Expedition*

The murky cloud with which reporter Underwood had surrounded me was not what I would have chosen to carry with me to New York. I had no more than eight months in which to complete the planning of my new expedition; find backers for it; recruit a staff of scientists and specialists; purchase ships, supplies, and equipment; and get off in time to beat the ice to the north coast of Alaska. There was, too, the matter of doing a book about my four-year sojourn in the Arctic.

I went immediately to the American Museum of Natural History, where I found that the cloud of controversy was not taken very seriously. Furthermore, most of the anthropological staff, as well as President Osborn, Curator Clark Wissler, and the new museum director, Frederick A. Lucas, also sided with me against Boas in my contention that Eskimos made and used pottery.

President Osborn was very much in favor of the concept of my new expedition, believed in my methods, and was quite willing to present my plans to the museum's board of directors. There was one thing, however, that he wanted me to do before asking the board to back me. This was to convince Peary, whose endorsement would be essential, that I had lived by hunting on the polar ice and could do so again. This amounted to convincing Peary that he would not have needed the twenty sledges and more than a hundred dogs that had made his North Pole trip possible had he known that there were seals and polar bears to be had for the shooting. Though Osborn was afraid that Peary would balk at admitting this, I went to call on him at his home on Eagle Island, Maine, and found it easy to convince him that there might have been seals near the North Pole which he simply had not seen. He even remembered that he had sometimes noticed his dogs sniffing at the ice. Neither he nor his Eskimos had connected this dog behavior with seals because they "knew" there could be no seals that far north. When I left Peary, he agreed to say to those with whom I was negotiating for support that there might well be seals under the ice at the Pole or anywhere else and that, if there were, there was nothing to prevent my using them as food.

So far, so good. The American Museum was definitely behind me. There was, however, another obstacle. There was another expedition in the making, and Osborn wanted to give it priority over mine. This was to be an expedition headed by two of Peary's former aides, Donald B. Macmillan and George Borup, for the purpose of investigating an unknown—and as it turned out nonexistent—land called Crocker Land, which Peary thought he had seen in 1906. Osborn wanted to send the Crocker Land Expedition off and have me wait a year or two.

I did not care to wait. I therefore went to see Gilbert Grosvenor, of the National Geographic Society, who introduced me to his father-in-law, the great Alexander Graham Bell. Bell made the interesting point that the airplane was coming into its own and would undoubtedly be widely used in the Arctic. If I wanted to show what a man could do on foot using Eskimo methods, I would be well advised to start doing it before my backers decided that arctic exploration could better be done by plane. The Geographic Society authorized me to go back to Osborn and tell him that they would put up $25,000 immediately and advised him to do the same. Osborn agreed. Actually, the Geographic and the museum were, in the end, only required to pledge $22,500 apiece, as the Harvard Travelers Club came through with an offer of $5,000.

All of this was highly satisfactory to me, but I soon realized that I was going to need additional funds very soon in order to pay for a ship. Anderson and I had decided that the whaler *Karluk,* which we knew well, would be an ideal vessel, and we knew that she was for sale at a relatively low price because of the decline in the whaling industry.

After trying several sources, among them my old friend Reginald Brock, whose Canadian Geological Survey had cooperated with my last expedition, I finally, through Professor James Mavor, got to the right place. Mavor and Charles T. Currelly of the Royal Ontario Museum called in Sir Edmund Walker, who had given me backing in 1906, and Sir Edmund Osler, president of the Dominion Bank of Canada. They suggested that I see the Prime Minister, Sir Robert Borden, and point out to him that as an American, which I had been since I was two years old, leading an American expedition, I would give the United States a claim to whatever lands I might discover. I was to imply that Sir Robert would not, of course, care for that. If he did not, could the difficulty not be avoided by allowing Canada to become an equal partner in the expedition?

Sir Robert referred the matter to the Canadian Cabinet that very afternoon. The Cabinet decided that it would be beneath Canada's dignity to go into partnership with others in such an expedition. Instead, they proposed that the Canadian government take over the entire project as planned, putting it under the control of the Department of Naval Service and outfitting and supporting it completely. Thus the Canadian Arctic Expedition came into being.

I reported to my United States sponsors as quickly as I could, and secured their consent to the change. Gilbert Grosvenor, who wrote the memorandum of agreement, said, to my great satisfaction, that if Canada could not or would not get my expedition under way by May or June of 1913, he still stood ready to do so.

The Canadian government acted quickly and efficiently. February, however, was more than half gone. I had articles to do for *Harper's Magazine,* I had a book—which turned out to be *My Life with the Eskimo*—to write and, most difficult of all, I had to comb Canada, the United States, and Europe for the best men to make up the large scientific staff that I planned to take along.

Sir Robert Borden suggested that I go at once to England to enlist the aid of Lord Strathcona, Canada's High Commissioner. Strathcona—the Donald Smith of Mount Sir Donald and Smith's Landing and countless towns and natural features throughout Canada—was over ninety but still active, and one of the richest men in the British Empire. I agreed to go, and thereafter accepted invitations to speak before the Royal Geographical Society in London, and at the International Geographical Congress in Rome. I sailed in early March, dictating on shipboard to my secretary, Gertrude Allen, the early chapter of my book. Because of fog and head winds, I almost missed my March 10 date with the Royal Geographical Society. I made it, however, though according to Ernest Shackleton, the antarctic explorer, whom I met at the meeting for the first time, I got off to a bad start with the society on two counts. In the first place, I made the audience laugh. Royal Geographical audiences were not supposed to laugh. In the second place, I praised the wrong explorer. Dr. John Rae had been dead nineteen years but was, it seems, *persona non grata* with the admirals who were still the backbone of the dressy and austerely social craft of polar explorers. It was the feeling of the top brass in the British Navy that Dr. Rae, in spite of his success in using the methods in arctic exploration for which I praised him and which I have tried to use, had lowered himself by being willing to go native in order to survive and succeed.

Looking back, I think that I probably did overemphasize my praise of Rae, perhaps because I had, to my shame, claimed for myself discovery rights in the comfort of Eskimo snowhouses, only to learn that in this, as in a number of other priority claims, I was sixty years behind Rae. He had found in 1848, wintering at Repulse Bay, that he was as comfortable in an Eskimo-style snowhouse as he had ever been in a British inn.

My talk before the Royal Geographical Society was, however, incidental. The main purpose of my visit was to enlist Strathcona's support. My first contacts with him were merely casual occasions for him to use his position as Canada's High Commissioner to expedite the work of the Canadian Arctic Expedition. It was not long, however, before there grew up between us the bond of a common interest —an interest in dietary matters. I told him what I had learned from the Eskimos, and he told me that years ago in Canada he had begun a regimen all his own by skipping lunch and ultimately breakfast too. Then he had begun to wonder why, since he liked some things better than others, he should bother to eat something different on Tuesday when he had liked what he had eaten on Monday better. This led to his questioning what he really did like and, when he got the answer, eating nothing else—eggs, milk, and butter. Although this combination would not have made up my favorite meal, much as I favor butter, the point was that Strathcona and I were in agreement on the feeling that the longer a man ate one complete food exclusively, the more likely he was to relish it.

I had many opportunities to observe the High Commissioner while I was in London, for he frequently invited me to dinner at his home in Grosvenor Square, saying that So-and-So would be present and he thought I would like to meet him. Strathcona, a broad-shouldered man taller than six feet, would be seated at one end of the long table, Lady Strathcona at the other. As course after course was served to the rest of us, he would converse, drinking a sip or two of each wine as it was poured. Sometime during the middle of the dinner, his tray was brought: several medium-soft boiled eggs broken into a large bowl, with plenty of butter and with extra butter in a side dish, and, I believe, a quart of whole milk, or perhaps half-and-half. My impression is that they also brought him toast, but that he barely nibbled it, using it a bit as if it were a napkin.

Strathcona, either personally or acting for Canada, financed my trip to the International Geographical Congress at Rome, which as a newsworthy event was being somewhat overshadowed by the fact that J. Pierpont Morgan, the elder, lay gravely ill in his suite at the Grand Hotel. The financier had been taken ill in Egypt, and his doctors had brought him on to Rome. My room, as it happened, was on the floor just above the two occupied by Morgan and his entourage.

Morgan died on March 31. I remember the day well. Walking down the broad flight of stairs past the Morgan floors, I saw a man in a tall silk hat and striped trousers going toward Morgan's door. Later, I realized that he was the United States ambassador. As I usually did, I asked the desk clerk how Mr. Morgan was. The desk had received no bulletin, and I hoped this was a good sign. When I returned from the congress session in the late afternoon, the doorman informed me that Morgan was dead. Later on, I heard that a hushed crowd was said to have waited outside the hotel for word of the millionaire's passing. I saw no such crowd either when I left the hotel or when I returned to it.

At the congress I again met Peary and his family. This meeting brought about a change in the personnel of my expedition that had a profound effect upon its fortunes. When Anderson and I had planned to purchase the whaler *Karluk*, we had expected to get with her the services of her able master, Captain Theodore Pedersen, who was one of the best ice skippers among all those who visited the Beaufort Sea coast of North America. While in Europe, I learned that Captain Pedersen had left the *Karluk* and was already at sea on another ship. He had given up the idea of sailing for me chiefly because he believed that if he held the position of master of a Canadian ship he would lose his United States citizenship. It did not occur to me at the time that I was about to lose my United States citizenship by taking command of an expedition under the Naval Service of Canada.

In Rome, I consulted Peary about the problem of a new master for the *Karluk*. In spite of the admiral's belief that it was unwise to take on an arctic expedition a man who had served under and had great admiration for another commander, he recommended that we offer Captain Robert A. Bartlett the *Karluk* job. Bartlett had commanded Peary's *Roosevelt* on the admiral's first two trips and was recognized as the most experienced and resourceful of eastern ice pilots. Though I could have wished that Bartlett had had some experience with western ice, which is quite different from that of the eastern Arctic, Peary's strong recommendation was enough for me. The Canadian government, at my cabled suggestion, offered Bartlett the job and he accepted.

When I returned to London, I found real trouble awaiting me in the form of a message from G. J. Desbarats, deputy director of the Canadian Department of Naval Service. Desbarats recommended that I get rid of my second-in-command, Dr. Rudolph Anderson, the man with whom I had amicably shared four successful years in the Arctic.

Anderson had married after his return from the north in the fall of 1912 and shortly thereafter had learned that, for reasons that seemed justifiable to the American Museum of Natural History, he was not going to get the permanent post in zoology that the museum had promised him before we went north in 1908. He had, however, been assured of work with the Canadian Geological Survey, and I had supposed that he was happy in his post under me. Now Desbarats said that Anderson was being uncooperative and arbitrary and making it difficult for the Naval Service to carry out the preparations ordered by the Canadian Cabinet. Anderson had, it seems, given orders that the expedition's purchase of pemmican be held up, pending the completion of scientific tests to determine the value of pemmican as a food for men and dogs on an expedition such as ours was to be.

This was so appalling to me that I boiled over in the presence of Lord Strathcona, who as former active head of the Hudson's Bay Company had signed orders for hundreds of tons of pemmican, the standard ration in the fur trade for more than a hundred years. Strathcona agreed that, while it was never too late to question the quality of any particular lot of pemmican, it was at least a century too late to question pemmican as a travel ration.

I did not hesitate, though I could not understand Anderson's position. I sent a cable, without waiting to put it in code: DAMN THE TESTS. ORDER PEMMICAN IMMEDIATELY. Much to my surprise, a messenger soon arrived from the cable office to say with some embarrassment that they could not accept the cable. I supposed that the stumbling block was the word "damn," but it was not. It appeared that they had never heard the word "pemmican" and so assumed that it was a dodge by which I was attempting to get through a code message at regular word rates.

After the cable had gone, I began to worry about the delivery of several thousand pounds of pemmican I had ordered from Bovril in England. Checking, I found that it was likely to reach Halifax so late that by the time it was shipped across the continent to the Navy Yard at Esquimalt, British Columbia, the *Karluk's* sailing date would be long past. I consulted the nonagenarian Strathcona, thinking that he might use his influence to speed things up. He did indeed. He went personally to the office of the London head of the Canadian Pacific Railway and arranged to have the entire shipment carried by railway express from Halifax to Esquimalt. For this extraordinary service the expedition was charged ordinary freight rates only. Strathcona was a pleased with himself as a boy who has just shot his first rabbit.

Before leaving for home, I had just enough time for a visit arranged by James Murray, the oceanographer who had been with Shackleton in the Antarctic and whom I had engaged for our expedition. He had had several conferences with the great oceanographer Sir John Murray (not related to him), whose work with the famous *Challenger* Expedition will never be forgotten. Sir John had asked James Murray to bring me to his house.

The old gentleman talked well, and with an obvious authoritarian dignity befitting the recognized dean of oceanographers. In the course of our conversation he told us about an occasion during the *Challenger* voyages when, at a point north of Russia, the ship's water-distilling apparatus broke down. Sir John said that he had known from the appearance of the sky—a condition known as "ice blink"—that there was ice beneath it. Realizing that they were north of the mouth of some great river whose ice had drifted seaward, he directed the ship's master to steer for the ice. Sure enough, said Sir John, it had proved to be river ice.

At this point I made the mistake of asking Sir John how he had known it was river ice. There was a sudden hush and the great oceanographer looked at me as if he was not sure that he had heard me correctly. Then he spoke slowly and distinctly, explaining that he had known it was river ice because the water on top of it was free from salt, and they had been able to fill the ship's tanks with it.

I should have kept quiet and let that pass, but I did not. I took the floor and told how I had learned from the Eskimos that all ice in the late summer is free of salt when melted—or at least no worse than brackish. James Murray looked at me as if I had just broken a piece of our host's best china. Sir John studied me for a moment, then turned away and changed the subject. It was plain that he did not relish having his scientific knowledge corrected by quotation from the lore of ignorant savages. On the way back to my lodgings I tried to explain to James Murray that I had on many occasions tested the truth of the Eskimos' statement and had satisfied myself that the water on top of all old sea ice is always fresh, the only condition being that it must be far enough from the edge of the floe to be unaffected by salt spray.

This brush with scientific conservatism added to the uneasiness I felt over the reports from Canada about Anderson. I was not entirely comfortable when I went to the offices of the Canadian High Commissioner to say good-by. Strathcona was outwardly as unemotional as I was, but I was not entirely calm within. The old man handed me his personal check for a thousand pounds, saying that it would be a good thing for me to have a little money for which I did not have to account to anyone. I protested, not too firmly, that the Naval Service had been very generous and would undoubtedly be considerate at all times. Strathcona said that I could not know much about auditors. They never felt, he said, that they were earning their salaries unless they were able to find some item to disallow. I laughed and said that I would report to him about that when I got back. He smiled and said, "I shall not be here."

He was not. He died the following January, when the expedition that he had substantially aided was just getting into the field and beginning to have troubles far greater than any I had imagined.

17 A House Divided

During the late spring and early summer of 1913, I continued to do as much writing as I could, both on *My Life with the Eskimo* and on my scientific report for the museum of the 1908–1912 expedition. Even after my return from Europe, I kept out of the Anderson controversy. I believed that there would be no difficulty when the new expedition was under way, with Anderson in command of a ship of his own.

The plan for the expedition called for two divisions. One was to be the northern party, of which I was to be the leader and which was to explore the ice north of Alaska, taking soundings, looking for signs of animal life, and searching for new land. The southern section, under Anderson, was to do anthropological, archaeological, geological, and zoological research in the vicinity of Coronation Gulf.

The Department of Naval Service had been concentrating supplies and equipment, including what I had shipped from Europe, at the Esquimalt Navy Yard, where the *Karluk* was being reconditioned. George Phillips, who had been put in charge of the logistics of the expedition by the Chief of Naval Stores, John Armistead Wilson, was most efficient. He had arranged for the purchase of several smaller vessels to support the *Karluk* and carry the supplies and personnel of the southern section to their proposed base in Coronation Gulf.

Phillips was very much disturbed about Anderson and kept urging me to get rid of him. He was even firmer on this point after the *Karluk* reached Nome, where I had preceded her to spend my

153

last days ashore working with my secretary and Bella Weitzner, of the American Museum, who had been helping to put my report into shape.

The cause of Phillips' final annoyance was a near-mutiny in which Anderson had a part. The trouble, which took me entirely by surprise, began with a message from the scientific staff asking me to meet with them. Captain Bartlett was not present at the meeting, nor was any member of his crew. It appeared that the staff was worried by what they considered the small size of the *Karluk's* fresh-water tanks. They were so concerned that they refused, to a man, to go north on the *Karluk* or any other ship unless she was equipped with larger tanks or carried a distilling apparatus. They might, they pointed out, be caught in the ice for an indefinite period and the ice would be salt-water ice. Where would they get fresh water?

I repeated to them what I had so brashly told Sir John Murray, keeping an eye on James Murray as I did so. The oceanographer spoke up. He had felt it his duty, he said, when the staff raised the question of fresh water, to tell them that Sir John Murray, Britain's foremost authority on the sea, had had nothing but scorn for my contention that one could get fresh water from sea ice. This was enough for the staff.

Since Anderson was present, I turned to him for support. To my astonishment, he said that all he knew about the matter was what he had heard from me, that as far as he could recall we had always used river water or snow. I had hired an expert oceanographer, he said, who had been with Shackleton on a polar voyage and who ought to know what he was talking about. Anderson was not going to argue the matter.

Exasperated and more than a little worried, I sent for Captain Bartlett, who supported me completely, saying that sealers in the eastern Arctic always got their fresh water from year-old or older sea ice and that we would do the same. The *Karluk's* tanks, Bartlett maintained, were large enough.

The scientists were somewhat mollified. Bartlett promised them that when we reached the ice he would pump our tanks full of "the sweetest damn water any scientist ever tasted." Unfortunately, the first opportunity to do this arose after a severe blow beyond Point Hope, three hundred-odd miles north of Nome. The first mate, whom Bartlett ordered to get a hose overboard and fill the tanks, put the

end of the hose in a pool at the very edge of the floe which the recent
high waves had filled with salt spray. The tanks had to be emptied
after Bartlett himself complained of the coffee made from water
taken from them. They were immediately refilled with convincingly
fresh water taken from a pool farther from the edge of the floe.

My misgivings about the scientific staff and particularly about
Anderson began to subside. When we left Nome at the end of July,
the expedition's fleet consisted of the *Karluk,* the thirty-ton power
schooner *Alaska* under Anderson's command, and the schooner
Mary Sachs, thirty tons and also gasoline powered, under Captain
Peter Bernard. Not far from Nome, the *Alaska* had engine trouble
and had to put into Teller for repairs. The *Sachs* became separated
from the *Karluk* in a gale shortly thereafter, and the *Karluk* never
saw either the *Alaska* or the *Mary Sachs* again.

Bartlett worked the *Karluk* slowly northward through heavy
ice. When she was about twenty-five miles southwest of Point Barrow, it occurred to me that I was wasting time sitting on board fret-
ting because my expedition was so well organized and equipped that
there was not enough for me to do. Taking with me our surgeon, Dr.
Alister Forbes McKay, who, like James Murray, had been with
Shackleton in the Antarctic, I went ashore over the ice and walked
all night—in bright daylight—to Point Barrow to arrange for the
purchase of some dogs and the hiring of additional personnel.

When the *Karluk* finally made the Point, McKay and I rejoined her. At first our prospects looked fairly good. We found an
east-moving current offshore and in spite of still heavy ice were able
to push eastward some two hundred and twenty-five miles to Camden
Bay. Here, a wind out of the east blew against us, moving the ice
and the helpless *Karluk* back toward Point Barrow.

I realized that if present conditions continued, the *Karluk*
would not make Herschel Island during the coming winter. We were
fast in the ice, and we had on board many of the southern section's
staff, who should be with Anderson farther east. I did not know at
the time just how far east the *Alaska* and the *Mary Sachs* had been
able to get, but I did know that they had passed Barrow. Since they
were following the north Alaskan custom of keeping between the
ice and the shore, I was sure they would be able to make good
progress.

I decided to send our two anthropologists ashore with instructions to work their way along the coast until they found Anderson

and his men. This turned out to be impossible because of ice conditions, and I had to recall them.

The *Karluk* was now definitely frozen in, and it was apparent that she would not break loose before spring. By mid-September it was obvious that we were going to need more food. The ice between us and the shore was safe enough by this time for a hunting party consisting of myself; Diamond Jenness, our anthropologist; Burt McConnell, my secretary and the expedition's meteorologist; George Hubert Wilkins, our photographer; and two Eskimos, Asatsiak and Pauyurak. The first night we camped on the ice, a new experience for the scientists and one that they accepted with some awe. The next day we reached shore on one of the Jones Islands, not far from Beechey Point and about a hundred and seventy-five miles east of Barrow. Here, before beginning our hunting, we sat out one of the worst storms I have ever experienced.

We had at first been able to see the *Karluk's* masts. The next time it was clear enough to look out to sea, she had vanished. Supposing that she would be stopped by thickening ice somewhere near Cape Halkett, we hurried westward, receiving only vague news of the ship from a few Eskimo hunting parties. When we reached Barrow, we learned that the *Karluk* had been seen about ten miles offshore from the Point but had soon disappeared. Although none of us really believed that she was in danger, I now gave up the notion I had had while on board her that our expedition was so thoroughly and efficiently organized that there was nothing for its commander to do.

In danger or not, the *Karluk* was gone, and with her some of the expedition's best men and all of the northern party's equipment. Those of us who were ashore were inadequately dressed and outfitted. We had not wanted to risk bringing our best sledges on this hunting trip, and now we needed them badly. We picked up what we could at Charlie Brower's trading station, and from there I sent to Ottawa a report of our situation and a statement of what I planned to do. I said that although the *Karluk* was no longer of any use to us and might be in danger of being crushed by the ice, I felt that the people on board her, being equipped with light skin boats, which were ideal for travel over sea ice, could easily make their way ashore. As for me, I intended to go on to the Mackenzie delta, get the work of Anderson's section going, and prepare for an exploration trip of my own northward over the ice of Beaufort Sea.

I hired an interpreter for Jenness and left him at Cape Halkett to study the Eskimos. The rest of us headed east for Collinson Point, where, I had learned, Anderson's two ships were safely wintering.

I should say here that the main purpose of the present expedition, a purpose that was recognized by my backers in Canada, had always been to explore the unknown Beaufort Sea north of Alaska, and in so doing to put to a real test my theory that an exploration party could support itself by hunting at sea as well as on land. I was interested more in proving that such a thing was feasible than in any new lands that the application of my theory might make it possible to discover. If the theory was sound, anyone applying it to travel could find whatever lands remained to be found in the unknown sea.

When we reached Collinson Point we found that the southern party had no intention of attempting any serious work during the winter. They had made a picnic-like attempt at hunting, with no success, and had notified Ottawa that there was no game in the area and that they could do nothing until summer.

Anderson was not at Collinson Point when I got there, having gone to Herschel Island with mail and dispatches for Ottawa. His second-in-command, Kenneth Chipman, was in charge. After persuading Chipman that there were many things that could be done in winter, I left him planning to do them and hurried east in the hope of overtaking Anderson before he got his mail to Herschel Island and of persuading him that the program I had sent to Ottawa from Barrow should be carried out.

When I met Anderson about twenty miles east of Collinson Point, it was too late. He had already mailed his report. I told him of my plans, which called for his cooperation in helping to outfit my party for the projected Beaufort Sea journey. He was unwilling to discuss the work of either his own section or mine. Since my supporting ship the *Karluk* had been lost, he felt that I was now a leader without anything to lead and that I had no right to take supplies or equipment from him or to spend any money to buy what I needed elsewhere. Nor did he believe that I had any right to tell him what to do.

He offered his resignation as second-in-command, but I refused to accept it and told him to go back to Collinson Point and take charge. In no very happy frame of mind, I left him and continued

east to negotiate for the dogs, vessels, supplies, and men that I knew
would be needed.

On the way I met Storker Storkerson, who had been with
Leffingwell and Mikkelsen during my first arctic venture. Knowing
he would be a perfect man for my sea-ice trip, I persuaded him to
join me and sent him west to Collinson Point with instructions for
making a winter survey in the Mackenzie delta, and for setting up
a base at Martin Point, from which I would take off for the Beaufort
Sea trip.

I went on to complete my organization work in the Mackenzie
region, and sent a further dispatch to Ottawa bringing them up to
date on what I was doing to carry out the plans I had outlined
to them from Point Barrow. This done, I set out westward from
Herschel Island feeling confident that, in spite of the Collinson
Point troubles, everything was now fairly well in hand. My first
disillusionment came about fifteen miles out of Herschel Island when
I saw coming toward me several sledges accompanied by a number
of our men who, according to my instructions, should have been
busy at Martin Point getting things ready for the ice trip. In
charge of the party was John J. O'Neill, our geologist, who handed
me a letter from Anderson.

As I read the letter, I realized, with an unpleasant feeling, that
instead of being well in hand the situation could hardly have been
much worse. Anderson acknowledged the receipt of my instructions,
but said that he had decided not to obey them.

He and the staff, he said, were of the opinion that my proposed
journey north over the ice was simply a stunt to get me newspaper
notoriety. It was his opinion that I had no intention of doing any
serious scientific work. If I did intend to do any such work, the
plans I was contemplating would make it impossible. Anderson and
his staff considered themselves justified, therefore, not only in with-
holding assistance for my ice trip but also in preventing me from
using any supplies that were at Collinson Point on either the *Alaska*
or the *Mary Sachs*.

The letter then referred to certain supplies of the expedition
that were being carried by the *Belvedere,* and said that the writer
and the scientific staff would protest against Captain Cottle's turning any of these over to me. They would take the position that if I
used any of them it would be "a criminal misappropriation of Government property."

The wording of this letter, while it plainly showed that it had been written in the heat of passion, left no doubt of the sincerity of its writer and his staff. In their own opinion, they were acting in the public interest by trying to forestall misuse of public property. In the interests of science, they were preventing a foray into a frozen ocean that could yield no knowledge, predestined as it was to failure because of inadequate planning. In the interests of humanity, they were discouraging a venture that, if carried as far as I said I intended to carry it, would lead to several deaths by freezing or starvation.

After I had studied the letter, a conversation with O'Neill enlightened me somewhat. Apparently, members of the expedition had been discussing my plan both with the local Eskimos and with the whalers. The Eskimos considered the project suicidal, saying that seals and polar bears would not be found at any great distance from land, and that we would inevitably starve if we did not lose our lives through some accident of travel over the broken and continually shifting ice. The whalers were of the same opinion. The members of the expedition accordingly did not doubt the foolhardiness of my project, and they believed themselves justified in taking steps to prevent me from carrying it out. They were quite sincere in their opinion that the government at Ottawa and public opinion in general would sustain them in the position they were taking.

A little quiet discussion with O'Neil shook him somewhat. Before we arrived at the police barracks at Herschel, he told me that his mind had been sufficiently changed so that, although he could not very well go back on his agreement to stand by the rest of the Collinson Point people in their opposition, he would at least go so far as to give me his pocket chronometer.

It came out, at this point, that one of the conclusions reached by the staff at Collinson Point had been that I would probably be unable to obtain a pocket chronometer. Though the expedition was under the Department of Naval Service, the chronometers had been given the men by the Department of Mines. It might be claimed, therefore, that they were not part of the equipment of the expedition proper and not subject to my requisition. If they were to refuse to turn one over to me, I would thereby be prevented from going out on the ice. Certainly to go without a chronometer not only would put our lives in extreme danger but would prevent us from being able to describe accurately at the end of the journey where we had been. This would, of course, mean that any soundings my party might take would have no scientific value.

O'Neill's decision to give me that chronometer turned the tide. We were to rely upon it for the next several years. Without it, our successful ice journeys could not have been made. I have always felt that O'Neill's turning it over to me without either request or demand was a fine thing, in view of the fact that he seemed to be sincerely convinced that our undertaking was stupid and doomed. He alone of all the southern party had the sportsmanship to feel that he did not want the mere lack of a reliable timepiece to keep me from having a chance to try out my theories.

O'Neill went on to carry out a survey of the Firth River, which runs into the sea at Herschel Island. This was one project on which Anderson and I had had no disagreement. I hurried west to Martin Point to join Storkerson, not daring to think what I might find when I got there. What I did find was that Anderson had refused to let Storkerson have any dogs or supplies and had also done his best to prevent the local Eskimos from offering to help him.

There were several ships in addition to the *Belvedere* wintering between Collinson Point and Herschel Island. The *Polar Bear* was one, carrying a party of Boston sportsmen who had been kept by the ice from getting out in time to go home. Captain Cottle of the *Belvedere* had given me a chance to buy from him supplies over and above the expedition's freight that he carried. He was doing the best he could without dogs to get them to Martin Point. The Boston hunters were appalled by Anderson's behavior, and offered what help they could give.

I had purchased the *North Star* from Captain Martin Andreasen for use as a support vessel in connection with my ice trip. She was a splendid iceboat, light and maneuverable. Anderson's men had tried to talk Andreasen out of selling me his supplies and his vessel, contending that the draft I had given him in payment for it would not be honored at Ottawa.

It was plain to me that, if I expected to get off before it was too late for favorable ice conditions, I would have to go to Collinson Point and have it out with Anderson and his staff. I knew from Captain Bernard, who had been with me on the trip from Herschel Island and accompanied me to Collinson Point, that I could count on the support of a few of the staff, notably McConnell and Wilkins. I hoped that I would prove to have still more friends in the group.

We arrived at Collinson Point at dinnertime. I told the men there that we would postpone all discussion until eight o'clock, when the evening work was done and everybody could be present. When that time came, I asked Anderson if he was taking the position I had learned about at Herschel Island: that there were two expeditions, he in command of one still in existence and I in command of the other, now defunct. I asked him also if he was taking the position that O'Neill and several of the other men assigned to the expedition by the Department of Mines were merely passengers and had authority from Ottawa to disobey orders whenever they liked.

The oceanographer Johansen answered for him. They considered, he said, that Anderson was in command of that part of the expedition which remained, that I had authority only over the *Karluk,* and none over the expedition at present. They felt that I had better go to Ottawa to report the failure of my part of the enterprise. Without replying to him, I insisted upon a reply from Anderson.

Anderson finally answered that my position was analogous to that of certain kings of England who had been undisputedly kings as long as their conduct was worthy of a ruler and as long as the people had confidence in them. When these sovereigns became either insane or criminal, he said, they had been deposed and in some cases executed. Although he generously disclaimed any intention of lopping off my head, he thought that I had already shown by what I had done and by the plans I had announced, especially the much-talked-of "ice trip," that I either was not quite sane or was outlining plans that I had no intention or prospect of carrying to any useful conclusion—plans that would, he said, use up a large part of the resources of the expedition. He considered himself responsible to the government for the carrying out of certain plans of theirs and his, and he felt that he would be unable to carry them out if he acquiesced to mine.

When Anderson had made his statement, I asked him if he intended to withhold by force supplies that my companions and I needed for the proposed trip. He replied that there would be no companions, for no one would go with me. Hereupon I made a sort of roll call of the men to find out from each if he would obey my orders and go with me out on the ice if necessary. I began with Captain Bernard, for I knew he would agree to go. Obviously, his prompt agreement surprised the others. I fear that some of the men had in a measure deceived Anderson, misleading him into thinking he would have the wholehearted support of the entire staff. Answering when their names were called, more than half were firmly on my side and a number of the rest wavering.

Anderson, somewhat shaken, now said that they would all cease opposing my project if I would sign a statement making certain promises. Asked what these would be, he said I must promise to let all the scientific men go on doing scientific work and not to hinder the various members of the party in carrying out geological, topographical, zoological, or other research. In general, the demands were merely that the plans that I had always wanted to carry out should be carried out. The evident purpose of the demands was to make it appear that I had been compelled to allow them to do these things, whereas it had in fact been my desire all the time that they should do them. I was more than willing to sign the proposed document. Luckily, I had sent out word from Point Barrow in October, or announced before the expedition ever started, that we intended to do all the things that the Anderson faction now asked me to promise I would not prevent them from doing.

It was a rather tense two hours, but before eleven o'clock a *modus vivendi* had been agreed on. By eight o'clock the next morning everyone was at work doing the things he should have begun doing after receiving my instructions from Storkerson a month earlier.

18 North into the Unknown

I felt somewhat easier after the momentous confer-
ence at Collinson Point, which certainly ended the delay in outfitting for the ice trip and seemed to promise a successful campaign of
scientific work while I was gone. Yet, the settlement of the difficulties with Anderson did not end our troubles. We met at Martin
Point another kind of opposition in the form of one of the north
coast's worst gales. After several days' delay caused by the storm,
Sunday, March 22, 1914, found us ready and able to go. The Boston hunters from the *Polar Bear* and many men from the *Belvedere*
were there to see us off.

To those who knew only that we planned to go north over the
ice to a point farther than any ship had ever penetrated and live
by hunting as we did so, the starting line-up of our ice party may
have seemed surprising. We left Martin Point with four sleds,
twenty-five dogs, seven men, and loads totaling nearly thirty-five
hundred pounds. However, nineteen dogs, three sleds, and more
than a ton of equipment were only to be used in helping us through
the incredibly rough shore ice. The final exploration party consisted
of six dogs, one sled, and three men—Ole Andreasen, Storker Storkerson, and myself.

We ran into difficulty at the very start when Captain Bernard,
driving his lead sledge over an ice ridge, fell against the handle bar
and ripped the skin from his forehead so that it hung down over
his eyes. He was in such bad shape from shock and bleeding that
after sewing him up we had to take him ashore. This cost us much

time, the loss of which might easily prove crucial, inasmuch as we had been a month late in starting. It was equally unfortunate that, following the resumption of our push northward, we received a further setback when, in the form of a spell of unseasonably warm weather, the thermometer did not go much below freezing. It was not cold enough to knit together the slowly moving ice that had been broken up by the severe storm of March 17, and we were therefore unable to leave the land-fast ice.

There was nothing to do but camp at the edge of the shore floe and wait for cold weather. I sent Wilkins and Castel ashore with Wilkins' motion-picture camera and equipment, which we could no longer afford time to use or space to carry. They also carried a leaky fuel tank that I wanted replaced. While they were gone, on what should have been a four- or five-hour trip, a second blizzard blew up that carried us at least forty miles eastward and fourteen or fifteen miles to the north. Wilkins and Castel were never able to rejoin us. We sadly missed their good dogs and the important tools that were still on their sled, although we had unloaded most of the surplus they carried before they left. We now had to leave Wilkins' supplies on the ice where they had been unloaded because we had no way of carrying them.

I needed Wilkins and Castel badly. I had not intended to send the support party back until we were at least fifty miles from shore. Now that we had lost the services of three men and a team of good dogs, we had to make what progress we could without them. The ice continued to be virtually impassable, and we could make little headway. Storkerson and I made a point of killing seals and bear whenever we could by way of encouraging the skeptics in the party to believe that they need never starve, although we still had more food with us than could possibly be hauled on the one good sled we intended to use on the advance journey. The other two sleds were so frail and broke so frequently that the delays in repairing them more than canceled any advantage resulting from their additional transporting power. I therefore made up my mind to send the support party back, not nearly as far from land as I had originally intended it to go.

I gave the men instructions for Anderson. These instructions are so essential to the understanding of later events that I summarize them here.

To guard against the possibility of our not returning to shore before the ice broke up, before leaving Collinson Point I had left with Anderson orders to be carried out if we were compelled to remain on the ice. My new letter to him emphasized the possibility that we might go to Banks Island instead of returning to Alaska, and instructed him more particularly than before as to certain things. The main point of both the earlier and the present instructions was that, in case I and my party did not return to Alaska in the spring of 1914, he was to assume that we had landed at the northwest corner of Banks Island or the southwest corner of Prince Patrick Island immediately north of it. He would then find himself in command of our various vessels, of which he was to make the following disposition:

With the *Alaska* and as much cargo as she could carry, and with certain members of the expedition, he was to proceed to the mainland shore of Dolphin and Union Strait. In that vicinity he was to select a winter base for the southern section of the expedition to occupy during the coming year and possibly a second year following. With the *Alaska* were to go two oil-burning launches, which I had purchased especially for use in surveying river deltas and the hundreds of small islands of Coronation Gulf.

The *Mary Sachs,* under Captain Bernard, was to take a cargo of goods into the same region, landing them there at the winter quarters of the *Alaska,* or at some neighboring point if Anderson found it preferable. The *Mary Sachs* was then to return to Herschel Island and, if the season remained open enough to permit it, was to take a second cargo from there to Cape Kellett at the southwest corner of Banks Island. If conditions seemed favorable, she might work up the west coast of Banks Island to Norway Island, but not farther. In other words, the *Sachs* was to establish, presumably at Cape Kellett but possibly farther north, a permanent base of supplies to which any party might retreat in case of shipwreck or other misfortune farther north. This would also provide a base to return to when the work farther north had been completed.

The most important item in my instructions was that the *North Star,* under command of Wilkins, was to proceed as early in the season as she could to Banks Island and was then to push northward along the west coast with the expectation of meeting us at Norway Island. In case she failed to find us or any records we might leave, she was to make her way, if she could, across McClure Strait to Prince Patrick Island, on the assumption that we would be waiting for her there.

Carrying these instructions to our men ashore, the support party left us at 70° 13′ N latitude and 140° 30′ W longitude on the afternoon of April 7. They had with them for the landward journey full rations for thirty-one days for the men and about twenty-five days for the dogs.

After some difficulty the party, as I later learned, reached shore on April 16. Here they met Constable Parsons of the Royal Northwest Mounted Police on his way to Herschel Island from a visit to the *Belvedere*. He told them that all the people along the coast, whalers and trappers and Eskimos alike, had given our party up for dead after the gale that carried us away from the shore ice. That was our first death. They killed us off again later on.

When the support party left us, Andreasen, Storkerson, and I were very close to the most northerly point ever reached by a ship in this sector of the Arctic. No human beings of any race had set foot on the ice in this longitude so far from the coast of Alaska. Our position was dramatic and we knew it. We were about to settle the great question: Is the Arctic a barren waste incapable of supporting life, or is it hostile only to those who persist in thinking and living like southerners?

We had an outfit calculated to last us a year and a half if necessary. By "outfit" I mean not food itself but the means of acquiring it—the clothing and scientific instruments, the necessary guns and ammunition. We had, in fact, food for ourselves for thirty days and dog food for about forty. We had two sextants and the tables necessary for determining our position. We carried two thermometers, an aneroid barometer, several prismatic compasses, and the pocket chronometer that O'Neill had given me. The dial of this was marked for twenty-four hours instead of twelve, a desirable provision in a latitude that offers about the same light in bad weather at three o'clock in the morning as at three o'clock in the afternoon. Our bulkiest piece of equipment was a sounding machine with several leads and what was left of our original ten thousand feet of wire. This wire had broken during a sounding made before the support party left. When we resumed our northern course on April 7, there was less than forty-five hundred feet left, and once we left the gradually sloping continental shelf, this did not always prove to be enough to reach bottom.

As the three of us started north, the ice was in a very unstable state. Repeated storms had broken up the largest floes and had ground them against each other so that there was scarcely a square foot of level going. During the first thirty-five or forty miles after leaving the coast we had found a great deal of young ice, sharp and thick, pushed up sometimes into ridges as much as fifty or sixty feet high. Often we had to use pickaxes to cut a trail for the dogs to follow. As we got farther out to sea the pressure ridges became fewer and the going was noticeably better.

There was still, however, great danger—or would have been had we not been alert to it—from cracks opening in the ice under pressure from all sides. On April 9 a new gale blew up and we had to camp after making barely two miles. We were just about to pitch our tent under a thirty-foot ice ridge when Andreasen noticed a crack opening across the very spot we had chosen. We lost no time in choosing another some distance from the ridge, feeling very pleased that the crack had given us warning before we were comfortably asleep. We set up the tent and built a snow barrier on the windward side of it, hoping to keep the worst of the gale from tearing the tent to pieces.

The wind increased, leaping the snow wall and shaking the tent top so that when Storkerson went out to take up a watch we could not hear him shouting to us. When he came in to ask why we failed to answer him, I decided that a watchman was not of much use if he was unable to make himself heard. We all lay down and tried to sleep, knowing that the ice, a good six feet in thickness, was breaking up all around us. Pieces, often as large as the gable end of a church, were piling themselves into ridges and marching like waves, frozen yet breaking, straight at us. Sometimes a fragment of the floe on which we were camped would be pushed up to a height of fifty feet, only to topple over when it broke near the water line. It was not difficult to picture what would happen to us if our tent happened to be under such a fragment when it toppled. Contemplation of such a possibility made it unpleasant to lie quietly in our tent, but we knew that to go outside and grope about in the darkness of the storm, blinded by stinging snow, would have been foolhardy. We had no choice.

The poets and journalists who still write about "the eternal silence of the frozen north" should have been with us that night. We knew that we were, so to speak, in danger as well as in bedlam, but one gets tired of staying scared, and too much noise can be as soporific as too little. All three of us were asleep by one o'clock. What woke us was the slackening of the gale, permitting the howling of a dog to reach us. Storkerson went out to see what the matter was. One of the dogs had been picketed to an ice block, which now had begun to move away from him. He was in danger of being dragged into a slowly widening crack.

Storkerson got the dog loose and came in to tell us that a pressure ridge some fifteen feet high had been thrown up within twenty-five feet of the back of the tent. It was necessary to pack up and move before it grew higher and fell on us. In the course of hitching the dogs, we found the track of a large male bear. Without even the dogs having been aware of his presence, and probably without his having been aware of ours, he had passed within fifteen feet of us while we slept.

The storm of that night left the ice a series of miniature mountain ranges, and the going was again bad. The temperature, however, had gone down, helping to keep the ice together. We were able to make from thirteen to twenty miles a day, in spite of some open water that forced us to detour until we found a tongue of ice by which we could cross. We were now a hundred miles from shore, and since the depth of the water beneath us was greater than our forty-five hundred feet of wire, we knew that we were not approaching land and that the possibility of finding any undiscovered territory in the Beaufort Sea was growing smaller.

Even here there were small scars in the comparatively young ice which indicated frozen-over breathing holes used by seals the fall before. We still had food on our sled, and I was sure that the seals would be back soon. All three of us, however, realized that at sea as well as on land there may be barren areas where life is not abundant.

With the colder weather that had set in came not only an opportunity to travel more rapidly but also a change in our camping habits. Although I had spent five winters in the Arctic and knew all about snowhouses, which most people back home think of as a symbol of the Eskimos, I myself had never built one. This was because many of the Eskimo groups with whom I lived were not snowhouse builders and because those who were, were so punctilious in the code of their hospitality that they would never let me lift a finger to help them when they built snowhouses for me. On the present trip, when snowhouses would have been comfortable and convenient, the weather had been so comparatively warm that what snow there was, was in no condition for block-cutting. I knew, however, that the impression given in many white men's books about the north—that there was something mysterious about snowhouse building that a white man could never learn—was incorrect.

In the evening of April 14, 1914, in a position roughly 71° N and 140° W of Greenwich, I had a slight touch of snow blindness. When in the middle of the night, although it was still light enough for travel, a wide lead opened up just ahead of us, promising to make travel the next day impossible, I felt that we had time, reason, and proper conditions for building a snowhouse. Since it would be practically opaque, it would give me a chance to rest my eyes from the glare. We accordingly found a suitably well-packed snowdrift, got out our long snow knives, and cut the drift up into blocks twenty inches high, from twenty to thirty-five inches long, and four inches thick.

The house is built preferably where the snow is four or more feet deep, thus allowing for the excavation of the entrance tunnel. The first block is set on edge as a domino might be. With his knife the builder slightly undercuts the inner edge of the block so that it leans inward. The angle of tilt is very slight if the house is to be a big one. It is considerable for a small house.

The oval or circle that is to be the ground plan is usually determined by the eye as the builder sets up the blocks one after the other. In practice, I found it more sensible to make an outline with a string having pegs at either end, one peg planted where the center of the house is to be and the other used to describe the circumference. Even the best of snowhouse builders, Eskimo or white, if they rely on the eye alone, will now and then make the house uncomfortably small or unnecessarily large for the intended number of occupants. With a string, a simple mathematical calculation tells one how many feet of radius will accommodate the intended number of lodgers.

When the first block is standing on edge, it is a simple matter to prop all the other blocks up by leaning each against the preceding one until the circle is complete. While the nature of snow is such that after the blocks have been leaning against each other for five or ten minutes they automatically cement themselves together and to the snow upon which they stand, it is actually the action of gravity upon the tilted blocks that gives the house its strength.

When the first tier has been completed, the second can be started in any of several ways. The simplest is to select any point in the circle formed by the first tier, and from the top corner of one of the blocks make a diagonal cut downward to its far corner. In the angle thus formed you place the first block of the second tier. After that, you lean the second block of the second tier against the first block of the second tier and so on, building up spirally. The blocks of each tier must be inclined inward at a greater angle than those of the tier below. The idea is to achieve an approximately perfect dome.

Building with snow blocks is simpler than building with masonry. Stone is an intractable substance and has to be shaped in advance according to a mathematical calculation, or molded in an exact form before it is placed in its intended position. Snow being a much more workable substance, such preparation is unnecessary.

If four men cooperate in the building of a snowhouse, one usually cuts the blocks, a second carries them, a third is inside placing them, and the fourth follows the builder around and calks the crevices between the blocks with soft snow. In ten minutes the soft snow in the crevices has become harder than the blocks themselves. The house, although fragile during the process of building, is moderately strong within half an hour.

When the dome itself has been finished, a tunnel whose entrance is below the level of the snowhouse floor is dug through the drift into the house. The floor covering is then passed into the house: a layer of deerskin with the hair down is spread over the entire floor except where the cooking is to be done. Over this layer is spread another layer of skins, with the hair up. The reason for the double insulation is that the interior of the house is going to become warm. Its inhabitants are going to sit around on the floor and later are going to sleep on it. If the insulation is not virtually perfect, the heat from cooking and from the bodies of the sleepers will melt the snow underneath and make the bedclothes wet. When the outside temperature is zero or lower, a double layer of deerskin will prevent any thawing underneath the beds, the snow there remaining as dry as sand in a desert.

When the floor has been covered and the bedding, cooking gear, and other things brought in, a fire is lighted. If there is enough fuel, it is desirable to heat the house until the snow roof and walls begin to thaw. The temperature in the house may reach 80° F. for a short time. The inmates keep feeling roof and walls to check the progress of the thawing. This, of course, is most rapid where the hot air accumulates. Usually the lowest tier of blocks, near the floor, does not thaw at all. The thawing proceeds without dripping, because dry snow is the best sort of blotter and absorbs the water as fast as it forms. When the inner surface of the roof and walls has become properly wet with the thawing, the fire is put out or a large hole is cut in the roof. This allows the walls to become glazed with a thin film of ice, giving it far greater strength and preventing loose snow from sticking to clothing that comes in contact with it. The house is now so strong that it would support the weight of a heavy man. As a matter of fact, bears occasionally walk over such houses. I have never known of one to break through. The strength of the house, however, is somewhat like the strength of an eggshell. It is difficult to crush with pressure but easy to break with a blow. A bear would have no trouble in getting into a house if it chose to, for one sweep of its paw would tear a great hole in wall or roof.

My first snowhouse, nine feet in diameter and six feet high, was ready for occupancy in three hours. During the rest of our ice trip we got so much practice as snow masons that we could put up a snowhouse in an hour.

It is not possible to give too much credit to our dogs for what success we had on our Beaufort Sea journey. On April 17 they were still hauling over two hundred pounds each. The snow was firm but rough, and the sled was continually going up and down over hard drifts. It is true that our six dogs alone could not have taken the sled over some of the pressure ridges we met. We helped them over such bad places, but that is all we did. The rest of the time Storkerson and Andreasen ran beside the sled, usually with their hands resting on it, while I ran ahead. On the seventeenth we averaged nearly four miles an hour, which meant that on level stretches we made at least five miles an hour.

Although the dogs themselves were excellent, much of their ability to carry on under the conditions we met resulted from our method of harnessing them in a single straight line. When dogs are harnessed fanwise, as they are in Greenland, it is only the dog in the middle of the team that can pull straight ahead. The others pull at considerable angles, and part of their effort is thereby wasted. This in some measure explains why it is that few explorers seem to have been able to haul more than a hundred pounds per dog, less than half of what ours hauled.

I believe, however, that the real superiority of all the dogs we used was in the breed—or, to be more accurate, the lack of it. Some were half Eskimo and half Saint Bernard. Others were half mastiff. Some appeared to have a considerable admixture of wolf.

In my arctic years I had experiences with dogs of all sorts. Some were brought from Greenland by Amundsen on his *Gjoa* voyage of 1903–1906 and left by him near the Mackenzie delta, where I used them. At different times I also made use of a hundred or more Eskimo dogs from the district around Victoria Island. Dogs from that region are presumably as pure-bred as any in the world, since they, like their owners, have been least in touch with the outside world. I have also used several hundred dogs of mixed Eskimo descent from the Mackenzie district and the north coast of Alaska, where the dogs as well as the Eskimos themselves have been subject to outside contact for from thirty to a hundred years. I have had a few Siberian dogs, and about fifty of the type most favored for driving by miners around Nome, Alaska.

On the basis of experience with all these varieties, I came to a conclusion on the whole very unfavorable to the Eskimo dog. For one thing, it is too small. Those I knew weighed from fifty to seventy pounds. The hauling of such a load as our six dogs were carrying would have required at least nine of the best Eskimo dogs. The disadvantage of having nine dogs instead of six is plain. There is the trouble of harnessing three more in the morning and of unharnessing, tying, and feeding them in the evening. True, a big dog needs a little more food than a small one, but six dogs weighing around a hundred and twenty pounds each will do well on less food than is necessary for nine dogs averaging seventy pounds.

One of the most spectacular ice crushes of our experience took place in our path on April 18. A floe to the north of us was moving east with reference to ours at a rate of about twenty feet per minute. The combined force of the two floes was so great that, although the ice was over six feet thick, their relative speed seemed undiminished even when they ground against each other and piled up a huge ridge. The ice buckled and bent for several hundred yards

—fortunately, to one side of us so that we could retreat. The toppling ice cakes half a mile away sounded like a cannonade heard over a stormy surf on a rockbound coast. The surf-like noise resulted from the actual grinding of the edges, where the ice was being powdered rather than broken. Mingled with this was a high-pitched screeching, like the noise of a siren, which rose whenever a tongue of six-foot ice from one floe was forced over the surface of the other. In about two hours the pressure ceased and we crossed the newly formed ridge and proceeded on our way.

Although we had been traveling in a direction a little west of north, frequent observations for longitude showed that our course was a little east of north. This could be accounted for only by an eastward motion of the whole surface of the sea. By April 20 we seemed to be entering a region in which game was scarce. We saw infrequent bear tracks, all of them a month or two old. The scars on the ice showing that seals had been there the previous autumn became fewer. We saw no seals in the leads, although we occasionally stopped for an hour at a time to watch for them.

We began to worry. As the signs of game decreased, we could not help remembering the statements of shore Eskimos that we would find no seals at any distance from land. My diary shows that our faith in the contrary view was at times shaken. We did not, however, seriously consider turning back.

My companions were as eager as I to make a success of the journey. What worried us more than the scarcity of game signs was the daily increasing height of the sun. There was no longer any darkness at night. The temperature still kept well below zero, but we knew that in a very few days the wind would change to the east and the first thaw of spring would be upon us. We said little about the danger of running out of food but a great deal about the necessity of hurrying on.

The scarcity of game signs would have troubled us less had we had the understanding of the polar sea that we acquired during the next four years. I now know what we then merely conjectured: that the presence or absence of seals has nothing to do with latitude. It is chiefly the result of the mobility of the ice. In any region where there is violent ice movement, and consequently much open water, there are sure to be a large number of seals. There is food for seals everywhere in the ocean, but in certain places the ice conditions are such that it is impossible for them to come up and breathe. During the summer they congregate in regions of open water. In the autumn, when the ice begins to form, they start gnawing at the covering overhead, as rats will gnaw at a floor board, making the breathing holes that they use all winter. If the young ice remains stationary, the seal remains stationary with it. If it floats in any direction, he travels along with it. His life depends upon his never going far from his breathing hole as long as the ice around it remains unbroken. If it does break and if leads are formed, he may do a certain amount of winter traveling. Ordinarily, he does not travel after the first hard frost comes and forms new ice over the leads.

We could not be entirely sure, in April, 1914, of the meaning of the scarcity of game. Yet, instead of restricting our rations, we ate three full meals a day and fed the dogs almost to surfeit, with the idea that the more rapidly the loads were lightened the greater our speed would be. We really should have thrown away one or two hundred pounds of food at the start, but we never had quite the strength of mind to do it. For one thing, Andreasen and Storkerson still thought chocolate and malted milk more palatable than seal meat.

We were making a new departure in polar exploration, not only in planning to live by hunting when our food was gone, but also in living well while we still had a chance to do so. We were traveling over ice floating over an unknown ocean, far from any known lands, and without any immediate intention of turning back. In all the polar literature I have read, I have never met with an account of any party the members of which, in like circumstances, would not have tightened their belts and saved every scrap of food. When I boasted of what we were doing, Storkerson seconded me. He, too, had lived by hunting for years and had acquired the hunter's temperament. Andreasen, however, was troubled by more doubts than he admitted.

By April 23, in latitude 75° 15′ N, we had entered an ice area of a new sort. Up to this point, every lead had given evidence of much lateral motion. That is, the floe on one side had been moving east or west with reference to the floe on the other side. Now we came to leads that had been opening and closing at intervals all winter without any lateral motion. A belt of three- or four-foot ice might have formed a little after Christmas. A belt of fifteen- or twenty-inch ice might have formed as recently as March. The center of the lead might be filled with five- or eight-inch ice not more than a week old.

One lead containing three such belts had evidently opened only three times during the winter. There were others, however, that showed that they had opened half a dozen times or more.

We were now getting light northwest breezes, and our sextant observations showed us to be drifting a very little to the east each day. We knew that Banks Island was to the east, not more than a few hundred miles away. This made us feel that the slight drift resulted mainly from the crushing of the sea ice against the Banks Island coast.

We had been traveling during the day and sleeping at night, but on April 25 we changed to night travel. The season was now too late for snowhouses, and the light at night was sufficient for traveling. Cold weather and westerly winds continued, but the temperature at noon was now such that although it might be below zero in the shade the snow melted where it was exposed to the sun. We were very comfortable in our day camps, for the tent, which kept the wind off, let the bright sunshine through. In fact, the interior was sometimes too warm. We no longer had to take pains to keep our clothing dry. By camping in the morning, we could hang any damp garments in the sun and find them dry before evening.

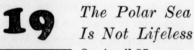

19 *The Polar Sea*
Is Not Lifeless

On April 25 we were two hundred miles north of the continental coast at the point where Canada and Alaska meet. A week or two more of cold weather would have enabled us to get as far north as 76°, opposite the southwestern tip of Prince Patrick Island. We did not get the cold weather. We did get an east wind, which I knew might easily send the floe we were on drifting rapidly westward. If that happened, we would have to try to return to the Alaskan coast, for the ice over which we could travel would be blown away from Banks Island, leaving more open water than we could cross. This would have been a very serious matter, for we might easily have been carried on westward, just as the *Karluk* had been, before we reached the coast.

This alarming prospect made me feel that we should change our course and head for Banks Island before it was too late. Storkerson and Andreasen had misgivings, largely based on the fact that the seal hunting where we now were had been poor and was getting poorer. They felt that, since we knew there were seals to the south of us, we should return to Alaska and not venture into a region where we might find none.

I was able to persuade them that we should keep on toward Banks Island or Prince Patrick Island as planned. The first ten days in May made it look as if I had sold my companions a gold brick. We ran out of kerosene, and there were no seals to provide us with animal oil for cooking. We took to burning hair clipped from two grizzly-bear skins which we used for bedding. The hair of half a

176

skin was enough to cook one day's meals, though the odor of burning hair did not exactly sharpen our appetites. We now went on half-rations for the first time, not entirely because of the absence of game. Our abstemiousness was partly the result of the compulsion we all felt to hurry onward rather than stop and hunt. The fear was in all our minds that the increasing warmth might make it impossible to reach land before fall and might keep us marooned on some drifting floe far out at sea while the *North Star,* following my instructions, looked for us in vain on Banks Island.

I still believed in my theory of ice travel, although my diary entries for this time show that it was somewhat shaken and that I even entertained the idea that perhaps the Eskimos and whalers had been right after all. We continued to skirt lead after lead without seeing a seal. I reminded myself as firmly as I could that I had had stretches of bad hunting luck in places where seals were known to be common. Yet, had not my luck always changed? Why should it not change here?

On May 7 it did change. I spotted a seal a mile away in mush ice. I shouted to my companions, not so much with the idea that it was time, so to speak, to set the table, but chiefly because my faith had been proved justifiable before I had lost it. Actually, that seal was as safe from us as it would have been if we had not seen it. We could not approach it, and could not have retrieved it even if we had been able to get near enough to shoot it. We contented ourselves with the certainty that there were seals in the waters we were crossing. The relief we felt did not last, for we saw no other seals for some time and the ice was getting worse, not freezing hard enough to allow the safe crossing of leads. Having to go around most of them made our progress very slow.

By May 13, we were **feeding** the dogs old skin boots and the grizzly-bear hides that we had sheared for fuel. We ourselves were down to three-fourths of a pound of food per day, and even at this rate our supply was going to last us no more than two or three days. It seemed to me that, haste or no haste, we simply had to stop long enough to look for seals. This we did, and were, in a limited sense, rewarded. We shot two, but both of them promptly sank. According to my theory, they should have floated, for here at sea there was no river water to make the ocean less buoyant. My theory was evidently wrong. This disturbed us very much, for it was obvious that if the seals we shot were going to sink there was no use wasting precious time waiting for them to bob up. We kept on going, hoping for a westerly wind to blow us toward the islands. By May 15, although we were making fair progress, we had to stop and make one more try for food and fuel.

This time I shot a seal that floated. From that moment on, we had no more worry about food. In fact, on May 20 we shot a young seal that was so tasty that we all ate too much of it and in consequence were unable to travel the next day.

On May 22 we saw a school of beluga whales blowing in the lead beyond us. During the following weeks we saw thousands of them, and it was at this time that I began to think of them as submarines making the Northwest Passage. Sometimes, when a lead was frozen over with six or eight inches of new ice, we noticed that the whales would come up under it with sufficient force to bend it upward until it broke and opened breathing places for them. It was because of my recording of this observation that the idea of crossing the Arctic Ocean by submarine eventually passed from George, later Sir Hubert Wilkins to the United States Navy, whose submarines *Nautilus* and *Skate* made the crossing, in opposite directions, in 1958.

On May 24 we found ourselves marooned on an ice island some four or five miles square. We could not cross the several miles of open water, even using the stratagem of wrapping our sledge in a tarpaulin to make it into a boat. The mush ice would have chafed a hole in the canvas and sunk us long before we could have reached the other side. Since the ice of our island was at least fifty feet thick and was under no pressure, we could consider ourselves safe for the summer, if need be. Should we not get off by winter, when the light would be too poor for hunting, our safety as island dwellers would be of no importance.

It was extremely unpleasant to know, as we did by measuring, that we were within fifty miles of the land we wanted to reach and yet were being carried steadily away from it by wind and current.

There were plenty of seals available, and the presence of their carcasses in our meat cache was enough to bring us all the bears in the vicinity. The bears were not educated in the ways of men and may even have doubted that we existed, just as men who had never seen the Copper Eskimos doubted that they existed. We found it hard to outguess these inquisitive animals, and both we and the dogs had several narrow escapes.

Our fifth bear turned up on June 3. I was away on a walk about our island, examining all sides to see if there might be a chance to get away from it. We usually tethered our dogs by making a sort of toggle in the ice with picks and passing the end of the tie line through it. Although ice is readily broken with a sharp blow, one of these toggles is unbelievably strong if subjected only to a steady strain. Half a dozen such toggles, for example, each one no more than five inches in diameter, will stand the strain of hauling a seventy-foot whale out of a lead onto the ice.

This time, thawing had weakened the ice, and when the dogs made a concerted rush toward the bear, pulling in unison, the toggles broke. Tied together as the dogs were, the bear would have had them at a great disadvantage had he stopped to wait for them. As soon as he saw them coming, he fled, making for the water as a bear always will when he thinks himself in danger. He did not dive, but started trying to climb back up on the ice, breaking some more of it as he did so. The dogs rushed up but had the sense not to go into the water.

Storkerson and Andreasen, out of the tent by this time, saw the great danger to the dogs, each one of which was priceless to us, and accordingly they began to shoot, although they had instructions that no bear was to be killed in the water because of the difficulty of retrieving him. Only the head of this bear showed above the water. Partly for this reason and partly because of the excitement, killing him required a fusillade.

When the shooting began, I was about half a mile from camp. As one shot after another rang out, I grew more and more worried. My companions knew as well as I did that our lives might depend upon the careful husbanding of ammunition. Yet there was Ole, standing up, wastefully shooting from the shoulder like a cowboy firing at Indians in a movie. My anger at this extravagance quickly changed to relief when I got home and saw what a narrow escape the dogs had had.

It was not until June 5 that we got a chance to leave the island, which we had begun to think of as home. On that morning we found at the edge of the floe about fifty yards of young ice and beyond it perhaps half a mile of open water. Beyond the open water the ice looked strong and old. We chopped a trail through the new ice, wrapped the tarpaulin about our sledge, loaded in the dogs, and ferried what gear and supplies we could manage to carry across in several trips.

Once on the other side of the lead, we found the going possible but slow. Sextant readings showed us that although we were traveling northeast at the rate of about ten miles a day our true course was southeast. On some days we could not travel in any direction and consequently lost ground because of the ice drift. However, we could tell from our soundings, which showed the bottom coming nearer as we proceeded, that we were inching toward land. By June 15 the depth beneath us was barely a thousand feet and land birds began to appear on the ice. A week later the depth was less than two hundred feet. On June 23, I climbed a hummock and saw between the pinnacles of a pressure ridge a dark line that I knew must be land. After two more days of slogging through wet, granulated snow in which neither we nor the dogs could get firm footing and which held back the sledge as if it had been sand, we came in sight of Norway Island, which is just offshore and about two-thirds of the way up the west coast of Banks Island. We were now on land-fast ice and no longer in danger of having to spend summer at sea. The going from this point on was exceedingly bad. Sometimes we waded through water nearly up to our waists, while the dogs had to swim with the sled floating behind like a log being towed across a river. When the miniature lakes on top of the ice were filled not only with water but with slush snow, the going was even worse. Though our feet went down through the mess to the bed ice, real wading was not possible, and either walking or swimming was quite impossible for the dogs. In such places I had to force my way back and forth through the slush several times, making a sort of canal, then take hold of the lead dog and drag the team after me while the other two men pushed the sled. This exhausting work gave us only six miles in a day.

Our first sleep on the land floe had a comfort and security about it that we had not known for over ninety days. No drift could now take away from us during the night the distance we had won during the day. No crack would open under us. No cake would tip on edge and spill us into the water.

At ten minutes past eight on the bright evening of June 25, ninety-six days out from the Alaska coast, we landed on Norway Island. This was a point-to-point distance of a little over five hundred miles. Counting the adverse drift, we had traveled about seven hundred miles.

From the time we first sighted land, our chief concern had been to get ashore. We had not stopped to pick up seal meat along the way. When we landed, therefore, we had no food for the dogs and only about half a meal for ourselves. Yet, while we were still a mile from shore, with the southwest slope of Norway Island conveniently spread out ahead, I saw through my glasses one wolf, one fox, eight hares, some king eiders, Pacific eiders, old squaw ducks, and three kinds of dark geese, one of which proved to be a Hutchings. After landing, we saw some willow ptarmigan, plovers, Lapland longspurs, snow buntings, and two or three kinds of sandpipers. We also found owl pellets and saw a few bumblebees and bluebottle flies. I am happy to add that there were no mosquitoes.

There were caribou tracks on the beach. While my companions made our first land camp and cooked with wood for the first time in months, I went to the top of the island to get a view of the far side. Norway proved to be about half as large as the old Admiralty chart indicated, and only half as far from Banks Island. I had climbed the most westerly of the hills, so that, turning to the east, I had to look first over three miles of the island and beyond that over three miles of sea ice to examine what I then thought was Banks. The land proved to be simply another small island, though more than twice the size of the one we were on. We later named it for Captain Bernard.

As I studied the landscape to the east through my glasses, one promising thing I saw was a half-dozen white specks. These might be geese, they might be caribou. When the six-power glasses failed to settle the question, I turned to the twelve-power, for, as usual when caribou hunting, I carried both. In these, everything quivered. The white spots sometimes looked round, like pillars, even seemed to move. In a few minutes they came back to where they had seemed to be at first. I gathered that the movements and changes of shape were atmospheric or optical. If the spots had been geese, I thought, they would have changed their relative positions. They must be either caribou lying down, or possibly just stones. Then, as I watched, one of the six moved in a way that was certainly not atmospheric, definitely separating itself from the other five. That was enough for me. I knew I had several hours of careful approach ahead of me. I signaled down to camp that I would not be coming home for supper, trying to convey the idea that, since I was off after caribou, they were free to eat all the food.

Going off after caribou was to be my principal occupation for the remainder of the summer. We knew that the *North Star* could not be expected so early in the season. After building a beacon on Norway Island and accumulating as much meat as we could carry, we crossed to Bernard, which Storkerson spent some time mapping. On July 31 we made the final crossing to the mainland of Banks, where we established our base camp.

It is hard to describe the feeling that possessed us as we settled ourselves on the shore that had sometimes seemed impossible of attainment as we traveled toward it. After our walk of some seven hundred miles we arrived at our destination in good health and with our dogs so fat that they were lazy. We had made a series of soundings, all over our limit of forty-five hundred feet, through four degrees of latitude and nineteen of longitude. We had established the line of the continental shelf north of Alaska and west of Banks Island. We had learned much—most of which was contrary to existing belief—about the currents in the Beaufort Sea.

Although all the evidence we had gathered pointed to the non-existence of new land north of the Alaskan coast, there was still a possibility that there might be undiscovered islands north or north-west of Prince Patrick. In addition to stockpiling food, which was essential, I planned to spend the summer carrying out geographical, geological, and archaeological work in Banks Island. For the following winter, if ice conditions permitted the *North Star* and the *Mary Sachs* to carry out my instructions, I planned two exploratory trips: one to the northwest from Cape Prince Alfred at the northwestern tip of Banks Island, the other north and east from the north end of Prince Patrick Island or Melville Island, depending on what wintering place the *North Star* was able to reach.

In the beacon at Bernard Island, which no ship going north along the coast could miss, I had left instructions and advice about suitable harbors, suggesting that if the *Karluk* was able to rejoin the working expedition she should, if Bartlett thought it advisable, try to reach Prince Patrick.

With the satisfaction of feeling that the first part of the mission of the northern section of the expedition had been accomplished, we relaxed and began our summer work. The environment and the conditions were ideal. There was plenty of game of all kinds except musk oxen, and plenty of fuel—driftwood, willow, and heather. We were in a beautiful region of rolling hills and fertile valleys, everywhere gold and white with flowers, green with grass, or mingled green and brown with grass and lichen. Sparkling brooks ran through the valleys, sometimes dipping into crystal rivers flowing easily over bright gravel bottoms.

This indeed was exploration to warm the heart. For the moment, the world could not have seemed better. It was as well that we did not know what was in store for us.

20 Banks Island on Borrowed Time

The summer passed rapidly, with Ole Andreasen keeping camp on the high land near shore while Storkerson and I hunted and explored the interior. Our only concern was ammunition; we had 109 rounds for the 6.5-mm. Mannlicher and 157 rounds for the Winchester. This would be ample to provide us with a winter stock of meat, but we would be in a serious position if our support vessel, the *North Star,* failed to arrive with a fresh supply.

A good hunter should be able, if he hunts from camp, to account for an average of 125 pounds of meat for each bullet. While traveling, with less time to spend on stalking and some waste of meat that cannot be carried, the average per bullet would be less.

We could not waste ammunition if we were to be prepared to spend the winter without reinforcement. We all knew this, and knew it meant that, however plentiful and tempting they might be, geese provided too small a target. Ole, however, had a hankering for goose that must have amounted to a compulsive craving. Upon returning from one hunting trip, Storkerson and I found that Ole had used up quite a large amount of ammunition with very little accumulation of meat to show for it. He explained to us that during our absence the camp had been beset by wolves. Since he knew that the dogs, aroused by their presence, might break loose and be killed or injured, he felt that it was his duty to kill the wolves or drive them away. This, of course, had required a great deal of offhand shooting. It was unfortunate that he had had to use up so many bullets, but at least the dogs were safe.

Ole did not stick to this story, but finally broke down and admitted that he had expended the ammunition on the slaughter of a single goose that he had been unable to resist. What bothered Ole most and probably made him feel guilty enough to confess was the fact that the goose had not tasted as good as he had expected it to.

Storkerson and I, in the course of our hunting, found some traces of former Eskimo habitation, but they were at least ten years old. With them we found bones of musk oxen. There were no Eskimo burial places, suggesting the probability that the people who had been here before us were hunting parties. They had apparently killed all the musk oxen on Banks Island. At least we saw none alive.

We expected the *North Star* by the first of August. By then we did not dare to venture far inland, for the water alongshore was opening up and we were anxious not to be away in the interior when she appeared. Throughout the month the shore leads were in perfect condition for northward navigation, but no ships came. On the twenty-second we cached our meat supply in a deep pit, where it would be safe even from bears, and started south along the coast toward Cape Kellett, at the southwestern tip of the island, hoping to find some message to explain the absence of the *Star*.

Storkerson and Andreasen followed the shore with the dogs, the dogs carrying our gear in packs. I kept along the ridges, from which I could get a better view out to sea. Since Storkerson and Andreasen had to accommodate their pace to the speed of the walking dogs, which was no more than a mile and a half an hour, they fell some distance behind me. The going was more difficult for all of us than it should have been because of the inaccuracy of our charts.

A very gloomy camp we made, our first evening on the way to Kellett. Here it was, almost September, when vessels even as far south of us as Herschel Island would ordinarily be thinking of getting out or choosing a safe wintering place, and our support had not put in an appearance. Storkerson and Andreasen now believed that no ship would come, and wanted me to agree to head for the mainland as soon as the ice closed in enough to permit sledging across Amundsen Gulf. I wanted to stay and continue the work that the northern section of the expedition had planned.

From the hills behind our camp we could see Cape Kellett, but we could see no masts nor any cairns on the hills. There was nothing to indicate that human beings were in the neighborhood. More than five months had passed since our departure from Martin Point. In that time we had done exactly what we said we were going to do. My companions felt that if our supporting parties had done what I had instructed them to do, and what they said they were going to do, they would be with us now. Since they were not, it must mean that they were not coming at all. I argued that even if they failed to appear we could carry on with our work, though we should have to change our plans somewhat. When we went to sleep that night none of us felt very buoyant.

In the morning I started for Kellett before the others got the dogs packed. I had not gone very far before I saw an unmistakable human sign—the imprint of a heeled boot—in the sand. I marked it with an upended stone and went on. As I crossed a small rise I saw two masts sticking up over the next ridge. The gloom of last night's camp immediately disappeared, to be replaced by a feverish apprehension. My first thought was that the ship, not having found us, might sail away before I could reach it. I made as good time as I could toward the masts. When I rounded the last turn and came out on the beach south of Cape Kellett, I stopped short in astonishment.

There before me was indeed a ship—but she was not the *North Star* and she was not in the water. There also were men, and to my amazement they were building a house. One or two of them looked toward me but showed no surprise, presumably thinking that I was one of their own party.

As I approached, I recognized Jim Crawford, who had been, before I left the mainland, the engineer of the *Mary Sachs*. It was the half-dismantled *Sachs* that lay hauled up on the beach between him and the water. Crawford looked up as I drew near. He dropped the ax he was using and opened his mouth. Then, after putting his hand to his eyes and peering at me, he shouted to someone behind him. As he came up, I recognized him as Captain Bernard. For a moment the two stared at me. I did not know what was wrong, but I saw plainly that they had not come to Banks Island with any idea of meeting me.

The two recovered their composure and shouted to the others, "Stefansson is alive! He's here!" and Bernard led me, as if I were something fragile that might turn to dust, into the tent that was their temporary camp. He seemed convinced that I must be starving and urged me to begin eating. I found it hard to make him understand that what I was hungry for was news, not food. I accepted some coffee and a piece of bread and butter and was rewarded with the news, which was not good.

There were several things that I wished to be told about. One was, of course, the whereabouts and condition of the *Karluk*. No less important was the whereabouts of Wilkins and the *North Star*. I was naturally curious to know why the *Mary Sachs* was at Kellett, dismantled, and what men and supplies she had brought with her.

It did not take long for me to realize that, in the eyes of the southern section of the expedition, I and my companions had been dead for at least five months. This not unnaturally seemed to me a quite unreasonable view of my situation. It was hard for me to realize that I must judge what the people of the *Sachs* told me in the light not of my own circumstances but of their belief in my death and my consequent inability to continue participation in the affairs of the expedition.

I was not greatly surprised to learn that the *Karluk* had finally been crushed by the ice and lost, and that her crew and the scientific staff had made their way to Wrangel Island, north of Siberia. I was surprised, and my surprise has never entirely been dissipated, to learn that Bob Bartlett, the *Karluk's* master, had made his way safely from Wrangel to Siberia and thence to Alaska with only a single Eskimo companion. I could not then—and still do not—understand why he did not take with him the entire personnel of the *Karluk*. True, he set rescue operations in motion when he reached the mainland, but rescue by ship from Wrangel might prove impossible or at least be greatly delayed. Sledging over the hundred miles of sea ice from the island to Siberia was not impossible, as Bartlett himself demonstrated. I considered Bartlett's procedure a mistake, but I was not greatly worried, having perhaps been made too confident by my own and my companions' ability to survive without help from the outposts of civilization. I was to learn that even theories that have been proved sound can fail those who do not entirely believe in them.

My desire to know what had happened to the *North Star* and Wilkins was at least partly satisfied by the answer to my question about the *Mary Sachs*. It appeared that, although even he believed me dead, Wilkins had planned to carry out my orders and sail the *Star* to Norway Island, where we had landed after our sledge journey across the sea ice. Wilkins had, in fact, been about to set out from Herschel Island but had decided to wait for mail. While he was waiting, Anderson, with the *Alaska* and the *Mary Sachs,* arrived at Herschel. Anderson had refused to let Wilkins have the *Star* and had taken her instead to Coronation Gulf with him, leaving Wilkins the *Mary Sachs* and a small launch. I felt that Wilkins should have stood up to Anderson. This he had not done. The *Sachs* had sailed for Kellett not to find me but to look for indications of my fate. Because a dead man could not conceivably have any use for them, several essential items of my equipment had been diverted to Coronation Gulf. One of these was a large tarpaulin, like the one we had worn out on our ice journey, necessary for converting a sledge into a boat capable of crossing leads. Another was the excellent, strong sledge that Wilkins had taken back to the mainland after escorting us out onto the sea ice. The third item that should have come north with Wilkins was sounding wire. Anderson had miles of it in the *Alaska*, but he had sent me none. We, who were to do the sea exploration, were left with the forty-five-hundred-foot remnant that was not nearly enough to measure the depths we knew we should find.

I did not know what to say about the situation with which I was confronted. It is hard for a live man to think like a dead one. Here I was, with two companions, ready to continue with the plans of which everyone was aware. Instead of having the supplies and equipment necessary, I had a land-fast ship that had lost one of her propellers and leaked so badly that she could not be refloated. And I had an unseaworthy launch that could not be made ready for use before the freeze-up.

The *Sachs* had brought food, but she had also brought people and dogs to consume it. There were ten altogether, including two women seamstresses and two children. One of the women was Storkerson's Eskimo wife and one of the children was his daughter Martina. Most of the ten were on hand when I put in my appearance. Wilkins, with the Eskimo hunter Natkusiak, my former companion, was off looking for game, something I knew that we should all have to be doing very shortly. The season of poor hunting light was barely two months distant. Although the *Sachs* had provisions sufficient for her personnel for a year, we would have to supplement them with fresh meat if we expected to avoid scurvy.

Once the small colony at Kellett had become used to the idea of my survival, Wilkins, Natkusiak, and I spent our time hunting.

It amused me to think that I, the supposed dead man, was now in the position of having to support my rescuers. The hunting itself was not amusing. We were working against time in a strange and difficult land, no longer beautiful with sparkling brooks and golden flowers but frost-bitten and rocky, the ponds freezing and cracking like artillery, the caribou growing leaner and more scarce, the light becoming briefer and thinner.

The winter of 1914–1915, after hunting became impossible, was a busy one. I had worked out a new plan for the next year's exploration, and the preparations for it gave everyone plenty to do. The women sewed skin clothing and boats. Captain Bernard made sleds, stripping the *Sachs* of metal and hardwood for his materials. Several of the men made pemmican out of mixed fat and lean meat to replace the commercial pemmican that had been lost with the *Karluk*. Those who were not otherwise occupied spent their time trapping.

Later in the winter came a serious and unexplained epidemic that cost us a number of dogs and delayed the start of the sled trip I had planned. When we finally did get off, we had more troubles. The condition of the ice gave the dogs sore feet, and our kerosene containers began to leak. Storkerson and Charlie Thomsen, husband of the second of our seamstresses, sledged back to Kellett for new containers and more kerosene while the rest of us waited and rested the dogs' feet. The result was that it took us forty-five days to get from Cape Kellett to Cape Alfred, at the north end of Banks Island, where but for the *Mary Sachs* our main base would have been. It was now April, too late it seemed to me to attempt a crossing of the deep and swift-running McClure Strait to Prince Patrick Island. I sent Wilkins and two other men back to Kellett with instructions to go to Coronation Gulf over the ice and take over the *North Star*, sailing her as far north as possible during the summer.

The rest of us, Storkerson, Ole Andreasen, Charlie Thomsen, and I, headed northwest out to sea on ice that was a little too thin to be comfortable. Taking soundings, we found an uneven bottom ranging from six hundred to twelve hundred feet down. We'd hoped to keep a northwesterly course, but the ice drifted steadily to the southwest. The sea began to grow deeper. It became increasingly evident that we were not going to get far to the northwest. On May 6 we turned to the east and headed for Prince Patrick Island, the west coast of which had been partly explored by Sir Francis McClintock and G. F. Mecham in 1853 in the course of their search for Sir John

Franklin. We hoped to map the unexplored section of the coastline, in spite of the fact that Mecham had reported that the absence of game in this part of Prince Patrick had forced him to turn back.

Mecham was right as far as land animals were concerned. The west coast of Prince Patrick is bad country with little or no vegetation. We had an advantage over the nineteenth-century explorer, however, in that we knew that we should find seals and bears if we went far enough offshore. While the weather was too foggy and generally bad for accurate mapping, we managed to traverse the unvisited part of the coastline.

On June 15, 1915, we had reached the extreme northern tip of Prince Patrick Island, the cape named after McClintock. As we had only one day's food supply on our sled, I climbed a small moundlike islet to look for seals. It was not difficult to find them. Three or four were out basking on the ice. Turning my glasses eastward to the Prince Patrick mainland, I saw a small heap that had a slightly artificial look about it. Crossing over to this, I found what had evidently once been a pile of gravel with a column of stones on top. Buried in the heap was a papier-mâché cylinder in which there was a rolled piece of paper bearing a partly printed, partly handwritten message signed "F. L. McClintock." The date it bore was "15 June, P.M." Sixty-two years ago to the day, McClintock had sat where I now huddled over the message he had written, telling of his fruitless search for traces of the lost Franklin Expedition.

The day before I found McClintock's cylinder, I left a message in a cairn on a small island a few miles to the south. Forty-six years later, in 1961, my message was picked up by a Canadian team of surveyors. It seems curious to me that tiny messages, a few inches long when rolled, can be found so easily in the vast expanse of the Arctic while a great expedition like Sir John Franklin's, with two ships and more than a hundred men, can be almost completely lost.

21 New Land and Old Troubles

June 15, 1915, a memorable day for us in the Arctic, was elsewhere the day on which a Mixed Claims Commission found Germany guilty of blowing up Black Tom Island in New York harbor, thus drawing the United States a little closer to the brink of a war of which we knew nothing. We did not even know of the sinking of the *Lusitania,* four months after the sinking of the *Karluk.*

On June 17, as we faced the unknown north from our camp off the shore of Prince Patrick Island, nothing seemed so important as what lay before us. We had found no new land to the west, and our soundings gave us some reason to believe that none existed there. If any was to be found it must be to the northeast, where no man, unless he was an Eskimo, had yet set foot. I sent the men and dogs ahead and went back to Cape McClintock, rebuilt the cairn there, and placed a record of our own in it. When I had done this I started north, a little east of the course of the dog team, and headed for some small islands that McClintock had seen and named Polynia Islands, perhaps having seen in the sky what he believed to be a reflection of open water. Beyond these islands I could see only the gravel reefs that McClintock had mentioned and which were shown on our chart.

I had made about fifteen miles when I caught sight of my companions making camp about five miles north of me. Climbing a small gravel mound, I surveyed the horizon all about, as anyone living by hunting would naturally do. To the north I could see no sign of land. Our camp was between me and the northern horizon. I could not see Andreasen or Thomsen, but as I swung my glasses a little to the

west I could see Storkerson climbing an ice hummock. He sat down
on the hummock, carefully wiped the lenses of his glasses, rested
his elbows on his knees, and began scanning the northern horizon.
I felt, as I watched him through my own binoculars, that I could tell
what he was seeing or not seeing. At first, to the northwest, it was
obvious that he saw nothing. He swung to the north and showed no
animation. Still nothing. The day was clear, the sky overhead strati-
fied with dark and light clouds, suggesting the water and ice that lay
beneath them. I was aware of the passage and occasional cry of sea
birds, but I did not take my eyes from Storkerson. His movements
were almost imperceptible, but as he swung his glasses into the
northeast and then moved them toward the east I got the impression that he was following something lying along the horizon
which he, having five miles advantage, could see but I could not.
Without taking the glasses from his eyes, he motioned with one
arm, and I realized that he was shouting to the men in the camp
below him.

Andreasen came scrambling out of the tent and Charlie Thomsen stopped feeding the dogs. Both stared at Storkerson. Suddenly
they started running toward him. Whatever he saw was important,
much more important, I was sure, than the gravel islands we had
been seeing. I did not dare, as I hurried toward the camp, believe
that it could be what I hoped. When I neared the camp, following
the sled trail, Storkerson came to meet me and told me what he
thought he had seen. Beyond him, I saw that Ole and Charlie had
opened up the sled loads that had been tied up for the night. Whatever Storkerson had seen had set off in these Norwegians an impulse
to celebrate.

Still prepared to believe that what had appeared on the horizon was a mirage, I climbed the hummock and, trying not to appear
as excited as the others were, fixed my glasses on the northeastern
horizon. In the tent below, Ole was jubilantly mixing biscuit crumbs,
scraped and shaken from a now empty package, with malted milk.
There was no mistaking what I saw. It was land—new, uncharted
land, stretching blue and white and tawny gray from northeast to
east by north.

I climbed down from the hummock, and we drank our crumby
malted milk, which was celebrative, not because it was better than
the seal meat we had been eating, but because it was different.
Privately, I got additional pleasure from the ceremony because I

was glad to see the stuff used up. It always made me nervous to hoard food.

We slept badly, being excited, and the next day started for our landfall. Seven and a half miles from camp we came to another small gravel island, which I judged to be about five miles from the new land. I climbed a hillock and tried to get a better view of our discovery, but fog had settled down and I could see nothing. We decided to wait where we were in the hope of getting a shot at the sun and locating our position exactly, but visibility on the nineteenth was as bad as it had been the afternoon before. Our travel time was getting short and we had to get back to Cape Kellett for a number of reasons. I decided that our compass bearings and the sights we had taken at Cape McClintock would have to do.

On June 20 we landed on the unknown coast of what we were to name Brock Island after the Chief of the Canadian Geological Survey. The land sloped upward from the coast, and we could see mountains in the distance. One of these I at first thought was a pressure ridge on sea ice beyond our island. When I decided that it was a mountain, I supposed it to be only six or seven miles away. It proved, when I set out to climb it, to be twenty miles distant, and I reached it too late to get the further view northward I had hoped for. After a brief glimpse of blue mountains stretching away into the distance in ever-higher ranges, the clouds shut in and I had to return to camp, where I found the men about to hitch up the dogs and start a search for me.

We did get a long enough, though hazy, view of the sun to determine the new island's position, but we could not wait to determine its extent. We did not find out until much later that what we had discovered was really two islands, the second, on which was located the mountain I had climbed, being much larger than the first. The nature of the ice that I had crossed to reach the second had not clearly indicated that it was sea ice. We named the farther land Borden Island, after Sir Robert Borden, the Canadian Prime Minister.

On the evening of June 22 we started south, not at all sure that the ice would hold out until we were able to cross McClure Strait to Banks Island. The journey southward along the coast of Melville Island had its difficulties, not the least of which resulted from the rotting of our dog harness. We made good progress, however, and left the southwestern corner of Melville on July 7. The ice in McClure Strait was still crossable although it was badly cut up and covered with water, through which the dogs sometimes had to swim. We hit the Banks Island shore at Mercy Bay, where Mc-Clure in the *Investigator* had spent two winters after his discovery of the bay in 1851.

During the twenty days following our landing, we made the first recorded crossing of Banks Island, reaching our base at Cape Kellett on August 19. We had been gone for six months and had suffered no real hardship, although I had had one unpleasant experience with an Eskimo family.

About halfway between Mercy Bay and Kellett, we had come upon the family in a hunting camp. They told us that Wilkins had been seen on his way to Coronation Gulf in the spring. During our stop Kullak, the husband, gave me a pair of sealskin slippers, saying that his wife was going to have a child in a few days and that he wished me to see that she had no difficulty. Further, he wanted me to see that the child would be a boy. This put me in a difficult position. If I refused the slippers, I should be regarded as showing ill will toward Kullak and his family. If I accepted them and anything went wrong with the birth, I would be held responsible. To accept the slippers, which I had to do, was in effect to bet against unknown odds that a boy would be safely delivered by Kullak's wife, Neriyok.

Some months later I learned that Neriyok had still not had her child. I realized then that she probably had been suffering from some pathological condition, and that my unintentional bet had been lost. Still later, I learned that although the child had been due in August, 1915, it was actually born dead in January, 1916, and that poor Neriyok did not survive the ordeal. Kullak charged me, as I had been sure he would, with murder, but suggested that I might atone for the deed by giving him a rifle. I did not approve of giving rifles to primitive Eskimos, who had proved able to live without them, knowing that to do so would be to reduce the number of caribou too rapidly. Kullak, angered, took a rifle from us by force. His fellow Eskimos, not wanting trouble, paid for the rifle with a dog, an act that caused Kullak to consider that his murder charge against me was still open. He never got around to killing me or any of my companions, however, perhaps because the other members of his tribe told him quite firmly that if he did they would make things very unpleasant for him.

The Kullak episode, as I look back on it, caused me more worry than I had ever felt over possible lack of food or any other of the supposed dangers of the Arctic.

Our arrival at Cape Kellett in August, 1915, marked a turning point in the expedition's fortunes. Confident that Wilkins had reached the mainland, I was sure that he would sooner or later come sailing up the Banks coast in the *North Star*. I hoped also, since the season seemed fairly open, that a whaler or two might reach Kellett and give me a chance to strengthen our outfit by trading. Meanwhile, everything at the base was in good shape. The men had collected food and driftwood and had even purchased a number of ethnological specimens from the Eskimos. The women, Mrs. Storkerson and Mrs. Thomsen, had been busy making clothing and boots, and a new sod house had been built.

My intention to wait at Kellett for Wilkins and the *North Star* was shattered by an important yet almost ludicrous event. A little before four o'clock one afternoon I saw a schooner coming in from the southeast and heading for the cape proper, which was a few miles from our camp. I thought at first that it was the *North Star*, but a good look through my binoculars showed it to be the *Polar Bear* of Captain Louis Lane.

I walked along the shore to meet the ship. Half a mile out she hove to and lowered a whaleboat. In it, as I approached, I recognized Captain Lane, Constable Jack Parsons of the Herschel Island police, and Herman Kilian, the ship's engineer. Presently, I could hear the men in the boat discussing my identity. "He's not an Eskimo," said one. "He's got field glasses." Then I heard Parsons: "That's Stefansson!" To which Captain Lane replied, "Don't you ever think it! The fish ate him long ago." A few yards from shore my identification was finally agreed upon, and Lane shouted an order: "Don't a damn one of you move till I shake hands with him!"

The boat touched the beach, and Captain Lane jumped out, showing all the enthusiasm of the heroic and successful rescuer. Starvation being the first thought of so many men in the Arctic, he could think of nothing better to do than immediately offer me food. As with Captain Bernard and my earlier "rescuers," I was hungrier for news than for food, but in the end I diplomatically settled for a can of corn, which was quickly opened for me.

Once again, it appeared, I was to be "rescued," along with any "survivors" of the *Mary Sachs* who still existed, for it seemed that Captain Lane and his party all believed that the *Sachs* had been wrecked in the course of her search for me.

I was unable to get any firsthand news of Wilkins and the *North Star* from Lane, but we now had our first account of the sinking of the *Karluk*. Not all of her crew had been rescued from Wrangel Island, Lane told us. Some of the men had died there, while others had become separated from the main party and were lost. Of those who had finally been rescued, several, we were told, had gone to the war. When we slowly came to realize that the repeated references to "the war" meant something more than the continuation of fighting in the Balkans, there was more astonishment from the *Polar Bear's* men. At first they had found it hard enough to believe that I was not dead; now it was almost too much for them to accept the fact that none of us knew anything of the World War, which had been going on for a year.

I gathered from Captain Lane that Anderson had not made public my message of instruction to him in which I had said that I did not intend to return to Alaska but planned to reach Banks Island and carry on my work from there. Since he had not, everyone supposed that I would have returned to Alaska had I not been kept by the accident of death from doing so. This supposition, which Anderson did nothing to correct, led Ottawa to cease communicating with me.

It was plain to me that I had to go to Herschel Island to straighten things out and get supplies, additional personnel, and vessels for the program of unfinished work that I had discussed with Wilkins before sending him south in the spring. For this purpose I persuaded Captain Lane to let me have the *Polar Bear* on charter.

When the *Polar Bear* reached Herschel Island, I had to go through the experience of returning from the dead all over again, without much heart for the ordeal, I must say. Things were in such a state of confusion that it was difficult to concentrate on what I must do. Neither Wilkins nor Anderson were at Herschel. Time was passing, and the period in which it would be possible to get back north and establish the bases for a continuation of our exploration of the northern islands and the sea to the north and west of them was growing shorter.

Since I was presumed to be dead, there were no orders for me to proceed with my work. There had been, I found, instructions from Ottawa for the southern section of the expedition to close up its work and, after sending vessels north to do what could be done to learn the exact nature of my fate, come home in the summer of the following year, 1916. In spite of lack of renewed authority, I decided that, since I was not dead, Ottawa would, if the facts were known, approve of my course.

I accordingly bought the *Polar Bear,* which on a charter basis was costing too much money, gathered together the necessary personnel and equipment, and, after leaving a message for Wilkins, headed north again. As the ice had closed in on the west coast of Banks, we tried to penetrate Prince of Wales Strait on the east side, hoping to reach Melville Island. We got no farther than Armstrong Point, about two-thirds of the way up Prince of Wales Strait. Wilkins, as I learned later, had with great courage and skill been able to get the *North Star* to the northern side of Banks Island, some twenty miles beyond Cape Alfred. We now had three bases— Cape Kellett, Armstrong Point, and the *North Star*—not all where we wanted them, yet near enough to the ideal to enable us to carry out our work.

If I were to be asked what I consider next in importance in arctic exploration to living off the land—which, in that winter of 1915–1916, was no longer in the experimental stage for us—I should say that it would be the ability to adapt to changed conditions. In the Arctic, plans very seldom work out exactly. The disappearance of the *Karluk* had changed mine once; Anderson's failure to permit my later orders to be carried out had changed them again. Yet here we were with our program intact, though the means of carrying it out had called for a lot of new thinking. There is never, in polar work, only one way of doing a thing. It was our firm belief in this principle that made the remaining years of our expedition successful.

22 *Triumph and Tragedy*

Our plans for further exploration of the northern islands and the unknown sea to the north of them depended on several factors, chiefly the division of our northern party into four sections, two exploring parties—one led by me and one by Storkerson—and two parties to maintain bases.

I sent to the *North Star* for Wilkins and discussed our project with him. He wanted to leave us and go outside for both family and military reasons. His father was dying and his country, Australia, was at war. Moreover, he had been originally taken on as a contract photographer, and there were no longer any supplies or equipment for photography.

We agreed that Wilkins would go to our Victoria Island base (Armstrong Point) and determine the state of mind of Captain Gonzales, now master of the *Polar Bear*. If he felt that the captain would make a determined effort to get the *Bear* north and establish a base at Liddon Gulf (Melville Island) in the spring of 1917, Wilkins would be free to leave. If he questioned Gonzales' intentions, he was to take command of the *Bear* and bring her north himself. Captain Joseph Bernard was to remain at Cape Kellett, look after the base there, and try to repair the *Mary Sachs* and get her into the water by August, 1917, by which time we should have returned from our northern work and be ready to head for home.

We decided to use the *North Star* on the northwest corner of Banks Island as an outfitting base and then abandon it, as we could not spare anyone to maintain it. A proposed surveying trip along the northeast coast of Victoria Island to be led by Storkerson would be outfitted there, as Wilkins would be for his journey southeast to the *Polar Bear*, and my party for the exploration of our newly discovered land and the sea north of it.

Things did not go as smoothly as I had hoped they would. They seldom do when many persons and unpredictable conditions are involved. Storkerson, coming from the *Bear*, had trouble with Captain Gonzales, who did not know how to take care of himself in winter and had to be carried back to the *Bear* in a sledge instead of acting as an escort for Storkerson. This delayed Storkerson's arrival at the north side of Banks Island, where we had agreed to meet him.

At Mercy Bay, in the center of the north coast of Banks, where we traveled in the hope of learning something of Storkerson, we found a note from him. He explained the delay and said that since he had lost so much time he had decided to go north and survey the new land instead of heading for the northeastern part of Victoria. It had been my plan to visit the *Bear*, but I now decided to head for Melville Island to join Storkerson. I hoped to catch up with him in the neighborhood of Liddon Gulf, where he said he was going.

I set out across McClure Strait with four companions, two of whom had recently joined the expedition—Harold Noice and Erol Lorne Knight, of whom much will be heard later. The other two were Charlie Thomsen and Emiu, our high-speed Eskimo dog driver whose celerity had earned him the name "Split-the-Wind."

Shortly after leaving Banks Island I had the only crippling accident of my arctic career. I went through a heavily crusted bit of ice and sprained my ankle. At first I thought little of the accident, but I soon found that I could not travel on foot. Since riding in a sled would slow us down and we would not be likely to catch Storkerson, I sent Emiu with his fast dogs on ahead to tell Storkerson, who would have passed Liddon Gulf by that time, to wait for us at Cape Murray, the place where we had made our landfall on Brock Island the year before.

My ankle did not improve much and travel was painful and slow, but we reached Cape Murray by May 3. Here I rested for three days and did a little rearranging of plans. It is wise in arctic travel never to let yourself reach the point of having only one string to your bow.

I sent Storkerson back to the *Bear* with positive instructions to the effect that, if Gonzales could not get the *Bear* north to Liddon Gulf, he was under no circumstances to go any farther south than her present position. On the way Storkerson was to stop at Liddon Gulf and then choose a site for quarters for the winter of 1916–1917. This done, he was to proceed to the *Bear,* pick up his family, and return to Liddon Gulf to supervise the hunt for winter meat. I asked Charlie Thomsen to go with Storkerson, but he would not unless he were allowed to return to Cape Kellett and bring his family back to Liddon Gulf. It was agreed that he should do this and carry with him the zoological specimens that Wilkins had been collecting. I had told Captain Bernard, before leaving Kellett, that he was not to leave that base even if mail or supplies for us should be delivered to Kellett by ship. Thomsen would therefore return to Liddon with his family as soon as he could get them ready. Charlie would have done better to have remained with us. I did not learn of the tragic end of his journey until the summer of 1917.

My ankle mended very slowly. After Storkerson and Charlie Thomsen had left, I sent Harold Noice, Aarnout Castel, and Karsten (Charlie) Andersen to begin the survey of the new land, the shape and extent of which we still did not know. Emiu and I set out a few days later.

While we were at Cape Murray we discovered that it was on a relatively small island some twenty or thirty miles across that lay, like a star in the sickle of the moon, in the mouth of a bay in what we then supposed to be a much larger island. The Leffingwell Crags, which I had climbed the year before, were on this larger island. After making as complete a survey of this land as was possible, I sent Castel, Noice, and Charlie Andersen on ahead.

Some sixty miles northwest of the larger island (Borden) lay an island known as Ellef Ringnes, which had been discovered some years before. At what was indicated on the charts as the northern tip of this island was a promontory known as Cape Isachsen, after Gunnar Isachsen, second-in-command of Otto Sverdrup's expedition, which discovered it in 1901. I instructed Castel and Noice to head for this cape, take observations, and leave a record, returning to Melville Island not later than July in the event that I was not able to join them.

In spite of the fact that, walking with some difficulty on snowshoes I fell fourteen feet into a crevasse, broke one snowshoe, bruised my hip, and did my bad ankle no good, and in spite of the fact that Cape Isachsen turned out not to be where the charts said it was, Emiu and I reached it before Castel's party did.

The shake-up from my fall and the persistent pain in my ankle had made me unusually peevish, and I was in no condition to appreciate Castel's and Noice's constant references to the deliciousness of food we did not have, in this case sardines and potatoes. Perhaps unjustly, I decided that for the time being I wanted no more of such talk. I ordered Castel and Emiu to go back to Melville Island, something I had intended doing myself. On the way they were to leave a cache of some items we would not need until winter on King Christian Island, which, according to the chart, lay a little to the east of a direct route from Isachsen to Melville. They were to instruct Storkerson to establish a base at Cape Murray as well as on Melville Island. I knew that Noice, without Castel, would not harp on the subject of sardines. This knowledge, and the consciousness that my ankle was really mending, brought me back to an even keel.

Castel and Emiu left for the south on June 4. Noice, Charlie Andersen and I headed north into the unknown region between Cape Isachsen and Axel Heiberg Island, which lay one hundred and twenty-five miles to the northwest.

Soundings and observed currents made us feel that we were approaching land when we were barely twenty miles from Isachsen. On June 12, Noice claimed that he could see land from a pressure ridge near our camp. Five miles farther on, land was unmistakably visible where no land appeared on the chart. On June 14 we camped on sea ice a hundred yards from the new land. It was like no land I had ever seen before, very high, snow-covered, and smooth with a peculiar oval skyline. Going ashore, Noice went inland and Charlie followed the shore. I remained on the beach taking observations and watching the birds, which were many and varied.

This island, which I called Meighen Island after Sir Arthur Meighen, later Prime Minister of Canada, was obviously quite recently formed. It was composed of gravel and erratic boulders, with no visible native rock. We found seashells some distance inland, quite far above the present sea level.

In eleven days we traversed the entire north, east, and west coasts. After this we set out to the south for Amund Ringnes Island, intending to cross the Danish Strait on our way to the land puzzlingly referred to as both King Christian Island and Findlay

Island. We found King Christian to be a very small island, smaller than Brock, and Findlay to be a group of three tiny ones nearly fifty miles south and west of it. Not unnaturally, we found no cache left by Castel. The spot at which he had been instructed to leave it did not exist.

What we did find, after twenty-five or thirty miles of westward travel over the worst slush ice I have ever seen, was a new, uncharted island some fifty miles long from north to south. This, which is now on the maps as Lougheed Island, was an arctic paradise, full of game and certainly capable of sustaining human life for a long time. From its central elevation we could see little King Christian Island, Ellef Ringnes to the northeast, Bathurst Island to the southeast, and our Borden Island to the northwest. We explored Lougheed as thoroughly as we could and on September 9 left, over exasperatingly bad ice, for Borden and Brock islands. On the fifteenth we reached Borden but found no indications of any attempt to bring supplies up from Melville. Without these it would be impossible to maintain a winter base at Cape Murray. We accordingly, somewhat depressed by this failure to carry out our instructions, left for Melville Island, reaching it on October 2.

At Cape Grassy, which is part way down the mouth of Hecla and Griper Bay, we found Natkusiak, the hunter, and several others on their way to Cape Murray. After much difficulty with overloaded sleds, one of which was wrecked, we were forced to make a winter camp at Cape Grassy. There was no news of the *Polar Bear*. We spent a rather rough winter ferrying meat from Winter Harbour, on the south coast, to Cape Grassy, while the Eskimo women at the harbour worked on clothing for the coming year.

It later appeared that, in spite of my instructions, Captain Gonzales had taken the *Polar Bear* south to Walker Bay on the east coast of Victoria Island, where she was of no use to us. Gonzales, anxious to save face, came by sled to see us in the last week of February, 1917. We learned from him that mail and supplies had arrived at Cape Kellett and that Charlie Thomsen had not left Kellett as he had been instructed to do. We sent the women and children back to the *Bear* with Gonzales and his people and turned again to the serious business of exploration.

Storkerson set out for his postponed exploration of the northeast part of Victoria Island and on April 12, I and my companions —Noice, Lorne Knight, and Emiu—started north again. As we proceeded over the ice of Hazen Strait and along the east coast of Borden Island, I discovered that Noice and Knight had joined the ranks of those who considered it unnecessary to obey orders. In winter quarters they had eaten only canned groceries and avoided underdone meat, with the result that they now developed symptoms of scurvy. This disobedience fortunately did not kill them, but it cut short our trip beyond the limits of discovered territory. At something short of 82° N, on April 26, it became obvious that we must turn back. Ice conditions now, however, were so bad that we could not return to Borden but had to head for Cape Isachsen instead.

On May 11 we reached the cape and set up what was named, appropriately enough, "Camp Hospital." Here we remained while I hunted caribou with gratifying success. The fresh meat soon had the two invalids on the mend. It was not many days before they were able to travel. We crossed Lougheed Island for the second time, finding plenty of food and available native coal.

The only difficulties resulted from a fall into an ice crevice while I was stalking a seal—a fall that came near to drowning me— and from our favorite dog Sapsuk's brush with a polar bear. Poor Sapsuk came out of the encounter with a bruised spine, which paralyzed his hind legs. We gave him the tenderest care, bundling him up on the sled and feeding him carefully, and he made what seemed like an impossible recovery, eventually being able to walk. He did not, however, regain sufficient strength to run with the other dogs. Had he done so, or remained unable to stand up, he might have lived. As it happened, he was left behind in camp when we went off hunting one day, and Emiu realized, too late, that he had left on the ground a greasy rag, which poor Sapsuk could not know was not the nourishing fat that it smelled like.

Emiu hurried back to camp, but Sapsuk had swallowed the rag. We did what we could to work it out of him, but did not succeed in doing so. Sapsuk did not suffer at first but in a day or so was in agony. I found his suffering too hard to take. Somewhat shamefacedly, I went off by myself, knowing that one of the boys would do the right thing to put poor Sapsuk out of his misery. When I returned, Sapsuk was gone, and there was a silence in camp for some time.

I reached Cape Kellett in mid-August, having gone on ahead of the others, walking steadily for more than twenty-four hours. I expected that the *Mary Sachs* would have been repaired and now be in the water, ready to go, and that the *Polar Bear* would have joined her there, ready to carry our now concluded expedition to the mainland and home. I did not want to risk having the un-reliable Gonzales decide that I had been lost on the ice and that he had better get out before he was forced to spend another winter on the islands.

What I found was more appalling than anything I had yet experienced : Gonzales had indeed been to Kellett and gone. He had found the *Mary Sachs* repaired and in the water but her captain, Joseph Bernard, was not with her. Bernard, I learned, had felt that circumstances made it advisable for him to disobey my orders for-bidding him to bring mail or supplies to Melville Island. He and Charlie Thomsen had set out with impossibly heavy loads, follow-ing the Banks Island coast north and west with increasing difficulty. For some reason, before reaching Mercy Bay the two had turned back. A party, alarmed by their failure to reach Melville, began a search along the north coast of Banks. At one point the searchers surprised a fox digging in the snow. They dug where the fox had been digging and found what they took to be a slab of salt pork. It was not. It was Charlie Thomsen's naked shoulder. They buried Charlie and set out in search of Captain Bernard, following occasional sled tracks until they finally lost them.

Neither Captain Bernard nor his load of mail was ever found.

As if this tragedy, poignant in its pointlessness, were not enough, I found that Gonzales had sailed away in the *Bear* after dismantling the *Mary Sachs* and leaving her a wreck in the hands of two men who wished to spend the winter trapping in Banks Island.

I and my three companions were left with no means of getting to the mainland until the Amundsen Gulf froze over in the coming winter. To cross the gulf would require sleds, and ours had been left at the northeast end of the island. It would take two months to go and get them.

The unexpected arrival of a strange ship made this trip un-necessary. The *Challenge,* under Captain Leo Wittenberg, with the former engineer of the *Mary Sachs,* J. R. Crawford, arrived at Kellett on August 26. Though she was not worth it, I bought her from Wittenberg for six thousand dollars, with the goods that had been left at Kellett thrown in for good measure.

The weirdness of the close of my expedition was made still

more weird by the fact that on our way south in the *Challenge*, as a result of a change in course necessitated by bad ice, we met and hailed the *Polar Bear*. Gonzales did not, of course, know that I was aboard the *Challenge*, but he stopped and both vessels made fast to the ice. Gonzales, told that I was present, came aboard and made a long-winded, thoroughly evasive, yet apparently plausible explanation of his implausible conduct. I took command of the *Bear* and we sailed her to Cape Bathurst, where I took great pleasure in leaving Captain Gonzales. The Eskimo families also went ashore there. The rest of us sailed west. Our great venture was over, though there was unexpected trouble ahead.

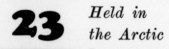

23 *Held in the Arctic*

It was now my intention to go home, report on our work of the last few years, and then return with several men for a project as interesting and ambitious as anything I had yet attempted. This would involve going north over the ice by sled—a journey we had already proved feasible—and establishing a camp on a suitable ice floe. Once we were settled on the ice, it was my intention to drift with the floe, spending at least one and if necessary two winters on it, living on seals and polar bears, taking soundings, and making other observations. We would be much freer than a party on a ship frozen into the ice would be, since we could move whenever we wanted to, come ashore if we had to, and get closer to the center of whatever mass of drifting ice there might be in the region north of the known currents by which Nansen in the *Fram,* De Long in the *Jeannette,* and Bartlett in the *Karluk* had been carried.

On September 13, 1917, on our way toward Nome, we arrived at the excellent harbor at the eastern end of Barter Island, a little west of the boundary between Canada and Alaska. Since the night promised to be stormy and dark, it seemed advisable to tie up for the six or eight hours of darkness and set out again early in the morning.

The wind blew hard all night from the northeast, but toward dawn shifted to the southwest without slackening. The *Bear,* without any of her crew noticing it, began to drag her anchor. Before we could do anything to save her, she struck a sand bar stern first and then swung around broadside to it and heeled over. When the gale blew out, we found ourselves high and dry. It might be weeks at this time of year before conditions would be right to get the ship afloat. It was obvious that, if we had to wait any considerable time, we should not reach the Pacific before freeze-up.

It did not take us long to work out new plans. Instead of sitting out the winter on the stranded ship, we would prepare for our proposed ice trip. We had, it is true, disposed of all of our dogs and most of our equipment, but I felt sure that we could buy enough of the dogs back to make the journey and that we could probably pick up adequate sleds and supplies.

Storkerson and I went off in different directions to make the necessary purchases and arrangements. Our hopes were high when, just after New Year's Day, 1918, we had completed all our purchases and had engaged Eskimos to help us through the early stages of our journey over the rough shore ice.

I had gone east to visit Herschel Island and then Shingle Point, and was on my way back to Herschel when I began to feel ill. In fact, I have never felt worse. Although I had no thermometer with me, I knew I had a high fever. I could not imagine what the matter was. An Eskimo at whose house I stopped wrapped me in blankets and carried me in his sledge to Herschel, where the two police constables Brockie and Lamont took me in. I was bathed, put to bed, and treated as a very sick man, which I certainly was.

No one, except possibly Henry Fry, the missionary at Herschel, realized in the early stages of it how serious my illness was. I myself expected every day that I would be out of bed the next. The days became weeks, I began to worry. It did not occur to me that I would not be able to make the ice trip, but only that the start of it was now going to be delayed until the temperature would no longer be as low as it should be for the best progress over moving ice. I sent for Storkerson and conferred with him about the change in plans necessitated by the delay.

Two weeks after our talk, I began what looked like a gradual recovery, hastened, I believe, by generous meals of the most substantial food. Feeling certain now that in four or five days I would be able to leave Herschel Island, I sent Storkerson off westward to get everything ready. A few hours after he left, I was taken with violent chills and a new fever. It was only at this point that everyone began to realize the seriousness of the situation, partly because Constable

Lamont had also become ill and his symptoms were similar to mine.

It was now Fry's opinion that I had had typhoid fever. When my friends thought of what they had been letting me eat, they were shocked and alarmed. During the first period of high fever I had been without appetite, but as soon as the fever dropped to 100°, I had begun to eat steaks and fried potatoes or whatever else the police were having for their meals. An hour before my sudden relapse, I had eaten a large meal of macaroni and cheese. There were some who believed that this heavy food was responsible. The relapse, they felt, served me right. What else could have been expected of a sick man who ate macaroni and cheese!

Anyone suffering severe illness in the far north does so under unusual conditions. This is the case even in an outpost of civilization like Herschel Island. My treatment had been in many ways opposite to the orthodox way of handling typhoid. Because no one had recognized my illness, I had mercifully escaped the starvation and milk-diet treatments prescribed by the home medical books available on Herschel Island. Constable Lamont's case was handled according to those antiquated ideas. He grew steadily worse, and just when I was lowest with the pneumonia that followed my typhoid, he died in his room across the hall from me. An Eskimo, apparently taken with the same illness and treated by the missionary as Lamont had been, died at about the same time.

Someone now started the rumor that what I and the two dead men had had was not typhoid but the much more serious typhus. This idea was the cause of a heroic effort to disinfect the police barracks with sulfur fumes. The door of my room was closed, and it was supposed that the fumes would not find their way in. Nevertheless, I was disturbed by the prospect of the fumigation. There was an Athapaska teen-ager waiting on me, and I asked him to keep my door and another door leading from a hallway to the outside open all night. Had this been done, nothing serious would have happened, but the Indian had not appreciated my reasons for wanting the circulation of air. Feeling that it was getting pretty cold in the barracks, he closed the outer door.

I awoke with my room full of sulfur smoke and had just strength enough to attract attention. Although the window of my room was quickly thrown open, the effect of the sulfur upon me was not beneficial. I commenced bleeding from the lungs, which may have been the result of the gas or possibly only a symptom of pneumonia. The bleeding lasted for several hours, and I had two or three relapses during the next weeks.

It was now decided to move me out of the police barracks to a separate building. Leo Wittenberg, one of the men who had been at Cape Kellett the year before, volunteered to nurse me. For the next several weeks he and the Indian boy were my attendants.

My convalescence was not going well. When it was decided that I must have had typhoid, I was put on the orthodox typhoid diet. Nothing but tinned and Argentinian powdered milk was available. My belief was that if I was allowed to eat the hearty foods for which I hungered I would probably have a better chance of getting well, and I used to reason elaborately and, it seemed to me, convincingly that I should be allowed a chance at a square meal. Arguments that seemed lucid to me were, unfortunately, considered the cunning of delirium.

I had been through pneumonia. Now I came down with pleurisy. I realized that even if I were to recover, I was in for weeks, perhaps months, of illness. I therefore sent a message to Storkerson directing him to take command of the spring exploratory operations and to undertake on his own the ice drift we had planned together.

Storkerson and most of our able men and all our dogs were off on the ice by the time I began to feel that my one hope of surviving was to get to the hospital at Fort Yukon. This, the most northerly hospital in North America, was about four hundred traveling miles south of Herschel Island. I felt that riding in a sled in the open air might not hurt me and that there was at least a chance of winning through.

Fry had told me that he was expecting his superior, Archdeacon Hudson Stuck, to arrive at Herschel in April. I hoped that he would not be delayed, for I felt sure that the archdeacon would take charge of my transfer to the hospital.

My condition kept growing worse. Finally, everyone agreed that I was going to die. At that point Police Inspector Phillips took the position that, if I were going to die, I might as well die as I wanted: in an effort to get to Fort Yukon. This did not meet the views of some of the others. There was at Herschel Island a very respectable graveyard where whalers and other white men had been buried with supposedly civilized pomp and circumstance. I felt sure that, if I died, there would be a thoroughly orthodox funeral. However, I preferred to die elsewhere and, if possible, later.

It was in the first week of April, 1918, that I left Herschel Island in a sled equipped with springs from an old cot. Constable Brockie, Henry Fry, my Indian teen-ager, and two Eskimos accompanied me.

Fry, now that we were away from the settlement, was less inclined to insist on the orthodox liquid diet for a typhoid convalescent. I was allowed to eat one of my favorite foods, frozen raw fish. This seemed to do me good, and my second day out from Herschel saw me free of fever. It seemed unnecessary for Fry to continue with us. He said that, since I apparently got along better the more my conduct differed from what his medical books said it ought to be, I might as well take the entire responsibility for doing as I liked. Having come to this conclusion, he returned to his mission at Herschel Island.

From then on, my breakfasts and suppers consisted of caribou and fish, sometimes frozen and raw, sometimes cooked. I felt better each day and regained weight until finally, when we arrived at the mouth of the Old Crow River, at the trading post of Schultz and Johnson, I was no longer in real need of the expert care that I could get from Mrs. Schultz, who before her marriage had been a trained nurse at Fort Yukon. While I did not need the care, I shall never forget the kindness of Mrs. Schultz and her husband.

Since it was now easy to engage local help, Constable Brockie and his men left me at this point, to carry back to Herschel Island my grateful thanks and the news of my recovery. I engaged a team and driver to take me on down to Rampart House, where I was welcomed even more warmly than I had been eleven years earlier when I had finished my raft journey down the Porcupine River. Dan Cadzow, who ran the place, told me that he had received news of my being ill at Herschel Island and had sent a messenger to the Fort Yukon hospital to notify Dr. Grafton Burke. Dr. Burke was now on his way to meet us. Hoping to cause the doctor as little trouble as possible, I did not linger at Rampart House but hurried on and met his party at Old Rampart, thirty miles downriver.

I at once had a foretaste of the comfortable time I was going to spend under Burke's care at Fort Yukon. One of my first questions was what I should eat and how much. His answer could not have been more satisfactory: "Eat whatever you like, as much as you can, and the oftener the better."

We were more than halfway from Old Rampart to Fort Yukon

on April 24 when Archdeacon Stuck and his mountaineer companion Walter Harper caught up with us. They had arrived at Herschel Island a few days after we left. On his way east along the coast from Point Barrow, the archdeacon had learned of my illness at Barter Island and had hurried on to Herschel with the intention of taking me to the Fort Yukon hospital. He had now come south by a different route and overtook us.

Three days later, when we arrived at St. Stephen's Hospital, Fort Yukon, I was so far recovered that I walked without assistance from the gate to the house. A month before, when I had been about to leave Herschel, Inspector Phillips had had to guide my hand as I made the penciled cross by which I agreed that if I died on the journey the responsibility would be my own. From the windows of my room in St. Stephen's I could look south across the Yukon River and across the Arctic Circle into the misnamed ''North Temperate Zone,'' which really is the least temperate of all the zones.

Thus, my polar expedition came to its end. From the isolation and peace of the north, I had come to a place that received a wireless news bulletin every day at noon. The Germans were smashing their way nearer to Paris every day, and their guns were shelling it. The electric sensory nerves of civilization had reached me in the far north, and I joined in the civilized world's breathless suspense. For good or ill, I was home after five years.

I spent three months at St. Stephen's, getting back my strength, a task in which I was very much helped by messages from Ottawa making it plain that the Deputy Minister of Naval Service, who was my immediate superior, approved and even applauded my conduct of the expedition during the years I had been out of touch with his office. He approved of the purchases I had made of vessels and equipment and of my disposition of them, and seemed particularly pleased that I had added new lands to the map of Canada.

During my convalescence I had plenty of leisure to think about my last five years in the Arctic. In conversations with Archdeacon Stuck, I learned that he and I had the same feeling about the average American's or Canadian's opinion of the north. The archdeacon had done a great deal of lecturing in the States in order to raise money for the Alaska Mission of the Protestant Episcopal Church. In these talks, being the forthright person that he was, he always minimized the northern winter cold, since it never bothered him, and stressed the summer heat and the mosquitoes, which did. No

matter how explicit he was in this, women would inevitably gather
around him after his lectures and say that they could not understand how he could endure the terrible cold of Fort Yukon.
"Madam," he would say to such a questioner, "we do *not* endure
the cold. We live in houses, we burn fuel, and when we go outdoors
we wear clothing."

I had time, too, while under the gracious care of the staff of
St. Stephen's, to consider my future. I was now nearly forty years
old. Up to this time I had always managed to get someone to pay
my way. I had gotten through the University of Iowa with a little
borrowing and a little teaching. At Harvard, I had waited on table
at Randall Hall and held small jobs in the Peabody Museum Library, although my chief support had come from my Divinity School
scholarship. When I had begun my career in the field, my expenses
had always been paid. After my first arctic trip I had started earning something by writing accounts of my work for magazines,
chiefly *Harper's*. After my second trip I had begun to get royalties
on my first book, *My Life with the Eskimo*.

Yet, I was now returning to civilization after the best part of
twelve years spent in the Arctic and was, as you might say, without
visible means of support. It seemed wise that I now turn to lecturing about my experiences. Ernest Shackleton had suggested to me
when I was in London in 1913 to make preparations for the Canadian Arctic Expedition that lecturing, under a good manager, was
the ideal avocation for an explorer. He had introduced me to his own
manager, Lee Keedick. The result was a contract for a series of
lectures after my return from the third expedition, which we then
supposed would be in 1916. Now it was 1918, and it seemed to me
that the interest created by my return was going to be overshadowed
by the impending close of the war. Nonetheless, I heard from Keedick while I was still in the hospital at Fort Yukon, and Desbarats
of the Canadian Naval Service, who still had the right to advise me
what to do, urged me to do what I could under Keedick's management to tell the public what our expedition had been like.

I left St. Stephen's Hospital in September and, after visiting
my family in North Dakota, went on to Ottawa to report. My first
lecture was scheduled for October 31 in New York City's Carnegie
Hall. I put up at the Harvard Club, where I was given a room in
which to meet the press. The reporters treated me very well, but I

was not entirely comfortable about the coming lecture, my first commercial venture on the platform.

My manager had seen to it that I had the right clothes, which included a white dress tie. At the last minute, while I was dressing, I realized that the clothes were so right that the tie that accompanied them was not the pre-tied kind, which could be put on and hooked at the back of the neck, like the collar of a fire-engine horse. What had been given me was the proper, nontied sort, which presupposes its wearer's possession of a wife, a valet, or skill at bow tying. I possessed none of these, and time was getting short. I hurried downstairs to consult the front desk. There was no time to buy a fake tie, so it was suggested that I canvass the club members who were in the house and find one who could help me. This I did, and fortunately found an old friend, Percy MacKaye—poet, actor, dramatist, and man of the world—a man who might very well have been born in a bow tie. Percy took care of me with a few nimble twists of his fingers and bundled me into a taxi in the nick of time.

Despite my apprehensions about the mood of the public, Carnegie Hall was filled. At first a little overawed, I gradually felt my way into the mind of the audience and was soon perfectly at ease, even able to handle and put down a bit of minor heckling. Isaiah Bowman, president of the American Geographical Society, was so pleased that he whispered to me after I sat down that he felt sure he would have no difficulty getting his board to give me the society's gold medal. I knew then that I was going to like lecturing.

24 *Honors and Lectures*

One of the most important occasions of my early days on the platform after my introduction to big-time lecturing at Carnegie Hall was my appearance at Massey Hall in Toronto on November 11, 1918. This was, in a sense, a report to the Canadian government and people on the expedition they had sponsored. It turned out to be a somewhat frantic competition between me and one of the great events of the twentieth century.

In Toronto, my host was the distinguished Canadian explorer, Dr. Joseph Burr Tyrrell, who lived some distance from the heart of the city. The Tyrrells and I—including a son who was the only licensed automobile driver in the family—spent a pleasant morning, which, however, went off like a skyrocket sometime before noon when the World War I armistice was announced. For a time, in the delirious excitement that prevailed, even I forgot the evening's lecture. Mrs. Tyrrell did not forget it for long, however. She assured me that her chauffeur-son, who had gone to town, would return in time to drive us to Massey Hall. She was overconfident. Conditions in the city were far more confused than we realized. No streetcars or buses were running, and although Mrs. Tyrrell tried to locate her son by telephone, none of his usual haunts answered. Needless to say, he did not appear at the house. Needless to say, also, we had to walk to the lecture, with the result that we arrived, somewhat blown, a half an hour late. Nobody seemed to mind, least of all my friend Sir Edmund Walker, president of the Canadian Bank of Commerce, who had helped to finance my first expedition on behalf of the University of Toronto. Sir Edmund, who was presiding, complimented us on our early arrival and seemed delighted that, under the circumstances, not more than two-thirds of those who had bought tickets failed to appear.

I talked against an accompaniment of whistles, bells, and shouting from outside, but the talk seemed to make an impression, though undoubtedly a slighter one than the armistice. This was my last lecture for some weeks because I had to spend considerable time concluding the expedition's affairs. This task included a trip back to the Navy Yard at Esquimalt, British Columbia, for a ceremonial paying off of the *Polar Bear's* crew, who, after disposing of the ship at Nome, had come south by commercial steamer.

When I paid off the men at Esquimalt I learned that on their way out they had heard some rumors, increasing as they got farther from the northern coast, to the effect that everyone, including the Herschel Island police, knew that we had made no long ice journeys and had discovered no new lands. The report was that we had remained in hiding in the Mackenzie delta area and bought from the civilized Eskimos in that region the seal and caribou meat that we claimed to have got by hunting.

I was deeply concerned at this time that these criticisms of the expedition and my conduct of it had found their way into the press. I should have preferred to ignore them, since it seemed impossible to get a sufficient number of members of the expedition together in Ottawa to give the kind of testimony in my behalf that would have made an impressive defense. The influenza epidemic that broke out after their return from the north had taken too many of them.

Now that many of the men who knew the falseness of these rumors were dead, I thought that it would be best to pay no attention to the slanderous stories. This was not so easy, and the Canadian government felt strongly that the charges should be answered, particularly in view of the fact that such an experienced and distinguished explorer as Roald Amundsen was joining in the chorus of dispraise.

Isaiah Bowman, as head of the American Geographical Society, told me that he thought that the best answer to all charges would be to elect me president of the Explorers Club, of which both Amundsen and Rudolph Anderson were members. Bowman knew that the board of directors of the Geographical Society was going to award me a gold medal. With the medal would go a citation, which would be worded in such a way as to serve as an answer to Amundsen's or anyone else's charges, though Amundsen, as I have said, did not put his charges in print until he published his autobiography in 1927. In this otherwise excellent book the explorer chose to refer to my account of the Copper Eskimos and of my method of traveling over ice as "harmful and dangerous nonsense."

On December 17, 1918, the American Geographical Society of New York gave me its gold medal, which bears the following inscription:

> *Vilhjalmur Stefansson*
> *1918*
> *He Learned the Way of Life of*
> *The Eskimo*
> *And in a Long and Hazardous Journey*
> *Discovered New Lands Beyond*
> *The Arctic Fringe of America*

With the medal came the citation complimenting me on doing the very things Amundsen said publicly that I could not have done.

Amundsen insisted that his reason for opposing me was that I was endangering the future of arctic exploration. The Geographical Society's award and my subsequent election to the presidency of the Explorers Club aroused him to renewed attack. In his campaign against me he had, perhaps without knowing it, the support of my former colleague Rudolph Martin Anderson. Anderson's attacks, which like Amundsen's were increased by the bestowal of honors upon me, were based on the belief that I was deceiving Canadians, in order to attract attention to myself, about the nature of their northern lands.

When Anderson heard that I was to be nominated for the presidency of the Explorers Club he wrote to Isaiah Bowman, secretary of the club, a something more than unfriendly letter conveying the idea that I was a complete charlatan and would soon be exposed as Dr. Cook had been. Anderson said—and in this he went further than Amundsen—that if I were elected president he wished to resign from the club. The board of directors had time to consider both Anderson's letter and Amundsen's charges before acting. Nevertheless, they rejected the charges and strongly supported me. I was duly elected president and Anderson's resignation was accepted.

This rebuff, however, did not keep him from continuing to try to make trouble, particularly between me and Captain Bartlett. I had sometimes questioned Bartlett's handling of the *Karluk* in the Beaufort Sea ice and had been puzzled by his decision to leave the *Karluk's* people on Wrangel Island after the ship was lost while he went ashore for help. I had not, however, criticized Bartlett publicly. Bowman did his best to keep Anderson from accomplishing his purpose. He wrote an identical letter to me and to Bartlett which, had there been any real hostility between us, would surely have suppressed it.

The Anderson-Amundsen attack upon me, although a handful of enemies kept it alive, did not have any effect upon my lecturing or upon the willingness of important societies such as the National Geographic and the Philadelphia Geographical Society to honor me. The National Geographic invited Admiral Peary and General Adolphus Greely, hero of one of the great arctic tragedies and holder, in 1882, of the farthest-north record, to be on the platform when Dr. Gilbert Grosvenor presented me with the society's Hubbard Medal. Admiral Peary, who was really too ill to have been present, made his last public address on that occasion, taking the opportunity to remind the audience that, using the methods I had evolved, I could have remained in the Arctic fifteen and a half years just as easily as five and a half.

In Philadelphia, I received the Elisha Kent Kane Medal, normally gold but this time, at my request, cast in bronze, the difference between the cost of the two medals being added to a fund gathered by the Explorers Club for the destitute mother of Henry Beuchat, who lost his life after the sinking of the *Karluk* in 1914.

After the Philadelphia award I set out on a lecture tour of one-night stands that carried me from Boston to Los Angeles, San Francisco, and Seattle. I have both a pleasant and an unpleasant reason for remembering the Boston lecture. Calvin Coolidge was Governor of Massachusetts at the time, very much in the public eye as a result of the Boston police strike. He was invited to be present at Tremont Temple. Unfortunately, both he and I were told to be on hand an hour too early. We both arrived at the appointed time but, there being no member of the committee present, had a hard time getting into the stage anteroom where we could sit down and wait. The Governor may have been displeased. He was certainly uncommunicative at the outset. Since I associated him—rather vaguely, I admit—with the police strike, I began to question him about it. This, apparently, was the right approach. From that moment until the committee members began to arrive, I could not get a word in edgewise. Later, when I heard Coolidge, as President, referred to as "Silent Cal," I supposed that the appellation was the result of the same quirk of human nature that impels men to call a fat man "Slim" or a tall man "Shorty."

My talk with Coolidge was a pleasant send-off for my lecture. The unpleasant incident that followed was one I could not have anticipated. It had been my custom to try to spice my talks with a sprinkling of something tart, usually by referring to a book about the north that seemed to me completely false. The book I chose for the Boston lecture was one that almost every child of the early 1900s will recall: *The Eskimo Twins.* I quoted from the book the author's reference to "the Great White World where the snow never melts." I assured the audience that there was fortunately no such place. I continued to make fun of the book while the audience applauded enthusiastically.

As I stepped down from the platform after the lecture, I saw approaching me a woman in tears, supported by several others who were attempting to quiet her. Oh-oh! I thought—the author of *The Eskimo Twins!* It was in fact the author's sister, who, as I later learned, had been telling her friends before the lecture how sorry she was that the author herself could not be at Tremont Temple that night to meet the distinguished explorer who had visited the very lands where the twins, Menie and Monnie, lived. From that moment, I gave up spoofing children's books about Eskimos.

I had a good time on this 1919 tour, meeting many charming and interesting people; but the succession of uneven audiences, sometimes good and sometimes poor, convinced me that Lee Keedick was not the best manager for me. He tried to persuade me to tell what he called "funny stories" and repeatedly urged me not to dwell so insistently on what a pleasant place the Arctic was. People wanted to hear about heroism, danger, and hardship, he claimed— not flowers, sunshine, and a surplus of food.

In Portland, Oregon, Roy Ellison of the Affiliated Lyceum and Chautauqua Association came to hear me talk. Afterward he told me about his organization, which had branches all over the West, Middle West, and Southwest. Ellison and his partner, C. H. White, offered me two thousand dollars a week over and above expenses, plus a companion who would take care of all the details of travel and booking. There would, moreover, be plenty of time in between trips for me to do my writing. This offer would net me three times as much as I was getting from Keedick.

I soon decided to write Keedick, asking him to sell my contract with him to the Affiliated Lyceum and Chautauqua Association. This he eventually agreed to do. I am happy to say that Affiliated paid him more for my contract than he had been getting out of me under its terms. This happy solution of my lecture problem, fantastic as it seemed both to me and to Keedick, was matched by another piece of good fortune.

It appeared that the Canadian Pacific Railway, which had sent a representative to my Carnegie Hall talk in the winter of 1918, saw in me a means of popularizing the northern lands that they owned and wished to develop. Canadian Pacific's representative, Max Enos, their public relations man, kept after me with an idea that from the first seemed interesting.

The Canadian government, as well as the railway's Department of Colonization and Development and my book and magazine publishers, agreed that it would be a good idea if I were to establish at Banff in the Canadian Rockies a sort of postexpedition headquarters. There, I and such members of the expedition staff as could be gathered together would have the peace and quiet necessary for concentration on writing about our accomplishments.

At Banff, the Canadian Pacific had a luxurious hotel surrounded by mountains and clear mountain air; the days were warm, the nights cool. The idea was that I, my secretaries, and my staff would have, somewhat removed from the hotel, a comfortable tent colony, with the privilege of using the hotel itself for important guests, conferences, and occasional meals.

I was apparently being offered this comparative paradise because I had pleased Colonel John S. Dennis, head of the Department of Colonization and Development, by introducing into my lecturing in the prairie states of the United States and the prairie provinces of Canada what he considered the best sales argument yet developed for Canadian prairie land. I had told wheat farmers about grain-killing midsummer frosts and how to avoid them: not by moving south to where the climate is warmer and the land prohibitively expensive but by moving north where farm land is cheap. People did not yet realize that by getting away from the midsummer night the farmer can make himself safe from that dreaded enemy of the wheat crop, the night frost.

The Canadian Pacific system of railways and steamship lines expected to profit by my ideas. It was the job of the Department of Colonization and Development to turn into ready dollars the latent resources of the millions of rich acres which the Canadian nation had presented to Lord Strathcona in the heyday of transcontinental railway building. I gathered that it was Colonel Dennis' job first to see that a stream of dollars poured into the company's treasury from farmers and others who bought the land and then to see to the development of each square mile sold. The land would be developed, according to its nature, into productive mines, forests, grasslands, and wheat fields. Trainloads of produce would then be shipped to the coastal cities and river ports of the United States and Canada, where their burdens of processed or half-processed wealth would be picked up by Canadian Pacific and other transoceanic liners bound for any market that existed in any part of the world.

It seems to me today that I got the best of the bargain when I accepted Canadian Pacific's offer and moved into Banff on August 11, 1919.

Somewhere between my last lecture stop and Banff, I lost the coat and vest of my evening clothes. Impressed with the notion that the Canadian Pacific Railway was a kind of Santa Claus, I tried to get them to arrange to have the new dress coat and waistcoat that I ordered from the United States admitted to Canada duty-free. In this I did not succeed.

I was to need the dress clothes often, however, for in spite of the tent-colony atmosphere there was a good deal of social activity. Almost immediately, I was interviewed by Cornelius Vanderbilt, Jr., and before I left both the Prince of Wales, later Edward VIII, and his brother, who became George VI, were visitors at Banff whom I very much enjoyed meeting.

There was work too. Immediately after my arrival I began to receive from Ottawa boxes of papers and other property pertinent to the expedition. The most important event of the first days in that delightful resort was the arrival of Storker Storkerson, who with all his men, dogs, and sledges had returned safely from an eight-month drift in the Beaufort Sea two hundred miles north of Alaska. Storkerson had now been ordered to report to me at my new headquarters. Ole Andreasen came with him.

Arctic
Journey

Below – The Leffingwell Crags

Facing page — My friend Storker T. Sorkerson
Below — Hanover, 1959

Chris Lund

Above — Copper Eskimos with bow-case and arrows
Below — The scientific staff of the Canadian Arctic Expedition

Department of Mines and Resources, Canada

Facing page — George H. Wilkins at Bernard Harbor

Above – The Klingenberg family
Below – Front row: Peary, Stefansson and Greely, and three members of

Harris & Ewing

ional Geographic Society. *Below* – A group of Copper Eskimos

Steaming up the Liard River rapids

Left – 1918: convalescing at Fort Yukon.   *Right* –   Charlie Brower – "T

g of Point Barrow"

Facing page – My wife, Evelyn, and I at our Vermont farm
Below – Ole Andreasen

W. Gibson

Margaret Bourke-White

Geological Survey, Ottawa, Canada

Making a boat-sledge

Getting ready to dine at the White House
with the King and Queen of Denmark

Owen Lattimore

25 *Orville Wright: A New Friend*

Storkerson's plan, as I have said, had been to test the ocean currents north of Alaska by living on the ice and drifting with it. There had been enough earlier evidence to make geographers and polar authorities believe that north of Alaska there was a strong current from east to west. It was supposed by those who believed that living on the ice by my methods was possible that Storkerson would ride the ice westward on a course roughly parallel with the coast of Siberia.

This did not prove to be the case. Storkerson and his men began their actual drift after reaching a point approximately 73° N latitude and 146° W longitude, which would be a little west of the Canadian-Alaskan line and some two hundred and seventy-five miles north of the coast. The drift from this point was not consistently east or west but resembled the travels of a leaf in an eddy. This unexpected behavior of the ice, apparently influenced more by wind than by current, continued for many months and was verified by constant astronomical observations. Storkerson's party also made an extremely valuable series of soundings ranging from 850 fathoms forty miles from shore to 2,500 fathoms ninety miles out.

Storkerson had intended to spend the winter drifting, but in August, 1917, he developed an acute form of asthma. In September, not caring to risk leaving his relatively inexperienced men without a proper commander, he decided to turn back, after 184 days of drifting. He and his men and dogs reached the Alaskan coast on November 8. I did not learn of the success of his venture until

February, when Storkerson reported by wire to Ottawa after wintering at Herschel Island.

This venture marked the close of the work of the Canadian Arctic Expedition. However, it did not receive its due amount of notice for many years—not, in fact, until 1959, when the director of the Royal Geographical Society in London wrote *A History of Polar Exploration* and in it gave Storkerson due credit. A year later, Commander James Calvert, who was the first submarine commander to surface his craft in heavy Arctic Sea ice, paid another tribute to Storkerson, giving him, and incidentally me, credit for originating the idea of using an ice floe as a drifting station for scientific observation. Years after the end of my expedition the idea was utilized by Russian scientists in 1937 and by Americans before and after the International Geophysical Year of 1958.

It was during Storkerson's stay at Banff in the summer of 1919 that I got the details of his remarkable ice sojourn to round out the material that was to become *The Friendly Arctic*. In my assimilation of this material I was helped greatly by a fortunate addition to my staff.

At Banff, I began to dictate the bulky report of my third northern journey, which turned out to be, though probably neither of us dreamed it, the first of more than twenty book-length manuscripts of mine transcribed and edited for publication by Olive Rathbun. This inestimably valuable young woman came to me through a misunderstanding. Her first job after graduating from the University of Wyoming had been as secretary to a number of naval officers during World War I. When that job ended, she remembered that her uncle, Edwin Embree, had become vice president of the Rockefeller Foundation. She felt that he would surely be able to find a job for her in that great organization. In this she was wrong.

Olive may not have known what nepotism was, but she soon learned that one of the first and firmest principles of the foundation was that no member of the family of a high official could hold even the lowest job within the organization. As it happened, my former secretary, Gertrude Allen, was now the secretary to the foundation's president, George Vincent. The Embrees accordingly turned to her for help in placing Olive Rathbun. Gertrude knew of many jobs. There should be, she was sure, one like that which she herself had held, helping the American Museum close the affairs of the Stefansson-Anderson expedition of 1912 and editing and typing its report. Now I would be closing another expedition and would prabably need similar help. She was aware that the American Geographical Society would know the answer.

Olive Rathbun applied, made a good impression on Isaiah Bowman's secretary, on Bowman himself, and on me. She was soon in advisory charge of whatever was going on at Banff. We agreed that, while Storkerson was with us, her most important assignment would be to learn from him whatever she could about anything related to the Canadian Arctic Expedition. Olive soon came to me with the idea that she could get a better grasp of expedition affairs, especially of the troubles it had encountered, if she had a chance to listen to Storkerson's northern stories and views when he was not inhibited by having me around.

During Storkerson's first month at Banff, I began to shift to him the responsibility for leadership in plans to promote the lands of northern Canada, partly as a result of Olive's suggestion. Olive reminded me that she was from the grazing country of Wyoming, that the people she was now meeting down in Banff village were an Alberta-type cattle and sheep group, and that Storkerson was himself a sort of cowboy, a Norwegian reindeer man. She thought that my idea of raising musk oxen and reindeer on arctic pasture lands would interest the local grazing authorities and that the resulting discussion would be of value to Colonel Dennis in pushing still farther north his scheme for increasing the value of Canada's idle lands. This expansion of the colonel's idea by Storkerson and me culminated in Canada's granting to us a lease of northern grazing land greater in area than England and Scotland combined. Of this enterprise I shall have something to say later on. The idea was born at Banff.

Olive was most eager for any and all information about the expedition, and kept trying to find out what had been our most difficult moment on land or sea. Storkerson and I finally agreed that it was something that had never happened, although it almost had. We had not known about it until the winter of 1915–1916, when we had time to go through piles of old newspapers that came into our hands when we bought the *Polar Bear*. Then we discovered that we had almost been "rescued" in 1915 by a well-intended airplane expedition commanded by my former secretary Burt McConnell.

I have mentioned the embarrassment that we narrowly escaped
in 1915 when we were "rescued" at Cape Kellett by Captain Louis
Lane in the *Polar Bear*. Now, on reading the old newspapers, Andreasen, Storkerson, and I saw that at about the same time we had
come very close to suffering the misfortune of being additionally
"rescued," this time by a former comrade whom we knew to be
loyal and of sound judgment. We realized that he must have been
changed to one of little faith by the public belief that our plans had
proved unsound and that we were either dead or in pressing need of
rescue. McConnell had, after all, been our youngest scientist, and
evidently he had come to see himself as a young Lochinvar, his
airplane a brave steed on which he would dash into the arctic maze to
the rescue of his former comrades.

At Banff, as Storkerson and I repeated our story to Olive and
described the predicament we might have been in, we became gradually more convinced that a 1915 airplane rescue would have created
an indescribably difficult situation. What had saved us from a lifetime of having to seem grateful to a high-minded but temporarily
misguided friend was, as we learned from the newspapers, chiefly
the intervention of two famous men, the discoverer of the North
Pole and the inventor of the airplane.

Peary, we read in the press stories, had explained to reporters
how difficult it would be for an aviator, though he were ever so safe
himself in a searching airplane, to find three lost men if they were
drifting somewhere among a million square miles of ice fragments.
Moreover, said Peary, Stefansson had never said that he was coming
back to Alaska. His absence from Alaska should be interpreted to
mean one of three things: either his sledging party had discovered
new land and was wintering upon it; or it was wintering on drifting
ice; or it had landed northeast of Alaska, presumably on Banks or
Prince Patrick, and should be looked for there by a ship sailing east
along the northwestern Canadian mainland and then north along
the west side of those islands. Peary had based his assumption on
plans that I had laid before him in 1912 and which he had approved.

Orville Wright upheld Peary by saying that he relied on Peary's
views and mine. In addition, he insisted that while without doubt
the airplane would eventually become good enough for the type of
rescue search that McConnell proposed, such a thing was at the time
out of the question. Thus Peary and Wright, well-meaning and

mature, saved us from the well-meaning youthfulness of McConnell.

I had not met Orville Wright at this time. My first personal contact with him resulted from a night letter from Dayton, Ohio, in March, 1919. That message had important consequences for me. It was addressed to Otis W. Caldwell, of the Lincoln School in New York, who knew how to reach me. It read:

I UNDERSTAND THAT MR. VILHJALMUR STEFANSSON IS TO BE IN CHICAGO NEXT WEEK. WILL YOU PLEASE EXTEND FOR ME AN INVITATION TO HIM TO STOP OVER A DAY IN DAYTON AS MY GUEST ON HIS RETURN TRIP. WE SHALL FEEL GREATLY HONORED AND HE MAY BE INTERESTED IN THE AERONAUTICAL DEVELOPMENT WORK THAT IS BEING DONE HERE.

Caldwell forwarded the wire but, much as I wished to meet Wright, my lecture schedule kept me from accepting his invitation until May, after I had become settled at Banff. From there, while keeping lecture engagements, I went to Dayton.

Orville Wright and his sister Katharine met me at the station and took me to their beautiful home, Hawthorn Hill, Oakwood. During the next several days I was introduced to the Dayton group of which they were the center. At that time most important, by reason of wealth and his recent war career, was Colonel Edward A. Deeds, among other things chairman of the National Cash Register Company, a director of the National City Bank of New York, and a partner with Charles F. Kettering in Delco. I soon gathered that Deeds had been the government's chief economic adviser in World War I.

I had a pleasant visit with the Wrights and their influential friends and was invited to come back to Dayton later. The opportunity to return came in July, and I wrote the Wrights. Katharine replied:

> . . . having received "due warning" of a second visit from you, we shall *expect* it. Please let us know a little in advance, if you can do so, that we may be sure to be at home. Orville is probably on the Pacific coast tonight. He is on a motor tour with Mr. Deeds and nine or ten other men. He has been gone eleven days and so far I have been favored with one telegram and one post card! When you know him better, you will know that you fared rather better than most people, in getting even that tardy acknowledgment of your book [*My Life with the Eskimo*]. He has almost an "inhibited will" when it comes to writing. It is really painful at times.

By the fall of 1919, I had reached the status of family friend. After one of my visits, a letter from Katharine said:

> When Carrie went up to your room to investigate, she found not only your dress shirt but also a silk one. Being a practical soul, she suggested that we sew on your buttons, which we have done, and keep the shirts here until you come in February. That struck me as being a sensible idea. If you are out on a long tour you may be glad to find a couple of fresh shirts waiting for you!
>
> I was reading not long ago about a lecturer who said that his price for a lecture was *one* hundred dollars, if he stayed at a hotel, *two* hundred, if he was "entertained"! . . . No one in this wide world understands that particular thing any better than we do. We would like to have you think of our house as a place where you can be sure not only of a welcome but of a chance to rest and relax from all strain. You'd never guess, from some of my past performances, that such a thought had ever entered my head, would you? I just *can't* forgive myself for the stupidity of not realizing beforehand that the talk at the Deeds's was sure to be *work* for you. It was *too* bad to pile that right on top of your long, hard tour.

It must have been overconscientiousness that made Katharine think I was tired at, or tired by, the party given by Colonel Deeds. My memories are of kindness and of a friendly interest in me and my affairs, and a keen appreciation of whatever I had tried to express. As for the story of the lecturer and his fee, I knew it was true, for once Elbert Hubbard and I had been a team at a lecture and he showed me his business card. As I remember, on the card was engraved: TERMS—$100 IF I STAY AT A HOTEL, $250 IF I AM ENTERTAINED. He had the technique that George Bernard Shaw developed later, and with equal charm, built on the principle that in the United States the lecture public loves to be insulted in the right way.

In January, 1920, I was to give a public lecture in Dayton. Colonel Deeds asked Katharine to find out if I could stay over an extra day and attend a very special party that he was giving. Henry Ford was to be among the guests. Orville urged me to accept. Enticing as the invitation was, it seemed impossible for me to consider. I was supposed to be in Chicago immediately after my Dayton lecture.

Katharine asked me to spend the night before my talk at Hawthorn Hill. As I look back on this occasion, it seems to me that I was feeling unaccountably apprehensive. The capacity audience in the city's largest auditorium was by turns quietly attentive and effusively demonstrative. Toward the end, however, I began to find it difficult to keep my bearings, and the Wrights and other close friends realized that something was wrong. A group of them rushed toward me at the close, and I was hurried to Orville's waiting car. Within half an hour the Wrights' family physician told Orville that I had the flu.

According to newspapers, the flu epidemic should have been a thing of the past. Dayton had been hit rather hard, and many had died there, including friends of the Wrights, although they did not mention that fact until my danger was thought to be over. Colonel Deeds, for whose dinner I stayed after all, though I did not attend it, brought a half-dozen of his guests to stand a moment at my bedside, among them Henry Ford. This was the only time he and I ever met.

Among the things about the Wrights that became clear to me during my convalescence was that Katharine was almost equally fond of and close to her two famous brothers during the years after their success when the three of them lived together. They were Will and Orv to her, Will—who had died in 1912—the senior by four years. To me, and doubtless to others, she held forth on how the brothers had differed, always with what seemed to me a balanced and impartial praise. I eventually came to feel, however, that she was a bit fonder of Orv. The two men, according to Katharine's account of them, had been about equally articulate, but in different ways. Will had made good set speeches at public gatherings and to engineering societies; Orv claimed that he never made speeches at all. Both had conversed well, but Orville was the better talker. In matters between conversation and speechmaking, Orv was distinctly the better, as he proved on the witness stand in numerous lawsuits, usually against Glenn Curtiss.

My convalescence at Hawthorn Hill was quick and easy. Carrie was the Wrights' only servant. She was really a member of the family. Orville was usually away during the day but home most evenings. In the daytime I talked with Katharine and, at my urging, mostly about her family. There were five Wrights altogether, the three well-known ones and two other equally loved brothers, Lorin and Reuchlin, whom I liked but met only occasionally.

When I felt strong enough to travel and lecture, Katharine and Orville talked me into staying with them still longer, although the doctor was ready to let me take up my work again. During that period our evenings were usually monologues by Orville, with Katharine chipping in occasionally and the hours gradually extending to and past midnight.

Katharine made it clear to me that the friendship and gratitude of the Wright family toward Edward Deeds was very deep. They despised Glenn Curtiss, and admired Octave Chanute and Otto Lilienthal as their greatest predecessors in the field of flight. They looked upon Curtiss as an active villain, and upon Charles Walcott, secretary of the Smithsonian Institution, as a passive one. Walcott's Smithsonian forerunner, Samuel Langley, they considered an honest and fair man who would never himself have claimed the invention of the airplane that Curtiss claimed for him.

During this period I was learning that the Wrights, Wilbur and Orville, were not so much *un*known to the public as *mis*known, and I formed a vague notion of becoming their biographer. Among the things I learned while with them, however, was that they had an admirer named Fred Kelly who was ultimately to do the authoritative biography of the brothers, the only one ever authorized by them.

26 Salesman for the North

My attack of flu and my pleasant convalescence at the Wrights' home cost me a good many lecture engagements, which could not be renewed. This left a gap in my schedule that turned out to be useful. While still at Hawthorn Hill, I received a message from the Canadian Prime Minister, who knew that I had been ill, saying that when I recovered he wanted me to go to London and present to the British Cabinet certain plans that he and I had considered.

Sir Robert Borden knew which side Canadian bread was buttered on. He was well aware that the British Prime Minister, Lloyd George, would not be as interested in our plans as the Parliamentary Under Secretary for the Colonies, Colonel Leopold S. Amery. Amery had not long since been on the staff of the Governor General of Canada and in that capacity had made a trip north from Lake Winnipeg. He was known to be very enthusiastic about the future of Canada's northlands. Sir Robert knew that Lloyd George, whom for reasons of protocol I would have to see if he were available, would be occupied with other matters during March and April. If I could get to London during that time, the way to Amery's more responsive ear would be open.

I had first mentioned my plans to Sir Robert in a letter written from Melville Island in 1916. In this letter, which reached the Premier sometime in the late summer of 1917, I presented the polar ocean as an arctic mediterranean, a hub from which the other oceans and the continents of the world radiated like the spokes of a wheel, with the powerful and populous lands of the North Temperate Zone forming the wheel's rim. Look at a globe, I suggested, and notice what the lands are. Canada and the northern United States. To the eastward, about halfway from the equator to the North Pole, lie the European lands of Britain, France, Germany, Italy, the Scandinavian countries, European Russia, and Turkey. Then come Siberia and India, and finally Japan and China.

The argument I had laid before Borden was to the effect that, in the dawning age of air transportation, the plane would take the place of the train and the steamship for all but heavy and slow freight. People would continue traveling east and west between places relatively close together. To distant lands, however, especially when in a hurry, they would fly north and south—straight north across the Pole from Chicago and Winnipeg to India, northeast to India from San Francisco and Vancouver, northwest to India from New York and Montreal. Flights from Washington to Peking would not cross the Pacific or even Bering Sea, but would traverse the Arctic Ocean. From Seattle or Vancouver to Siberia or India, planes would cross the polar mediterranean. People would worry less and less over east and west and whether they were ever likely to meet. Travelers would think more and more about north and south and their possible meaning—the Asiatic peoples crossing the Arctic Sea and Canada on their way to the United States, and, in turn, fliers from Mexico and the United States crossing Canada and the Arctic Ocean on their way to Asia.

The polar mediterranean, I had argued, was going to be crossed at all seasons, the traffic going by air above the floating ice, by submarine through the water beneath it. Swift cargoes would go by airplane, slower ones by submarine. This would be true in war as well as in peace. In this commerce, whether peaceful or military, the islands of every sea would retain whatever values they had always had and would acquire new ones, especially as airports and as weather and rescue stations. The islands of the North Atlantic and North Pacific had long been known and securely owned. The ownership of many islands around and in the Arctic Ocean was uncertain. For instance, who owned northern Greenland? Greenland had been discovered by Scandinavians, but in the main had been explored by nationals of the United States: by Kane, Hayes, Hall, Greely, and Peary. Who owned Grant Land, named after a President of the United States? It had no doubt first been sighted and cultivated by the Icelandic colonists of Greenland in the late Middle Ages, and then by the British in Elizabethan times. It was, however, known to the world chiefly through the explorations of Kane, Greely, and Peary, and those of the Norwegian *Fram* Expedition of Otto Sverdrup. Who owned Heiberg Island, named by Sverdrup for a Norwegian brewer? And who owned the Ringnes Islands, discovered by the Norwegian Gunnar Isachsen and named for other Norwegian brewers, the brothers Ringnes?

Was it not mostly because these lands had been considered worthless that nobody had challenged British ownership of them? Britain had historically been mistress of the seas, frozen or not, but now the power of the United States was developing. If Americans once got the idea that northern lands and seas were valuable, what then would be Canada's position? Would it not be well for Canada to build up more and better arguments? It had been largely due to Borden himself and his Conservative party that Canada was able to claim by right of discovery a few marginal islands of the vast archipelago north of Canada. Why not make Canadian rights additionally secure by further exploration of the islands that the Canadian Arctic Expedition had discovered and by some form of occupation, such as weather stations and police posts? There also remained the possibility, however remote, of discovering new islands in the as-yet-untraveled sections of the Arctic Ocean.

If these ideas had not been in Borden's mind already, the seeds of them had been planted through the talks we had in 1912 before his government took over Anderson's expedition and mine from the National Geographic Society and our other United States backers. My letter from Melville Island had been intended to revive them. In my first postwar conversations with him, Borden had been alive to these views and seemingly eager to implement them. He told me that he had been mulling them over ever since his government took over our expedition. Since receiving my letter with its added arguments, he had begun to feel even more strongly. On one or more occasions he had said to Desbarats that we ought to give the surface impression that the Canadian government considered these notions visionary. He had, however, instructed Desbarats to intimate to me that Canada would take up such matters as soon as the most pressing problems of peacetime adjustment had been met.

Now, in 1920, I was informed that the time had come for me to go to London. I understood this to mean that I was free to begin

talking openly about plans for a continued northern exploration,
which Canada might support, and that I should feel free to discuss
the aviation angles of such a project with Orville Wright if the
occasion should arise.

During what I expected to be the last days of my recuperation
I told Orville and Katharine about many of my ideas, but said
nothing about this international political aspect, although I knew
the Wrights did not think in political terms. Borden had asked me
to leave that angle out of all my talks with anybody but himself
and his designated associates. It was his expectation that, if there
was an expedition in 1921–1923, the government of Canada would
again be its exclusive backer.

There were, I believe, only three or four men in Borden's
Cabinet who understood that when he thought of a new northern
expedition he was thinking mainly of discovering new islands in the
Arctic Ocean, and that he was thinking about them from the aviation angle as possible stations in a world-wide network of great
circle flying routes. I feel sure that his top secretary, Loring Cheney
Christie (later Canada's ambassador to Washington), was completely in Borden's confidence in this as in other matters. I knew that
Desbarats knew everything I knew, and I believe nobody tried to
keep any of what was going on in Borden's head from J. B. Harkin,
commissioner of Dominion Parks. Desbarats was the logical man to
handle Borden's ideas. The new expedition was to be announced as,
and was really to be, a continuation of the one that the Deputy Chief
of Naval Service had been managing. I never knew why Harkin was
brought in, but I do know that he came to be the best-informed man
in Ottawa, or anywhere, on both overt and secret matters connected
with our plans. I was told that the only files our project ever had
were in either Harkin's private apartment in Ottawa or his office.

I think that Borden believed that I would go to London anyway
in the early months of 1920 to collect a British medal. This was a
possibility of which Isaiah Bowman had made me aware. I know
that both Desbarats and Harkin took pains to mention whenever
possible my prospects of being a medalist.

Bowman was as interested as I in getting geographers, particularly geographic explorers, to accept my view that it was easy for a
healthy and intelligent man to live comfortably and be well fed on
the local resources of the Arctic Sea. The stronghold of conservatism
in this field, to Bowman's way of thinking, was the aristocratic Royal

Geographical Society of London, within which polar exploration was regarded as an exalted sport for the nobility and the gentry.

I have told how Shackelton had warned me that I would have difficulty getting much support from the Royal Geographical in view of my having praised Dr. Rae in my first London talk in 1913. He had said that I would forever have against me Sir Clements Markham, then president of the society, a perfect example of the gentleman polar explorer. When, on my return from the abbreviated lecture tour that followed my illness, I told Bowman that I had been ordered to go to London in April, he returned to his idea that it would help the cause of northern exploration if people who thought as we did could get the British to follow the American, French, and German geographical societies in giving me a medal. He thought that it would be best to try to popularize Dr. Rae's ideas and mine by getting me a chance to lecture again before the Royal Geographical. This might be managed, he felt, through the society's recently retired secretary, Sir John Scott Keltie, who was much more a scientist and less a fashionable sportsman than the former president had been. Bowman said that he would be writing Keltie about another matter and would slip in the news that I was coming to London, hinting that it might be possible to get me for a lecture.

In London, I at first stayed at Claridge's, which is not exactly the hostelry for a nongentleman explorer, although I did not quite realize it at the time. It was not I who chose the Claridge. My friend Fred Walcott was an investment banker, a partner in a Wall Street firm whose London representative was Lord Fairfax, descendant of those Fairfaxes who were so prominent around Washington's time in Britain's most fashionable colony, Virginia. When I wrote Walcott from Dayton in late January that the Canadian government wanted me to visit London, he offered to have his bank get accommodations for me on a ship that was taking him over for one of his frequent trips. Warning him that I wanted to travel in the cheapest first-class room available, I thanked him and accepted. We met frequently on the way over, but not until the British Isles were practically in sight did it occur to me that I had made no hotel reservation. When I spoke of this, Walcott suggested that I might as well come with him to the hotel where he always stayed, which was Claridge's. The name meant nothing to me, and he did nothing to explain its significance.

I had at first been told that it would be all right for me to take

Miss Rathbun to London as my secretary. This had seemed to both Olive and me an excellent idea, for she had in England a classmate who was a Rhodes scholar from Wyoming, Horace North Wilcox, in whom she was deeply interested. Her sister would go along as chaperone. It was decided, however, that I would do better to engage a male secretary and have Olive remain in the States to continue work on the *Friendly Arctic* manuscript. Sir Robert Borden told me that, as the government's representative, I would no doubt be dining often in London with Cabinet ministers, perhaps even with the King. He said I would need to have proper clothes made by a London tailor and that there would be amenities to observe. Borden's right-hand man, Loring Christie, suggested one of the wounded war veterans for whom the government was trying to get jobs, a good shorthand-typist who knew the ropes in social London—was in fact a French nobleman reared in Britain—the Baron de Grandcourt.

As anticipated, my new secretary was most presentable, had good French and flawless public-school English, and knew how to find me what was supposed to be the right Bond Street tailor. It was from the Baron that I first learned the real status of Claridge's. Grandcourt stared when I mentioned the hotel, and asked me what sort of allowance we were traveling on. I told him that my directive from Christie had been that my accommodations in London ought to be "good but not extravagant," whereupon Grandcourt suggested that perhaps since Walcott was so used to staying at Claridge's he could get me reduced rates. I decided that the Baron and I would go along with Walcott and check out after the first night if our accommodations proved to be too expensive. I put off speaking to Walcott about the possibility of reduced rates, however, for he had many friends aboard ship and was always busy.

What happened was that Lord Fairfax came to meet the boat train from Southampton. He shook hands with me warmly and said that in a day or two, after at least a night in the country, he and Walcott would look me up at the hotel. We were decorously welcomed at the superhotel but told that there was only one suite available, the one that had been reserved for me on Walcott's order. This consisted of three magnificent rooms for me and a single adjacent room for the Baron. Without food or service, the rate was eleven guineas per day, and that was when the guinea was worth five dollars.

For three days I did not hear from Walcott and Fairfax. Fortunately, Walcott, in his radiogram to the hotel, had made the reservation for only three days. My first caller at Claridge's was a friend of mine who had been described to me as one of the richest Welsh coal-mine owners. He stared when he found where I was lodging and said that he hoped the news of it would not spread. According to him, nobody stayed at Claridge's except Indian princes, American millionaires, and deadbeats who were trying to borrow money. Perhaps unconsciously putting me in the last category, he offered to lend me money if I needed any. I said that I would stay the three days and pay for them personally in order to teach myself a lesson.

My next visitor was Sir Arthur Conan Doyle, whom I had met during my first stay in England in 1913. Doyle suggested that I end my jeopardy by moving to his hotel, the Grosvenor. This I did. In the meantime Grandcourt had telephoned the colonial ministry, had found that they expected us, and had explained that I hoped to call on several old friends before turning up for my regular duties. This was his way of getting the needed time for the Bond Street tailor to work me into shape.

On my second day in London, I dined with Ernest Shackleton at the Marlborough Club. He thought the Claridge episode such a good joke that I regretted having told him about it. I was afraid that he would spread the story, though I asked him not to.

I had some free time during the first week in London. One day I lunched at the Royal Societies Club with Sir Richard Gregory, editor of *Nature*. Sir Richard and I had what was to me a memorable two hours together, partly because he made it clear to me that what Bowman and I thought of as a weakness in the British attitude toward polar exploration was recognized as such in some British circles. Many Englishmen felt that the code behind this attitude was not that of science but rather that of lawn tennis. This British view of arctic exploration I summarized in a letter to Bowman.

Sir Richard pointed out that the reason for so little advance in the methods of exploration was exactly this sportsman's attitude of never pointing out the errors made by one's competitors. He said that there was a small group of men in England who felt that the truth should be told, even about explorers, for the sake of the advancement of knowledge and for the sake of preventing failures and tragedies in the future. These men were former members of the expeditions of Shackleton and Sir Robert F. Scott, all then connected with the faculty of Cambridge. Two of them, Priestly and

Debenham, were working mainly on the Antarctic; but another, Wordie, was devoting himself to the Arctic. The funds available for their use were partly furnished by Cambridge University; there was, however, some ten thousand pounds left over from the funds raised for the Scott Expedition.

I told Bowman that I thought Lady Scott's attitude toward the activities of this group was admirable. Not only had she taken the side of Mawson, who was being denounced for having pointed out some of the mistakes made by Scott, but she seemed not to have the least desire to have Scott's mistakes covered up, and was quite willing that some of the Scott funds be used for an investigation that she well knew might point out some serious mistakes made by him. Her point of view was that it was quite possible for us now to see the mistakes made by Napoleon and to point out why he lost the Battle of Waterloo, without abandoning the position that Napoleon was, nevertheless, a great man. Lady Scott thought that after her husband's mistakes had been pointed out, there would remain enough real achievement to leave him occupying a very high place.

That Shackleton, too, was dissatisfied with British polar exploration, though for a different reason, I indicated in another letter to Bowman. I said that Shackleton condemned vehemently and even profanely in private the conduct of the men whom he praised in his lectures. This might be good platform etiquette, but it was the very thing that prevented us from exposing the ludicrous and sometimes almost criminal mistakes of commanders of some arctic expeditions, and from pointing out the unnecessary pitfalls into which expedition after expedition fell because criticism permitted among bankers and politicians and military leaders was not permitted in the very artificial game of polar exploration.

My talk before the British geographers must have fallen on more fertile ground than Bowman and I had feared it would. In any event, I did become a medalist of the Royal Geographical Society in 1920. My other business in London was not brought to so successful a conclusion.

27 Feuds and Favors

I felt pleased and rewarded by the conferences I had with Sir Richard Gregory and Sir John Scott Keltie at the Royal Societies Club. I took still more pleasure in occasional lunches and dinners with Shackleton at the Marlborough Club.

The Marlborough Club was a unique institution. Nobody belonged to it except by courtesy of King Edward VII, who, having been the eldest son of long-lived Queen Victoria, had spent almost a lifetime as Prince of Wales. His long tenure in this high but subordinate office may have given him a special point of view. With a wit amounting to wisdom, Shackleton said, with a wink, that he thought it possible that King Edward favored him because he was a roughneck and offered him membership so that the club would have a higher percentage of men of his own kind.

One privilege allowed members of the Marlborough was permission to buy the very special port wine that King Edward liked best of all drinks. Over this orthodox beverage of the gentry, on the fringe of which class Shackleton claimed that he belonged, the explorer explained his dream of future expeditions to the Antarctic, in which he would surpass even the great achievements he tells about in his truly magnificent *Heart of the Antarctic*. It did not occur to me during those pleasant meetings—nor did it, in fact, until I had left the British Isles—that Shackleton was having me on, playing the spy in true storybook fashion.

I have said that from the time Desbarats first told me that Borden supported my schemes for the transpolar use of airplanes and submarines I never ceased being secretive about Borden's plans. Yet, there I sat at Shackleton's club, talking freely and behaving like a simpleton, lulled by the feeling that he was an antarctic man who cared nothing for anything but outdoing Scott and Amundsen. It is possible that my memory deceives me, but I do not remember a word spoken at the Marlborough Club about any serious interest that Shackleton may have had in the northern polar region. I do remember, however, that I revealed to Shackleton the very plans that I had so meticulously hidden from Isaiah Bowman and from Katharine and Orville Wright. I tell my side of the story all the more readily because Shackleton's side of it has been so well presented by Margery and James Fisher in their fine book *Shackleton*.

Though their story is very different from mine, I feel sure that the Fishers must have known what they were talking about when they said that Shackleton lectured at the London Philharmonic Hall twice a day, six days a week, for five months, and that when the lectures finished in May, 1920, he was readying for a new venture that he had been planning. Late in 1919, apparently, he had talked to one of his former colleagues about a new expedition in the Arctic. He seemed to feel, according to the Fishers, that the Beaufort Sea, then the last completely unknown part of the Arctic, was a real challenge. Shackleton appears to have told this man that he intended to operate in the "Zone of Inaccessibility," the name that Bowman and I invented in 1918, but that he might also try to reach the North Pole.

Although Shackleton gave me no such impression at the time, he nevertheless wrote the Royal Geographical Society at the end of February, 1920, about his arctic plans. The Fishers say that he received a general approval, the council advising that he should consult the Canadian government at once. By that summer Shackleton was able to say that the government was interested in the plan, though no definite promises had been made. The most surprising thing was for me to read, in the Fishers' book, that in the spring he also conferred with the explorer Stefansson, who had wide experience in the Arctic, and received cordial offers of help from him.

A news story in *The* (London) *Times* said that Shackleton had told a certain Norwegian that he had given up the idea of exploring the Antarctic "and in future will devote himself to the Arctic." The Fishers say that this "was still so in March when Shackleton returned from Canada assured of support from the Government."

But after further details the Fishers continue: "A change in government in Canada, marked by a strict economy drive, had put an end to Shackleton's hopes in the immediate present of exploring the Beaufort Sea."

This is no doubt the impression that Shackleton gave to others, but there was, as I say, no hint of it in his talks with me. I certainly made no "cordial offer of help," because I was entirely unaware of his plans.

The one man who knew all sides of the official Canadian government position, or at least a great deal more than I did, was James Harkin. At first I felt sure that he would eventually release his information, but the last time I saw him his position still was that Borden had trusted him to keep certain matters secret. He had not been released from that pledge during Borden's lifetime. With the Prime Minister's death, Harkin felt, the secret became inviolate. Ambassador Christie meant to tell the whole story, insofar as he could, in his life of Borden, but he did not live long enough after his chief to get a chance to write what I feel would have been an adequate account.

There were, as I have said, many in Canada and elsewhere who thought me a faker and who said so, among them my former second-in-command Anderson and my distinguished contemporary Roald Amundsen. It is possible that others, including Shackleton's friends, agreed with them. When Shackleton arrived in Canada, he was hailed as an explorer planning to penetrate the Beaufort Sea, and was given a dinner in Montreal by Canadians who believed that the charlatan Stefansson was about to be stopped in his attempt to get away with the plum of another northern expedition.

It was plain, at that point, that Shackleton had double-crossed me. Surprised and troubled, I consulted Desbarats, who confirmed my fears. Desbarats said that, worst of all, the Minister of Naval Service, his own superior, was one of those sponsoring the Shackleton dinner. Gradually, we came to believe what was at least partly true: that many prominent Canadians felt that a second-rater like me should not be supported by the government when it was possible to get an authentically great man in my place. There were rumors and counterrumors, but the essence of the whispered story seemed to be that a faction of the Canadian government had sent me to London to promote their scheme, that in Britain the truth had leaked out (as I admit it had), and that some of Shackleton's

friends had gone to him to see if he were not willing to step into
my shoes. To organize a really great arctic expedition seemed to
these Canadians a good idea, but it ought to have a good commander.
The Shackleton group, however, overplayed its hand.

Sir Robert Borden had asked me, much to my delight, whether
I would not like to belong to the Rideau Club, most distinguished
of Canadian clubs. He proposed me, and Speaker Rhodes of the
House of Commons was my seconder. When this became known, it
struck somebody on Shackleton's side that if I were to be blackballed by this famous organization it would mark the end of my
influence in Ottawa.

The blackballing was easily managed, but it did not have the
expected effect. Though Borden was no longer Prime Minister, he
was influential, and he realized that the command of an arctic expedition was the real issue. So he cautioned his successor, Arthur
Meighen, not to believe what a lot of people were saying about me,
and said he felt sure that I was the best man available for this
northern journey. Meighen thought so too, but when they came to
reckon their strength it proved that about half the Cabinet were
already pledged to Shackleton. There was either an actual or a near
tie. Eventually, the two factions said to each other that, if they
could not agree, perhaps they had better do nothing.

As to what the world lost, if anything, by the Canadian government's deadlock, there probably cannot even now be agreement.
What Borden's hopes and mine were I have tried to explain. What
Shackleton planned, if the Fishers' report of him is correct, was
something like this: He believed, though his belief has been proved
unjustified, that the Beaufort Sea contained "land masses larger
than the whole of the United Kingdom or else a cluster of islands
of the same dimensions." It was his idea that he would find and
present to the Empire this mythical territory. He also planned to
study the magnetic field in the polar region and to have a look at
"Eskimo tribes hitherto unknown." He seems to have believed that
there was land in the vicinity of the North Pole and that he was
about to become its discoverer. In the course of his discovery, he
felt that he would clear up once and for all the great Cook-Peary
controversy—which had already been cleared up to the satisfaction
of most serious geographers.

In the 1920s a sort of infighting through character assassina-
tion was practiced by those who engaged in the extremely competi-

tive vocation of polar exploration. When need for justification arose, it was explained that the hostility was for the good of the sport. For instance, it will be remembered that Amundsen explained that he denounced me in his autobiography because my "prattle" was injuring the causes of polar exploration.

Amundsen was not alone in attacking me. Others, instead of ridiculing me in public, used the expedient of trying to keep me out of socially desirable clubs. Sometime after I had been proposed for the Century Club in New York City by Henry Fairfield Osborn, president of the American Museum, my sponsor wrote that he was very sorry but that he had felt obliged to withdraw my name from the Century Association. He assured me that I should not take the matter too seriously. He had been kept out of the Century for a year by verbal attacks made by one of the opponents to his candidacy. He supposed that an opponent of mine had been writing to a member of the Committee on Admissions. He had, he said, no information about the matter at all, but asked me not to mention the difficulty, since these club matters were considered confidential.

A number of Century Club members who had written in to support my candidacy now insisted on taking up the issue. After months of haggling, Osborn resubmitted my name and after a lot of further delay I was elected. I am today an honorary member. At the Rideau Club in Ottawa, the struggle was more bitter. We lost the first round, and Sir Robert Borden and Speaker Rhodes wrote me chagrined letters accepting defeat. A curious sort of vindication came forty-one years later when the issue was accidentally revived.

In 1960 Donat Marc Le Bourdais, who had traveled with me on the lecture circuit in the 1920s and had become a well-known Canadian journalist and author of books about northern Canada, was asked by the Royal Canadian Geographical Society to write for their *Journal* an article that was published in August, 1960. As preparation for this, he wrote to ask me on just what date I had been blackballed by the Rideau Club. I never knew the date, and as a nonmember I could not get the information myself. I wrote to an old friend who was a member, the Honorable Joseph T. Thorson, president of the Exchequer Court of Canada, telling him what Le Bourdais wanted, and asked if etiquette permitted him to ask the proper officials for the date. Mr. Justice Thorson saw no etiquette in the way.

The secretary-treasurer of the Rideau Club, Mr. C. C. Fair-weather, soon wrote that the record showed that I had been proposed for membership on February 19, 1921, by Sir Robert Borden and seconded by the Honorable Edgar N. Rhodes. The ballot was cast on March 1, 1921, and I failed to be elected. Particulars of the vote were not available, he said. The correspondence had, however, been brought to the notice of the president and the committee, who were pleased to offer me honorary membership in the Rideau Club.

I have mentioned these social incidents by way of illustrating the fact that all factions in Britain and Canada were not in agreement either about my status or about what should be done to strengthen Empire and Canadian claims to that northern region which I had insisted was to become extremely important. My mission to England in 1920 ended in apparent failure, partly because of unresolved opposition in Canada and partly because I had been taken in by Shackleton in London.

Seeds had, however, been planted, though they were destined to bear bitter fruit.

28 On the Border of the Academic World

My disappointment at the outcome of my London visit made me look forward eagerly to the work for the summer of 1920 which had been planned at Banff the previous year. This period was to be, although I did not realize it at the time, the transition from my life as an explorer of unknown arctic territory to a new life as an explorer of human error.

Raymond Pearl was head of the School of Hygiene and Public Health at Johns Hopkins University in Baltimore. I had been told that he would be interested in my experience with a meat diet in the north, and had met him in Washington after my return from the north in 1918. He was interested, and to such an extent that he suggested that he and I collaborate on a book about nutrition. He had questioned me and had his questions and my answers taken down in shorthand. These notes were transcribed and sent out to twenty-odd nutritionists, with a request for their comments. Most of those scientists had only unfavorable things to say, adding up to the belief that I was either a liar or a teller of fairy tales, or both. There were, however, a few in addition to Pearl who were genuinely interested in what I had to say about my arctic diet, and Pearl felt that an attempt to convince the skeptics would be extremely valuable. I liked his idea of our doing a book together.

In the summer of 1919, he and his wife had come to Banff, where we, with Olive Rathbun's invaluable help, made plans to spend the following summer at the camp in Vermont planned by Pearl and administered by Lowell J. Reed, then associate professor of biostatistics at Johns Hopkins and later president of that university.

Although the plans for the summer were largely based upon the prospect of a collaboration between Pearl and me, it soon became apparent that the report of the Canadian Arctic Expedition which I had promised Sir Robert Borden, and of which *The Friendly Arctic* was a by-product, would have to have priority over the nutrition book. Pearl understood this, and not only agreed to put off our collaboration until 1922 but allowed me to use the Vermont camp as I had used Banff the summer before, as a headquarters for the preparation of my report. He and his wife and their associates gave me much sound counsel, without which *The Friendly Arctic* might have been quite a different book.

The Hopkins camp consisted of three rented houses stretching along the eastern shore of Lake Memphremagog from North Derby to Derby Line on the Canadian border. Olive Rathbun, who by this time had married Horace North Wilcox, Bella Weitzner, and I shared one of these houses. In it we spent a great deal of our working time, I dictating, Olive taking down what I said and typing and correcting, and Bella Weitzner coordinating and checking the anthropological details.

In the evening we usually went to the Pearls' and read them what had been done during the day, listening to their comments, adding, altering, and deleting. Raymond Pearl put so much detailed attention and effort into my book that I do not understand how he could have done any work of his own. I was so carried away with what I was doing that I do not believe that I was very considerate of Raymond. He, on the other hand, seemed to want things to go the way they were going. At least I was ready to believe that he did, and I took some justification from the fact that he often said of some point about the primitive life I was trying to describe that we must develop it more fully in our proposed nutrition book.

In the delightful atmosphere of a northern Vermont summer, with quiet for work when needed, with exactly the right kind of help, and with stimulating conversation when desired, *The Friendly Arctic* grew. It grew to be as much Olive Wilcox's book as mine.

It was not finished in the summer of 1920 but carried over into 1921, when, between lectures, I was back in New York City. Gilbert Grosvenor, of the National Geographic Society, who wrote the foreword, provided the title, which turned out to interest many and infuriate others. The book had an immediate success.

While I was working on *The Friendly Arctic,* Alfred Harcourt of the publishing firm of Harcourt, Brace and Howe, had been reading my earlier book, *My Life with the Eskimo.* He wrote me, while I was at the Johns Hopkins camp, that he would like me to do a book aimed at young people about my experiences with Eskimo life. I was busy at the time and not especially interested in juvenile books. A couple of years later I did do a book for Harcourt, *Hunters of the Great North,* which, although Harcourt apparently thought of it as a juvenile, was a perfectly straightforward adult account of my experiences as a member of the Anglo-American Polar Expedition of 1906 and not at all the juvenile version of *My Life with the Eskimo* that Harcourt apparently had wanted. I am sorry to say that because of the way it was promoted it was a long time before anyone discovered that the book was an account of my first expedition.

Before *Hunters of the Great North* was published, however, Harcourt had another idea. He felt that my view of the Canadian Arctic and its potentialities had been lost in the bulk of *The Friendly Arctic,* which although a best seller at the time, seemed to be constantly out of stock as a result of the cautiousness of the publisher. Harcourt felt that I should do a book about my feeling that the Canadian north was a land of destiny, and that he was the man to sell it. The book was to be called *The Northward Course of Empire,* paraphrasing Bishop George Berkeley's line, "Westward the course of empire takes its way."

I did the book, and it appeared a month after *Hunters of the Great North.* A large part of it was serialized in *The World's Work,* and another section appeared in the *National Geographic Magazine* under somewhat unusual circumstances. That section, "Transpolar Commerce by Air," was one of two chapters—the other being "Transarctic Commerce by Submarines"—that Harcourt thought too fantastic to print in a serious book. I talked him into letting me try out the air-commerce chapter on the *National Geographic.* He agreed that if they would print it he would let me include it in the book. Gilbert Grosvenor liked it and showed it to Alexander Graham Bell, who also approved of it. It appeared in the *Geographic* for August, 1922, and I took great pleasure in showing

Harcourt the thousand-dollar check I got for it. But when Harcourt still held out against the submarine chapter, I inserted a few comments on submarines into other chapters.

In spite of our hopes for *The Northward Course of Empire,* it sold less than two hundred copies in Canada and so was, at that time at least, not a very successful missionary. In fact, although I was born a Canadian and had returned to Canadian citizenship in 1913 after thirty-odd years as an American, Canada has often seemed bent on ignoring my work on her behalf. It is interesting to note that the University of Manitoba, which may have felt some responsibility since I was born in that province, was the only Canadian university ever to honor me with a degree, although I have been the recipient of seven other honorary degrees from institutions elsewhere than in Canada.

It has sometimes been assumed that the books I have written have been the cause of these honors. I like to think that this is not entirely true. Certainly it is not true of the first one I received, in 1921, from the University of Michigan, the machinery for which was set in motion before *The Friendly Arctic* appeared. This degree resulted from the friendship of Admiral Peary with a Michigan professor, William Herbert Hobbs. Peary realized and made Hobbs believe that when I said that Peary could have reached the Pole without his elaborate support, had he thought of trying to live by hunting, I was criticizing not Peary but conservatism in arctic exploration. My Michigan degree was recognition of a victory over this conservatism. It pleased me to know this, although the victory was still only partial. It will later appear that the Michigan degree came at an opportune time and was important for other reasons.

A year after the Michigan doctorate, the University of Iowa, our alma mater, offered both Rudolph Anderson and me honorary degrees, mentioning *The Friendly Arctic.* I am sorry to say that I had to stand up alone to receive the honor. Anderson said that he disagreed so thoroughly with what I had to say about the Arctic that he could not accept a degree if I were given one.

The remaining six doctorates that were awarded me were spread over a period of nearly thirty years, beginning in 1930 with the University of Iceland and the University of North Dakota, which I had been asked to leave when I was a student there. These were followed by the University of Manitoba in 1937, and the University of Pittsburgh and Florida Southern College in 1945. It was pleasant to note that the latter took no offense at my obvious feeling that Alaska had as much to recommend it as Florida. Dartmouth was the last to honor me, in 1959.

In addition to the academic honors that came to me as a result of my work, I had several narrow escapes from the pack ice of academic life which, had I once been frozen into it, might have held me permanently.

During the years after my return from the expedition of 1913–1918, I had become acquainted with a very remarkable woman whose chief interest for me was that she was the widow of that poet who had had such a negative effect upon my early aspirations as a poet—William Vaughan Moody. Harriet Tilden Moody, a shrewd businesswoman and a member of the board of trustees of Cornell University, had been appointed to a committee to select candidates for the office of president of Cornell. Mrs. Moody had taken a fancy to me and formed an opinion of my potentialities that was extremely flattering. She informed me that I was her choice for the presidency of Cornell and that three of her colleagues on the committee knew of her intention to nominate me and believed that they could get the rest of the group to agree.

I had the feeling that a college president's job was largely that of fund raising, a task for which I had no talent. I asked my friends Isaiah Bowman and Raymond Pearl for advice. The advice I got prompted me to turn down Mrs. Moody's offer. I did refuse it, but had to do it twice before my refusal was accepted. In 1921, Livingston Farrand, another anthropologist, became president of Cornell.

It is interesting to note that the two men who advised me to avoid becoming a college president themselves failed later to take their own advice. Isaiah Bowman became president of Johns Hopkins, and Raymond Pearl narrowly escaped becoming president of Harvard, losing out to James B. Conant.

My other brush with academic life came a little later, in 1924. This, like the Cornell episode, left me where I was, but had circumstances permitted it to draw me in, I should have been highly pleased.

During one of my visits to the University of Michigan I had told President Marion Le Roy Burton a story of the disagreement at Harvard between the astronomers who claimed that the sun could not be over ten million years old, and the geologists who knew that certain rocks in the earth were much older than that. This story of academic conflict, confusing to students, gave President Burton the idea that such differences in a university should be worked out in amiable conference before opposing ideas were presented to the student body as truth.

It was Burton's idea that there should be a "Professor of the Coordination of Knowledge" who would moderate all discussions about disputed truths. Burton offered me the job at Ann Arbor, inviting me to give a lecture at Michigan, after which I would sign the necessary documents. Since this was, in a sense, the long-deferred establishment of my "school of unlearning," I was delighted with the prospect.

I gave the lecture and the president walked with me to my lodgings, telling me as we said good night that he would hand me the papers at breakfast the next morning. Just before breakfast, however, Mrs. Burton telephoned to say that her husband had been taken ill and could not meet me. I offered to stay over, but she, knowing more than I did, advised against it. I never saw President Burton again, for he never recovered from his illness. With him died the idea of a professorship in the coordination of knowledge. My school of unlearning, it seemed, would have to be a private one.

Three

29 New Arctic Ventures

During these crowded years of rapid-fire book publication—which I could not possibly have managed without Olive Wilcox—I kept on lecturing, averaging something like twenty-five thousand miles a year on the circuit. It was a period of what seemed to me extraordinary affluence.

For the first time in my life I was earning much more money than I needed for my living expenses. My temperament induced me to look about for creative ways of spending the surplus. I tried financing a relative from Iceland who was a gifted tenor, not discovering until I had sunk some ten thousand dollars in his career that he was too lazy to achieve real success.

A more satisfactory way of disposing of my wealth had begun to develop in my mind. I had formed the habit, while on lecture tours, of visiting secondhand bookstores in towns where there were any to visit. I had found, often in unlikely places, an extraordinary number of valuable but usually inexpensive items about the polar regions. When I told Isaiah Bowman about this developing interest, he encouraged me by offering me a collection of more than two hundred duplicate volumes from the library of the American Geographical Society, which the society would otherwise have sold to some dealer for practically nothing. This formed the nucleus of my polar collection, which was to use up most of my spare earnings for the rest of my life and which was to give me, in my later years, educational opportunities that no ordinary academic connection could have provided.

In 1921, I gave up my residence at the Harvard Club in New York and took an apartment with two close friends, Carl Ethan Akeley, the famous African traveler, sculptor, and taxidermist, and Herbert Joseph Spinden, a Harvard classmate of mine famous for his archaeological and anthropological work in Mexico, Central America, and South America. Carl and Joe were, like me, frequently away but needed a base in New York.

The apartment we found was at the corner of Central Park West and 89th Street. It had something like ten rooms, which allowed for plenty of guests. It had also a most extraordinary housekeeper who had a completely undisciplined and unceasingly noisy son of about six. She was a widow but, being Irish, was never without men friends in police uniforms, all of whom seemed to hate the English and particularly that Welshman Lloyd George. Our housekeeper supported them in their animosity, even going so far as to declare—without worrying us much, I confess—that when she got around to it she intended to assassinate Lloyd George.

What really did worry us was her policeman guests, not because of their antipathy to the English, but because of their predilection for ham. Baked Virginia ham was the housekeeper's specialty. Since we all liked it, we did not care how often she served it. We did, however, note with some alarm that, no matter how large a ham was provided, we never saw the same joint more than once. This had a social effect upon our lives because, although we could not curb the appetites of the police, we could, by inviting guests whenever ham was served, see that as little as possible of it got back to the kitchen.

The Ellison-White organization, which had taken over my lecturing from Lee Keedick, was interested in the summer business provided by the Chautauqua circuit, an American institution now almost, if not entirely, extinct. Chautauqua, which takes its name from Chautauqua Lake in western New York, where it first appeared, was a movement begun in the 1870s on a largely religious basis. It sought to make use of the North American's instinct for summer recreation by combining it with useful education. The movement began with summer sessions at Chautauqua Lake but spread throughout the country in the form of traveling tent shows. It provided a wide range of entertainment from vaudeville acts, magicians, singers, and travel lecturers, to great personalities such as William Jennings Bryan and Russell H. Conwell with his famous "Acres of Diamonds" lecture.

Chautauqua was at its height in the 1920s when I was a part of it. Before I transferred from Keedick to Ellison-White, a young man who had been with me during the last part of my final expedition, Erol Lorne Knight, was working on a small Chautauqua circuit, advertised as one of the two white men who had been on my expedition's farthest-north journey in 1917. Knight's talks were accompanied by motion pictures that Wilkins had taken while we were together in the Arctic. When I was free to go with Ellison-White, I was put on the big-time Chautauqua circuit and Knight was hired to travel with me to run the projector and answer questions, after my lecture, about what he thought of what I had said. This use of Knight as an accessory to my talks was so successful that we later engaged Fred Maurer as an extra. Fred, a brilliant young man who had been on the *Karluk* in 1914 and was later rescued from Wrangel Island, did all kinds of odd jobs helping to set up and take down tents, and he was always available as an extra question answerer during lecture time.

Another young man working with Chautauqua was Milton Galle, a likable and able Texan whom I had not known before but who became associated with us as a result of the stories that he heard Fred Maurer tell of the days on Wrangel Island.

It was Fred's idea that the *Karluk* disaster had prevented Wrangel Island from being known as it should be known: as a place where willing and able men could live indefinitely off the land without real danger or discomfort. Maurer wanted me to organize a party to colonize the island and explore the sea to the north of it. Knight also was enthusiastic about the idea, and the two men had little difficulty winning over Milton Galle. Backstage on the Chautauqua circuit, they talked almost constantly about their hoped-for trip. The idea of the expedition kept getting more firmly rooted in my own mind as I saw how it tied in with my views of the future of the Arctic and the development of the Canadian north. It seemed to me that such a project would help to break the deadlock in Canadian arctic matters that my conflict with Shackleton appeared to have set up.

Fairly early in 1921 we had agreed that the Wrangel Island project was feasible. Knight, Maurer, and Galle were determined to be the colonizers, but there was a hitch. They were all Americans and I was trying to persuade the Canadian government to take possession of the island in the name of the British Empire. This meant that the expedition should have a Canadian or British leader. We were all agreed upon this point.

J. B. Harkin, the Prime Minister's delegate in the Wrangel Island matter, and I drew up a letter that we sent to several Canadian universities asking them to recommend recent graduates or seniors who might qualify for the post of leader of the expedition. The candidate who seemed most likely was Allan R. Crawford, of the University of Toronto, who had a good academic background and had done fieldwork with the Geological Survey of Canada.

I could not very well hire him until the Canadian government made up its mind whether or not it intended to back our project. This decision I thought had been reached when I received a letter from the Prime Minister saying: "I have discussed the matters which you laid before me today and desire to advise you that this Government proposes to assert the right of Canada to Wrangel Island, based upon the discoveries and explorations of your expedition. I believe this is all that is necessary for your purposes now."

This hopeful message was unfortunately followed by news that our expedition to Wrangel would not be authorized for 1921, but might receive approval for 1922. This left me without much to offer Allan Crawford, but I wanted very much to meet and talk with him.

It was at this time—June, 1921—that an offer of an honorary degree came from the University of Michigan. The university insisted that I come to Ann Arbor to receive it. I was, however, very much tied up with my Chautauqua lecturing, and the management did not seem disposed to release me. I pointed out to them that they had been billing me as "Dr." Stefansson when I was no such thing. How would they like it, I asked, if someone got up at one of my lectures and said, *"Dr.* Stefansson, my eye! This man is a fake!" I got time off to go to Michigan.

To kill two birds with one stone, I asked Crawford to meet me at Ann Arbor. This he did, and we had a very satisfactory and conclusive talk. Since Wilkins was also there at the time, he was able to give Crawford much advice and information about life in the Arctic in addition to supporting what I myself had to say.

Sir Auckland Geddes, the British Ambassador to the United

States, was also getting a degree from Michigan that June. I therefore had an opportunity to sound him out unofficially on the subject of Wrangel Island. Sir Auckland expressed great interest. Although he naturally could not commit his government to support of the proposed colonization, I took great encouragement from his intelligent and enthusiastic attitude.

This was still not sufficient justification for a definite commitment to Crawford. I was satisfied that he was the right man, but I had to let him go with nothing settled.

It was not long, however, before I decided that if the Canadian government was going to defer action for a year I would go ahead on my own, believing that once the expedition was under way I could win government support. I therefore set about organizing a stock company and making preparations for the voyage north.

30 The Wrangel Island Tragedy

Wrangel Island, about two thousand square miles in area, lies on the 180th meridian approximately one hundred miles north of Siberia. It had been seen by Captain Henry Kellett of H.M.S. *Herald* in 1849 from a small island named after his vessel which lies some thirty miles to the east of Wrangel. No one is recorded as visiting it until some American whalers went ashore in 1867. One of these whalers, unaware of Kellett's sighting of the island, thought that he had discovered it. Russia being more popular in the United States at that time than Great Britain, he named it after Baron Wrangel, the last Russian governor of Alaska, who as a young man had heard and tried to verify Eskimo rumors of an arctic continent north of Siberia. Lieutenant De Long, in the *Jeannette*, passed north of the island in 1879, thus proving that it was not a continent. The island was mapped by Lieutenant R. M. Berry of the USS *Rodgers* in 1881, and the name Wrangel Island was confirmed by him. No one considered it of much importance until the *Karluk's* crew landed on it in 1914 and spent the summer there, establishing the fact that there was abundant game and suggesting that, if imported, caribou would thrive on it. The island's prime importance was, to my way of thinking, as a possible station on one of the polar air routes. This was my chief argument in trying to persuade Canada to colonize and claim the island.

By September, 1921, the Stefansson Arctic and Exploration Company's party, under the leadership of twenty-year-old Allan Crawford, was at Nome outfitting. They had been, as instructed,

very secretive about their plans. The only basis that Nome old-
timers had for judging what their plans might be was the size and
nature of the outfit that the explorers purchased to take with them.
Since I had stressed the fact that anything other than basic hunting
and camping equipment must be considered a personal luxury, and
their personal resources were meager, they bought little more than
the absolute essentials.

The sourdoughs had expected to see quantities of lumber and
tar paper, cases of canned goods, and slabs of bacon going aboard
the small schooner *Silver Wave,* which the expedition had purchased. When they saw no such thing, it was argued that my men
were either foolhardy or up to something very secret. The only
thing likely to be very secret, according to the citizens of Nome, was
a gold strike. Since the outfit that the exploration party was taking
was very modest, it followed that the strike must be somewhere on
the coast east of Point Barrow, a region in which supplies could be
obtained from the many trading posts there.

Captain Jack Hammer of the *Silver Wave* would not have let
our men have his ship if he had not been told where he was supposed
to sail it. He was duly advised and told to keep the destination secret. He was told the truth, but like many other Alaskans, he did
not believe what he was told. When the *Silver Wave* left Nome on
September 9, carrying Crawford, Maurer, Knight, Galle, an Eskimo seamstress named Ada Blackjack, and seven dogs, Hammer
expected to be ordered to change his course as soon as he was out of
sight of land. He was astonished to find that he was not.

The party had been advised of the importance of taking with
them an Eskimo umiak, or skin boat, but they had decided that
those available at Nome were too expensive and that it would be
better to pick one up at East Cape, Siberia, on the way. They never
visited East Cape, however, and arrived at Wrangel Island on September 15 without the skin boat—a far more important piece of
equipment than they realized.

Captain Hammer helped the party to unload and get ashore.
Still bewildered and suspicious, and disturbed by the raising of the
British flag on the island, he then sailed back to Nome, carrying a
few personal greetings and a letter from Crawford addressed to me.

Everything had gone well, and there was every reason to suppose that the purposes of the expedition would be carried out. The
flag raising, however, caused a furor when Captain Hammer re-

ported it in Nome. His crew was worried because they, being Americans, might be considered renegades as a result of helping another nation take possession of an island that the United States could have claimed. The Nome newspaper printed a story and stirred up enough public opinion to make me and the colonizing party appear to have done something underhanded. The result was that a number of Alaskans joined in a protest that was sent to Washington.

The *New York Times* learned of this protest and, wishing to have as much as they could of the real facts, asked me for a statement. This I gave them. By this time, several months had passed. I felt very comfortable about the colonizing party at Wrangel, and I was not greatly worried about the uproar at home.

The *Times* story, although I should have preferred to keep the whole thing quiet, was fair enough and did not falsify our intentions. Unfortunately, other papers, picking up the *Times* story, made their own additions. The impression they created was that there was something felonious in the activities of a British subject living in the United States who used his residence there as a springboard to launch the dive of another power into territorial expansion.

Yet, it was not only the American press that criticized me and my arctic activities. The Canadian press continued to insist that Wrangel Island was of no value and that I must be crazy to think of colonizing it. The British press took a slightly different tack, saying that our venture was a mistake because it might jeopardize British-American relations.

Although I had not at first been worried about the unfavorable notice my venture was getting, I now saw that it might have serious consequences. The time had come for me to approach the Canadian government with a request that they send a supply ship to the Wrangel Island colony in the summer of 1922. The public view seemed to be that, since I had stressed the party's ability to live by hunting, no supply or relief ship should be needed.

I told the Canadian government that in addition to the supply ship which I had assured my men would be sent—although they were quite prepared to spend a second winter without help from the mainland if weather conditions made it impossible to reach Wrangel in 1922—all I wanted was to get back the money I had advanced and borrowed to promote Canada's claim to the island. I offered to accept, in the event that no money could be found for me, a lease on Wrangel Island which I could then sublease to the Hudson's Bay

Company. I should have much preferred a direct refund, however, for I knew that the very papers that declared that Wrangel Island was worthless would loudly affirm, if I were given a lease, that I was fattening at the public trough.

The predicament in which the continued amicable inactivity of the Canadian government left me promised to become serious. My personal resources were now exhausted. I could not myself hire a relief ship, even if I thought of it as a "rescue" ship, which my own past experience kept me from doing. I was, however, with the promise of some financial help from New York, able to make a deal with Captain Joseph Bernard, master of the *Teddy Bear*. Bernard made an earnest but unsuccessful effort to reach Wrangel in August, 1922. While he was at sea, the Canadian government finally voted me three thousand of the five thousand dollars I had asked for. After that time, ice conditions rather than money made a call at the island impossible.

The winter of 1922–1923 passed without adding anything to my worries. I felt better for having been able to send a ship out in 1922, even though it had not been able to get anywhere near the island. I had told the colonizing party that, if it proved necessary, they were at liberty to make a trip to the mainland, but I advised against doing it before a second winter had passed. I felt—and as it turned out correctly—that the second winter on Wrangel Island should present little more difficulty than the first, barring accident or illness. It would, however, be imperative to send a relief ship in 1923 if for no other reason than to find out whether the party had decided to stay on or come home. I had promised them that they would be given this choice, and it had been my intention to send others, including Eskimo families, to replace them as colonists in the event that they felt they had had enough.

In April, 1923, I was given an opportunity to make a statement before the Cabinet in Ottawa. The Cabinet courteously and attentively considered what I had to say. Their answer was that, although they agreed that Wrangel Island was a part of the British Commonwealth, they were not so sure of either the validity or the desirability of a claim that it was part of Canada. This, they felt, was for London, not Ottawa, to decide. It was suggested that I go to London, representing the Canadian government, and take the matter up with the Minister for the Colonies, the Duke of Devonshire.

I sailed to London in May and found the Colonial Office helpful and well informed, as were the Foreign Office, the Admiralty,
and the Air Ministry, all of which were made part of the discussions about Wrangel. I found no one in these departments opposed
to my views about the Arctic and the ownership of Wrangel Island.
I even found, in Commander John Graham Bower, an expert who
supported my belief that submarines could operate under the arctic
ice. Bower and I agreed that submarine men ridiculed this notion
because they knew nothing about arctic ice and that arctic experts
ridiculed it because they knew nothing of submarines. I asked
Bower which he thought would be more uncomfortable and dangerous: a voyage across the Arctic in a submarine or a trip in a Viking
ship such as the Norsemen used in the eleventh century? Bower did
not hesitate. The submarine, he was sure, would be more comfortable and less dangerous.

Conversations such as this one with Bower and other high
officials gratified and informed me, but the matter of getting help
for Wrangel Island moved slowly. It is not unlikely that the Foreign Office wished, before committing itself, to sound out other
nations as to what their attitude would be. This was a tedious
business. The summer came and I had no commitment. I got in
touch with *The* (London) *Times* and the *Manchester Guardian*,
both of which gave me open support in my campaign, as also did
The Spectator. The London *Observer* felt that the Empire was large
enough and chose not to help me.

Eventually, I got a partial decision. The government felt that
I was doing the right thing in Wrangel, but believed that for the
present it would be wise to continue the occupation on a private
basis. Nothing could be done, in any case, until the Prime Minister
of Canada arrived in London for the Imperial Conference of Prime
Ministers in September.

September would be too late. I therefore went to my friend
Colonel Leopold Amery of the Admiralty and put my cards on the
table. I agreed that private management of the Wrangel Island
venture was sound. I, however, who had put it into operation, was
a poor man and now a heavily mortgaged poor man. Could not some
wealthy Briton be found to help? Amery and his friends raised
money, but the funds that finally sent a ship to Wrangel came in
another way.

Griffith Brewer, the London representative of the Wright interests, came to me in July with an offer to raise the necessary money personally if I would allow him to ask in *The Times* for public funds with which to reimburse him. *The Times* was willing and so was I. Brewer advanced twenty-five hundred pounds. I immediately cabled to Nome, with the result that the only available ship, the *Donaldson,* was chartered.

It happened that at this time Harold Noice, who had been with Knight and me on our 1917 arctic sledge journey, was in New York and looking for a chance to go north. I knew that he was an able arctic traveler and that he would like to take the *Donaldson* to Wrangel. This I arranged for him to do, with the understanding that he would, on reaching the island, discuss the situation with the colonists and allow any to leave who wished to leave, he to provide others—Eskimo or white—to take their places. If Noice himself did not wish to stay and command the new party, he was to find someone else on the mainland who would do so.

While Noice was in Nome late in July, he learned that the Russians were asserting a claim to Wrangel Island and demanding not only that any vessel going there ask permission of the Soviet government but that in exchange for such permission it call in at Siberia and pick up a contingent of Red Guards to police the island on arrival there. After consultation in London, I cabled Noice to pay no attention to these Russian demands and to keep as far away from Russia as possible on the trip to Wrangel.

The *Donaldson* sailed from Nome on August 3. While she was making her way northward, *The Times* was conducting its successful campaign for funds. Approximately eighteen hundred pounds was raised. I was touched to see that one contribution came from a granddaughter of Sir John Franklin.

I was beginning to feel quite buoyant when, on September 1, tragic news came from Nome. The *Donaldson* had reached Wrangel without difficulty, but, according to Noice, he had found only the expedition's seamstress, Ada Blackjack, and its cat, Vic, still alive. Lorne Knight had died at the camp on Wrangel a month or so before the *Donaldson* reached it. Crawford, Maurer, and Galle had set out for Siberia half a year earlier, in January, but had never reached their destination.

The news stories that immediately began appearing gave the impression that starvation and the party's lack of experience had been the causes of the disaster. I found this hard to believe. Game had been abundant during Maurer's earlier sojourn on the island, as I knew it to be in most parts of the Arctic, and Maurer and Knight were certainly not inexperienced, both of them having traveled and camped with me under conditions far more difficult than were likely to be found on Wrangel Island. Something was wrong. The facts, I felt, simply could not be as Noice had represented them. Yet, these were the facts that had been given to the public—the facts that would be remembered.

An investigation conducted after my return to New York from London conclusively proved that Harold Noice, for reasons that are still hard to understand—he attributed his behavior to a nervous breakdown—deliberately concealed facts that were known to him, and even made alterations in Lorne Knight's diary, which, if left as written, would have disproved many of Noice's contentions. Noice gave the impression that the three men who had left for Siberia did so because of lack of food on the island and that they died of starvation during their attempt to reach the Asian mainland or Alaska. We now know that this is not so. There had been, according to Knight's diary, sufficient food before the trio left. We know also that Knight's life might have been saved had one of the men who left the island remained to hunt for him. Knight was ill with scurvy, which perpetuated itself because it kept him from being able to hunt the fresh meat which was available and would have cured him. Ada Blackjack was afraid to hunt and could not, by trapping, get enough fresh meat to keep Knight alive. It is probable that none of Knight's three male companions would have left him had they known the real nature and severity of his trouble.

Noice, under pressure, made an explanation of and apology for his conduct. Unfortunately, this did not erase from the public mind the feeling that the Wrangel Island episode was one more example of a foolhardy attempt to prove the Arctic less cruel and uncompromising than it is. The general impression was that all I had learned and tried to teach about the Arctic had been proved of no value. The fact that a new party consisting of Eskimo families and a white trapper named Charles Wells was left by the *Donaldson* on Wrangel Island made little difference to the public. Neither did it matter that Carl Lomen of Nome was so convinced of the value of Wrangel, in spite of what had happened, that he was willing to buy my interest in the island with a view to developing it for reindeer production.

The Wrangel Island venture, so confidently begun, ended as a fearful blow to me. The last of my purposes in attempting to colonize it went by the board in August, 1924, when the armed Soviet transport, *Red October,* reached the island, landed a force of guards, ran up the red flag, and arrested Charles Wells and his Eskimos, shipping them to Siberia and thence to China, in the course of which journey Wells and several of the Eskimos died. After their seizure of the island the Russians developed and maintained a station on Wrangel to serve the very purpose for which I had always imagined the island to be suitable.

The story of Wrangel, including the diaries of the men of the 1921–1923 expedition, is recorded in my book, *The Adventure of Wrangel Island,* published in 1925.

31 Caribou and Baffin Island

It seemed, in 1924, that, although I had proved to the satisfaction of most of those whose opinion on the subject might be valuable that the Arctic is not inhospitable and that much of it is suitable for development in the production of food, forces were at work that tended to convince the public of the opposite.

Accident and a certain amount of miscalculation had canceled the success of the Wrangel Island party. The peculiar behavior of Harold Noice set public opinion against us despite the fact that men and women were still living on Wrangel Island.

Another plan in which I had had equal interest should have succeeded, but for a number of reasons did not. Early in 1919, I had begun an attempt to convince the Honorable Arthur Meighen, then Canadian Minister of the Interior, that his government should undertake the breeding of reindeer and musk oxen as a national enterprise. Meighen was interested and asked me to present my case before a joint session of the Senate and the House of Commons on May 6, 1919.

This gave me the chance I wanted. I pointed out that in the settled parts of the world more and more land was being devoted to the raising of cereal and fruit crops, and that the acreage available for meat production in the form of meat cattle and sheep was being steadily cut down. I said that this fact was only one of several that pointed to northern Canada's lands, which were too far north for cereal crops but which provided a magnificent year-round grazing area. Reindeer (the domesticated form of caribou) and

musk oxen, native to the area, were, I said, splendid meat animals.
The musk ox had the additional advantage of producing high-
quality wool. The development of the Dominion's million square
miles of unused grazing land would, I declared, soon make northern
Canada the great wool-, meat-, and milk-producing area of the
Western Hemisphere.

As I spoke I felt that my hearers were being affected, and indeed they were. Within two weeks a royal commission was formed to
study the possibilities that my talk outlined. On the commission
were the Dominion Railway Commissioner, the manager of Canada's greatest meat-slaughtering concern, the Commissioner of Dominion Parks, and myself. Things at first moved rapidly and well.
During the early part of 1920 a number of hearings were held and
thirty-five witnesses were asked to give their opinions.

Before the commission made its report, I felt it necessary to resign from it. I had too much of a personal stake in what was being
considered, inasmuch as I had applied to the government for grazing privileges in the southern half of Baffin Island. Although the
commission showed interest in my ideas, it was plain that they
regarded them as highly experimental and would be willing to proceed only with the greatest circumspection. Believing that this was
the case, I decided to try to get private capital to back me in a
large-scale development.

The logical place to look for this capital appeared to be the
Hudson's Bay Company. I approached the New York agent of the
company and through his interest was able to have my plan put
before Charles Sale, deputy director of the Hudson's Bay Company
in London. He wrote that he was very much attracted by my proposal and that he would be able to talk to me about it in the spring
of 1920. This was convenient for me, for it was at that time that the
Prime Minister of Canada asked me to go to London to lay before
the British Cabinet the northern schemes I had presented to him.

At this time I was successful in persuading the company to
back me in a somewhat roundabout way. I was to get my grazing
rights from Ottawa and then transfer them to a Hudson's Bay
subsidiary to be set up as the Hudson's Bay Reindeer Company.

The Privy Council decided that my lease should be granted.
I was given thirty years' grazing rights to more than a hundred
thousand square miles of Baffin Island, all of the island south of
60° N latitude. In exchange for this, I was to see that a thousand im-

ported reindeer were on the leasehold by 1924 and ten thousand (which might include 40 per cent wild caribou) by 1932.

I assigned this lease to the Hudson's Bay Reindeer Company, of which I was to be a director and technical adviser. From the outset my advice consisted of an effort to get the company to begin operations on a large scale immediately and to put Storker Storkerson in charge of buying the deer, getting them from Norway to Baffin Island, and managing the herd when it was established.

I immediately ran into difficulty. The company moved very slowly, although I warned them that the success of the reindeer business in Alaska was likely to increase the price of deer. During the summer of 1920, I was busy with so many things—lecturing, writing *The Friendly Arctic,* planning the Wrangel Island expedition—that I could not, aside from a barrage of letters, push the Baffin Island project as it should have been pushed.

The company hired Storkerson, as I suggested, and in late summer he went to Baffin Island to make a study of the grazing prospects. Storkerson was very much in earnest. In fact, he had decided to make large-scale reindeer herding his lifework, and if the company had not hired him he would have found other backing and gone into it on his own. He made a report to the directors of the Hudson's Bay Reindeer Company in November, 1920, speaking in enthusiastic terms of the vegetation on the grazing lands. On the strength of this and of what I knew of the Alaskan reindeer project, I urged the company to increase its capital and jump in with both feet immediately.

It was decided, however, to begin with a small herd. Early in 1921 Storkerson went to London to talk over his plans with Charles Sale. Sale was enthusiastic about Storkerson and sent him with instructions to investigate the reindeer situation in Norway. I began to feel that we were getting somewhere.

Storkerson returned from Norway in April, 1921, and made his report to Sale. For reasons that are not entirely clear, Sale had by this time decided that he would like to have someone who had had actual experience in buying deer negotiate for our animals. He therefore appointed Francis H. Wood, who had purchased reindeer for Dr. Wilfrid Grenfell in Labrador some years before. Storkerson apparently knew of this without at first realizing its import. He gave Sale the impression that he was willing to let Wood handle the purchasing. Within twenty-four hours, however, Storkerson had had time to consider the threat to his own authority. He then wrote that Wood's appointment made his own position untenable and was "a grave injury." He offered his resignation, to take effect immediately.

I heard about this while on a lecture tour, and did what I could by cable and letter to get the company to make it possible for Storkerson to reconsider his resignation. The company had gone so far, however, in perfectly good faith, that I came to feel that it could not retrace its steps. Storkerson's resignation was accepted. The death knell of the Baffin Island reindeer experiment was sounded, though we did not hear it at the time.

Francis Wood and an associate went to Norway, where they purchased as many deer as the company's *Nascopie* could carry— less than seven hundred. Sixty-two of these never reached the ship, and seventy-seven died on the voyage to Baffin Island. When the deer were put ashore, they immediately scattered in a search for food. The Lapp herders who had been brought from Norway with the shipment recovered only 260 of them.

The grazing was, according to the herders, not at all as Storkerson had pictured it, and the Lapps themselves had no taste for wandering far in search of better pasture in the severe weather that followed the landing on Baffin Island on November 1. They did not seem to care very much whether the herd was preserved or not. They were lazy, unimaginative, and incompetent.

I did not at first realize how bad the situation was, being in 1922 much concerned with my difficulties with the Wrangel Island enterprise. By 1923 the state of the Baffin Island herd was so bad that I suggested to the company that it would be wise to get an experienced reindeer man from Alaska to help save the project. The man recommended by Carl Lomen, Alaska's reindeer king, refused the post offered him on the ground that the experiment had already failed. No one else was available.

In the fall of 1923, to no one's regret, the Lapp herders called it a day and returned to Norway. They were replaced by Eskimos, who seemed much more interested in preserving the herd than the Lapps had been. I again urged the hiring of a capable manager and the purchase of more deer, but the company did nothing, leaving the herd to its post manager at Amadjuak Bay.

By 1924, with the Wrangel Island catastrophe still fresh in my mind, reminding me of my failure to prove what I knew to be true, I saw the handwriting on the wall and knew that another hope must be deferred. The Hudson's Bay Reindeer Company's entire herd of deer had disappeared, and its two-hundred-thousand-dollar capital investment had disappeared with them.

It is probable that Storkerson had misjudged the character of the vegetation on the Baffin Island range, but it is certain that had he remained as manager he would, with his skill and resourcefulness and knowledge of arctic conditions, have worked out a better system of herding than the company, without him, was able to devise.

I felt a deep sense of frustration over the double defeats of Wrangel and Baffin islands, coupled with a sense of regret that I had taken on so much that I could not give personal attention and direction to all my projects at the same time. Neither of these failures changed in the slightest degree my feeling about the principles behind the enterprises.

Storkerson, too, kept his faith and continued in the reindeer business in Norway, with high hopes of expanding it. His experiences had, however, begun to break him down. He was saddened and confused by the public belief that I, with whom he knew that he had shared journeys that were now said to be creations of my imagination, was a complete charlatan. In his native Norway, his faith in me turned many against him. He began to go downhill, to neglect his business obligations, and to act strangely in other ways.

When I heard that my old companion had been declared insane and committed to an asylum, I tried to figure out in what way I had failed him. I sometimes still have sleepless nights filled with doubt and worry over what his association with me may have done to destroy him.

32 *London Friends*

The years following my return from the 1913–1918 expedition were years crowded with negotiations concerning the two unsuccessful enterprises that I have described and with the arduous routines of writing and lecturing. Yet, it was during these years that I had an opportunity to develop my affection for British people and their ways.

Almost everything with which I was associated took me to London for periods ranging from weeks to months in almost every year. Although I was of Icelandic descent—which means that I had a touch of Irish in me—and had been educated as an American, my association with the British, which really began under the warm and endearing tutelage of Lord Strathcona in 1913, had developed, by 1921, into a sense of belonging that possessed me whenever I visited London. However, after my unhappy experiences with the official apathy that helped to defeat my intention to add Wrangel Island to the Empire and the equally defeatist reception of my attempt to develop the grazing lands of northern Canada, I was not at all sure that I wanted to be British if it meant joining the ranks of the Kipling imperialists.

I first met Kipling at the Strathconas' in 1913 and found him sharply and ingratiatingly interesting. Our first meeting, arranged by Strathcona, was typical of that great old man's way of bringing compatible people together. While I was in his office one day, talking over my projected expedition, Strathcona heard me quoting some lines from Kipling. He said nothing at the time, but a few days later phoned to tell me that he had invited Kipling to dinner and thought I might like to come too.

I sat beside Kipling at dinner. We immediately discovered a mutual friend in William B. Cabot, who had known the poet in Vermont and who had been instrumental in getting support from the Harvard Travelers Club for my 1913 expedition. The subject of Vermont having been brought up, Kipling asked if I knew his brother-in-law, Beatty Balestier. I did not know Beatty at the time except through having heard Bill Cabot speak of him. I later learned a great deal about the Balestiers, and what I learned gave me considerable insight into Kipling's character. At our first meeting, however, he talked and questioned me chiefly about Eskimos. Kipling had read about the "Blond Eskimo" furor and listened attentively to my explanation. By the time dinner ended, I had grown quite eloquent on the subject of Dr. Rae and his adoption of Eskimo ways while traveling. In the midst of my description of Eskimo snowhouses, we had to get up from the table, and Kipling was soon lost among other guests who wanted a word with him.

He found his way back to me, however, and continued his questioning about snowhouses. How were they furnished? How many people lived in a single house? Did Eskimo snow villages have any places for social gatherings? I told him that the largest snowhouse I had ever seen could hold two dozen standing spectators and leave room in the center for half a dozen dancers. Kipling wanted to know how big such a house would be. When I told him, he spun on his heel and started to pace off the distance. This ended our talk, for as he paced, watching his feet through his thick glasses, he entered a circle of women guests who immediately claimed him.

It was at a later dinner in London that I had an opportunity to talk with Kipling about the strange family feud that drove him from his adopted country. I had, since my first meeting with Rudyard in 1913, met Beatty Balestier and learned from him of the Vermont trouble. Beatty had given me the impression that his sister Caroline, Kipling's wife and five years older than her husband, had been the cause of the rift. Caroline had apparently driven Rudyard to ask her brother for an accounting of the money put in his hands for the construction of Naulakha, the Kipling house in Dummerston, Vermont, near Brattleboro. This Kipling did with shy embarrassment. He would have let Beatty's explanation be sufficient had Caroline allowed him to do so. Instead of accepting Beatty's statement, she insisted to her husband that Beatty could not be trusted with other people's money. Kipling, against his better judgment, confronted his brother-in-law again, again with embarrassed apology. Beatty, according to what he told me, realized that his sister was behind Rudyard's attitude. He claimed that he said some very harsh things about Caroline to her husband without feeling animosity toward Kipling himself. He gave me the impression that he was devoted to Rudyard and that he had never altered his devotion, even after Caroline's nagging had driven the Kiplings to, as Vermonters would say, "have the law on" Beatty, binding him to keep the peace. In spite of Beatty's warm feeling for his brother-in-law, and even though Beatty had the upper hand in the lawsuit, the situation got out of hand. The Kiplings, after four American years, left Vermont, never to return.

On several occasions I had a chance to talk with Kipling fairly intimately. I told him frankly that I felt that his quarrel with his brother-in-law had been tragic for Beatty Balestier. I said that I doubted that he ever had a more devoted friend or greater admirer than Beatty. I even ventured to say that I hoped the breach between them might be healed. Kipling let a murmured suggestion of assent come through the front of his British reticence. I formed the conclusion that the quarrel had been entirely Mrs. Kipling's doing and that Rudyard himself would have welcomed a reconciliation with his brother-in-law.

Whenever I had an opportunity to mention the Balestier feud to Kipling, I found in the poet's manner a distinct wistfulness. Once, when Rudyard mentioned that he was about to take a trip to South America, I said that I hoped it would be followed by one to North America. Again I saw that pensive, faraway look. I got the impression that when Caroline, who was in poor health, died he would visit Vermont and put an end to the estrangement between himself and Beatty. Caroline, however, continued her domination of the situation, outliving Rudyard by three years.

Another friend I made in London was Sir Arthur Conan Doyle, whom I found immensely congenial in spite of a preoccupation with spiritism that often appeared to do strange things to his character. We became quite close—so much so that when Sir Arthur came to New York later he regarded me as his best friend there and even asked me to take on the responsibility of telling him whom he should or should not see from among the host of applicants for his time.

He had been a firm believer in the spirit world for many years. People said that the death of his eldest son after World War I had turned him to spiritism. That this was not true I know from his own statement and from the fact that he wrote books on the spirit world before his son died.

Doyle was an enormous man, six-feet-four or -five and built in proportion; but a heart ailment, which limited his activity, made him seem almost frail. I attended a number of séances with him and found his ready acceptance inconsistently naïve. Confronted with the spirit world, Doyle was more like Dr. Watson than Sherlock Holmes.

On several of my visits to London, I occupied Stephen Coleridge's New Court flat. Arthur Page, of what was then Doubleday, Page and Company, was at the time busy with the details of buying up the old London publishing house of Heinemann, and he and his wife Mollie sometimes joined me in giving elaborate parties at New Court. These affairs were joint in everything but the bills, all of which Arthur Page paid.

One summer I sublet New Court to a pair of American girls, Fannie Hurst, the novelist, and Ruth Bryan Owen, daughter of William Jennings Bryan and later United States ambassador to Denmark. While they occupied the Coleridge flat they gave many parties, to most of which I was invited, thereby widening my acquaintance among Londoners.

Among my new acquaintances was Agatha Christie, creator of her own Sherlock Holmes in the form of Hercule Poirot, who was tremendously popular with readers of detective stories. Agatha came to a luncheon party that I gave one day at New Court. I had given her a memo with the address and rather complicated instructions for reaching the place. She was living in the country at the time and, on arriving in town, discovered that she had lost my note. This was serious, for she knew little about me except that I was a friend of Conan Doyle and that I had sublet a flat from someone in one of the Temples. She had no recollection of what my note had said. Nevertheless, she arrived at the luncheon only an hour late, proving herself to be better than Conan Doyle at playing the role of her fictional detective. She told me that she had simply put herself into the character of Hercule Poirot and worked out what he would have done in a similar situation.

My plan to add Wrangel Island to the British Empire induced

some of the most dedicated imperialists to take me up and regard me as one of them. This interested me more than it embarrassed me, for I was glad to learn the views and feelings of such people as Lord Milner; General Bobbie White, who had been mixed up in the celebrated Jameson Raid in South Africa; Geoffrey Dawson, editor of *The Times;* and the Dowager Countess of Dudley, mother of the Governor General of Australia.

Such embarrassment as I felt resulted from my somewhat confused nationality, and from the fact that my imperialist friends were likely to be on the side of the full-dress British explorers while I was doing my best to publicize and praise the work of low fellows like Thomas Simpson and John Rae.

A curious tie between the two camps was Lady Kathleen Scott, who had been very kind to me on one of my early visits to London in sending to my hotel an invitation to visit her. Lady Scott might well have felt bitter toward those who went so far as to believe that her husband's heroic death in the Antarctic had been unnecessary, the result of scurvy brought on by putting too much confidence in the medical profession's belief that lime juice, fruit, and vegetables were all that were needed to prevent the ravages of the disease. Lady Scott, however, took the position that she did not wish to protect her husband at the expense of the safety of future explorers. Her kindness to me, whose theories of polar travel she knew well, proved what a broad-minded and generous woman she was.

If I was acceptable to Lady Scott, I was, without being two-faced, acceptable also to the Kipling type of imperialist. I was acceptable enough at least to be commanded one day, on one of my first visits to London, to appear at Buckingham Palace before His Majesty George V, who was technically my king, although my efforts to extend his Empire were more the result of a belief in travel across the polar regions than of a devotion to the principles of empire or of loyalty to the crown.

Before going to the palace for my audience I had a talk with Shackleton, who knew how the common man was supposed to look and behave in the presence of royalty. Shackleton said that the prime requisite was a good tailor. I mentioned Hill Brothers, the firm that had been recommended to me by my former secretary, the Baron de Grandcourt. Shackleton seemed to think that I could not do better.

I took his advice and was measured for a complete morning costume: striped trousers, coat, four-in-hand tie, spats, and top hat.

Everything was ready on time. On my way to Buckingham Palace, I went over Shackleton's instructions in my mind. When the King sits down, I sit down. I do not speak until the King speaks. When the King rises after fifteen minutes, I rise and leave. George V, Shackleton had told me, was noted for his punctuality. He never kept anyone waiting. That is what Shackleton said.

I soon learned that, in my case at least, he was wrong. When I entered the palace, I was met by a very ornate Lord Ponsonby, who reported to me with the most elaborate courtesy that due to unforeseen circumstances His Majesty had been delayed. Would I be kind enough to be seated.

I sat and thought about things for a while, mostly about what I was doing there and what the King would have to say. Would he talk about my Wrangel Island project, about my Baffin Island reindeer scheme, about my latest expedition, or what?

After twenty minutes His Majesty appeared. I noticed, with something of a start, that he was dressed exactly as I was from top to toe. Hill Brothers must have an inside track, I thought. I must have been a trifle flustered at the time, for I do not remember what the King said by way of greeting.

He immediately sat down and I followed suit. He broke the ice by saying that since it was his duty to meet great numbers of people he was necessarily thoroughly briefed before an interview. "But," said His Majesty, "I know something more about you, Stefansson. I read in this morning's *Times* an interview with you. You spoke enthusiastically about the possibility of domesticating an animal called the musk ox. Now I fancy myself a naval man, and one of my naval friends has just been made governor of the Falkland Islands in the sub-antarctic region. I'm eager to have my friend do a good job and would like to help him in some way. Do you think that the musk ox would do well in the Falkland Islands?"

This opening would have been hard to resist. I began to list the musk ox's virtues. The King followed what I said with questions, all of which I answered. Apparently he had forgotten about Shackleton's fifteen-minute rule, for almost an hour went by before there was any break in the conversation. Then the King rose. The interview was over.

That evening I ran into Shackleton at the Athenaeum Club. As I approached him I saw that he was laughing.

"What's the joke?" I said. "Did I do anything wrong?"

Shackleton said that the joke was really on my tailors. "Do you know," he asked, "why you were kept waiting at the palace this morning?"

I said that I did not.

"Well," said Shackleton, "believe it or not, Hill Brothers are a whole year behind the times. They dressed you in spats and a four-in-hand, and neither of those adornments are being worn with a morning coat this year. Some noble lord saw you in time and warned the King. The reason you were kept waiting was that the King had to go back to his dressing room and put on spats and a four-in-hand. A matter of courtesy, you know. He couldn't embarrass you by making you feel that you weren't properly dressed."

This little incident made me feel more at home in London than I had ever felt. Even if few Englishmen were ready to do anything about my ideas, they did not hesitate to try to make me feel that I was one of them.

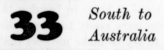

33 South to Australia

The Wrangel Island and Baffin Island failures had not, as I have said, caused me to lose faith in the north. Yet, for the time being my efforts to publicize that faith seemed wasted. I wanted to throw myself into something else—not necessarily an entirely new career but something with a different emphasis.

Ever since 1910, when I first gained enough command of the language of the Eskimos to begin thinking like one of them, I had been gradually acquiring the belief that a desert as an unlivable and worthless region was not a reality but rather a state of mind. For instance, without having to do more than stop thinking like a European and start thinking like an Eskimo, I had been able to portray what had long been considered a frozen desert as a productive and comfortable region. Might it not be possible to do the same thing for the dry, hot deserts of Africa, Asia, and Australia?

If I were going to do this, the place for me was plainly Australia. When studying comparative religions in 1903, I had learned something of the life in the interior of Australia from Sir Baldwin Spencer and F. J. Gillen. Between 1913 and 1916, I had spent months at a time with George Hubert Wilkins, who had been born and reared on the southern edge of the Australian desert. He had recently informed me that during 1923–1924 he would be on the northern edge of that region in charge of a British Museum natural-history expedition. He offered to help me get started with any desert studies I wanted to make.

If I intended to study Australia, it was probably now or never.

In another year Wilkins might be in another continent, and I would not be able to have his on-the-scene help and advice. Moreover, the project would take money, and I could probably get more now than I would be able to get later. Ellison-White had an Australian office and wanted to book me for a lecture tour in Australia and New Zealand. Wilkins advised me, however, that an even better agent would be an Australian named Carroll. I had heard the same thing from an Australian journalist friend of Wilkins, Freda Sternberg. She was anxious to take a vacation from her regular work in London, where she represented Australian newspapers. Her urging, combined with that of Wilkins, convinced me. Freda would arrange the tour, and Wilkins would come down from the tropical and humid north to spend some time with me when I was lecturing in Sydney, Melbourne, and Adelaide. I was pleased that he wanted to introduce me to his hero, Sir John Monash, under whom, as commander-in-chief of Australian forces, he had served on the Western Front after leaving our Canadian expedition in 1916.

I had books to write and I could not afford to delay the writing of them. Wilkins and Freda saw no problem in that. All I had to do was take along two secretaries. Olive Rathbun Wilcox's husband Jack agreed to go along as the operator of my lecture stereopticon. He would also look after the details of our traveling. Olive would take my dictation as usual—magazine articles, book chapters, correspondence.

Freda Sternberg left several weeks before we did. The Wilcoxes and I sailed from San Francisco and stopped to visit my Harvard classmate Alfred Lowrey Castle and other friends in the Hawaiian Islands. We also spent a day with my friend James Norman Hall in Tahiti. Wilkins met us in Sydney.

One thing I very much wanted to do was investigate something that Wilkins had told me in the course of our work in the Arctic between 1913 and 1916. He had remarked on the similarity between the food tastes of early European pioneers in South Australia and his own food tastes and mine while we were living by hunting on the sea ice north of Alaska. Almost from the first June day on which we met at Sydney, his older friends and he began to review and confirm or contradict what he had told me in the north about dietary matters. Many of these reports of his are contained in *The Friendly Arctic* and in more detail in my *Not by Bread Alone,* published in 1946.

There are many interesting things about Australia that one seldom finds mentioned in print. Everyone has heard about Australian kangaroos, but not many have heard anything about Australian camels. I had known Wilkins for nearly ten years before I heard him mention these camels. I stood gaping when for the first time I saw a train of them winding over hill and dale—these trains were almost everywhere except in the cities. Olive and Jack found them equally surprising. It is not that Australians are ashamed of their camels. Their reticence about them reminds me of the medieval Scandinavians' reticence about seasickness. In the vast and detailed saga literature of Iceland, in which no topic recurs more frequently than seafaring, I do not remember a word about seasickness. Were the early Icelanders, perhaps, free from this affliction? Not at all. They were seasick all over the place—so frequently and conspicuously sick that they said nothing about it. It was like breathing. A person breathes millions of times for every one time he mentions it. It is when he stops breathing that it becomes news.

Another thing the Australians did not write about—perhaps in this case because they were a little ashamed—was their cockney way of speaking. I felt sure that their teachers must long have been trying to fight against it. Yet, while I was there a convention of schoolmasters passed a resolution saying that this was their speech and that they might as well admit it.

Australians are not slow to criticize and poke fun at foreign accents, particularly the American. When we were there, American speech was a favorite subject for jokes. The first journalist who heard me talk in Sydney commented on my funny accent. He thought particularly amusing the way I pronounced "water" and "coffee." With that common word, water, we certainly had our troubles. Olive's accent, though she was from Wyoming, was very much like my Dakota way of speaking. We both became self-conscious about "water" and in restaurants usually had Jack Wilcox speak for us. I remember very well an early breakfast we had at the railway station in Adelaide. The waitress had not put any water on the table, and Olive tried to ask for some. She had trouble. Jack tried to help her out but did no better. We called the head waiter, who explained that he was sorry, but they did not serve such things before noon. What sort of exotic wine he thought we were asking for I cannot imagine.

Wilkins, although he never thought of telling us about camel trains, had coached us on some of the peculiarities of Australian speech. From my youth I had known that a bush ranger was a country highwayman, but Wilkins cautioned us that a bush nurse was a rural nurse. A ranch was a station.

It was news to all three of us that in Australia many trees shed their bark but relatively few shed their leaves. We were surprised to find that a tree that from a distance looked to a European or a North American like a shade tree is unlikely to furnish any shade under Australia's nearly vertical noonday sun, since its leaves stand on edge and give little more shade than a wire fence.

We met many interesting and delightful Australian people. I had expected much of Sir Douglas Mawson, the antarctic explorer, and I was not disappointed in him or in Lady Mawson, who I learned was Dutch.

By a lucky chance, on entering a lift at the Hotel Australia in Sydney, I ran into my old friend Percy Grainger, the pianist. Once in every five or ten years Percy visited his native land. He told me that I must meet Nellie Melba who, named for Melbourne, was now living in retirement near that city. He instructed me not to be bashful. He said that she would perhaps take the initiative.

She did. After lecturing in and around Sydney, usually to full houses, I went to Melbourne, where the hall was also sold out, though only half the people who had bought seats came. Although the temperature was above freezing, the Australians thought it cold and most of those who came to hear me were bundled up in steamer rugs. Some actually carried braziers. I hoped that Melba was in the audience. I did notice, without at first realizing that it was the great singer, a slightly stout woman who leaned forward from her front-row seat. She seemed not to be missing a word and laughed at all the right places. At the close of my talk she rushed forward, shook my hand warmly, and almost shouted, ''I know one thing about you, you must have had a wonderful voice teacher! You place your voice just right!'' I had been flattering myself that she was appreciating my sense of humor. Instead, she had been listening to my voice. Perhaps she had not heard a word I said. While I was stammering my disappointment, somebody came up and introduced us.

The impression that Melba's first words made on me gave me a wrong view of her. When I visited her home, at her invitation, on my first free afternoon, I changed that view. I then saw that she was quick-witted and less self-centered than is usual with singers. In fact, she turned out to be one of the most intelligent women I ever met. In my esteem she did not rate quite as high as General Monash and Sir Baldwin Spencer, but she did leave an indelible impression upon me.

There was one way in which most Australians we met disappointed us. Many had traveled widely about the world, but few had seen the interior of their own continent. They knew San Francisco, Detroit, and Atlanta, Dublin, Moscow, and Budapest, but they had not bothered to visit Alice Springs or the Macdonnell Ranges, and they were puzzled when we asked them about such uninteresting places. Most Australians in Sydney or Melbourne thought of the natives only as blacks who could not learn anything, many in fact, dismissing them as animals rather than people.

Sir Baldwin was, of course, an exception. We visited the Spencers in their country home among well-watered woodlands and magnificent trees. Sir Baldwin had been everywhere in the interior and the north of his own country, and we did not hear him carry on about the marvelous instincts and deplorable stupidity of the blacks. On the contrary, he maintained that what city-dwelling Australians regarded as mere instinct in Australian aborigines was really evidence of native intelligence. He declared that, as far as he knew, the brains of the natives were about as good as ours. Spencer, it seemed to me, knew more about the blacks than anyone else I met. He agreed with the usual city dweller that a family group of natives could with relatively little trouble travel in places where whites would probably die of hunger and thirst. He attributed this aptitude, however, to extraordinary intelligence and a kind of Sherlock Holmes intuitiveness rather than to primitive instinct.

I enjoyed the lecture tour, but with the exception of occasional engagements in such fabulous gold towns as Ballarat, I was seeing and learning little of the desert that I had come so far to study. The problem of seeing the desert to advantage, Spencer assured me, would solve itself. He had already heard, and perhaps had helped to make it come true, that the government would fall in with my idea of a desert expedition. He had in mind a foremost authority on water, a geologist, who, he said, should travel with me. He particularly wished me to cultivate a desert botanist named Osborn. If I were really lucky, I might even get Osborn to join my party.

My first real preparation for desert studies came when I lectured at Adelaide. After I had spent part of a day with Douglas

Mawson, I went to an appointment with Sir Baldwin's Professor Theodore Osborn, who told me many fascinating things about the relation of Australian plants to water. The problem of grazing there is not so much one of finding grass, I learned, but of finding water for animals to drink. I gathered that artesian water, which was the only water available, was likely to be brackish. For that reason sheep made the best grazing animals, since they could tolerate more salt, though they had a disadvantage, said Osborn, in that they were unable to travel as far as cattle could from a source of water in search of food. Horses were even better at this than cattle. For every mile from water that a sheep could travel in search of grass, a bullock could go two miles and a horse three or four.

Professor Osborn seemed pleased with a rumor he had heard that a party would be made up to take our group by special train north from Adelaide to Oodnadatta. There we would be met by Dodge cars, which were then supposed to be especially good for travel across country where both water and roads were scarce. If I wished, the party would take me right across the Australian desert beyond the Macdonnell Ranges out across the Berkeley Table Land, where agriculture and stock raising really began. Most fortunate of all, the government would assign to the party Dr. Keith Ward, reputedly the country's highest authority on artesian water.

Our party did not have any official head, unless I was it. The most influential member was probably the Countess of Stradbroke, whose husband was Governor of Victoria. Another, of almost equal if different influence, was Vera Burns of the Burns-Phelps steamship line. The husbands of both these women were too busy to join us, but I felt sure that it was they who took care of the bills. What made everything so easy for us may perhaps have been the influence of Lord Foster, the Governor General of Australia, who was much interested although he was also unable to accompany us.

After two nights in our special train on a northbound narrowgauge railway, we took to our cars. After driving for several days, we finally reached Alice Springs. This settlement looked to me so much like the sort of desert resort we now have in Arizona and New Mexico that I actually bought a corner lot and paid taxes on it for some years. I perhaps do not need to add that I sold it just before an astounding rise in value.

From Alice Springs we took a day's ride out over the Berkeley Table Land, and another side journey to the Hermannsburg Mission

of the German Lutheran Church, where we had a glimpse of an
interesting battle of culture. This mission existed, of course, for the
conversion of the heathen, the Australian blacks. The missionaries
had discovered what everybody in Australia seemed to know—that
in a dry land the best domestic animals are horses. Being German,
the missionaries fed their native converts on horse meat. This horri-
fied the British Christians, who questioned whether the benefits of
Lutheranism were adequate compensation to the natives for the
degradation of eating horses. Public opinion, we were told by the
missionaries, swung more and more against horse-meat eating until
the powerful Anglicans and Roman Catholics forced the mission to
sell and kill the horses. We heard much, and smelled more, of the
decaying beasts as they were being sacrificed to save the natives from
a degrading diet.

At Hermannsburg we saw a score or more natives who had just
come in from the northwest. Their clothing could have been hidden
under an ordinary postage stamp. Interesting to see were naked
women walking about carrying live dogs, dingoes, across the small of
their backs. A missionary told me that unmarried, or at least child-
less, women carried dogs instead of babies. It seemed to be customary
to hold the dog's forepaws in one hand and to let its head hang in
the crook of one elbow while the tail hung from the crook of the
other.

Interesting as this trip was, my mind was not entirely on what
I was seeing. I could not get Wrangel Island out of my head. I did
not then know the complete story of what happened to the Wells
party after the Soviet guards took over the island. My book, which
Olive and I had written and which we knew was now going through
the press, worried us a lot. I realized that I had bitten off more than
I could chew. I had enough to do to write and lecture about frozen
deserts, I now saw, without going off on detours through hot and
dry ones.

There was another important thing bothering me. In talking
with Baldwin Spencer and with true pioneers who had in some cases
been brought up to speak the native tongue of the Australian blacks,
I became convinced that it would be as unsatisfactory to deal with
Australian natives without knowing their language as it would be to
deal with Eskimos without knowing theirs.

Olive, Jack, and I conferred and agreed, over the protests of
Mr. Carroll and Miss Sternberg, that we would have to cut the

Australian tour short and omit the New Zealand visit. Both parties would lose. We could only try to compensate our managers for their losses and hurry anxiously back to New York. We came home to face a difficult situation in which both Olive and I were needed: the final collapse of the Baffin Island reindeer experiment of which I have already written.

34 The Bellevue Experiment

Like my views on arctic travel and the importance of developing the north, my ideas about diet were an attempt to correct what I saw as human error.

My real introduction to the medical profession came with my article "Observations on Three Cases of Scurvy" published in the *Journal of the American Medical Association* for November 23, 1918. The story of how close that paper came to being rejected reads like fiction. One day in his office Dr. Morris Fishbein, the *Journal's* editor, overheard his assistants talking about an article that had been submitted. It was curious, they said, how men good in their own field go off the beam when they venture into another field. Fishbein asked what they were talking about. They told him that they were discussing a manuscript that they had just thrown in the wastebasket because it was not accompanied by return postage. They said that, postage or not, the wastebasket was the place for it, since it was completely crazy. It had come from the polar explorer Stefansson, who was a good enough explorer but obviously knew nothing about medicine. His attention drawn to the paper, Fishbein read it, decided that it might not be crazy, and sent it to the Nutrition Department of the Yale Medical School. Yale wrote back that the article sounded as if it might make sense and, if it did, it could be important.

Though Fishbein later confirmed this story, I first heard it from Dr. Alfred Hess of New York, famous in the early days of vitamin discovery for applying a diet of fresh and raw fruits and vegetables to the treatment of scurvy, adult and infantile. Dr. Hess telephoned me to say that if I would come to his house for dinner he would introduce me to the Yale professor who had saved my manuscript, Dr. Lafayette B. Mendel. That evening Mendel and Hess cited numerous case histories involving the ravages of scurvy during World War I, especially among British soldiers. The British had been in the war longer than the Americans, and their army cooks were said to be even more likely than ours to overcook foods, thus depriving them of what antiscorbutic value they might have had.

Dr. Hess said that what impressed him most about my paper was that I had reported approximately the same time values for symptomatic change from a diet of fresh raw meat that he had been obtaining from a diet of fresh raw fruit and vegetables. This was, in each case, about four days from lethargy and deep gloom to cheerful optimism. It would seem, then, that in the treatment of scurvy the important thing is that the food be fresh, and whether a doctor should prescribe, in his therapy, raw fruits and vegetables or underdone and raw meats would depend on such considerations as convenience, cost, and individual preference. Some patients might prefer to be cured by eating medium or rare steak. Some might choose an endive and grapefruit salad.

I have already told how the famous nutritionist Raymond Pearl became interested in my idea that diet should be taken out of the realm of theory and folklore and put into the field of common sense and practical experience. Pearl and I never got around to writing our projected book on the history of man's diet from the Stone Age to the beginning of agriculture. We had too many other irons in the fire. We did, however, continue to believe in and talk about our ideas.

Most practicing physicians and teachers in medical schools were against us. The doctors had patients whom they had been treating in the firm belief that a varied diet was the only diet suitable for human beings; they could not very well afford to do a sudden about-face. The professors and students who sat at their feet believed that nutrition was a science, a science that was perhaps responsible for the success of the human race. Not unnaturally, when I published, or spoke of, experiences that questioned the very foundations of that science, the science was given the benefit of the doubt and what I had to say was either disbelieved or disregarded.

Occasionally we made converts. I remember once visiting Dr. Frederic M. Hanes of Winston-Salem, North Carolina. One of Dr. Hanes' guests loudly declared that even the best foods would sicken a man if he had to eat the same thing every day. He offered to bet anything that nobody could eat one quail at each meal for ten consecutive days. I offered to take the bet—even up to a thousand dollars. I might have won some easy money if I had not gone on to say what I already knew to be true: that I could eat three properly cooked quail at each meal with no side dish except perhaps a little butter. The company seemed to think I was joking, so the test never took place. It did, however, lead to further conversation that gave me a chance to expound my views. I was finally able to make a favorable impression upon the company. I regarded that evening as a victory in a minor skirmish, but I was still far from having won the war.

The transcripts of my first talk with Pearl had aroused some interest on the part of the Mayo Clinic at Rochester, Minnesota. Dr. Charles Mayo invited me to come to the clinic to have a thorough physical examination with the idea of discovering whether my supposedly unorthodox arctic diet had done me harm or good. I was delighted with the offered opportunity, but was unable to find the two or three weeks' time necessary for the experiment.

One day at the Harvard Club in New York I happened to mention my disappointment at not being able to get to Rochester. The friend with whom I was talking, Dr. Clarence Lieb, said that New York doctors would also be able to examine me as thoroughly as the Mayo brothers had proposed to do. He persuaded me to let him organize a team of doctors interested enough in my ideas to give me a thorough going-over. This he promptly did, and I began dropping in at the offices and clinics of his expert colleagues, paying for the tests they gave me by giving talks before their medical societies. After these tests and observations were completed, Dr. Lieb wrote and published a paper in the *Journal of the American Medical Association* for July 3, 1926, "The Effects of an Exclusive Long-Continued Meat Diet." This was, in effect, a signed statement by several eminent doctors that after rigorous examination they had found me to be in a state of health equal to or better than the average man of my age who had followed a mixed diet.

Some weeks after the publication of Dr. Lieb's article I received from the American Meat Institute in Chicago one of the most important letters of my life. The writer, Wesley Hardenbergh, a public relations man for the institute, not unnaturally thought that, although I might be overstating my case, my insistence on it might be good public relations for the Meat Institute.

Hardenbergh's letter asked whether Lieb and I would permit the institute to reprint ten thousand copies of Dr. Lieb's paper for distribution to doctors and teachers specializing in nutrition. We telephoned Pearl and he took a night train up from Baltimore. At breakfast the next day we chose others who would meet for a real strategy session at lunch. At that session we reached a decision.

We told the American Meat Institute that just printing one more article, however excellent it might be, would not satisfy the general feeling that, so far as the Stone Age diet was concerned, I had to ''put up or shut up.'' In our opinion, the demonstration should be more dramatic and more conclusive than that. We suggested that two experimental subjects, men who had already lived for a year or longer on meat alone, volunteer to subject themselves to a preliminary study of several weeks while living the usual white-collar city life on an ordinary diet. After those weeks, the volunteers would shift to a diet of nothing but meat and water and remain on it, under strict medical routine, for just over twelve months. Then the subjects, myself and one other, would continue under medical observation for two or three further weeks for a readjustment from meat alone to an ordinary mixed diet.

Following up our proposal, we said, among other things, that, while we would grant no reprinting privileges on anything already written, we would go through a thirteen-month test under prearranged conditions to be agreed upon at a New York meeting between representatives of the meat industry and ourselves. We would agree to all customary publication privileges of the results, favorable or unfavorable, after the tests had been completed and the results studied. During the test itself, and for a short time afterward, only we and the American Meat Institute would be free to issue bulletins.

During the next several months we had many conferences. The governing committee of about a dozen physicians and scientists of recognized reputation would receive no pay, because they would all be attached to one institution or another. Of the members of this experiment committee, only one, Clark Wissler from the American Museum, was a long-time friend and associate. Newly made friends in the group were Ernest Hooton, Clarence Lieb, and Raymond Pearl. All the others were strangers, most of whom I had not previously known even by name. Raymond Pearl was chairman. I would receive no pay, for I would have a special unrestricted right to say or write what I liked about the experience. My partner in the experiment would receive nominal pay and travel and living expenses. Nurses and technicians, chiefly chemists, would be paid at standard rates.

The most important man in the whole setup would be the other subject of the experiment. I chose Charlie Andersen, a Dane of business college education who had been with me for three years on the Canadian Arctic Expedition. On that expedition he had lived on fresh musk ox, caribou, seal, and polar-bear meat. Since about 1920 he had been self-employed, working his own orange grove at Weirsdale, Florida.

As to choice of meat, we were to be free to eat any fresh meat we liked so long as it had not been chemically preserved or overcooked. We knew that we would be getting more than half our calories from animal fat, the rest from animal lean. The total intake would be variable. One of the jobs of the technicians and nurses would be to determine what proportion of fat and lean we consumed.

The purpose of our test was to learn the truth, but we did pay some attention to theories. We kept the controversial ones constantly in mind. This was at a time when lean meat was looked upon by many as unwholesome. Animal protein was supposed to promote hardening of the arteries, high blood pressure, and breakdown of the kidneys— in short, to bring on premature old age. For this reason the technicians were particularly concerned with the lean portion of our diet, especially the muscle tissue. Even those who half believed what I had been saying in praise of meat often supposed that what had saved me and the men of my expedition from its dread effects must have been the glandular portions. I had explained that only when living on seals had we eaten liver, it being the Eskimo custom to give all other internal organs to the dogs. There was, accordingly, considerable discussion about whether or not we should include liver in our experimental diet. As a matter of fact, we seldom ate any, though it was not forbidden.

One of our committee, Dr. Eugene Du Bois, a physiologist on the staff of the Russell Sage Institute, was the administrator of the test. For the first half-year Charlie Andersen and I slept in the Nutrition Ward of Bellevue Hospital, and most of the technician work, such as calorimeter studies, the weighing of the meat, and the determination of how much lean and fat we consumed, was also done at Bellevue.

I had forecast that we would be getting more than half our calories from fat. Most of us were surprised at the final computation, which was that about 80 per cent of the calories came from fat and 20 per cent from lean. The daily intake varied between 2600 and 2800 calories. There was, of course, no carbohydrate except what is normally contained in whole meat, perhaps 50 calories per day. If it is true that liver is higher in carbohydrates than are other meats, I repeat that we seldom ate liver. Some of the committee urged liver upon us, while others suggested that we avoid it. We probably ate no other organs except perhaps an occasional kidney. We were permitted to eat brains, and once, for a special reason that I will mention presently, I consumed a considerable amount of brains fried in bacon grease.

There appears to have been no rigid timing or other surveillance during the preliminary stage, when Andersen and I were being observed at Bellevue on the "normal" or mixed diet. We took our meals in the Nutrition Ward with the nurses, eating just what they did. We were usually free from hospital routines. Some days, however, were heavily occupied with such things as the calorimeter studies. When these were scheduled, we ate no food the evening before. In the morning, attendants would ease us into the calorimeters, which looked like roomy coffins. Once inside, lying comfortably on our backs, we were cautioned to think only pleasant and placid thoughts. Andersen and I had been impressed by numerous stories of previous tests that had been ruined by subjects who thought of something funny and laughed, or by others who thought of something that angered them. Both hilarity and hatred, it seemed, generated a lot of body heat. After the first hour on our backs the calorimeters were locked, the electric gadgets, breathing apparatus, and such were adjusted. We then faced three hours of tranquillity, during which time we were supposed to keep awake. Those were tedious days, rewarded by large meals of anything we liked.

During these first weeks we were examined by our doctors and by any other medical men or nutritionists who wished to do so. At this time we received our last barrage of warning letters and telephone calls. Personal friends, especially women, were worried that we were making ourselves ridiculous by being experimented on like animals.

One of our most prominent opponents, Dr. Nikel Hindhede, professor of physiology at the University of Copenhagen, visited us at Bellevue to say again that he had tried the all-meat diet upon both impartial subjects and others who held views similar to mine. All the experimenters, chiefly medical students of the University of Copenhagen, had given in within four or five days. My view was that Hindhede's results had been obtained in what was really a psychological rather than a nutrition test, and that his results showed only the power of imagination and suggestion. Karsten Andersen stuck with me, even against the advice of his internationally famous countryman.

We began our all-meat diet on February 28, 1927. At first we were somewhat worried about Andersen, since his preliminary examination had showed a blood pressure higher than the doctors liked, and our specialist in lower-colon diseases, Professor John C. Torrey of Cornell, said that if Andersen had come to him as a patient he would have advised him not to eat any meat. Lieb and our other observers were ready to stop the test if Andersen reacted unfavorably. To the surprise of some of the doctors, and the gratification of all, Andersen's health began to improve on all points, moderately so as to blood pressure and decidedly so as to colon. Torrey said jubilantly that he had never seen a more favorable response in any treatment he had ever prescribed. This is referred to, though not as extravagantly as in his conversation at the time, by Torrey and Montu in "The Influence of an Exclusive Meat Diet on the Flora of the Human Colon," *Journal of Infectious Diseases,* August, 1931.

My start was not so auspicious. Du Bois had been impressed by what I told him I had learned along the Mackenzie and Horton rivers about "rabbit starvation." He wanted me to go directly from the mixed diet to a heavy one of exclusive lean meat. I protested that the experience of missionaries and traders, as well as Athapaskans, Eskimos, and my own group on the Horton, combined to make me believe that headache and diarrhea would soon develop. Du Bois countered that I had myself indicated that the symptoms would not appear before a week or two. As he wanted only forty-eight hours, we went ahead. I felt discomfort after twenty-four hours and before forty-eight I was so much worse that Du Bois and his associates agreed to cease and asked me what I suggested. I suggested brains cooked in bacon fat. It worked. Within seventy-two hours after leaving the mixed diet I was back on an even keel. I remained there throughout the experiment.

Hindhede had predicted that we would give up as early as four days after starting. Other skeptics allowed us as much as three weeks. For at least six weeks Du Bois saw to it that we were never out of the sight of a doctor or a nurse. Visitors were watched to see that they smuggled nothing to us. Doctors, technicians, nurses, and all concerned kept repeating to Charlie and me that, while each of them trusted us, they had to be ready to testify that they knew positively that we had not cheated.

Before six weeks had passed, they were all telling us that they were convinced not only that we had not cheated but also that we had no desire to cheat—that if we were hungry it was only that we had a hankering for more fat meat. After the first six weeks the experiment was altered a bit. I was let out for hours at a time, and later for days on my own responsibility; Charlie remained virtually under lock and key for three months. If we wanted a boneless sirloin, Charlie and I each picked a raw steak we liked, and it was then weighed and fried medium or rare. We ate every bit, cleaning the platter of all grease or juice.

The technicians sometimes offered to walk with us for exercise. I think Charlie often accepted their offers. I always declined, explaining that in a city I never walked if I could take a subway or a taxi. This is what an Eskimo would have done. Any Eskimo is always prepared for maximum walking, but nobody does it for fun or for "exercise."

After the first three months Du Bois made us take a long trot every month in order to test our fitness. At his private house, east of Central Park, he had doctors meet us in midafternoon and examine our breathing, pulse, and blood samples. Then, in shorts and sandals, we would run along the side street, across Fifth Avenue, into the park, and around the reservoir. Returning, we would run up a flight of stairs and plump ourselves down on couches to be examined again. Du Bois reported a steadily improving performance. He took this to mean that the longer we were on a diet of 80 per cent fat and 20 per cent lean meat, the more nearly we approached 100 per cent fitness.

After our first half-year at Bellevue, the New York summer was at its hottest. We noticed a special solicitude on the part of one of the doctors, Graham Lusk. Du Bois interpreted this to us. Lusk's fame rested in part on his having reported upon the heat-producing factor in various foods. He had found meat notably high. It was now understandable why Lusk looked disappointed on very hot days when both Charlie and I said we were finding the heat no more bothersome than during other summers, perhaps less so. I do not remember, however, that either at Lusk's or Du Bois' insistence any tests of our ability to stand heat were made.

Everyone agreed that summer is the time when no one remains in New York City by choice. There was a meeting of the supervising committee at which a vote indicated that nobody was skeptical any longer. Everybody agreed that meat was still our favorite food. There was no objection to our moving to a small house in the woods behind Croton-on-Hudson. There, Charlie and I proposed to live chiefly on our favorite domestic meat, boiled mutton, drinking the broth, as we used to do with caribou. I explained to the committee that the Eskimos boil caribou until it is done no more than is usual with our roasts and steaks in New York. We would cook our mutton as if it were caribou.

In that little Croton house we had some of the most delicious meals I can remember. Charlie, however, while praising our boiled mutton, would often remark that it was not quite as good as caribou. We agreed on that. It was not quite as good as mountain sheep, musk ox, or caribou. I do not remember during any of this period any hankering for forbidden foods, such as fruit, pastries, or bread and butter.

Toward the end of the all-meat year, Charlie had a worse set-back than I had at its beginning. He was again living at Bellevue. The hospital was struck by an epidemic of pneumonia, and Charlie was not spared. Du Bois found it encouraging, however, that his case was lighter than others in the hospital and that he made a good recovery.

After a year and some days on meat alone, we were put back on a mixed diet and given a round of transition tests. As part of it, we were given what were called glucose meals, drinking a kind of sugar syrup as if it were a pint of beer. It was perhaps two weeks before our sugar tolerance was certified as back to normal. I believe that in all other respects our condition was thought to be equal to what it had been in the beginning. A few judges considered it better. To me this had been an anthropological and physiological study, and in it I was not impartial.

The evidence and opinions of the group of physicians observing us were summarized by Dr. Lieb in *The American Journal of Digestion and Nutrition* * as "A Year's Exclusive Meat Diet and Seven Years Later." Here Lieb points out that my periods of exclusive meat diet total about nine years and that during these my "sense of physical and mental well being was at its best." Lieb adds: "He found that the exclusive meat diet worked as well when he was inactive as when active and as well in hot weather as in cold."

With this I agreed and agree still. Dr. Lieb's summary for the seven years following the Bellevue year coincides with my opinion for the thirty years that followed.

* XI, No. 8, 473–475.

35 Over and Under the Arctic

In 1928, I was still busy with the Chautauqua circuits, but was beginning to consider the possibility of acquiring a new main source of income. The Chautauqua booking organization, however, persuaded me to stay with them for another year. They contended that what I had to say in *The Northward Course of Empire* should be very important to my native land of Canada, even though Canadians had thus far turned a deaf ear to me. I still hoped to arouse Canada's interest in her northern lands and waters, and now my manager, Ellison, claimed that this was the way to attract Canadian attention. That was enough to make me sign up again with Ellison-White, or rather with that branch of the Affiliated system which was run from Calgary, Alberta, by J. M. Erickson and called the Canadian Chautauqua.

I was to join the Canadian Chautauqua as promptly as I could after a final talk at the University of Cambridge, England, where I had been lecturing. I was supposed to reach Cabri, Saskatchewan, on the morning of May 29, 1928, and to speak that evening from the first tent of the six-tent Chautauqua. I took the SS *Majestic* from Southampton to New York and the first and fastest train from there to Minneapolis. Then, making a slight detour that had been suggested by Orville Wright, I spoke on the transpolar role of aviation at a national conference of the American Aeronautical Society in session at St. Louis. The society agreed to pick me up by airplane and fly me the rest of the way to make my date. They kept their promise.

In my lifetime effort to keep in touch with my own past, I have remained in touch with much of Canada through the dispersed Chautauqua staffs with which I once worked. The active manager of the Calgary section of the tent empire was Nola Erickson, whose husband J. M. Erickson was the titular and legal head. I seldom saw Erickson himself because he was busy in the Calgary office. Both Ericksons were from California, and when Chautauqua collapsed, they moved back to that state.

Although a venerable institution in the United States, Chautauqua did not reach Canada until World War I was several years under way. In 1917, J. M. Erickson decided that the time for Canadian Chautauqua was at hand and that it could be made extremely profitable. He borrowed money, tents, and equipment from Ellison-White, but was eventually able to buy them out.

At first no one could be found in Canada who knew the ropes. For three or four years Erickson had to hire trained American workers. Once established, however, he and his wife began to train Canadian college students. He needed two for each tent and a director for each town in which a tent was set up. Advance workers visited the booked towns to inject life into the local committees and make sure that they did not forget the contracts they had previously signed. Most of this foundation work was done by girls, who, Erickson felt, had a better chance of getting action and money out of local businessmen.

In 1929, the top year for Canadian Chautauqua, Dr. Wilfred Rusk Wees and his wife, Frances Shelley Wees, managed the Peace River Circuit, which, since there were very few towns in the district, was good for only three weeks. Wees had begun in Chautauqua in 1922 as a crewman, earning twenty-five dollars a week and sleeping in the tents as the tour went along, buying his own meals at Chinese cafés, where you could get steak, fried potatoes, pickles, coffee, and pie for twenty-five cents. Wilfred Wees moved steadily upward until in 1929, when I was part of the program, he was the local manager. I had my meat-experiment partner Karsten Andersen with me on the circuit. I was finishing a book on the side and too preoccupied to worry about the bad food and poor audiences which constantly worried Mrs. Wees. Even in Edmonton, although I was the number-one speaker on the circuit, I attracted only sixty people. Frances Wees was determined to stir up the Canadians.

When we reached a place called Kindersley, Saskatchewan, she decided to try the experiment of needling the town beforehand. Kindersley was a good choice, for there were a number of Icelanders there as well as the brother of my friend Carl Akeley. Mrs. Wees went about telling everyone who I was and how important to all Canadians my message was. The result was that I talked to a packed tent and everyone had a good time, including me.

I recently corresponded with Mrs. Wees and was glad to have her remind me of a typical Chautauqua stand.

> My last tour with you (there were several intervening) was
> Fort Francis, Ontario, August 17th, 1929 [she wrote]. It was
> raining cats and dogs on your night. I had to walk four blocks
> to the tent, carrying my heavy cash case (you remember, about
> 2½ feet square, padlocked, bound with metal, full of heavy
> ticket rolls and stuff) and nobody even thought of that but you.
> I was tucking up the skirt of my blue beaded evening dress (be-
> cause of course I had to be on the platform later) and dreading
> to struggle through the mud. . . . You knocked at my door,
> looking very elegant in your dinner jacket. And you asked if
> you could escort me to the tent (a whole hour before you needed
> to go) and carry my cash case for me. I never forgot. I had seen
> . . . your sympathetic understanding of people. And I made up
> my mind to work so that others should see it too.

The year 1929 was my next-to-last Chautauqua year. During 1930 Wilkins and I were busy attempting to carry out the ideas about underwater travel that we held in common. When 1931 came along, I was feeling desperate about the inattentiveness of Canadians to what I had been preaching—chiefly the importance to them of the extended arctic use of submarine and airplane. I thought I might have just one more try at arousing them. In 1929 my Chautauqua tour had covered midwestern Canada, a triangle from the southern boundary of Alberta north to the Peace River and east to southwestern Ontario. Now I would cover the rest of Ontario, western Quebec, and the western Maritime Provinces.

The story in these new regions was not very different. My "message" about the inevitable greatness of northern Canada was growing stale; the Canadians had heard it from me so often before. If greatness was inevitable, why not just wait for it?

That summer, while I was lecturing in Ontario and Quebec not far from Ottawa, I used to drop in at the Parliament buildings to buttonhole my old Harvard friend Mackenzie King, who had become Prime Minister. I could not help noticing that even he was beginning to avoid me. Others were palpably bored and made signs and grimaces as they got out of my way, as if it were one thing for country Chautauqua yokels to take my northern prophecies seriously but another to expect politicians like themselves to do so. The new islands that the Canadian Arctic Expedition had discovered and added to Canada were pointedly referred to as "the Conservative Archipelago," the ruling party now being Liberals who considered themselves above concern about such worthless things as a few barren islands.

I then and there made a resolution that had been too slow in coming: I would keep away from Canada and Canadians for a decade or so, until the value of their northern resources became apparent even to them.

In Alaska as well as in Canada no progress was being made. The reindeer industry was being blocked, or strangled, in both countries, but I was hearing wonderful things about it from northern Scandinavia and from the Soviet Union, where reindeer were being cultivated as cattle were in Alberta, Montana, Texas, and the Argentine. The rest of the world seemed not to be turning such a deaf ear to my message. My books were being translated into a dozen languages. Russian editions of them began to appear.

I found the rivalry between capitalism and communism depressing. To me, as a student of comparative religions, these -isms were just two more in the nearly infinite complex of faiths. I thought I could already detect on each side a willingness to get along with the other —a willingness that did not lose sight of the fact that each expected to triumph over the other in the end. This was the sort of half dog-eat-dog and half live-and-let-live spirit that had developed two hundred years earlier between Lutheranism and Romanism, though each of those factions still talks of eventual world supremacy.

It was obvious that world cooperativeness would be a long time coming. Meanwhile, we would lay the groundwork for a submarine commerce in heavy goods to supplement the air commerce that had been established to take care of lighter goods. It would be a freight service supplementing an express service. The pattern of our collaboration had been established. My responsibility would be the necessary propaganda. Wilkins' would be the direct action.

Not that either of us would keep out of the other's field. Both of us were already lecturing, both writing. But the emphasis had differed and would continue to differ. While I stressed lecturing, writing, and the building of a polar library, Wilkins would write and lecture also, but his main role would be negotiating, organizing, and doing. There was no written agreement to this effect. It was an arrangement that came about naturally.

From the beginning of our acquaintance in 1913, when he joined the Canadian Arctic Expedition as photographer, Wilkins was a loyal supporter. He was, however, a man with a strongly independent mind impelled by a great driving force. During our first years together we had many differences, though whatever real conflict there was between us was always frank and open. The differences grew less as our common experiences rubbed down the sharp edges of our personal communion, and we ultimately worked together in the smoothness engendered by mutual respect and confidence.

A great deal of the early friction between Wilkins and me got into the diaries kept by Wilkins himself and by his close associate on the *Karluk,* Burt McConnell. McConnell's Canadian Arctic Expedition papers are now at Dartmouth College, in the Stefansson Collection of polar material, of the formation of which I shall have something to say further on. It is perhaps unlikely that many students will try to decipher McConnell's shorthand diaries, but a large part of Wilkins' diaries are also in the collection and perfectly legible. These diaries, although they give good pictures of the early stages of our relationship, are far from sufficient to give a real picture of Wilkins' greatness.

Most of his most notable achievements belong more properly in the autobiography that he never wrote than they do in mine. Yet, the greatest of them are so linked with my career that it would be impossible not to mention them.

I should say that Wilkins and I became, during my abbreviated Australian venture, closer than we had been before, and that was very close. It was at this time that he began to talk to me about the impression that my article on transarctic air commerce, published in 1922 in the *National Geographic Magazine,* had made upon him.

After Wilkins left Australia and finished his book about his zoological expedition to the antipodean tropics, I was not in close touch with him for some time. Then one day he wrote me from London that he was planning to make exploratory airplane flights north

of Alaska and then cross from Alaska to Norway on a great-circle
flight. In his letter he asked my help in finding a suitable pilot. He
himself planned to act as navigator.

I knew of a young North Dakotan who had been a pilot in
World War I and then given up schoolteaching to become the first
air-mail pilot in Alaska. His name was Carl Ben Eielson. Everything I learned of him was good, especially that he was eager to
become not only a pilot in the Arctic but an arctic explorer by air.
I wrote Wilkins about him, and as a result Eielson was soon hired.

As Wilkins' plans went forward, he secured the financial backing of the North American Newspaper Alliance and the Detroit
Daily News, and I presently found myself, with Isaiah Bowman,
William B. Mayo, Henry Ford's chief engineer, and a number of
others, on the board of directors of the Wilkins-Eielson project, officially known as the Detroit Arctic Expedition.

Wilkins and Eielson carried out the first phase of their work
with remarkable success, considering that aviation, in 1926, was still
a long way from maturity. They had some bad luck at first, but it
was not in any way caused by arctic conditions. After several crack-
ups at Fairbanks, on a regular landing field, they flew thousands of
miles over ice and open water, without any real difficulty. They
proved conclusively what I had long been asserting: that flying
in the Arctic over land or sea, in winter or summer, would be possible. In March, 1927, at a point six hundred miles north of Point
Barrow, they were forced down on the ice by engine trouble. While
Eielson was repairing the motor, Wilkins cut a hole in the ice and
sounded the depth below. He found it to be more than three miles.
This was on the very edge of the region that Shackleton and others
had expected to find filled by a great land mass. On this flight,
incidentally, Wilkins and Eielson made the first known landing on
and take-off from sea ice.

More important than these pioneering flights from my point of
view was the great achievement of April 15–16, 1928, when Wilkins
and Eielson flew from Point Barrow to Spitsbergen, following the
route that is practically the same as that now regularly used by
Scandinavian Airlines. It was Wilkins, therefore, who after my
failures at Wrangel Island and Baffin Island realized an important
part of my 1922 prophecy that the Arctic would prove to be a
natural air route.

The Wilkins-Eielson achievement, among the greatest in all

arctic history, was acclaimed as such even by the unpredictable Amundsen, who had publicly expressed the belief that any attempt to make such a flight would be foolishness.

Wilkins emerged from his arctic work with honor, distinction, and unimpaired health. Ben Eielson was not so fortunate. On a rescue mission in late 1929, from Alaska to Siberia, in terrible weather, which as one pilot said, made flying seem like traveling through a bottle of milk, Eielson wrecked his plane on the ice. Searchers found his body, which had been thrown clear of the plane, some time afterward.

Hubert Wilkins was to be instrumental in confirming, in 1931 and again in the 1950s, the second part of my prophecy, which resulted from my observation, in 1914, of a school of beluga whales breaking through the ice with their humped backs. If whales could break through ice and come up for air, why could not submarines do the same? Wilkins decided that he would put a submarine to the test.

It appeared that my idea was not entirely new. Wilkins had, without being aware of it, a namesake, Bishop John Wilkins, who in 1648 had published a book called *Mathematicall Magick*. When Wilkins' name and mine began appearing in the public press connected with the idea of submarine exploration of the polar sea, someone gave me a copy of the bishop's book, calling to my attention the fifth chapter, entitled "Concerning the possibility of framing an Ark for submarine Navigation. The difficulties and conveniences of such a contrive." The bishop, a man well ahead of his time, pointed out that his "Ark," traveling submerged, would be safe "from ice and great frosts, which doe so much endanger the passages towards the Poles."

Wilkins went at the preparations for his trial by submarine with the same determined thoroughness that he had applied to his expedition by air. He bought, for one dollar, from the United States government a thirteen-year-old decommissioned submarine, organized a crew and scientific staff, and in August, 1931, got his "framed Ark," not without difficulty and delay, to Spitsbergen, where he was to dive beneath the ice. In spite of the fact that the stern diving fins had been removed, no doubt by a member of the expedition in the hope that the voyage would be abandoned, and that the special auger for boring holes in the ice overhead had become stuck halfway out of its sheath, Wilkins managed to get below the ice and travel for some distance under it. He was also able to get some remarkable motion pictures of the underside of the ice, taken through a porthole.

The obstacles were so great, however, and the *Nautilus* so un-fitted to deal with them, that after an under-ice journey of about twenty miles Wilkins gave up and returned to Bergen, Norway, where, in fulfillment of an agreement on which the U.S. Shipping Board had insisted, he sank the old ship in two hundred fathoms.

Twenty-seven years later, two American atomic-powered sub-marines, the *Nautilus* and the *Skate,* made two successful voyages under the northern ice, completing the work begun by Wilkins in 1931 and suggested by me privately in 1914 and publicly in 1922. The *Nautilus* traveled without surfacing from Bering Strait to the open ocean north of Norway. The *Skate* sailed under the ice to the Pole, where she surfaced after the manner of beluga whales, then submerged again to complete her voyage without a hitch.

It is interesting to note that the skipper of the *Skate,* Com-mander James Calvert, did not know until he returned to Norway after his visit to the Pole anything of the history of my idea or of Wilkins' application of it. At Bergen, Calvert met friends of Wil-kins—long since Sir Hubert Wilkins—who gave him a copy of *Under the North Pole,* Wilkins' book about the 1931 venture. After reading the book, Calvert was so impressed that he sent Sir Hubert a cable complimenting him on his insight and vision and adding, ''The majority of your aims and predictions of nearly thirty years ago were realized this summer. The men of the *Skate* send a sincere salute to a man who has many times shown the way.'' With his char-acteristic generosity and modesty, Wilkins forwarded the cable to me, reminding me that it was I who had really started the whole thing.

In thanking Calvert for his cable, Wilkins made the wise sug-gestion that the commander repeat in midwinter the voyage to the Pole that had been made during the summer. In December, 1958, before Calvert had had a chance to discuss the winter voyage with him, Wilkins died suddenly of a heart attack. In January, 1959, Calvert came to see me. We had a long talk about the problems in-volved, and I gave him a copy of *The Friendly Arctic* to carry with him to the pole.

A few months later I received the following letter. Though I wear no beard, it made me feel like a genuine prophet:

USS SKATE (SSN–578)
Care of the Fleet Post Office
New York, New York

Tuesday, 17 March 1959

Dear Dr. Stefansson,

Well, here we are at the North Pole, having broken
through the ice at the exact spot. The beluga whales
have nothing on us—we have been up 3 times in 3 days
—each time through the ice!

Seriously, the information you gave us was of great
help. *The Dynamic North* particularly good.

Conditions today at the Pole about normal except
wind high (30 knots). Air temp. —24° F. Visibility
poor in the blowing snow.

We conducted the memorial services for Sir Hubert.
We used red torches in the dim light—most impressive.
Much to tell you, but I must close now. Please
give my best to Mrs. Stefansson.

Sincerely,
Jim Calvert

P.S. I read *The Friendly Arctic* on the way
up—enjoyed it tremendously. We'll be on the
lookout for life—none yet.

My cup, once drained by disappointment at the failure of two
of my northward ventures, was filled to overflowing a year later
when the USS *Seadragon,* a sister ship of the *Skate,* under Commander George Steele, who consulted with me and borrowed books
and reports, made a successful voyage from the Atlantic to the
Pacific via the North Pole and the Northwest Passage, the first
complete transit of Parry Channel by any ship and the first east-
west crossing of the Arctic by submarine.

36 Arctic Fantasy

Wilkins' triumphs, although I could regard them privately as a vindication of a great many of my views about the destiny of the far north, did not make much of a dent in the public attitude toward the Arctic. Ignorance of northern conditions seemed to remain very dear to those who should have been most interested in knowledge of them.

One of the most amazing illustrations of public ignorance about the polar regions appeared in 1932. One morning in January of that year I answered my telephone in New York and heard the somewhat awed voice of my old friend Harold Strong Latham, chief editor of the Macmillan Company. Latham told me that he had discovered an almost unknown arctic explorer who had written a book —a book certain to change the author from an unknown to a celebrity. Had I ever heard of a Czech named Jan Welzl? As it happened, I had, but I knew of him only that he had once been on the Mackenzie River, in what capacity I did not know, and that on his way out to civilization he had given a sketchy interview about himself to an Edmonton newspaper.

This just fitted, Latham said. Welzl had gone home to his native Prague. There he had met the playwright Karel Čapek, who had been impressed with his stories and was now sponsoring a volume by the old man to be called *Thirty Years in the Golden North*. It had already been published in London by Allen and Unwin. Would I join Čapek, Latham asked, in allowing the use of my name on the jacket of the American edition? I said that I would, if I liked the book. Latham immediately sent me a copy.

In a few hours I called him back and told him I would be delighted to endorse the book if it was to be promoted as a parody. Latham protested. Welzl's book was no parody. It had been brought out as an authentic account by a reputable publisher, and it had been vouched for by one of Europe's foremost dramatists, a man who was to the Continent what Shaw was to Britain. To this I replied that I might have the wrong idea about the publishers, but not about Čapek, who, I believed, was the real author of the spoof, not its mere sponsor. I told Latham that I was willing to bet that Čapek, not Welzl, had written *Thirty Years in the Golden North.*

It seemed to me that Čapek probably believed that the real Jan Welzl was dead—or at least beyond caring what was done with his reminiscences. Otherwise, even a sardonic genius like Čapek would have hesitated to produce such a lampoon. Over the telephone I described what I thought must have happened. The real Welzl, who had apparently dropped out of sight, had been cast in the role of an arctic Baron Munchausen. Čapek had found himself an uninhabited group of arctic islands, invented grotesque, impossible inhabitants for them, invented voyages that Welzl could not possibly have made, and so produced a real thriller.

For his purpose the New Siberian Islands, the center of which lies on approximately 145° E longitude and 76° N latitude, were a good choice. Since they had never been inhabited, they could, in fancy, be populated with any sort of imaginary beings. No voyages had ever been made to or from them, so why not create an imaginary traffic between them and some real place like San Francisco? Everything connected with the imaginary population might have some relationship to real things and real events but would never be wholly accurate or wholly real. The second sentence of the introduction sounded this note:

"In the year 1924 Welzl was carrying supplies from San Francisco to his friends in the New Siberian Islands on board the small vessel *Seven Sisters,* when he was wrecked on some rocks off the Pacific coast of the United States." Just as San Francisco and the New Siberian Islands existed, so there had been a *Seven Sisters.* She had not, however, been lost in 1924 but about twenty years earlier; and she had not been wrecked on some rocks "off the Pacific coast of the United States," but beached in sand on the coast of Alaska.

Farther down on the same page, Welzl was said to have needed a visa "for the purpose of getting back to New Siberia, where he had a considerable amount of property stored up in a cave. He also owned a number of whaling vessels jointly with some of his friends." This considerable property, it was implied, he got from trading with his aboriginal friends. What he did with his whaling vessels I found hard to imagine, since no whaling had ever been done by anybody near the New Siberian Islands.

The opinion I gave Latham on the phone was that *Thirty Years in the Golden North* should be published as a glorious hoax, outranking the then well-known Trader Horn and Joan Lowell stories. Latham felt that this would never do, especially in view of the book's publication in England as an authentic narrative. Inasmuch as his company had contracted for only five hundred copies of the book, Latham felt that it should now simply be withdrawn.

This seemed to me the best move for a reputable publisher, but to my astonishment the withdrawal order was never given. Before the Macmillan Company could act, the Book-of-the-Month Club decided to make *Thirty Years in the Golden North* a selection. The question now was: should the publisher sacrifice not merely its initial five hundred copies but the more than fifty thousand that the Book-of-the-Month Club would distribute to its members? Moreover, would not Henry Seidel Canby, the club's chief judge, take grievous offense if the book that he and his fellow judges had chosen were to be branded as a manifest hoax? At this point the Macmillan Company's honest misgivings were dispelled by the pressure of the huge potential sale.

What followed was a four-act tragicomedy. The curtain went up with Canby's public endorsement of the Book-of-the-Month Club's choice. Dr Canby swallowed the hoax—hook, line, and sinker. He referred to the book in his review in the *Saturday Review of Literature* as a story worthy of Hakluyt—which, incidentally, did not eliminate the possibility of a hoax. It was Canby's opinion that the preposterous story was a genuine account of experiences that might have taken place. In his review he cited as impressive, incidents described in Welzl's book that would make anyone familiar with the Arctic roar with laughter. The chief of the Book-of-the-Month Club's board of judges and editor of the *Saturday Review of Literature* closed his review by saying that he was "willing to certify to the excellence and to the apparent sincerity . . ." of

Welzl's story, but admitted the possibility of inaccuracy. "We have, he said, "persuaded Dr. Stefansson to comment on the scientific aspects (if any) of this book."

It is indeed appalling that an educated doctor of philosophy, an eminent literary critic, could be so ignorant of the geography, meteorology, and anthropology of the polar regions that he could for an instant accept *Thirty Years in the Golden North* as anything but a farce. That he could do so is an indication of the general public's ignorance of the north.

As rebuttal to Canby's endorsement, I published in the *Saturday Review of Literature* an account of what I had told the Macmillan Company in advising Latham to publish the book as a parody. My comments did not seem to injure the book at all. For two years it enjoyed wide acclaim. Many people seemed eager to accept such "facts" as that Eskimo girls mature at the age of six and that the inhabitants of the New Siberian Islands must not sneeze after being out in the cold lest the jar break off their solidified noses and they go rattling across the floor—as those of the Icelanders, according to European folklore, used to do in the Middle Ages. Now and then some spoilsport would point out that Eskimo girls mature very little earlier than girls of other regions do, that it never is quite as cold in the New Siberian Islands as it sometimes is in parts of Alaska, and that in any case the New Siberian Islands had never been inhabited. Such things ruffled the book-buying public hardly at all, and in due time I heard from my friends at Macmillan that sales had passed the hundred-thousand mark. The acceptance in England was equally enthusiastic.

At the height of the book's success I received a letter, long, involved, and written in bad German, from Jan Welzl. The letter had been mailed in Dawson, in the Canadian Yukon. This was the beginning of act two.

> I, Jan Welzl, am a pauper [said the letter, in effect], and I am here at Dawson living on the charity of the Canadian government. The other day, on the street, I heard a man saying that there went that liar Welzl. So I asked him why he called me a liar. "Well, you wrote that book, didn't you?" I could not deny this. For once in Prague I knew some journalists who said I ought to write a book. They helped me write it and it was printed but it did not sell, so I left Prague and am now here. I thought this might be the book they were talking about. But when I saw *Thirty*

Years in the Golden North I recognized nothing in it except my
own name on the title page and Karel Čapek's, for he was one
of the journalists who helped me in Prague.

The letter ended with a plea for advice. I took it to Harold
Latham. He told me that there was not much he could do at this
stage. Welzl did not specifically claim that the book had injured
him, only implied that it had impaired his reputation for truthful-
ness. If he felt that his character had been injured severely enough
to warrant action, it seemed that the papers would have to be
served against the original publisher in Prague. I transmitted this
information to Welzl.

A year later, act three began. Again writing from Dawson and
stating that he was still living on relief, Welzl complained that,
while his Canadian neighbors had first denounced him as a liar,
lawyers from the United States were now calling him a thief. The
lawyers insisted that he had falsely claimed to be penniless while
he was really a wealthy man, concealing the vast income he must
have received as author of the international best seller *Thirty Years
in the Golden North*. Welzl wanted me to tell him what to say to
the lawyers.

Offhand I did not know. I decided that my friend Charlie
Hamel, the head of a firm of Washington lawyers specializing in
taxation, might have an answer. I wrote Charlie, told him the story
of the now-recognized hoax, and asked him if he could not do
something for the hapless victim. Charlie wrote me about a week
afterward that he had looked into the matter and found that it was
being handled by a Treasury Department lawyer whom he knew.
He would ask the man to lunch with him.

Here began the fourth act. After lunch and over coffee, Charlie
asked the lawyer if he was in charge of the Jan Welzl case. He certainly was. Where was he bringing action? In Dawson, Alaska,
where this tax dodger was in hiding. Dawson, *Alaska?* Charlie had
always supposed that Dawson City was in Canada. Was that within
the jurisdiction of the United States courts? The lawyer blinked,
said he'd be damned, and left no doubt about his eagerness to cancel
whatever steps he had taken.

It appears that, following the collapse of the case against him,
Jan Welzl had several pleasant and relaxed years as "Eskimo
Welzl" back in his own country, though without the benefit, it is
true, of the many thousands of dollars that the book published

under his name had earned for someone. I myself still cling to the notion that *Thirty Years in the Golden North* was to Karel Čapek, as it was and is to me, a satire on a small but prolific and successful class of arctic writers, and a poke at those who swallow their yarns.

Amusing as the book's history was, it had its serious overtones, for it emphasized the willingness of even educated men to believe anything and to know nothing about the north.

37 With Pan American Airways

By the early 1930s my polar library had developed into one of ten thousand books, pamphlets, and manuscripts relating to the Arctic and adjacent regions. The growth was primarily the result of my habit of making book collecting a by-product of everything I did. I had built up a small staff to take care of the collection and handle research. As the library grew, it drove me from one apartment to another in New York's Greenwich Village, looking for more space in which to house it.

Originally, the library had been my personal hobby, but it was to become a semipublic institution. In February, 1930, I received a letter from Ralph Lomen, younger brother of Carl the Reindeer King. Ralph had been field manager of the search for Ben Eielson. Pointing out that the concentration of efforts to find the lost pilot had revealed the dearth of readily available written information about the special conditions and problems of the Arctic, he suggested that some sort of arctic manual was needed and that I was the man to write it. Nothing came of this suggestion immediately, although it did become a reality some time later.

For some years I had been adding to the library items on arctic aviation, being not unaware of the growing importance of the subject. As a matter of fact, I had for some time been giving advice to individuals contemplating journeys in the north. Among these was a flier known as "Fish" Hassell. As an American of Swedish descent, Bill Hassell was determined to do some pioneering that would lead to the establishment of an airline between his favorite country,

Sweden, and his favorite American city, Rockford, Illinois. The advice I gave him, unfortunately, was not enough to get him and his navigator, Parker Cramer, beyond Greenland. His plane had to be abandoned on the Greenland ice-cap, and his attempt to establish an airline came to nothing.

International aviation was, however, in the air, in more senses than one. Cramer, working with a Cleveland, Ohio, company known as Transamerican Air Lines, hoped to establish a service connecting the United States with Copenhagen, Denmark, by short hops to Labrador, West Greenland, East Greenland, Iceland, and the Faroe and Shetland Islands. Because I was acting as adviser to Transamerican, Cramer came to me. My advice was not to try any such flight. I pointed out that the route he planned to take had already been proved sound both by scouts for the German Lufthansa and by the English pilot John Grierson. A new flight over the same route, if successful, would impress nobody. If unsuccessful, it would depress everybody and Transamerican's prospects would suffer.

I do not know whether or not Cramer asked anyone else's advice. I do know that he did not take mine. After flying safely as far as the Faroes, he was lost in the North Sea. This was a serious blow to Transamerican. The company did not, however, give up its hope of securing rights to fly the route that Parker Cramer had attempted and which I had advised them to consider satisfactory. I felt that they should not try to negotiate with Iceland through Copenhagen. The Danes had little love for Icelanders, and Icelanders felt similarly about the Danes. In late 1931, Transamerican asked me to negotiate with the government of Iceland for a base there, but I felt that, in spite of my Icelandic background, I would not be as good a negotiator as someone with legal training would be.

The ideal man for the job, it seemed to me, was an old friend from college days in North Dakota, a lawyer, born in Iceland, who had been Chief Justice of the North Dakota Supreme Court and who had represented the Congress of the United States at the millennial celebration of Iceland's Parliament. Judge Gudmundur Grimson had been so successful as an ambassador of the world's most powerful republic to the world's oldest that he had been showered with honors, including a doctorate from the University of Iceland.

Transamerican accepted my suggestion and sent Grimson to

Iceland, where he arrived in January, 1932. Though Grimson was perfectly qualified for his new mission, it was a tense situation for me when he and Mrs. Grimson sailed from New York for Iceland. The judge was to deal with Iceland for Icelandic flying rights and with Denmark for rights covering the Danish colony of Greenland. On my advice, concurred in by Grimson, we planned to negotiate with Iceland first. According to our judgment, a predetermined situation in Greenland, whether favorable to us or not, would irritate Iceland. On the other hand, a success in Iceland would help us at Copenhagen.

When Grimson got to Reykjavik, he found a considerable bulk of opinion favoring our route. To some extent this was attributable to the arguments raised in my book and magazine articles. One of the Icelanders ready to cooperate was the Prime Minister, Tryggvi Thorhallsson. He warned us, however, that there was no law to cover the sort of agreement between Transamerican and Iceland that Grimson recommended and which he himself considered equitable and desirable. He felt that, in view of Judge Grimson's familiarity with the legal practices of both Iceland and the United States, it ought not be too difficult to have a satisfactory law drafted, although considering the meticulous caution with which the Icelandic Parliament, the Althing, had to move, it might be some time before it could become law.

The Prime Minister's suggestion was adopted, a committee of jurists was set up, and soon a proposal was ready for submission. The Althing, however, is a bicameral legislature, like the Congress of the United States, and each house is jealous of its own prerogatives, which involve various prescribed hearings and mandatory delays between successive readings of new laws before a vote is taken. Iceland's first aviation law, applicable to international as well as domestic flying, was submitted to the upper chamber on February 27, 1932, and passed by the lower house on March 20.

With this success behind him, Grimson went on to Copenhagen. There were still a number of arrangements to be made, most of them under my supervision but carried out by Transamerican's Danish representative, the noted aviator Captain A. P. Botved, who was known as "the Danish Lindbergh." Their business was concerned more with Greenland than with Iceland, and included a Danish meteorological survey. I remember, in connection with this,

that our New York office was startled by confirmation through field
studies of the fact that the flying boats that we then planned to use
would have less trouble from ice forming on Greenland harbors in
winter than they would have from the same cause in New York.

In spite of the rights that Judge Grimson secured for the
company, Transamerican had been so hard hit by Parker Cramer's unsuccessful and fatal flight that it never operated overseas.
Shortly after Transamerican's negotiations abroad were concluded,
Pan American Airways purchased their assets and began a study
of the transatlantic plans that were in its files.

It was at this point that, thanks to a Harvard classmate of
mine, Robert Grant, I became an adviser to Pan American. Grant,
who had been a banker but had like many others been taken in by
Ivar Kreuger, the Swedish "Match King," had joined Pan American. In going through Transamerican's files he found my notes
advising against Cramer's flight but insisting that the route chosen
had been a good one. My association with Pan American, which
lasted from 1932 to 1945, was a very happy one. I had no office
hours but was available on call, and it was agreed that the rights
to any memoranda that I might write for my employers were to remain mine and might become a part of my polar-aviation library.

At Pan American, I was assigned to Evan Young, vice-president. After several weeks of learning the ropes from him, I started
giving advice whether it had been asked for or not. I began by
persuading the company to consider carefully before firing Transamerican's staff. Later I worked also with John Cooper, another
Pan American vice-president.

One of the tasks that I carried out in the early days of my
association with Pan American was the business of putting the
company straight about the relationship between Scandinavians and
Finns. This was chiefly a matter of explaining the shifts of north
European domination. The Finns had, in 1932, bitter memories of
their centuries of subservience to the Swedes. Their newer domination by their neighbors to the east was less galling: they had been
under Russia's thumb for only a century. There were points of
sensitivity between the Danes and the Swedes also, and these, I
knew, would be important if Pan American put into effect the projected air route across the North Atlantic, the rights to which had
been inherited from Transamerican.

Pan American needed Greenland as much as it needed Iceland as a step in its transatlantic route. For this reason I was able to convince Evan Young that we badly needed Captain Botved because of his standing in Denmark and its importance to us in our negotiations about Greenland. I also succeeded in persuading Pan American that Reginald Orcutt, overseas vice-president of the Mergenthaler Linotype Company, who had many and widespread associations in Europe, would be an invaluable adviser for us.

My first project as Pan American's adviser on northern operations was a study of the results of a flight made by Charles and Anne Lindbergh as a survey of possible air routes through Alaska to Asia. The Lindberghs were a memorable team. Their Asiatic venture has been described by Anne in her best-seller volume, *North to the Orient*. I liked the Lindberghs and they liked the northern people and the land. Once, when I heard them declare that Greenland was the most beautiful country they had seen in any climate, I asked them to put the statement in the form of a letter, which they did. That letter is one of my treasured keepsakes.

Four of us worked on the Lindbergh North Atlantic flight of 1933—the Lindberghs, Colonel Robert Logan, and I. Logan, a Canadian pilot in World War I, had been sent north after the armistice by the Canadian government and became the first Canadian airman to report on far northern flying conditions. He had spoken favorably of airfield locations as far north as Canada's most northerly island, Ellesmere. Now, the two of us were to recommend airport locations on Canada's eastward route. For such a study we needed marine as well as aeronautical knowledge. Pan American accordingly chartered for our use a Danish freighter, the *Jelling,* which, under Logan's command, was to carry supplies for the Lindbergh plane and to sound channels and harbors with a view to future airport supply by ship.

This projected trip, in spite of the Lindberghs' skill, was a dangerous one, as must be all air voyages into regions where conditions are unknown. I was anxious, though not skeptical. The day before the Lindberghs took off, I wrote to Charles:

> I have studied all the authorities I could; the advice I have given you has been a condensation of theirs. Nevertheless, I feel responsibility in passing it on, which worries me more at second hand than if this were an expedition which I were leading. In

spite of my decade and more of planning and dreaming about a northern commercial airway, my chief concern, till you are back safe and successful, will be your safety rather than your success.

As a result of their crisscross flying survey, the soundings and other observations of the *Jelling,* and the meteorological and other reports of the governments involved, the Lindbergh expedition recommended that on operational flights along this route Newfoundland should be avoided because of its weather. A more northerly take-off point from North America for Greenland, such as the Labrador mainland, perhaps near Northwest River—the site of the present Goose Bay airport—was recommended.

Eastbound from Labrador, both the flying boat and the *Jelling* headed for the capital of Greenland, Godthaab. The *Jelling* steered south around the tip of Greenland and went on to Reykjavik, while the Lindberghs flew both up and down Greenland's west coast before crossing the inland ice and Denmark Strait and making for Iceland. In Reykjavik they met the *Jelling* and sent her back to New York while they went on a flying public relations tour of the Scandinavian countries, the Soviet Union, and the British Isles. By way of adding an additional string to our transatlantic bow, the Lindberghs made a reconnaissance flight to the Iberian Peninsula and northwest Africa, returning to New York by way of the Azores.

While the information gathered and the good will built up by the flights of 1933 were useful to Pan American, the earlier flights and Anne Lindbergh's book about them, *North to the Orient,* were far more interesting to the public and therefore additionally valuable to Pan American. True, Europe had understood in Shakespeare's time the mariners' slogan that "The near way to the Far East is north," but meanwhile the distortions of the Mercator map and some significant events, such as Columbus' voyages, had made us forget this truth. Everybody was sure that Kipling was right when he said that east and west were not likely to meet. The public was therefore both enlightened and jolted by a book that told them that the direct route from New York to Peking is north, and that if a nonstop plane were available and you flew by the shortest distance you would cross the Arctic Sea but not the Pacific Ocean. I had long ago explained in my *Northward Course of Empire* that this sort of flying would be advantageous, and had argued that weather conditions would average better the year round on the northern route than on the westward. The Lindberghs did not argue the point. They simply reported that they had flown both routes and found that the northerly was the shorter and better way.

All this was good news to Pan American, which hoped to use the sphericity of the earth not only on its northeastern routes to Moscow and Berlin but also on the northwestern to Tokyo and Peking.

My work with Pan American was intermittent, giving me plenty of time for other pursuits. Early in 1935, brought to a head by the belief in Washington that war might be in the offing and that if it were the north would be highly important, Ralph Lomen's idea of an arctic manual was presented to me once more. This time there was action, although it turned out to be somewhat confused.

Funds for the production of the manual were put into an army appropriation bill and General Oscar Westover was authorized to hire me and my growing research organization to prepare a report of living and operating conditions in the Arctic. We immediately took steps to increase the library by some five thousand volumes and to undertake much more detailed cross-referencing in the catalogue.

What I proposed to do was prepare an exhaustive report, running to perhaps two million words, of which the arctic manual would be a by-product. From the first it was clear that the manual should try to give, in reasonably small compass, those underlying facts and principles which would be most useful to men who had to travel or live in the Arctic, whether in peace or in war.

The form and length of the manual was something of a problem. Should it be a booklet, giving concise directions for specific things to do under specified conditions? If so, it could be carried in the pocket and, when its possessor got into trouble, it could be pulled out and thumbed through for a solution. Perhaps, however, the book should undertake to explain things at such length, and so clearly and interestingly, that a man would remember what he had read. In that case, instead of carrying the manual in his pocket, he would carry with him a still more portable memory and would have such a grasp of fundamentals that he could while in the field devise the appropriate solution for any problems that might arise.

General Oscar Westover, as chief of the Air Corps, considered this matter of format so important that he carried it up to the chief of staff, General Malin Craig. I never talked with General Craig about it, but the deputy chief of staff, Major General George S. Simonds, informed me that the manual was to be written in topical form, with a narrative trend similar to that of my published books and with an attempt at such lucidity and human interest that the manual might be read for pleasure, or at least without mental, distress, by anyone who was interested—as any reader had better be if he was going north. Later, said General Simonds, I might be employed to make a supplementary abridgment for carrying in the pocket.

After the death of General Westover in an airplane accident, our work went forward, with some modification, under the direction of his successor, General H. H. ("Hap") Arnold. We were to prepare four exhaustive "guides"—to Alaska, arctic Canada, Greenland, and arctic Siberia—each ranging from one thousand to five thousand typewritten pages in length. In addition, the smaller *Arctic Manual* would be prepared at the same time.

By the end of 1939, war had descended upon Europe as well as Asia, and clouds were gathering over the United States. There was much to do in Washington, and General Arnold, who could not spare the time for conferences with us in New York as General Westover had done, assigned the work first to Colonel H. H. C. Richards and then to Colonel R. C. Candee.

It had been my understanding that, when the *Arctic Manual* was to be printed, I would be asked to get it ready for the press. This would have involved further editing and the preparation of an index. The first thing I knew, however, a printed copy turned up on my desk.

It had also been my understanding that, if a pocket manual was to be produced by condensing the original 536-page publication, the condensation would be done by me. However, a 74-page condensed version soon came along, later available as the Army's *TM-240*. I was surprised both by its sudden appearance and by its quality. I am not sure even today that I could have condensed the material so well.

I continued to be involved in Pan American's negotiations with foreign countries in preparation for their transatlantic services. In mid-August, 1937, I had received an urgent telephone message from Constantin Oumansky, then ambassador from the Soviet Union, with whom I had previously had some dealings on behalf of Pan American. Oumansky, who knew that I had been instrumental in forwarding to Moscow the United States request for help in finding the lost Ben Eielson, appealed to me in my capacity as president of the Explorers Club, asking me to set in motion a search for the famous Soviet aviator Sigismund Levanevsky, who, with five companions, was missing on his flight from Moscow to Alaska. His four-motored plane was known to have passed over the Pole, but no later word had been received from him and it was assumed that his plane was down on the ice.

Two months earlier, in June, the United States had been thrilled by the arrival in Oregon of a Soviet plane that had flown nonstop from Moscow by way of the Pole. Many Americans had been struck by the fact that the fliers Chkalov, Baidukov, and Beliakov reported the flying conditions worse in the Oregon Mountains than they had been while crossing the Arctic Sea.

In July, three more Russians, Gromov, Ymashev, and Danilin, had taken off from Moscow and flown by the same route to northwestern Mexico. There they had turned around, not because of bad weather, but because they wanted to land in the United States. Even San Jacinto, California, where they came down, was so distant from Moscow that the Russian plane was found to have broken the long-distance record by 658 miles. The flight, not counting the loop into Mexico, was certified by the National Aeronautic Association of the United States at 6,295 miles.

Both these flights had been accomplished in light, single-motor planes. The real object, however, was the flying of passengers between the Soviet Union and the United States, and so, on August 12, Levanevsky and his companions had taken off from Moscow in a passenger-type craft.

Oumansky told me over the telephone that his government would meet all expenses, but it was hoped that the Explorers Club would coordinate the rescue efforts, which no doubt would come from many nations, as they had when Umberto Nobile and his dirigible had gone down in the Arctic some years earlier. Oumansky suggested that I take a room in my regular hotel, the Carlton, which was almost next door to his embassy and would be convenient for consultation. I took the first train to Washington, checked in at the Carlton, and walked over to get the latest news. There was none.

I saw only one hope. In the gathering polar twilight and inevitable darkness, that hope depended on George Hubert Wilkins. If I could persuade him to undertake the search, there would be a chance. I reached him by phone, and he took the midnight train from New York. At breakfast he told us that he was ready to start at once if he could get the only plane then in the United States suited for the job, one that our friend Richard Archbold of the Explorers Club had outfitted for a projected trip to New Guinea. We both felt that Archbold would either lend us the plane or sell it to the Russians.

I told Oumansky that morning what I still believe: that only Wilkins and his pilot Hollick-Kenyon had the competence, the knowledge, and the faith that could lead to finding the Levanevsky party. Because of the lateness of the year, any rescuers would have to depend chiefly on moonlight, starlight, and scattered auroras. For the searchers themselves, if they should be forced down on the pack ice, there would be no hope except through the use of their skill in hunting and in snowhouse construction. Only Wilkins had the necessary combination of these skills.

The story of the search has been told in detail by Wilkins himself. From their base in the Mackenzie delta and elsewhere, he and his pilot repeatedly took off before the first glimmer of dawn in the arctic sky. By noon they were too far north to see the daylight when it came. It was over by the time they returned to their base. These repeated flights, up to seventeen hundred miles long, crossed and recrossed a vast area to within two hundred miles of the Pole. Only such maps as Wilkins and I have published on Northern Hemisphere projections can convey the real nature of those heartbreaking and seemingly impossible flights.

The Levanevsky search, though seen by me only from the remote side lines, was the most notable event of my second presidency of the Explorers Club or, for that matter, of my years with Pan American Airways. The fact that no trace of the Levanevsky party was ever found does not minimize the greatness of Wilkins' achievement. Had it not been for the war which was even then threatening us, the greatest series of arctic flights ever made would undoubtedly have led to a knowledge and use of the Arctic that even today has not been entirely realized.

38 Bureaucrats and Bibliographers

That the Eskimos or their ancestors were the real discoverers of the Northwest Passage is certain. They established in remote times a regular traffic between the Atlantic and Pacific oceans around the north end of North America. I learned this from Charles Brower at Point Barrow in 1908 and confirmed it from the Eskimos themselves in 1911. For them it was all in the day's work. They got neither reward nor rank for their enterprise.

The British naval officers who, unaware of what the Eskimos were aware of, rediscovered the Passage piecemeal were rewarded handsomely by promotion. American naval explorers were as a rule less fortunate. Peary was, it is true, made a rear admiral by act of Congress, but only in the face of bitter opposition from the Navy. One of the British pioneers in northern waters from 1818 to 1828, Edward Parry, who was the first European to attack the whole Northwest Passage, was quite rapidly jumped from lieutenant to admiral, reflecting British respect for explorers' achievements.

The United States did not show an equal respect. Not until shortly before World War II, when the importance of arctic work became apparent, was recognition of it a foregone conclusion. One man who benefited by this change in the attitude of the United States was Commander Edward H. Smith, master of the light ice-breaker *Northland*.

Smith came to me to discuss the advisability of constructing heavy-duty icebreakers with a view to testing the possibility of opening the Baffin Bay-Bering Sea route—the traditional Northwest

319

Passage—to wartime navigation. We talked about icebreakers, the Soviet experience with them, and their possible uses as supply ships for northern bases and as convoys for naval vessels. Although Smith had prepared for the Coast Guard a *Greenland Pilot,* he was unaware of the northern guidebooks that we had just turned over to the Army. Since he was about to cruise along both the west and the east coast of Greenland, we decided that it would be a good thing if he got the Army's permission to study my Greenland material.

During our conversation Smith and I discussed the possibility of setting up an arctic-information organization which would answer the needs of the different departments of the government and save useless duplication. We concluded that we might start by establishing a coordination committee with one member from the Army, one from the Navy, one from the Coast Guard, and one from the State Department. As the nucleus of the organization, I of course had in mind my polar library and its staff, which was already an available source of arctic information but provided no means of breaking through the barriers of protocol, which kept the various branches of the armed forces from using it.

I continued to be frustrated by confusion in Washington and in the services. I spent a great deal of my time watching for good and bad things in the publications of the various branches of the government. I found both good and bad, and evidences of the old, wasteful duplication of effort were constantly cropping up.

Smith and I continued to push for experiments with the Northwest Passage, but we ran into trouble with Ottawa, where the feeling was that Smith was not going through proper channels in arranging important meetings to discuss this problem of Canada's northland. Such meetings, Ottawa felt, should have been arranged through the United States Secretary of State and the corresponding officer in Canada.

I succeeded in getting a liaison officer appointed to handle the delicate threads of communication. He was Richard Finnie, author of an important book, *Canada Moves North.* Smith and I were looking forward to getting somewhere with Finnie's help, but unfortunately it was discovered that his appointment had not been made at the right level and he had to be let go. Smith and I continued to run into obstacles. We never did get anywhere with the idea of using the Northwest Passage. Smith, however, did not let his disappointment interfere with his Greenland work, for which he was rewarded by being made a rear admiral. Before the war he might have made similar contributions and remained a commander until his retirement.

These were discouraging days for me. One of the most disheartening situations of this period arose during the Depression, when Colonel Brehon B. Somervell was Works Progress Administrator, from 1936–1940, for the New York area. The Explorers Club had welcomed the WPA as a means of accomplishing something that was closely tied up with the advisory work of our library and with the idea of an arctic institute. Under professional bibliographers we would recruit from unemployed clerical workers a gradually larger and more competent staff to canvass the libraries of New York for what was known or thought about the region north of the civilized world. Within government circles the support for our plans was strong from the beginning. This support was most noticeable in the history and geography sections of the State, Interior, Army, and Navy departments, in the higher ranks of which we had many active backers.

The WPA of New York authorized us to hire a chief bibliographer at a fair salary. We chose one who was also a Sanskrit scholar. We wanted to reach back as nearly as we could to the beginning of human progress. Among our early sources would be the Bible, Homeric poems, and the rest of the classics of Africa, Asia, and Europe. We worked slowly, for only thus can one hope for quality. We had access only to the unemployed, for this was strictly a Depression project. During our second year we had over a hundred workers, some good, some poor.

The Explorers Club pledged its help in the project by canvassing club members for information that would then be turned over to my staff. Part of the service of the Explorers Club members to the coordinator was the furnishing of information on the availability of Canadian oil for Alaska. It was argued that such oil, descending the Mackenzie by downstream barges or by pipeline parallel to the river north of Norman Wells, crossing a low divide to the head of the Lewes or some other branch of the Yukon, and then to Fairbanks and the mouth of the Yukon on the Bering Sea, would make military operations in the north feasible. Our arctic bibliography offered supporting information. It should have been clear sailing from then on. It was far from being so. We ran into serious difficulties that could not entirely have been due to malice, or even to lack of interest. They resulted in large part from misunderstandings for which I was not blameless. They were caused by my poor liaison work between the Army and the WPA, especially where Colonel Somervell was involved.

After a lapse of more than two decades I find it difficult to believe how unprepared those of us working on the bibliography were when the final blow struck. We had been deceived, I suppose, by the general WPA amity. I was conscious of a change in WPA administration and of a rise in the animosity of certain classes toward the New Deal. We heard increased talk about boondoggling. Still, it was to me a storm from a practically clear sky when we were told that Colonel Somervell felt that we had been coddling our bibliographers far too long. He had fired them all so that they could be replaced by a more deserving and less pampered group of workers. We learned that the colonel thought that a bibliography of the arctic regions was not real work that could be of use to anybody. It was, he felt, a benevolent make-believe on the part of the government designed to preserve the self-respect of the poor—to make them feel less like paupers.

When I finally realized that Colonel Somervell really meant what he had been saying, it did not immediately occur to me to go to him and talk him out of his naïveté. Instead, I proceeded to get him overruled and humiliated. I belonged to the faction that admired what the WPA was doing for painting and sculpture and the other arts. I was one of those who thought it a silver lining to the Depression cloud that at last the United States was subsidizing drama, the writing of history, and painting and sculpture that was meant to adorn public buildings. It seems to me now that, through our self-righteous scorn for diplomacy, we not merely failed to win the colonel over but almost tricked him into hostility. When we finally attempted to placate him, it was too late. The WPA administrator for New York simply told us that we did not understand the benevolence of Washington. He intimated that there was a fundamental usefulness in building golf clubs for suburbanites but not in compiling a bibliography of a worthless and remote Arctic!

The lines of conflict were drawn. Our side tried to bring reason, even scholarship, into what Somervell felt was a situation requiring ''just plain common sense.'' The Explorers Club appealed to those already committed to bibliographies and to the systematizing and preserving of all knowledge, knowledge of things even more remote than the polar regions, such as planets, stars, and nebulae. Too late, Somervell discovered that the Air Corps, Engineers, and many other groups really wanted an arctic bibliography. Because of Somervell's intransigence they did not get one.

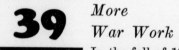

39 More War Work

In the fall of 1940 the War Department asked Pan American to let me help give the new head of the Alaska Defense Force, Brigadier General Simon Bolivar Buckner, an arctic education. Buckner had never been farther north than West Point, having been stationed during the years of his service in such places as Texas and the Philippines. He had been given the Alaskan job in July, and had heard that winter comes early in the north. The general had already left for Anchorage, and the Army wanted me to get there as soon as possible and give him some advice before he was called upon to make any important policy decisions.

Pan American was glad to oblige the Army. The company had, in any case, been thinking of sending me to their office in Fairbanks so that I might become familiar with its operations. I left New York at once and went by train to Seattle; from there I flew to Juneau and then to Fairbanks, where I was to spend a week with my friend Joe Crosson, Ben Eielson's successor as manager of the air operation that Pan American had taken over from the Aviation Corporation.

One of the reasons for the Army's desire to have me confer with Buckner was that I was supposed to know something about permafrost. I am in a way being anachronistic in speaking of permafrost by that name in 1940, since the term was coined by a man whom I did not meet until 1945 and who appears to have first used it in print in 1943, when the Intelligence Branch Office, Chief of Engineers, printed the book *Permafrost or Permanently Frozen Ground* by Professor Siemon Muller of the Department of Geology, Stanford University. Muller, who was born in Russia, used "permafrost" as a translation from his native tongue. In 1911, I had used the term "permanently frozen sub-soil" as a translation from the Eskimo to explain an archaeologically troublesome condition that I first encountered when digging up ancient Eskimo house ruins.

Permafrost, or permanently frozen ground, is a common phenomenon in the northern parts of Asia and North America. It is now known that there are islands of permafrost in the lowlands of Minnesota, on the upper slopes of Mount Washington in New Hampshire, and in other apparently unlikely places. Permafrost does not behave the way seasonally or occasionally frozen ground does. Where it occurs, its peculiarities must be taken into account because they present special construction problems. Soon after starting my job as adviser to Pan American, I had realized that we were going to have in arctic airport construction the kind of trouble I had met in my early work in archaeology, and I had done what research I could on the subject. In 1940 there was still not much known outside Russia about the peculiar qualities of permafrost, but anyone hoping to build barracks and airports in the north needed to know what had been learned by those who were aware of its existence and its effects. Joe Crosson brought me up to date on the subject. After my conference with him I felt that I could be helpful in preventing engineering errors. I therefore went down to Anchorage, where I was presented to General Buckner.

I found him one of the most delightful men I ever met. Like the Australian Wilkins, Buckner thought of himself as a Southerner and did not have preconceived notions about arctic conditions. Instead, he tried to understand them and to deal with them as he met them. In a few months, as had been the case with Wilkins, Buckner was having less trouble with the climate and its effect on human life than most Northerners. He and I kept in close touch after the month I spent with him. In a year he was writing me that the Alaskan was his favorite climate. After four years' experience of it, he wrote me that he preferred it to that of either Hawaii or the Philippines. The general backed up his statement by the purchase, in 1944, of a farm at Homer, Alaska.

When I was associated with Buckner, the Army had just published my *Arctic Manual*. Buckner and some of his officers questioned me on points made in the manual that they wished to have amplified. Some things they did not quite understand; others they doubted. Among the book's great variety of subjects was arctic village planning and house building. In this section I had described how animals, and especially men, produce fog, which I referred to as "human-and-animal fog." While I was discussing the subject with Buckner and his aides, I hit upon a happier term: "biofog."

The first mention of this phenomenon in print may have been in the narrative of Baron Ferdinand von Wrangel describing a journey in the 1820s. Wrangel was sent by the Russian government to investigate rumors of land north of northeastern Asia, the land that eventually received the name of Wrangel Island. Wrangel noted that a raven, flying in midwinter near the region now called the Pole of Cold, at perhaps −70° or −80° F, left a fog trail behind it in the air. I have described in an earlier chapter of this book how in the still air of the forest north of Great Bear Lake, during the winter of 1910–1911, we used to see the smoke of even a single caribou rising through the woods as if it came from a small campfire. The combined smoke of many caribou gave the impression of a burning forest. In spite of earlier observations of biofog, I was to hear men saying in Alaska in 1940, as if it were a new discovery, that aviators could see villages if they flew right over them, but could not see them from an angle when half a mile away at an altitude of a thousand feet.

I explained to Buckner that, in view of all this, it was necessary to be particularly careful in locating airfields and in placing buildings about them. On days when the temperature gets below −40° F, airport buildings may be completely obscured by a dense human and animal fog, especially if there should be a slight movement of air from the buildings toward the field.

I mentioned that I agreed with a number of local fliers that the power station and hospital at Ladd Field had been so placed that there was always danger that the field would be partially obscured by biofog. I suggested that, while these buildings could not be moved before the following year, it would be wise to think twice before locating any new construction, and to avoid building expensive buildings that might later have to be moved. In making this sort of suggestion I was a little afraid that Buckner might take offense. He never did.

I returned from Alaska late in 1940, having promised Buckner that, with the cooperation of his friends and mine in the government, we would establish what we both wanted: a center of arctic studies **in the** United States similar to that which the British already had in the Scott Polar Research Institute of Cambridge. After some eleven months I had made no progress toward this end. Then, unexpectedly, I received a letter from the very man whom I had feared I could not reach, one believed to have the confidence of President Roosevelt and therefore the power to overcome the opposition of the chief of the Construction Division of the Quartermaster Corps, the official who had been thwarting us. We had heard that the President, angered by the conservative opposition he was meeting, had set up an agency of open-minded scientists and statesmen, calling it the Office of Coordinator of Information. The rumors gave way to something substantial in October, 1941, when a letter arrived from William J. Donovan, Coordinator of Information, suggesting the establishment of my proposed center of arctic studies. I suggested that we have a conference in New York, with the idea that there we could discuss to better advantage the possible use of my arctic library in connection with the plan.

Donovan, tied to Washington, sent a deputy, David Bruce. We were delighted with him and with his understanding of what was being proposed. The result was that I and my entire staff and library were to be retained as advisers to the Office of the Coordinator of Information. We were to furnish, on request, complete information —geographic, economic, political, social, or religious—about any country in the world extending north of a line drawn at about 60° N latitude. We were to do research on any such countries at the Coordinator's request and to make available to his office any research we might do independently for others. This agreement was to run for six months, subject to renewal.

The contract was signed and we were in business. Bruce concentrated on what Donovan had said in his letter to me about "the establishment of a center of Arctic studies." He explained that the Coordinator wanted us to work out a plan for freeing Alaska from dependence upon remote sources of petroleum such as Venezuela, Texas, and California. As a result of Bruce's suggestion I wrote my first direct memorandum as a government employee, a letter of December 10, 1941, which was headed "Local Petroleum for Alaska and Bering Sea." In this letter, with which I enclosed an article from the July, 1941, *Foreign Affairs* entitled "Routes to Alaska," I made some suggestions as to the best, though not the cheapest, way of meeting Alaska's wartime need for oil. I pointed out the advantage of my proposal over a plan proposed by the Army to ship oil north from California. I recommended a conference on the subject at which the government and the Standard Oil Company of New York should be represented.

This letter, together with the *Foreign Affairs* article, created much excitement. Within twenty-four hours I was told what would be done. There would be no meeting in Washington such as the one I recommended, but it might be a good thing to have one in New York. The really important thing would be to hand my letter and the accompanying article to a genius whom the Coordinator had hired to dress up proposals for presentation to those at the top. This individual would turn my material into a marvelous illustrated prospectus by means of which it was hoped that the Vice President would be convinced. If he liked the ideas, Mr. Wallace would get the President to read the prospectus. If Roosevelt also liked it, orders would go out to have Norman Wells and other Mackenzie River properties expanded and a downhill pipeline laid connecting them. This would mean that Alaska and northwestern North America generally could dispense with, or at least greatly reduce, the importing of petroleum from Venezuela and California.

The prospectus was ready for my first inspection within two days. I considered it a very good promotional job, truthful and easy to grasp. I made a few suggestions and approved a slight modification the next day. My hopes were high, but I never saw the memorandum again. This was, however, the genesis of the misunderstood and now almost forgotten project that came to be known as Canol—short for Canadian Oil.

This was not a vague plan but an actual network of some sixteen hundred miles of oil and oil-derivative pipelines and a refinery at Whitehorse, Yukon Territory, constructed between 1942 and 1944 at a cost of 130 million dollars. This great and useful system, though built to serve emergency military purposes, was not developed at all along the lines I advised.

The reason for the existence of such a project should be obvious. The North Pacific sea lanes were vulnerable in case of war with the Japanese. The United States and Canada were constructing air bases in the extreme northwest and some of them were already completed. These were along a line from Edmonton north through Fairbanks and west to Nome. Parallel with the Canol project of developing local oil to service them was obviously the project of building a road to make them accessible by land.

It was my opinion, and I said so, that the road should follow the Mackenzie Valley, making use of the river for boats and barges in summer and for tractor trains to run on the river ice in winter. I believed that the highway should pass close to the oil region of Norman Wells, just west of Great Bear Lake, and then head for Mayo or Dawson, four hundred miles northwest of Whitehorse, from which the Yukon River would provide the highway to Circle, already connected to Fairbanks by road.

With my suggestions for the location of the road, I also forwarded to General Walter Pyron, the Army's petroleum expert, a proposal for developing the Norman Wells oil area. General Pyron attended a conference in late April, 1942, in which the Canol project became a living, if somewhat lame, enterprise. The general's notion of the geography of Alaska and northwest Canada was something less than sharp. He had heard of Whitehorse, though he was not sure whether it was in Alaska or Canada. He did know that it was on the proposed Alaska Highway.

The conference that set Canol in motion resulted in a memorandum from Professor James H. Graham, dean of engineering at the University of Kentucky, who was an assistant to General Brehon Somervell, by that time chief of the Army Service Forms. This memorandum, which contained several geographical boners, authorized the extension of the Norman Wells field but called for a pipeline from Norman to Whitehorse over terrain that no one really knew and about which almost everyone but Professor Graham had great misgivings. The die was cast, although I did not know of this memorandum until mid-May. In the meantime, I had been working on my own plans.

The Alaska Highway was built over what I still believe to have been the worst possible route, and the Canol project was put into action. It was not the project that anyone but the Army would have chosen, but it did produce and deliver oil, although at enormous cost. It served a useful purpose, not the least of which was the introduction of its thirty thousand employees to subarctic conditions. My friend Richard Finnie, who was closely associated with the venture, has said, ". . . though it matured differently from the way he anticipated, Canol undoubtedly sprouted from a seed planted by Stefansson."

The Office of Coordinator of Information had big enough things to worry about. There were also small ones. Donovan began to be concerned about the multiplication of requests for help made to my arctic center. Some of the increasing requests for northern information and opinion that worried the Coordinator came from his own office.

The kind of thing we found difficult to handle is illustrated by an army publication that came to my attention. It was entitled "An Advance copy, subject to Correction of 'Glossary of Icelandic and Eskimo Words Commonly Used on Maps.' " Two main things were wrong with this vocabulary. It contained linguistic errors, and it committed the unpardonable sin of grouping Eskimos and Icelanders together, a juxtaposition that would have aroused ridicule in all Scandinavian countries and perhaps resentment in Iceland. When I received this pamphlet, I immediately noted my comments on the first four pages. Then I held it up, thinking that I should first handle the matter through the naval officer from whom I had received the booklet. He felt, however, that I should take my comments directly to the Army.

I therefore asked the Office of the Coordinator of Information to submit to the Army my attached notes and to ask if they would care to have me either correct the present vocabulary or make up another more adequate for the purpose. My staff and I could easily do that. I said that the two vocabularies, Eskimo and Icelandic, should be published separately, since there is no political, linguistic, racial, or other relation between the two peoples and languages. The Eskimo vocabulary was not quite so bad as the Icelandic, but it was not good enough to be printed. Had we been asked to prepare the pamphlet in the first place, or finally allowed to revise it, the Army would have been spared being made to look ridiculous.

On June 4, 1942, Donovan telephoned me about the possibility of a Japanese attack upon North America through Alaska. After we hung up I wrote him, saying, "When you telephoned I am afraid I did not express what I meant . . . I now try to." I then reviewed previous conversations, his and mine, and closed with:

> You remember, this was practically what you and I discussed with the Vice President in relation to an oil pipeline from Norman to pour fuel into the Yukon River, and a road from the Mackenzie basin at Norman to the Yukon. To fight the Japanese effectively we must apply our strength from the interior, as the Soviets do, rather than having our main strength coastal and thus depending on the outcome of a naval warfare.

It now seems to me doubly urgent to speed up the production and refining of petroleum at Norman. As you know, the plans to that end, upon which I have been working under your direction, are now being carried out. The only fly in the ointment is that, in my opinion, the work is being done the hard way. I do not worry about what seems to me an unnecessary expenditure of millions; but I do worry that while we are spending the extra millions we are also losing a lot of time.

Donovan merely replied that he found my memorandum interesting, and was sending it on to the War Department.

Alcan and Canol were beyond my reach. These projects were carried out, not only the hard way, but, in my opinion, in the wrong way. My opinion was shared by many others who were in a position to judge.

40 A New World

These were crowded but discouraging days. Had it not been that certain developments in my private life provided me with a lightning rod, I might have felt in danger of being struck down by the thunderbolts of officialdom. My library staff provided a strong foundation for the many harassing exigencies of my somewhat confused and often confusing contacts with government departments, and formed a collective alter ego for me while I was away from New York lecturing.

In spite of my continuing preoccupation with matters of national defense and development, there was time for social life. I was living in the heart of Greenwich Village. I had become, following an impulse that first struck me when I lived at the Judson in Washington Square in 1907, a Villager. As a Villager, I met all kinds of interesting people, interesting in ways that differed markedly from the interest I found in the political, scientific, and military figures with whom my work brought me into contact.

One of my early friends was a charming and vivacious young woman named Betty Salemme, born Betty Hardy, married to a brilliant Italian-born sculptor. Betty told me that she had attended my Carnegie Hall lecture in 1918 and that I had made a lasting impression on her. What she had remembered for more than twenty years was not the substance of my talk. As with Dame Nellie Melba in Australia, she had been struck by something else. With Melba it had been my voice. With Betty it was my head.

When I met Betty in the Village she was planning a year's work for her husband, Tony. This was to consist of two parallel projects, one a full-length study of a man's body, the other a sculpture of a man's head. Paul Robeson, the ex-football star, actor, singer, and friend of Eugene O'Neill, was providing the body. I was to pose for the head.

Betty told me that she knew a successful man when she saw one, mentioning O'Neill and Robeson. She suggested that I was headed for success, if I had not already achieved it, and that I was therefore a logical subject for her husband's skill. I do not know exactly how I found the two hours that I spent in Tony Salemme's studio every morning, put pose I did, while Betty kept me from going to sleep by making both coffee and conversation.

In the course of my developing acquaintance with the Salemmes, I was introduced to a charming young woman named Evelyn and to a remarkable Village night spot called Romany Marie's. Which introduction came first I cannot to this day remember, so closely are the young woman and Romany Marie's associated in my mind. It seems surprising to me now that my first impression of Evelyn was not indelibly memorable. The score is even, however. Evelyn's first impression of me has been lost among later, more vivid ones.

Perhaps the first time I made a distinct impression on Evelyn was during an evening at Romany Marie's. Marie's, for the benefit of those who never knew it, was more a social center than a night spot in today's sense. Marie herself dominated it. As hostess, she welcomed for tea or coffee and talk all the interesting people who lived in or came to the Village. Among these were Robeson and O'Neill, the Millay sisters, Edna and Norma; poets Witter Bynner and Arthur Davison Ficke; Stephen Vincent Benét; his brother William Rose Benét; and Bill's wife, Elinor Wylie. Singers came and sang, if asked to, although Paul Robeson's attendance fell off because he was asked to sing too often and hated to refuse. Poets read poems (I remember especially Harry Kemp), and Bobby Edwards, the lineal descendant of an early Massachusetts governor, sang his own songs to the accompaniment of a ukulele fashioned out of a cigar box.

The occasion that was the first to make me remember Evelyn— with some embarrassment, I admit—resulted from a certain unperceptive clumsiness on my part. One evening Marie was short of waitresses. Evelyn, among other guests, offered to help her out. In the first place, if I had been more observant, I should have noticed that nobody at Marie's ever paid for anything more than he ordered, even if it was only a cup of coffee and he sat over it all evening.

Tipping volunteer waitresses was bad manners and I was foolish enough to offer Evelyn a tip and stupid enough, when she refused it, to insist that she keep it. At least my gaucherie made Evelyn remember me, and my annoyance with myself made me remember her.

What really focused my attention on Evelyn was her singing of folk songs. A wonderful mimic, she could sing perfectly in languages she did not know. She was especially good in French and Spanish—so good at the former, in fact, that she once got a job in a well-known Broadway restaurant, the French Casino, singing as a country girl fresh from France. Her repertory consisted of old French songs and some popular new ones, which she learned by listening to Maurice Chevalier, then at the peak of his career. A newspaper columnist who learned Evelyn's secret thought it would make good copy. When the story appeared, Evelyn felt that she had better quit. She did not stay away from the Casino for long, however. Her employers began to see that there was something to be said for a Brooklyn girl who knew no French but could successfully explain to those who did that she had a sweetheart to whom she had sworn that she would not speak a word of her native tongue until she had completely mastered "zis deeficult Anglish."

Some time before, Evelyn had married Bil Baird, the puppeteer, with whom she toured the country with a very successful marionette show.

Then one day I heard from Romany Marie that Evelyn was in a New York hospital with a ruptured appendix and was not expected to live. With the death of my Harvard roommate, Valdi Thorvaldson, suddenly sharp in my memory, I went to the hospital and was allowed to see the patient briefly. Evelyn, I discovered, seemed more concerned about her husband and the news that he might be getting of her—he was out of town with his marionette show—than she was about herself. She wanted to be sure that the messages he got cheerfully assured him that she was receiving the best of care and that he had nothing to worry about.

Apparently, Evelyn sensed more about herself than the doctors did. On my next visit to the hospital I found her recovering. When she was able to leave the hospital, friends of hers took her away for a long convalescence.

It was the New York World's Fair of 1939 that brought us together again. Grover Whalen, as head of this venture, had invited the government of Iceland to participate. With customary American ignorance of Scandinavian relationships, however, he had implied that Iceland might share an exhibition building with Denmark. Iceland wished to be represented at the Fair, but not in cohabitation with Denmark, and I was asked by Icelandic officials to explain the situation to Mr. Whalen. The result was that Iceland was offered a separate building site.

At about the same time the Icelandic government asked me to prepare a book on Iceland that they could sell at the Fair. I agreed and began looking for a publisher willing to handle a rush job. Through Theodore Roosevelt, Jr., I managed to get Doubleday to do the book. It was called *Iceland: The First American Republic,* and it appeared with a preface by Ted.

It happened that, shortly after I had signed the contract for this book, I was walking south on lower Eighth Avenue, wondering how I could get the manuscript finished on time. I was then living at 67 Morton Street. A block or so from my apartment I was surprised and pleased to meet Evelyn. She was on her way to Tony's Garden Restaurant at 48 Barrow Street. I joined her, and we sat down at Tony's to catch up on news of each other. Evelyn confirmed something that I had heard from Romany Marie—she and her husband were separated and she was consequently no longer in the marionette business. In fact, she was looking for a job. I was aware that David Gaither, whom we both knew, was in charge of exhibits at the Iceland building. I knew, too, that he was short of help. Moreover, I knew that Evelyn could do anything she set her hand to. I asked her if she would like me to get her a job helping with the Icelandic exhibits. She would, and I did, although she had to join the Painters, Paper Hangers, and Scenic Designers Union in order to qualify. This presented no real obstacle. She was soon making models of the hills and dales and the ponies and sheep of Iceland. As the work continued, she picked up—as I had suspected she would —a good deal of knowledge about Iceland's culture.

More than her occupation at the Iceland pavilion, it was Evelyn's interest in a favorite book of mine that brought us permanently together. The book was *Life on a Medieval Barony,* by William Stearns Davis. I had known of Evelyn's love for the music and song of the Middle Ages. I now found that she was interested in learning about every aspect of medieval life. She was eager to

learn about the whole era, about its social and economic organization, its law, and its religion; she excluded nothing from the range
of her interest.

It occurred to me that this many-sided young woman would
make an ideal librarian. She could not have enough of books, and
was as conversant with their folly as with their wisdom, forming no prejudgments as to what was or what was not important
enough to be preserved. I knew she would be as sympathetic with
David Starr Jordan when he denounced what he called "the higher
foolishness" in education as with George Lyman Kittredge when he
urged libraries to save shelves and stacks of educational foolishness
because it could be regarded as folklore. Such catholicity of intellectual taste in Evelyn was a revelation to me, who had originally
thought of her as a folk singer, a mimic, and a marionette player.
I felt that, when we got the Iceland building opened and the Fair
off our rather crowded agenda, she might fit into the information
service of our polar library.

The library now had a staff of ten, with a steadily growing
reference section for that region around the North Pole which has
for a boundary the southern edge of permafrost on land and the
farthest limit of drifting ice at sea. We had undertaken to counsel
the Army, the Navy, and corporations like Pan American Airways
on the climate, nature, and resources, as well as on the politics and
cultural history, of a third of the Northern Hemisphere. Our territory covered Iceland, the northern halves of Norway and Sweden,
all of Finland, the northern third of the Soviet Union, and the
northern Pacific Ocean, including the Sea of Okhotsk and the Kurile
Islands. East of this, our field included the Aleutians, all of Alaska,
the northern third of British Columbia, Alberta, Saskatchewan, and
Manitoba, and all the lands in North America north of the transcontinental railways of Canada. On our eastern coast we went as far
south as the Gulf of St. Lawrence and Newfoundland. We covered
all of Greenland, and were not unaware that ice has been observed
at sea abreast of Palm Beach.

We foresaw the growth of our service and the need of fluency
in many languages. We already had, of course, through me, Latin
and Old Norse. We had employed bilingual and trilingual personnel fluent in French, German, and Russian, and we were building
up our library in these tongues. As book collectors we covered all
languages that have printed alphabets.

Evelyn did join the library staff and proved indispensable in more ways than one. Without her I should have found the difficult war years very hard going.

We were married on April 10, 1941. Our first joint action as a couple was to establish a summer headquarters in Vermont. Olive and Jack Wilcox had for years been reminding me of the advantages of Vermont for summer work and pointing out that there the telephone service was practically free. Evelyn volunteered to find a place for us, and soon found one. It belonged to two brothers, Edgar and Benny Dearing, who, though we never saw them, left a wealth of legend and folklore that added greatly to the charm of the place. What we still call the Dearing Farm is, after two decades, beginning to be called the Stefansson Place. It is on the divide between two branches of the White River, about five miles northeast of the Wilcox farm and perhaps six miles west of our post office, Bethel, at the head of Camp Brook. We have 210 acres, of which only 40 are field or meadow.

We soon decided to move our duplicate books up from New York, and also the bulky, inactive items such as sets of *Atlantic, Century, Harper's, North American Review*, and *Scribner's*, to make room for more active books at St. Luke's Place, to which we had moved from Morton Street in order to get more space. These and other magazines we indexed for pertinent articles. We stocked the farm with dictionaries, encyclopedias, and reference works generally and, of course, with favorite authors and with the classics of exploration.

For a decade beginning with 1941 we shifted our main activities for a little more or less than half the year from 5 St. Luke's Place in Greenwich Village to Dearing Farm. There was the slight handicap that Olive could never leave Brooklyn until Jack's teaching job at Brooklyn Polytechnic freed him, so they were at Gaysville, Vermont, only from early June to late September. Yet Olive, more nearly than I, was the active head of our project, and it was valuable to have her in New York for contacts with the various government departments and with Pan American.

Meanwhile, Evelyn was learning more and more about my chief fields of interest and proving every day that I had not been wrong when I had thought that I saw in her the qualities of a superb librarian as well as a superb human being.

41

Pemmican and Candy Bars

It was early in June, 1942, that I received new instructions from the Office of Coordinator of Information in Washington, with whom my six-month contract had not yet run out. I was to see Colonel Georges Doriot in the Quartermaster General's Office. When I called on the colonel, I found that I had been sent for to talk about both pemmican and suitable clothing for soldiers stationed in the Arctic. I was impressed with the department's interest. The Quartermaster had heard from old-timers that pemmican was the ideal ration and from up-to-date nutritionists that, as a food, it was scientifically unsound. They asked me to give an hour's talk, to be followed by a question-and-answer period.

The conference with Colonel Doriot and his Quartermaster group that followed my talk was the first of any kind that Evelyn attended with me. We got a warm reception, somewhat Gallic in its style, although Doriot was already a highly regarded member of a New England institution, the Harvard Business School. He said, in effect: "You are the master. We are here to sit at your feet. We want you to suggest any line of research you think we should follow, but especially we want your suggestions on food for the Army in its northern operations. Your least suggestion will be translated into command."

I reconstruct as best I can what I said to an audience that represented many shades of opinion. It was the most important conference, I think, that I ever addressed in connection with World War II. As a student of North American frontier history, I reviewed what Canadians have named the Pemmican War of 1814–

1821, which was the first struggle between commercial giants on our continent and was based on food—as, indeed, was the war that Canada had entered in 1939 and the United States in 1941. That early struggle was for commercial dominion over the fur trade from the Gulf of Mexico to the Arctic Sea, the only business of financial consequence in America at that time. The protagonist was a company that had most of the money and prestige and nearly all the law on its side. The antagonist was a loose conglomeration of trading upstarts, mostly Yankee and French but some British. The heavyweight business champion who had held the title since 1670 was the Hudson's Bay Company, which traded from London by ship through Hudson Strait and Bay. The challengers were not even a company but a federation of semi-independent partners who traded from Montreal along the St. Lawrence River, the Great Lakes, and the Mackenzie River system; they came to be known as the Nor'westers.

The Hudson's Bay Company had everything in its favor, and true gamblers would normally have bet on it. But the independents had one thing on their side: a better diet, and that turned out to be the decisive factor in the war. I pointed out to the Quartermaster Corps, since they had called me in as an adviser on food, that the winning food in that early nineteenth-century struggle was pemmican, which is why English-speaking North America's first internecine struggle is known to historians of the frontier as the Pemmican War. Pemmican, the best and lightest food ever devised for men on the trail, was invented by the North American Indians. Its use gave anyone traveling in the north a distinct advantage. The company had hoped in the early 1800s to starve their competitors by making it a crime for anyone to make, import, or sell pemmican in its territory. I suggested that English-speaking North America should now consider the use of pemmican to make it easier to win the war in which we were engaged. Thereupon I went briefly into the history of the Hudson's Bay Company and of the Nor'westers, which I do not need to repeat here.

In sketching the seven years of the Pemmican War, I explained that since pemmican was regarded by the fur trader as a summer or hot-weather ration, Sir John Franklin had not planned to use it even on his second expedition, 1825–1827. Its extensive winter use in polar exploration actually began with the Franklin Search, which started in the late 1840s. Since that time it has been a standard for both summer and winter arctic exploration. I went on to explain the experience and opinion of all those, including Admiral Peary, who had used pemmican as a complete, all-things-in-one food, whether in the Arctic or in the tropics. I explained the ideal composition of it: roughly a pound of dried lean meat to a pound of fat.

Having established that to the Indians, pemmican was from the start a hot-weather military ration and that the fur trade began its use in summer in the late 1700s, I went on to explain that since I had lived mainly by hunting in the Arctic I knew pemmican only by hearsay. The pertinent evidence of its excellence was, however, available, condensed, and quotable, and convincing to me, as I hoped it would be to the Quartermaster Corps. I began by citing what the commander-in-chief of the Canadian forces in World War II had recently said. Then I quoted some of the favorable testimony of Major General Sir Samuel Benfield Steele about this North American emergency ration as used when he was in charge of Canadian participation in South Africa's Boer War.

Everyone seemed impressed, and Colonel Doriot followed his kind words with a letter of appreciation after I had left. I supposed that we were off to a good start in our effort to win the war by feeding the armed forces compactly and promptly.

I was asked to follow my talk and the ensuing conference with some written statements and recommendations. One of my suggestions was that the department add to its staff of nutritionists drawn from academic circles at least one good man from the meat industry. I recommended either a chemist, Dr. Roy C. Newton, a vice-president in charge of laboratories at Swift, or Colonel Edward N. Wentworth, a biologist and head of Armour's Livestock Bureau. Both men were taken on by the department, but Newton was consulted more frequently because Wentworth was reported to be "too fond of pemmican." It appeared that conservatism is especially powerful in the field of diet. Mothers, startled by what the nutritionists said, wrote letters to their soldier sons telling them how their family doctors were running down pemmican, saying that it was a dirty native food and had too much fat in it. They kept repeating the old saw: "Fat burns only in the flame of carbohydrates." Interpreted, this means that there is no use trying to get nourishment out of things like butter and suet unless you eat at the same time a lot of bread or other carbohydrates to help metabolize the fat.

All of us who were working on the pemmican problem agreed on the advisability of being ready to meet the tests likely to be demanded by a generation that knew nothing about pemmican as a standard food. We planned to have on hand sample quantities of standard pemmican and also of varieties of pemmican designed to meet tests to satisfy the victims of the rising fear of dietetic fat. Both Armour and Swift offered their facilities. We decided on Swift, who made up what we called Type A, or Standard, and Types B and C. The chemists and technicians saw to it that A would meet the fur-trade standard of half-rendered fat and half-desiccated lean, by weight. The chemists told us that in heat units this would yield about 80 per cent of calories from fat and 20 per cent from lean. Type B would give 70 per cent of calories from fat, and C about 60 per cent.

In September, 1942, we began to hear complaints from nutritionists that they and their science were being disregarded by pemmican fanatics who ignored such well-known facts as that eating fat foods makes you fat and that everybody dislikes fat in hot weather.

Among other witnesses whom I had selected to support my views were both tropical and polar experts of the Explorers Club and Chicago meat-industry executives, heads of departments and vice-presidents of such firms as Armour, Mayer, Swift, and Wilson. The rumble of mutterings from professional nutritionists, however, kept growing louder. By early spring of 1943 we felt that citing authorities who were historians of the fur trade was not enough; nor was it enough to quote expeditions like those of Peary in the Arctic. The most telling blows against us, we felt, were being struck by nutritionists. They kept digging up family physicians who operated through the mothers of enlisted men to protest against a nonscientific attitude in feeding the Army.

In order to counter this, we naïvely decided to use "unassailable up-to-date facts." We felt that we had an unassailable demonstration place in notoriously hot midsummer Washington, and the perfect demonstrator in the person of Earl Parker Hanson. Earl did have against him the fact that he and I had been friends for a dozen years, since I had met him when he was a senior at the University of Wisconsin. Apart from this drawback, which I explained to my colleagues but which they agreed to discount, Hanson was an engineer and geographer who was in the spring of 1943 an adviser

on jungle warfare to both the Air Force and the Quartermaster
Corps. He had never used pemmican before entering upon his test
for us, but he had known many who had used it and had read of its
use in both polar and tropical regions.

We used Hanson as a guinea pig, keeping him on an exclusively pemmican diet for nine weeks in the hot summer of 1943.
This test showed conclusively that a properly proportioned pemmican constituted an excellent food for hot weather, resulted in no
vitamin deficiency, and disproved the nutritionists' contention that
a percentage of more than 35 per cent of fat in the human diet is
dangerous and possibly fatal. Hanson's test also proved that pemmican is a kind of self-regulating food as far as quantity is concerned. If you eat the right amount you are well, happy, and strong
and don't crave more. One pound of fat pemmican per day was all
Hanson needed even when taking strenuous exercise.

In 1944 there was a newspaper flare-up over the pemmican
controversy. The details seemed childish to me and I wrote to the
Surgeon General of the Navy about it. Though long, his reply is
so material and clear and presents such a sharp picture of confusion
that I quote it:

> This letter is an answer to yours of March 3, 1944. In it you
> ask concerning the reason for removing "pemmican" and choc-
> olate from the Navy aircraft emergency ration. You also ask for
> the formula of this "pemmican" and inquire why the Navy uses
> this term for the product.
>
> The statement which you quote concerning the reason for
> the removal of the "pemmican" and chocolate from the aircraft
> emergency ration appeared also in Naval Aviation News for
> March 1, 1944. The reason presented therein is not the correct one.
> Actually, these two items were removed from the ration because
> the majority of reports indicate that the "pemmican" is diffi-
> cult to swallow when the mouth is dry, and that the chocolate
> increases thirst, as well as being distasteful to some. . . .
>
> One ¾ ounce can of each of 3 slightly different types of
> "pemmican" was formerly provided in the aircraft emergency
> ration . . . [consisting of] rendered kidney fat, prime oleo oil,
> seedless raisins, evaporated apples, crisp bacon, peanuts, dex-
> trose, shredded coconut, vanilla extract, salt.
>
> It is not clear from our records whether the designation "pem-
> mican" was given these products by the Navy, or whether the
> experimental samples were already so designated by Armour
> and Company when they were first supplied to this Bureau in
> 1938.

This letter shows that the Navy had not been using pemmican at all, in the sense of an exclusive meat preparation, but had been using instead a sort of candy bar, which was, no doubt, the invention of some dietitian and to which the name of pemmican had been given. The name had no more to do with the contents of the bar than Babe Ruth's name had to do with the candy bar somewhat obliquely named for him. It is small wonder that pemmican, in spite of the obvious advantages of its slight bulk, high food value, and antiscorbutic qualities, never became a standard ration, nor even an emergency ration for the armed forces. The armed forces went to a great deal of trouble to get my advice, but made no effort to take it. Others who were called in as experts in one field or another had similar experiences.

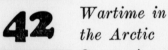

42 Wartime in the Arctic

One morning early in July, 1943, the telephone rang at our Vermont farm. It was Hap Arnold, Commanding General of the Army Air Forces, asking me if I would, at noon the next day, fly in one of his planes to Presque Isle, Maine, to spend a month at the headquarters of Brigadier General B. F. Giles, commanding the North Atlantic Wing, Air Transport Command (ATC). I was to take Arnold's word for it that I would not be sorry if I did this. Giles would get in touch with me immediately and explain everything. I agreed to go if Arnold would get permission from the Quartermaster General, for whom I was still working in spite of the dim prospects for pemmican and good arctic clothing. Arnold had thought of that and had already done so. What, he asked, was my usual daily charge? I said that it ought to be higher but it never had been more than forty dollars plus expenses. Arnold promised that it would not be less. That being the case, I agreed to go. I mention my price and Arnold's agreement because of what happened later.

I was ready to leave immediately, and would have done so had I not received a further message telling me to wait for a letter. The letter, signed by General Giles, duly came. It was simply an invitation to come and talk to the staff of the North Atlantic Wing of the ATC about forced landings and rescue work in northern latitudes.

I wrote Giles that I could come any time they wanted me, the sooner the better. They immediately sent a car all the way to Vermont to pick me up. I was in Presque Isle on the eighteenth. General Giles introduced me to his chief of staff, Colonel Milton W. Arnold, and to his wing quartermaster, Major D. J. Matthews.

After a preliminary three days at Presque Isle, Giles let me go back to the farm for a day to prepare for my month's absence. The general had three main jobs for me: (1) to help him get pemmican as an emergency ration for his North Atlantic Wing, (2) to make an inspection trip in a PBY flying boat with six or eight men under the command of the general's chief meteorologist, Colonel A. F. Merewether, (3) and to report on whether or not anything could be done to correct what he had already concluded must have been a mistake—the Army's willingness to use the head of Frobisher Bay as an air base on a route from Winnipeg and Churchill, Manitoba, to northern Europe by way of Greenland.

The first of these jobs would be the PBY survey of the weather stations that were already functioning in Quebec and Labrador. The first one we visited was run in typical Canadian fashion by a civilian meteorologist, his wife, and her brother, who was an all-purpose handy man able to make or repair anything. Mr. and Mrs. Theriault and her brother Blanchet spoke both English and French. The setup made a favorable impression on Colonel Merewether and me, but it worried the colonel for a reason that I did not at first understand but which he explained as soon as we were alone. He knew that the civilian informality of the Canadian arrangement would not fit into the United States Army's scheme of things. He would recommend no change unless requested to do so by the Canadians, and he hoped that I would back him up; but he was quite certain that we would be overruled. It would probably be decided that the three local people should be replaced by a dozen enlisted men from some southern part of the country, or even by civilians. In any case, there would be an officer or boss, and under him a cook and cook's helper, one or two waiters, and a miscellaneous staff who would spend their time grousing about how lonesome and miserable it was to be stationed in the wilderness.

This elaborate setup of malcontents, said the colonel, would replace three local Canadians who knew and loved their job. In their spare time throughout the year the three Canadians hunted and fished; in the summer they also did a bit of gardening and prepared for winter—chopping firewood and making and mending snowshoes. They kept busy at things they liked to do and for which they had been trained. They loved their garden produce, and the fish they caught made our mouths water—trout eighteen or more inches long which they took in nets.

The Theriault place at Lake Norman was our only stop between Presque Isle and Goose Bay, Labrador, at the head of Lake Melville, some six hundred and fifty miles northwest. We reached Goose on the morning of August 13. It was a bustling place with transoceanic planes going and coming constantly. The new hotel was not yet serving meals, so we ate at the military mess. Most of the personnel were enlisted men from the United States who did not seem to object to the war as an institution but were sourly critical of nearly every detail of its operation. The Canadians, who had been at war since 1939, complained less and were generally more mature. Those whom we met, whether from the States or from Canada, were mostly connected with the ATC, either in the Labrador-Hudson Bay region or in Greenland.

With one form of grousing my personal bias made me sympathetic. This was the common complaint that modern nutritionists were upsetting the commissariat. Many of the complainers were veterans of one sort or another—some had been on polar expeditions, some were employees of the northern fur trade, others had been gold miners in Alaska or whalers in Canada. One of those whom I met at Goose Bay introduced himself as Canadian Flight Officer Scott E. Alexander, who had been in the far north with the Royal Canadian Mounted Police for nine years, four of them near Coronation Gulf. He knew Ole Andreasen, my companion of drift-ice travel.

Our PBY left Goose at nine-thirty in the morning, Presque Isle time, flew north along the Labrador coast at five thousand feet and was at Hebron four hundred and fifty miles away by eleven-thirty. There were eight of us, counting myself, with Colonel Merewether in command and acting as copilot. The pilot was Captain C. E. Barnes. We were guests at the Moravian Mission for lunch. At one-thirty we took off from Hebron. By five-twenty we reached the first of the three United States Army stations that we had been directed to visit, Crystal 1, on Ungava Bay. It was commanded by Major Norman D. Vaughan, an antarctic veteran. Major Vaughan was an old friend of mine and so was his second-in-command, Captain Edward E. Goodale, grandson of the famous Harvard botanist, whom I had known. Crystal 1 was a large establishment, the details of which are not interesting to me now although at the time I occupied myself in writing long memos about them.

Crystal 2 was our next and main destination, the station already known as Frobisher Bay and already an issue upon which I had been asked to make a report. It was a location at the head of a 150-mile fjord in the southeastern part of Baffin Island, which Lindbergh, Logan, and I had condemned when we were mapping the proposed Pan American route across the North Atlantic. The choice of this unsuitable site was blamed, according to gossip that I never investigated, upon Elliott Roosevelt. He was said to have chosen it upon my recommendation. If there is anything behind this rumor, it could perhaps have been that Elliott once heard me mention the name of Frobisher Bay and neglected to notice that I did so disparagingly.

On August 17 our PBY started from Ungava toward Frobisher at one o'clock in the afternoon. Half an hour after we crossed Hudson Strait, we began seeing tiny bits of floating sea ice. I began to feel quite at home. At four-fifteen we were down at Crystal 2 and met Captain William L. Bunting, of the Al Johnson construction firm of Minneapolis, a company that was already spending enormous amounts of government money on a job that in my opinion should never have been undertaken. I found several of my old friends around, many of whom were doing good work in a bad venture.

There was one achievement about which everybody was talking. Twenty or thirty dogs had been sent to Frobisher for rescue purposes. In winter, forced landings are numerous and dog teams are needed to bring in stranded crews. For these dogs a lot of highly advertised packaged foods had been supplied, the kind that were even then, as they are now, touted as "rich in nourishing proteins, essential vitamins, and minerals." These poor dogs had been mangy and wretched until Willie Knudsen, a Norwegian who knew dogs, arrived from Greenland. At first Willie could find nothing wholesome for the dogs to eat except when the construction company's kitchens compassionately donated eggs, lard, or other good human food. Willie finally located some cord, which he knit into fish nets. He found a boat and rowed it out into the bay. By the next morning his nets had provided quantities of splendid fish, and he was able to get some seal blubber from local Eskimos. By the time we saw them, his dogs had regained their health and were sleek and frisky.

At first the dogs got all the local fish. Gradually, however, both Johnson's construction men and the soldiers began to consider that fresh local fish was better food than that shipped in from New York. Others joined Knudsen in setting nets. The cooks, at first reluctantly but to everybody's delight, including ours, began to serve the Baffin Island catch. There was general approval when it became known that Knudsen had requested the Army to furnish six nets with which he might supply fish for men and dogs, as well as two of larger mesh to get seals, which would provide blubber for the dogs. The dog teams need fat along with their lean meat to maintain their health and strength for the winter rescue work.

Our PBY planned to go farther north along the east coast of Baffin Island, for the crew wanted to reach Crystal 3 at Clyde River, which is just across Davis Strait from the center of Greenland's west coast. I did not go along on this flight, thinking that nothing I could learn at the old trading and whaling location there would be as likely to interest General Giles and the Army as much as what I might pick up and report from Frobisher Bay. When the PBY returned that evening, she reported having failed to penetrate the clouds. Merewether said I would have to go along on the next flight, for, whether or not he was able to reach Crystal 3, he would have to return directly from there to Goose Bay in one jump.

Not knowing where we would come down, we left Frobisher Bay the morning of August 21. After flying thirty miles northeast we could see enough of Clyde River and Crystal 3 to make out that Captain Bob Bartlett's *Morrissey* was there. As our pilots agreed that it would be risky to descend, we turned and headed for Goose, which we reached in the evening. The next days were spent in conferences and the evenings in lectures, which I gave before considerable audiences. On August 24, I met Captain D. S. Traub, a doctor from Louisville, Kentucky, and was gratified by his report that his friend Dr. Michael Somogyi had published in the *Journal of Biological Chemistry* an article in which he declared that, instead of fats being burned in the flame of carbohydrates, the truth was that "carbohydrates . . . inhibit the burning of fats."

During my month with General Giles, I interviewed or chatted with at least a hundred knowledgeable men and did my best to distill their observations and ideas for his benefit. I found him good at digging out what he wanted to know. My report on my trip with Merewether was long and detailed, and Giles questioned me keenly about it after we got back to Presque Isle on August 26. He was chiefly interested in Crystal 2.

What I had to say to Giles was essentially contained in the report that Lindbergh, Logan, and I had made to Pan American in 1934. Our main points then, as mine had to be now, had been two. Apart from its general climate, a northern airport must first be easy to fly into and out of; secondly, it must be easily supplied with heavy items by regular surface transportation, either land or water. On both counts, Crystal 2 was undesirable.

First, the lowland at the head of Frobisher Bay is surrounded on three sides by mountains that are frequently shrouded in fog. Sometimes the fourth side is fogged in also. On this score alone, the location should have been avoided. Second, the airport, if at the head of Frobisher, would be almost the most difficult place to supply in all of southern or eastern Baffin Island. For, in addition to the long season of ice cover, the tide is one of the heaviest in the world—we were told the range was from thirty to forty-five feet. Residents told us that, with the ebb and flow, huge blocks of ice were tossed about helter-skelter. For two-thirds of the year, therefore, freight supply by steamer would be impossible.

Why face these difficulties when near at hand were vast regions in which they were not present? Hudson Strait is almost as far north as Frobisher Bay, and the strait is flanked on its Baffin Island side by extensive lowland. The strait's season of navigation is longer, the tides lower, and the land almost ideally flat to make airplane approach safe from collisions with mountains when visibility is bad.

To complement the discouragement of my Frobisher report, Giles told of the exasperating and yet amusing adventures that Lieutenant Murray Weiner had on his fourth attempt to get pemmican for the North Atlantic Wing. He had secured several thousand pounds, but each can had been conspicuously labeled *Second Class Beef*. The meat was not second-class in any respect that Giles could discover, but perhaps it was so labeled to give the impression that it was dog food. Indeed, it is one of the merits of sound pemmican that it is suitable for both men and dogs, being equally good for men who are being rescued after a forced landing and for the teams rescuing them. I heard later that although quantities of this pemmican were carried in transport planes back and forth across the

North Atantic, and must have given the pilots some reassurance, the contents of very few cans were used by humans for food during the remainder of the war.

Our agreement on pemmican as an emergency ration was only one of the many opinions that Giles and I found ourselves sharing. It was on my third day with him, July 24, 1943, that the general gave me a carbon of a letter he had already sent to the commanding general of the ATC, Major General Harold L. George. This turned out to be the determining factor in fixing what I would be asked to do after my assignment with the North Atlantic Wing. Giles asked to have me made available for future conferences with his wing and to have me sent to the Arctic Training School at Buckley Field, Colorado, to help train and indoctrinate Air Force personnel for work in northern latitudes.

I had spent some weeks during the spring of 1943 at Camp Hale, Colorado, helping to instruct Mountain and Winter Warfare troops in camping technique, including the building of snowhouses. My wife was with me on that trip, the work of which is described in the appendix of the second, or Macmillan Company, edition of my *Arctic Manual*.

On returning from Presque Isle, I went, after a short rest at our farm, to Camp Buckley and teamed up with my old friend Belmore Browne in conducting a course in medium-altitude mountaineering. In theory, and pretty much also in practice, we worked in the vicinity of the tree line of the Rockies, he below and I above it. The instruction of troops took place during autumn and was handled chiefly by talks that Belmore illustrated by sketches. I delivered most of the lectures and he answered most of the questions.

The soldiers, chiefly officers, were in numerous camps of a few men each. Belmore and I wandered about from camp to camp, climbing and descending peaks and ridges by way of example. In the evening we sat with the soldiers around campfires, discussing the day's work. This was a pleasant and I hope profitable reliving of my arctic experiences. The Colorado mountain seminar certainly indicated a growing awareness on the part of the Army of the role that the north and winter conditions were to play in the war.

At the beginning of this chapter I told of my early July telephone conversation with the commanding general of the Army Air Forces in which I mentioned my usual fee of forty dollars a day. Several months after my conversation with Arnold, I got quite a shock when I learned that because of the general's informal ways I could not be paid at all. There was no official record that I had been asked by the proper authority to perform this service. Nobody questioned anybody's word. General Arnold said that he had asked for the service and had promised a per diem of not less than forty dollars. General Giles testified that I had performed the service for the required time. However, there was no proof of what I had been promised. The decision that I would not get paid, and the suggestion that I would have to meet my own out-of-pocket expenses, came in a letter of March 18, 1944, from Headquarters, North Atlantic Wing, Air Transport Command, Manchester, New Hampshire, signed by Colonel R. C. Hutchinson, Executive. It was a masterpiece of casuistry, but it made the facts plain. Even a five-star general in the stress of a world war must go through proper channels.

Arnold was furious, and determined that somehow the Army must live up to his unquestioned telephone promise. The best he could do was suggest that everybody pretend that what I had done and was supposed to be paid for was a job under the auspices of not the Air Force but the Quartermaster General of the Army, who owned a hundred and fifty days of my time per year and might, if he wished, have asked me to do all the things that I had done for the Air Force. And this is the way it was finally settled.

43 An Aleutian Junket

Although the tide had turned in the war in the Pacific with the Battle of Leyte Gulf in October, 1944, and the Germans' last-gasp drive in the Ardennes had been stopped on Christmas Day, the war was not over in either theater.

The United States Eleventh Air Force was hammering at Japan through the Aleutians without very much recognition by the public. Someone in Washington conceived the idea of a heroic story about the forgotten men of the Eleventh. Late in December, 1944—on the twenty-eighth to be exact—I discovered that I was a part of the project. On that day my office had a phone call from Lieutenant Colonel William S. Carlson, of the Air Force, who said that he was coming up from Florida to New York to talk with me about plans for an Alaska trip. He and I were to be members of a team of historians charged with the responsibility of collecting, writing, and illustrating a human-interest history of the Army Air Forces in Alaska, including the Aleutian Islands. For the next two months there was constant discussion of this trip.

My companions and I were to cooperate with the Alaskan Department of the Army, the Eleventh Air Force, and the ATC. We were to see everything we could, learn everything we could, and even fly on combat missions. We were to live with the men of the Air Force and get the spirit of their day-to-day tasks. We were not to get into any discussions but, as Colonel Hans C. Adamson, who gave us our orders, said, were "to write history, not make it."

I was the team leader, charged with directing the others, Lieutenant Colonel Carlson, Major D. Brodsky, and an artist, Mr. Clayton Knight. General Hap Arnold, was, of course, technically our boss. He was pretty busy, however, helping to run a war. Our real bosses, we learned early in January, 1945, were to be Colonel Adamson and his assistant, Bernard A. Bergman, deputy chief of the Personal Narratives Office, War Department, Headquarters of the Army Air Forces, Washington, once a member of the editorial staff of *The New Yorker*.

The first worried letter in my file dealing with this project came from Carlson at Orlando on January 9. It referred to a letter he had just received from Bergman about our prospective colleagues: "If Adamson and Bergman expect from us a book written in the style of the stories which you might find in *Liberty Magazine*, I am afraid I must disappoint them. Their concern about Brodsky seemed to be his ability to popularize. The approach, I think, is entirely wrong and it may be that we will have some trouble."

Our chief trouble, however, was that, although we had full authority to investigate classified matters concerning the Eleventh Air Force, and we did learn some interesting things, we were not authorized to make them public. The result was that our trip was largely wasted. We accomplished practically nothing.

The plane assigned to our party of human-interest historians was to be a Lodestar, the pilot of which had telephoned from Edmonton that he would come to fetch us when informed of my arrival there. Brodsky announced my arrival and in the evening a Lieutenant Robbins introduced himself. Next morning at Edmonton we met several officers whom Carlson and I knew personally and many whom all of us knew by reputation. Especially interesting to me were Lieutenant Colonel Boyd Yaden of the Alaska Division, ATC, and his subordinate Simeon W. Muller, the permafrost authority.

At Edmonton we received news of the death of Charlie Brower of Point Barrow. It had been my dream to introduce our party to him and for as many as possible of them to hear his fascinating narratives and philosophizing. For Carlson and me, most of the interest of a Barrow visit disappeared with Brower, so we gave up our planned trip there and headed northwest toward Fairbanks. At several stops on the way, we picked up information about Canol and lesser associated engineering follies of the sort mentioned earlier.

Leaving Brodsky at Fairbanks, Carlson and I headed west for

Nome, where Carlson lunched and dined with one or two dozen men and women, most of them officers handling airplane transport to the Soviet Union. I went home with Ralph Lomen, and he and I joined the rest at the Army's guest house for coffee at 9:00 P.M. The Eleventh Air Force was still fighting the war without our help.

According to the officers with whom Carlson dined, and according to the librarians we met the next day, the Army chiefs in Washington were wrong in thinking that soldiers in Alaska wanted to read mostly books about the tropics or Europe. Given the chance, these Nome officers said, troops who are stationed in the north want to read about the north. This sort of discussion I had heard in 1943 when I was with the North Atlantic Wing. I was to continue hearing it in southern Alaska and the Aleutians, with the same criticism of those in Washington who selected the men's reading material.

With the freedom conferred by having our own plane, we saw many places between Fairbanks and Bering Sea which I do not mention in this summary. On the afternoon of February 20 we took off from Nome for Galena and Fairbanks. From Fairbanks we went south to Anchorage, where I breakfasted with my former secretary, now Captain Burt McConnell.

At Anchorage, I met perhaps the most impressive personality of the trip—Davenport Johnson, commanding general of the Eleventh Air Force, to which we had been specially assigned. We were told that we would dine with still-higher-ranking Lieutenant General Emmons, commanding general of the Western Theatre, and other dignitaries. There we would meet my old friend retired Colonel Otto E. Ohlson, the manager of the Alaska Railway. There was a big reception after dinner at which Colonel Ohlson starred. That dinner and reception provided probably the best conversation of our whole tour.

The two powers with whom we dealt in Alaska were the Army and the Civil Aeronautics Board. I was still on the staff of Pan American, which was expanding in Alaska and so had to deal occasionally with CAB people. Four-fifths of my notes, however, were made along the lines mapped out for us by the Air Force.

On February 24, I had my first chance to dine alone with Colonel Ohlson. Among the things he told me was that his railway was now between six and seven million dollars in the black. As a result he had asked the Interstate Commerce Commission to study his rate schedule, for he did not want the road to make too much money. His great triumph was that he had finally arranged for a portage by tunnel through the mountains at Whittier. This would save the government money, speed up service, and lower both passenger and freight rates for all Alaskans.

Ohlson went at length into an issue that was controversial at the time. He wanted to discontinue the several-score miles of track leading south from the Whittier tunnel to Seward, replacing the railway with a road. The building of that highway would cost two million dollars, but this could be saved in two years by not having to maintain the snow fences, trestles, bridges, and other costly features of the present railway operation. Ohlson said that most or all Federal agencies are compelled by law to turn their profits, when there are any, into the Treasury. His railway had been made an exception to this rule, perhaps because nobody expected that there ever would be any profits. Now that he did have more than six million dollars, he was going to ask permission to use it to buy two fine Pullman trains. The Alaska Steamship Company was about to shorten its time from Seattle to Anchorage by two days. Ohlson wanted his new trains to match that improvement. We discussed his ideas far into the night.

Ohlson told me that the Whittier cutoff involved two tunnels through 13,090 and 4,966 feet of solid rock. These tunnels had increased his freight capacity into Anchorage from the south by more than 75 per cent and eliminated delays. They had cost five million dollars. The Army was now thanking him for having foreseen war needs. He claimed that that was not what he had done. He had merely foreseen what would be good business resulting from inevitable peacetime growth.

The cooperation of the Eleventh Air Force and the Alaska Railway was the most favorable instance I saw in Alaska of collaboration between civil and military authorities. Thus, it was a pleasant note upon which our party turned west toward the Aleutians and the Kuriles, the area of struggle with the Japanese. What a pity it was that it had to be a military struggle and not a peaceful blending of cooperation and competition.

Monday, February 20, we left Anchorage and headed west. This was to me the beginning of our trip, for I had understood from the commanding general of the Air Forces that our book was for the most part to describe the region out of which we were pushing the Japanese. Having spent most of my time from 1907 on in or

near Alaska, I was supposed to know the entire Territory. I knew
less about the south coast west of Anchorage and the Aleutians,
however, than I did about the rest of the region.

On our Aleutian flight I sat beside General Johnson. He was
naturally frank. It helped that he was a Texan and that I was able
to talk with him about Maury Maverick and several other friends of
his. Besides, he knew from General Arnold that the Air Forces
wanted our group, particularly Carlson and me, to be informed
about anything that was not top-secret.

I had a premonition the first day out of Anchorage that in
Davenport Johnson I had met another case of a Southerner taking to
the north as a duck takes to water. When I came to know him better,
I asked him how Southern whites like the Aleutians. The enlisted
men, he said, didn't really like any place in the world. The officers
from Oklahoma or Texas liked the north better than those from
the Old South. Some of the men he knew who were enthusiastic
about the Aleutians were Texans. He knew about Buckner's having
bought land at Homer, south of Anchorage, and said he felt the
same way about that region, though he himself had not bought any
land as yet. He agreed that the one unpleasant thing about the
Aleutians was the sandstorms, but even those were not as bad as
those in the Texas Panhandle. He was also aware that the blowing
sand here in the islands was the Army's own fault. It resulted
from their passion for using bulldozers to tear away the turf, which
paved the way for erosion.

The untouched islands were a delight. At first the land over
which we flew was forested, with beautiful mountain fishing lakes
and woods full of moose, the beaches prowled by bears searching
for fish. At the few places where we stopped, the people were delighted to see us, and we enjoyed the spirit of hospitality and the
flavor of the fish. There was less visiting as we continued west along
the island chain. At Adak it stopped entirely. We were now all
one family—the Air Force, the Navy, and the construction people—
for here was the main base of the Eleventh Air Force. Carlson and
I never got farther in the direction of Japan, but Brodsky did continue to the west end of the chain.

During our time at Adak, the Aleutian climate impressed me
as unique in Alaska. The coldest it had been the winter before
was 28° F, only four degrees of frost. The wind was persistent and

gusty, snow rare but rain frequent. Some of the troops who were
used to sunshine groused about the dull skies, the fog, and the rain.
If they came from Seattle, they liked the climate because it was
much like home. The morale in the Aleutians was about the best
of all World War II theaters, according to the officers. According
to the doctors, the health of the troops was the best of any about
which they had any knowledge. The most common grievance was
lack of action. Johnson said, however, that mail from men transferred out of Alaska indicated that those who had been getting in
other theaters the action that they thought they craved were soon
wishing themselves back in the Aleutians.

For what little action these islands saw during the first year
of United States participation in the war, it was generally agreed
that we had been badly prepared psychologically as compared with
the Japanese. In some cases we had been incompetently led, handicapped also by the information we had picked up in school and
college and from newspapers and radio. On February 26 my diary
has a paraphrase from Johnson in which he discusses morale: ''Of
course fellows like Corey Ford at first got them to feel pretty sorry
for themselves, but we are getting them out of that.'' According
to Colonel Thorne, adjutant of the Eleventh Air Force, both officers
and men liked being stationed on the Alaska mainland better than
on the islands. ''But even on the Chain the troops don't feel sorry
for themselves by reason of the climate.'' My entry for February
26 also includes:

> Johnson feels Ernie Pyle does harm to discipline of the Army
> by inventing or selecting and emphasizing out of true propor-
> tion stories of how officers and enlisted men are just buddies,
> informal and not much discipline, saying this in further comment
> on men like Corey Ford who exaggerate hardships, injuring
> morale by making men sorry for themselves. The General added,
> however, that if Ford and Pyle gave things in true perspective
> and stuck to facts the editors might not buy their stories and sub-
> scribers might not want to read them.

On the evening of March 2, 1945, we were saying farewells in
the most nearly formal room of the Adak headquarters. I felt that
although our tour was over we had still seen little of what we
came to see. While we were saying good-by to General Johnson, a
telegram was brought to him. He passed it to me. It was from

Orlando, Florida, where Carlson had been stationed, asking that he be informed that on February 13 he had been promoted from lieutenant colonel to full colonel.

Johnson sent for Carlson and spoke to him severely, reminding him that, since he had come up here representing the War Department, the Eleventh Air Force had a right to expect proper conduct from him, including the wearing of the proper uniform and insignia. Johnson said he was afraid that he would have to take steps. The general then walked up to Carlson, removed the oak leaf from his collar, and pinned on the colonel's eagles. Carlson's worried and flustered look disappeared.

So our Alaska mission ended as something of a wild-goose chase. We made some interesting contacts and saw some new and interesting country, but nothing of real importance came of our trip. By four-thirty on the afternoon of March 3 we were back at Whitehorse. Just after midnight we were at Edmonton. The Army flew us back to Chicago, where we were turned over to a commercial airline on the morning of May 7, 1945. Far to the west, men were still being killed. We did not then know how soon the end of the war was to come.

In a book that Carlson wrote in 1962, *Lifelines Through the Arctic,* he says truly that "with the end of hostilities there was little interest in war narratives." Our *No Mean Victory* was never published. The story of the Air Force in the Aleutians has been told by others who knew it firsthand. Carlson and I would have felt embarrassed indeed to produce a book in order to justify our trip.

44 The Rise and Fall of Encyclopedia Arctica

In 1946, I was approached by the Office of Naval Research with the suggestion that the wartime alliance of the circumpolar countries should in some way be perpetuated. After several months of discussion a three-part program was proposed, comprising the preparation of a roster of the men of all nations who were students of the Arctic and the sub-Arctic, whether by experience or by reading; the compiling of a bibliography of all recorded knowledge and opinion about the northern polar regions from the earliest possible dates; and the compiling and publication of a multivolume *Encyclopedia Arctica*.

There were two candidates for these three jobs. One was the private group that, with corporate and government help, I had been building in my library. The other was the Arctic Institute of North America, which was a recent creation resulting from my recollection of a suggestion made in Alaska by General Buckner, who had found useful in the Philippines a central information agency on tropical problems set up by the United States government to serve the Army, the Navy, and civilian employees. Everyone concerned knew about the Scott Polar Research Institute of Britain, and we were aware that the Soviet Union was organizing a similar body at Leningrad. There was the Army's Arctic, Desert and Tropic Information Center, whose arctic branch was headed by a civilian, Dr. Laurence Gould. Its military head was the companion of my Aleutian flight, Colonel William Carlson. It had become evident, however, that in the United States such departments as Interior, State, and others were reluctant to consult this branch of the Army. For this and other reasons, it was decided to set up a North American Arctic Institute for Canada, Greenland, and the United States, with headquarters in Montreal and branch offices in the United States.

After much discussion, both in Montreal, where I sat as a board member, and in our New York office, we concluded that the roster and the bibliography could best be handled by the institute. For the *Encyclopedia Arctica* I personally would sign a contract, renewable yearly, with the Office of Naval Research. The Navy really had complete control, but it was understood that I would have freedom similar to that given university presidents by their boards of trustees. The estimated time required for preparation was two years, but this might be extended by mutual agreement. The probable cost would be around two hundred thousand dollars, exclusive of final editing. A further understanding was that I would do as much of both writing and editing as I could and that all authors of articles and all staff members, including translators, would be chosen by me or by my representatives.

During my financial negotiations with the Office of Naval Research, I discussed with many persons familiar with encyclopedia financing the terms I was accepting from the Navy. I was usually told that I should ask for three to six times the amount that I had myself proposed and which the Navy had accepted. I stuck to my figure, however. I felt that commercial publishers had overlooked the potential money-saving factor in man's fundamental desire for the increase and diffusion of knowledge. I knew that we would secure without cost the help not only of geographical societies like the Royal of London, the American of New York, and the National of Washington but of private corporations that carried on exploration or did other scientific work as part of their regular business, the Hudson's Bay Company for one. Such corporations, my staff and I were certain, would be glad to check for accuracy anything in their special fields that we might wish to submit to them. As it developed, our optimism was more than justified.

Northern Canada and the corresponding sections of the northern Atlantic were covered at government expense and without cost to us. The Provinces gave us their best historical and scientific personnel to cover those parts of their own areas which are underlain by permafrost. They provided the history of exploration from the earliest times and an account of their resident aborigines: what could be learned of their earliest-known days and primitive culture, their current education and health and welfare programs set up for them. For the same areas the Provinces gave us information about climate, agriculture (both primitive and current), mining, general geology, and soil science—in short, every kind of knowledge, leaving it to us to select, abridge, or emphasize.

The national government of Canada could and did give us priceless information for nothing. Especially valuable was their coverage of the topic of arctic and subarctic aviation. In this field they gave us the services of an officer of aviation rank equivalent to that of major and set him up for a year in a suite of rooms with an adequate clerical staff. We had just been through a war that we had won, with less ease than many imagine, by helping each other. In that spirit Canada now helped us.

As for the Hudson's Bay Company, they submitted material from their records going as far back as 1670, including such hitherto-unavailable information as the company's version of the career of Samuel Hearne, who on their behalf located the Coppermine River in 1772. They prepared for us a life of Alexander Mackenzie, who discovered the Mackenzie River in 1789 and who later crossed the widest part of North America some years before Lewis and Clark got around to making their crossing farther south. Among many other biographies, the company gave us that of their employee Thomas Simpson, who in 1837 found the Colville River and the same year reached Point Barrow, thus discovering the north tip of Alaska from the east as the Admiralty had already done from the west.

Corporations in the United States were equally generous with their help. For example, the Western Union Telegraph Company described for us how, shortly after the Civil War, they surveyed an overland route through Alaska and across Bering Strait to connect with the Russian transasiatic route to Moscow. This provided the groundwork for a survey of the route that E. H. Harriman and others, shortly after 1900, planned to use for a round-the-world railway connecting New York and Paris. Pan American Airways told me that I might use Lindbergh's, Logan's, and my own account of how we surveyed the steppingstone route across the North Atlantic by way of Greenland and Iceland.

When I signed the encyclopedia contract with the United States Navy, I counted on Soviet help almost as much as I counted on

British or Canadian. I hoped that Russian cooperation would give us as good coverage for the northern U.S.S.R. as we could get for any other parts of the world that I had not myself visited. We had some hope that Soviet scholars would write articles for us in English, as the Scandinavians did, but we expected to have on our staff at least one person who knew Russian. We did secure a superb staff member who was multilingual; she was fluent in Russian, English, and French and spoke Italian and other non-Slavic languages as well as some basically Slavic. She was Beatrice Olkhine, whose sister we knew as Professor Volkonskaya of Vassar. Immediately following the 1917 revolution, Beatrice had secured a job at Geneva as correspondent at the League of Nations for several British newspapers.

We knew, of course, that both before and after the Bolshevik revolution much of the best scientific writing of the Russians had been done in German. Since we feared that we might have to do a good deal of our encyclopedia writing by translation of northern Siberian material from the German, we secured Felizia Syed, a writer who was born in Ohio of German-speaking parents.

At the beginning of the encyclopedia's second year we began ruefully to realize the many disadvantages to us of a cold war with the Soviets. They controlled about 49 per cent of the irregularly circular boundary of the Arctic, whether that boundary was measured by the northern tree line, the southernmost permafrost line, or the farthest limits of drift ice in the sea. They controlled three-fourths of the land surface north of any of these boundaries. I figured that if we were to project a circle on our globe with its center at the North Pole and its boundary drawn through the northern suburbs of North America's most northerly large city, Edmonton, we would have less than one hundred thousand human beings north of that line, while the Soviets would have more than one hundred million. They were an arctic-minded, arctic-inhabiting people. An arctic encyclopedia could hardly do without them.

Both parties to the encyclopedia contract, the Office of Naval Research and the Stefansson Collection, decided to ignore when possible the ideological split among the northern nations, but our staff would have to compile its own material on the Soviet sphere. We would get it from books and other published sources, though at many times the expected cost in money, time, and labor. From people who were still on our side of the intellectual fence we would secure what we could. Since most of the material would have to come from printed sources translated from the Russian, we had to increase our staff from about ten to more than twenty. We scoured the world for those, gratifyingly numerous, who would charge us nothing or who would work at the inadequate rate authorized by Washington. The quality of the manuscripts we received ranged from the worthless to the nearly perfect, which could be submitted to the printer with a minimum of editing. The in-betweens had to be licked into shape somehow.

It was our expensive but otherwise good fortune that the Russian language contains one of the world's best encyclopedias, the *Bol'shaia Sovetskaia Entsiklopedia* in sixty-odd volumes, which are as arctic in orientation as the *Britannica* is European. We had to spend considerable amounts of money for copies of the Russian encyclopedia. Then, of course, we had to do the translating, adapting, and editing.

Few can have known better than we the difficulty of battling with the double-edged sword of the cold war. At first the basic morality of both sides made us all trusting. Distrust soon grew, however. In Washington, and I suppose also in Moscow, it seemed to be a first principle that nobody was to be trusted if he was well informed about the other side. This attitude had amused more than impressed me when I first encountered it back in 1940. In that year the State Department asked me how it might secure good representatives in Iceland, a country that both the democracies and the Nazis were courting. I suggested that this was a simple matter, since the universities of Minnesota, North Dakota, and Wisconsin had many graduates born of Icelandic parents in the United States. No, I was told, these could not be used. Because they would have loyalties divided between their countries of ancestry and of birth, they could not be trusted to be wholly on ''our'' side. I offered a second suggestion. Such universities as Columbia, Cornell, Harvard, Iowa, Johns Hopkins, Minnesota, Wisconsin, and Yale had fine Old Norse (that is, Icelandic) departments, and therefore had properly trained alumni who were not Icelandic, or even Scandinavian by descent. But even these born citizens of the United States, it seemed, were not safe enough for the State Department's needs. The mere fact that they had selected for study a language so obscure as Icelandic tended to show that they were biased.

The comic side of this attitude began to appeal to me less when

I came up against Washington's screening of our encyclopedia translators and contributors. My first serious difficulty was with a native American citizen who was as fluent in Russian as he was in English, as one would expect of a man who had taken the last years of his undergraduate study in Moscow. Why would a man want to do such a thing when it would have been cheaper and easier to continue his education where he had started it? To the guardians of our safety in the Office of Naval Research, my translator's behavior appeared highly suspicious. Such a man, it was said, must have had some communistic leanings, if he was not actually a Communist stooge.

Here, I am afraid, I took the wrong tack. I reminded the Navy that I myself was probably suspect, having publicly praised the accomplishment of the Soviet aviators Gromov, Yumashev, and Danilin when, in 1937, they had captured the long-distance flying record by a 652-mile margin. I gave our Navy further offense by suggesting that it was not an adequate comment on a nonstop airplane flight of 6,195 miles from Moscow by way of the North Pole to southern California to say that communism was an unsound theory and that the Soviet Union was teetering on the verge of bankruptcy. With some show of alarm, my friends in the Navy told me that the fact that I could say such things suggested that I myself was tainted. They wanted me to clear myself by firing the American translator who had studied in Moscow.

Here again I took the wrong turn. I went to General George Marshall because I knew that one of the Soviet polar flights had ended at Vancouver, Washington, while he was in command there. I asked him whether or not he thought it wrong for me to employ on a government contract an American who had studied in Moscow, or wrong for me to admire the Russians' aviation achievements. Marshall replied, as I had expected he would, by asking how I thought I could get better Russian translations than by employing the man I had chosen. He said emphatically that he felt I was right to admire the Russians' transpolar flights not on political but on engineering grounds. I felt cheered by this interview with the Army's chief of staff. I was crushed later on when I learned that these views of Marshall's, which I was in the habit of repeating, were used against him when he was himself charged with treason by Senator McCarthy.

The clouds were gathering. We had administered the spending

of more than three hundred thousand dollars of the Navy's money in order to secure more than six million words for the twenty volumes that were to be the foundation stones of our northern polar knowledge. We had decided to make the arrangement of material topical, and as publishers we selected the Johns Hopkins University Press. We shipped them the first two volumes; the others were to come at the rate of four a year.

By the autumn of 1948 we had cleared most of the hurdles that had been set up in the Soviet Arctic as a result of the cold war. The embassy of the U.S.S.R.—through a succession of ambassadors, Litvinov, Oumansky, and Gromyko—had actually said to us in friendly conversation, later implemented by deeds, that they would help us to secure any northern information ever printed or mimeographed in Russian or any other of their languages. The most important of these we were able to handle through our regular staff, which was then functioning smoothly. Under Olive Wilcox's direction and mine, more than a hundred volunteer scholars were gathered in New York to tackle the final editing of the manuscript, which was being shipped steadily to Baltimore. We were busy, and still hopeful.

A few months later, not entirely to my surprise, I was told that the Navy could not renew our encyclopedia contract.

The Navy never told me why. The nearest I ever came to an explanation was when the director of the Canadian Meteorological Service, Dr. Andrew Thomson, offered to try to get some indication of the cause of the Navy's action from Dr. Francis Wilson Reichelderfer, chief of the United States Weather Bureau. It seemed to me that Thomson might be able to do this, for he and Reichelderfer were the chief figures in the volume of our encyclopedia that deals with arctic meteorology, and for three years both of them, with their staffs, had been giving us service beyond price. So I welcomed Thomson's offer, and was delighted when he told me in the late forenoon that Reichelderfer had said there would be no secrecy but that the right man could not be reached until after lunch. About three o'clock of the same day, however, Thomson called my hotel room. He said he was dumfounded, as I gathered Reichelderfer also was. It appeared that when he reached the key man in Washington he had been told that there would be no comment. No comment, that is, except the statement that orders had come from higher up to cancel my contract after one year's terminal arrangement.

There was nothing to do but reduce our staff, give up what we could of our New York accommodations, and thereafter do practically nothing except type, file, and otherwise try to salvage manuscripts, notes, maps, and pictures. We found that about a third of our six million words were practically ready for the publisher's copy editors. With the two completed volumes, we were therefore ready to publish at least six of the projected twenty, another six were nearly ready, and a final six or eight were in various stages of outline and notes, chiefly the work-in-process of Miss Olkhine and Mrs. Syed. Those two devoted workers were, I feel, even more depressed by the events than I.

As to what really happened, I can only offer an informed guess. After more than a decade of listening to theories, hunches, and supported conclusions, I am increasingly in favor of a view of my own that developed while McCarthyism was collapsing and the fires it started were cooling off. I feel that at first the Navy higher-ups did not take McCarthyism much more seriously than I did at the outset. Yet, when they saw McCarthy, in Senate committee hearings, riding roughshod over the Army, they got the idea that it would be wise to sever connections with me, as one of McCarthy's possible targets, before they were accused of having anything to do with me. They could then admit ruefully, if accused, that they had at first been taken in but that they had fired me before I had had a chance to do any harm. They might then pride themselves on their performance of the noble task of preventing, by having stopped the publication of the encyclopedia, the spread of arctic knowledge potentially helpful to the Soviets.

When it finally dawned on us that the *Encyclopedia Arctica* was going to be sacrificed, I knew that the expense of maintaining my now enormous library in New York was going to be more than I could carry. Evelyn and I considered the matter carefully. By thinking first of our Vermont farm, we thought of something else. Following up the thought, I telephoned an old friend, Rolf Syvertsen, the dean of Dartmouth College's Medical School. Reminding him that our farm was only about thirty miles west of Hanover and that I knew Dartmouth's Baker Library had unused shelf space, I asked him to find out if the college would consider housing my library in exchange for the use their faculty and students could get from it. I also suggested an option to purchase the library at a price to be agreed on, which I assured Syvertsen would not be a tenth of what it had cost me over the years.

Syvertsen came at once to New York and spent some hours with us. A few days later he telephoned me that Dartmouth was not only accepting my proposal but would pay the cost of packing and truck transport.

So it was that Evelyn and I, and what had come to be known as the Stefansson Collection, left New York City for Hanover, New Hampshire.

45 McCarthyism in New England

When Evelyn found and I bought the 150 acres that comprised the buildings and land left behind by the Dearings, I knew that we should need someone to help develop the property. In this connection I thought of Charlie Andersen, my companion on the arctic ice as well as in the Stefansson meat-eating expedition to Bellevue Hospital in 1927. Charlie was at this time living in Florida, managing his own orange groves, but I had an idea that he might be free in summer. My proposition appealed to him, and he was soon installed at the farm, renewing fences, rebuilding stone foundations, and reminiscing with me about our northern experiences. Charlie cast longing eyes at various properties in the neighborhood. This delighted me, for I hoped to lure him away from Florida and have him as a year-round neighbor with a farm of his own. One day he came in with the report that the Stoddard Place, adjoining us on the west, was going to be sold for whatever it would bring in its ravaged state after the timber had been cut off.

We were greatly concerned over this news, for the property included a beautiful young grove of sugar maples, known to Vermonters as a "sugar bush." Charlie and I talked each other into buying the place, which included a livable house, somewhat smaller than ours at Dearing, and another "150 acres more or less" of land, bordering ours. This gave us a total of more than three hundred acres of land with a half-mile path between houses—two miles by road. Our plans for this property did not work out quite as we had expected. During the next years Charlie had to give all of his attention to his Florida acreage. I had promised to buy his land if at any time he felt that he wanted to quit. That time came, and Evelyn and I found ourselves owning two complete farms. We were thus able to consider an idea that had been germinating for a long time.

I had known Owen Lattimore and his wife Eleanor for some years, admiring him for the scholar that he was and liking him for his companionable geniality and friendly openness. He was an expert on China and Mongolia, had been Director, Pacific Operations, Office of War Information, and President Roosevelt's chosen advisor to Chiang Kai-shek, and was, at the time Charlie Andersen and I acquired the Stoddard Place, director of the Page School of International Relations at Johns Hopkins.

Evelyn and Eleanor Lattimore had become close friends. When we bought out Charlie Andersen's interest in the Stoddard Place, they decided to go into partnership in the development of it. The Lattimores were to spend as much on refurbishing as we had paid for the property. Both families then would become joint owners.

Eleanor got her son David and some of his schoolmates to come to Vermont to help do the place over for use as a summer center of Asiatic studies. The young people camped in and about the farm, where several of Owen's Mongolian associates were staying and where Mongolian language and culture were being studied by a few scholars under Owen's supervision. The elder Lattimores slept at our Dearing place and made their trips between the two houses on foot.

In the winter of 1949–1950 the United Nations induced Owen to head an economic mission to Afghanistan. At that time Senator McCarthy was boasting in Washington that he was about to reveal his great secret: the name of the man in the United States who was the head of the secret apparatus of the Soviets for undermining the United States. We all wondered who this might be. We had come to no conclusion when we saw Owen off on his mission. To our amazement, while Owen was in Afghanistan, in March, 1950, McCarthy announced that the chief secret agent of the Soviets in the United States was Owen Lattimore!

Owen completed his mission in Afghanistan and then took the first plane for home. We all knew that Senator McCarthy could have based his announcement on nothing but false information or misunderstanding. There was obviously a fight ahead, however, and it was going to be costly. One of the best law firms in Washington undertook to help Owen in his defense against the McCarthy charges, showing its confidence and public spirit by waiving all legal fees. There would, however, be many incidental expenses which he and his friends would have to meet. One day Eleanor telephoned us from Baltimore that all they owned would have to be turned into cash. Therefore, would we please sell the Stoddard Place? Of course we would. We called Mrs. Bundy, who agreed to get the papers in order, and we put several advertisements in the most likely publications. One of these was the *Saturday Review of Literature.*

Two friends and former staff workers on our *Encyclopedia Arctica,* Helen Iseminger and Ruby Collins, were still living in New York. Ordway Southard, a former student at the University of Alaska who had done some reading in our library, happened to call on them one night and while with them looked at a copy of the *Saturday Review.* He asked if the farm being offered for sale could by any chance be the one he had seen once when, while in the trucking business, he had taken a load of freight to the Stefanssons. Helen and Ruby said that it must be. Southard got in touch with us, and I invited him to come and look the place over. In two or three days he came, agreed to the terms we had advertised, and closed the deal to the satisfaction of Mrs. Bundy. A few days after this he moved into the Stoddard Place with his wife and daughter.

One night some weeks later Evelyn and I were alone at the farm when the telephone rang. Evelyn answered and found that it was the Hearst newspaper in Boston asking to speak to Mr. Southard. Evelyn explained that he lived on a neighboring farm, half a mile away, and had no phone. She could not very well call him in the middle of the night, since she would have to go by car and the road was roundabout and not very good. Well, then, said the caller, was there anyone who could reach Mr. Southard? Evelyn gave him a nearer neighbor's telephone number. The reporter then wanted to know if Southard was the man who, some years before, had run for governor of Alabama on the communist ticket? If he was, we had never heard of it. We said so. Well, was this Southard's wife the one who had run for lieutenant governor in Alabama? Again we did not know.

Next morning we learned that our neighbor had carried the reporter's message, as requested, but that Southard had refused to get up and take the call. Later he came to see us. He had not intended to make a secret of his past, he told us. The point simply had not come up. We asked him if he hadn't given a thought, ahead of time, to the possible consequences of his purchase of Owen Lattimore's farm. Well, yes, he had considered the matter, but the fact was, he said, that none of us had done anything illegal. On this point, naturally, we had to agree. At the same time, Evelyn and I considered the situation, innocent though it was, most unfortunate for the Lattimores.

This experience tainted the farm for us and the taint was aggravated by the attempts of a woman named Lucille Miller to tar me with the pink brush which many irresponsible people had taken to wielding. As a young girl, Mrs. Miller had belonged to a group that included Alger Hiss. She had, however, renounced communism and taken up with the McCarthyites. Unsympathetic people implied that she was getting off the Black Maria and boarding the band wagon, thereby getting publicity and perhaps even money. She was now boasting that she had been one of the first to expose Hiss and others. The Southard trouble induced her to train her sights on me. At first nothing came of this.

Happily, the Lattimore situation grew less tense, with Owen's lawyers successfully refuting the charges against him. It could hardly have been otherwise, since the charges were fabrications. Then, just as Evelyn and I thought we were getting out of the woods, we found ourselves in the thick of them again, this time with the attack directed against us.

The situation was colored by the fact that Evelyn and I owned, in addition to our Vermont farm, a house and lot in New Hampshire. Had we owned either of these without the other, it seems to me that the case would have been simple. I had, during the course of my war work for the United States government, been renaturalized as an American citizen. After we left New York, Evelyn and I had had a mild family difference about where we should vote. I admired both Vermont Senators, Aiken and Flanders, and wanted to support them. Evelyn contended that our chief breadwinning job was in Hanover, where our library was, and that that should be our legal residence.

One evening when we were dinner guests at the home of George Rublee, a lawyer-friend, in Cornish, New Hampshire, there was another guest, a man I admired as much as any I ever knew, Judge Learned Hand. With equal respect for him as man and as lawyer, and with my mind on our family voting problem, I asked Hand if he felt that in the light of Vermont law I could legally and ethically continue voting in Vermont while Evelyn voted in New Hampshire. To my surprise he seemed to feel that there was some question about this. However, with a judicial look that he assured me was serious, the judge told me that if the matter ever came before him, if I had selected the right lawyer to plead my cause, and if both Evelyn and I agreed that we wished to vote in different states, he would decide in my favor. He suggested, however, that I would do well to act and talk as if I were living on our Vermont farm and just visiting New Hampshire. Although I felt sure that he considered such a position both legal and ethical, I meant to talk it over with him at another time. That opportunity never came, however.

The day after the dinner party, my Hanover workroom telephone rang and I found myself in conversation with Louis Wyman, the attorney general of New Hampshire. Would I come to Concord, he asked, and cooperate with his office? I asked him what he meant by cooperate. Tell all I knew about communism, he replied. This I said I would be delighted to do, to the proper officer and in the right office. Since I was a Vermont resident, however, he must give me time to decide whether a Vermonter ought to accept this kind of invitation from Concord or await one from Montpelier. Wasn't I a Dartmouth professor, Wyman demanded. Unfortunately, I said, I had not that status. Wyman then said he could see that I wanted to be difficult. He would act, he said, accordingly.

As soon as he rang off, I called my friend Justin Stanley, who was taking a year off from his Chicago law office to act as vice-president of Dartmouth College. I was surprised to find that he sounded quite worried about what I reported. He told me he would at once call the attorney general and tell him that I had not understood what he wanted and that I would appear in his offices at any convenient time.

In half an hour Stanley called me back to say that he had been unable to reach Wyman or anybody in authority in his office. We left it that he would put in a call early the next day. Going to the Hanover post office a little later to pick up my mail, I found a process server waiting at my box. He handed me a summons commanding me to appear at the attorney general's office. On being consulted, Justin Stanley said that I should accept the summons but that I should appear with an attorney. He would go with me himself, he said, but it might be better if I were represented by a Concord man. He recommended Dudley Orr, a trustee of Dartmouth. I spent that evening with the Orrs, discussing the situation.

When we appeared at the attorney general's the next morning, Wyman seemed surprised that my attorney was about the best, legally or socially, that Concord could produce. The examination began. Did I know much about Communists? Of course I did, for I was an alumnus of the Harvard Divinity School, where they considered Jesus a Communist, and we knew a lot about Jesus. That was not what he meant. Did I know anything about American Communists? I replied that I had lived for years with the North American Eskimos, who were all formerly communist, though some were now becoming quite capitalistic.

Wyman suggested that I stop play-acting and start telling him about ordinary American Communists. I said that I knew only one, a classmate of mine named Crosbie. I had seen an interview with him in the *New York Times* in which he admitted that he was a Communist. After reading the *Times* story, I had telephoned Crosbie and asked him if he were the Crosbie I used to know. He said that he was. Would he lunch with me and tell me about himself? He would be delighted. Now, if the attorney general cared for hearsay evidence, I would be glad to report what Crosbie had told me.

Wyman did not follow this up. Instead, he asked me about my wife. How old was she when she left Hungary? I suggested that the question would be hard to answer. So far as I knew, Evelyn had never left Hungary because she had never been there. But was she not Hungarian? Yes, in the sense that her parents had been born there. She herself had been born in New York City.

At this point Wyman requested a private conference with my attorney. I asked and was granted permission to leave the room, and when I was called back a half an hour later the atmosphere seemed to have cleared. Orr and I took our departure, having agreed on a second meeting the following week.

Walking with me to the railway station, Dudley Orr gave me his view, which was that the McCarthyites were not after me at all. Instead, they had thought of me as an elderly fool who had been hoodwinked by a scheming wife. Now, continued Orr, they were a bit upset to find how young Evelyn was, for she was at least twenty years too young to be as experienced as they had assumed. During my absence from the room Wyman had showed Orr his correspondence with the informer who had set him after us. It claimed that Evelyn had been a high-ranking communist functionary before she left Hungary and that she was now indoctrinating Dartmouth students and misleading me while masquerading as a teacher of the Russian language. Orr had assured Wyman that, while Evelyn's Russian was pretty good, she was not teaching it to anybody and that it was not native but had all been learned in American schools, first in New York and than at Middlebury College, Vermont.

In spite of what Orr told Wyman, Wyman wanted Evelyn to appear for a hearing. The week of waiting was difficult. Nothing gave me such a keen awareness of the horrors of McCarthyism as Evelyn's sleeplessness and her obvious worry during that week. Innocent as she was, she must have feared they might set some kind of trap for her. I imagine that the tension and uncertainty of the accused must have been similar during the Salem witchcraft hysteria, in the Know-Nothing era, and during the Palmer raids after World War I.

The second hearing in the attorney general's office was an anticlimax. For some reason Wyman himself did not appear. His deputy seemed satisfied after he had studied a certified copy of Evelyn's birth certificate.

The story of our troubles with the McCarthyites ends with a return to the scene of its beginning. Evelyn and I again dined at the Rublees in Cornish. Judge Hand was once more a guest. His cheerful greeting to Evelyn was, "Well, what have you been doing since last we met?" When she replied, with a laugh, that she had been on the carpet before the attorney general of New Hampshire, he looked first startled, then stern. This was no laughing matter, he said. His reaction caused a brief return of her nightmare. Even today, it sometimes reappears, reminding us that the McCarthy type of persecution is a sinister poison that affects the innocent perhaps more than the guilty.

46 Iceland and Greenland

Our postwar years, many of them made uncomfortable by experiences with bureaucratic fumbling and public cowardice in the face of such threats as McCarthyism, were not all nightmare. Our summers at the farm were a delight, and the friends who visited us there helped to make us forget the exasperating difficulties in which we were often involved. I lectured occasionally. Evelyn, developing into an arctic authority in her own right, produced several books about the northland. In 1949 we were invited by the government of Iceland to spend a midsummer month there as guests of the nation. We were pleased that the letter of invitation suggested that Judge and Mrs. Gudmundur Grimson accompany us.

The four of us flew from New York, arriving at Reykjavik's Keflavik Airport after midnight, too late for any formal reception. Grimson's cousin, Steingrimur Jonsson, a former Pan American representative, met us at the field and took us to the Hotel Borg. The Borg was owned by an Icelander named Josephson who had earned his money in the United States by traveling with Ringling Brothers' circus giving exhibitions of the Icelandic form of wrestling called *Glima*.

I had not been in my ancestral home for thirteen years, and, closely as I had kept in touch with the country's development, I expected to find some changes. An uncle of mine who as Freeman B. Anderson had been the first Icelandic graduate of both Manitoba and Toronto universities, back in Iceland as Friman Arngrimsson, his original name, had sponsored the development and modernization of Iceland's electrical system. My uncle's successor was Grimson's cousin, the master electrician of the country, Steingrimur Jonsson. He and his wife Lára were our guides.

As author of several books wholly or in part about Iceland, I learned few things on this tour. I unlearned several. I learned that trees were fewest and most difficult to cultivate where the winter climate was warmest, apparently because warm winter spells were followed by killing frosts that were most harmful to those plants which blossomed in winter while the sap was running. The largest and most numerous trees were therefore on the northern east coast and on the north coast—at Hallormsstadaskogur and near Akureyri. I also verified what we had reported to Pan American as early as 1934: that the company needed two airports. Thick weather is seldom reported on both sides of the coast at once. When the south coast is cloudy, the north coast is clear, and vice versa.

As if not to be outdone by Iceland, the Greenland Department of the Danish government invited Evelyn and me to spend the summer of 1953 in Greenland as their guests. Since neither of us had ever been there, we accepted eagerly.

Europe's first knowledge of Greenland, or rather of its location, came from the reports of many historians and cosmographers who had read the now-lost book *The Ocean* by the famous mathematician and navigator Pytheas, who is believed to have discovered England, visited Iceland, and tried as early as 330 B.C. to go even farther north. He did sail northward from Thule for a day, but was turned back by ice and dense fog. This, and everything else reported by and about Pytheas, I had discussed in my *Iceland* (1939), *Ultima Thule* (1940), and more fully in *Greenland* (1942). Ever since the publication of these books the Danes had been saying that I ought to come and have a look at the regions about which I wrote so much. They redoubled their pressure in 1943 when my wife published her *Here Is Alaska,* which describes the American north and its Eskimos without including much about the oldest and best-known arctic colony, Danish Greenland. Both Evelyn and I saw justice in the Danes' mild criticism. We were eager to make up for our long neglect of the Danish Arctic.

I wanted to visit Greenland chiefly because it was, and had been since 1721, the only large theocratic dependency of any European power. Other states such as Portugal and Spain had based their colonization on gold and on missionary fervor, or on the fur trade, as Britain had done in Canada, or on agriculture, as in the United States. In Greenland there existed a country that had been colonized not for any of these conventional reasons. The Danes insisted that they were concerned simply with the physical and spiritual welfare of the natives. I have touched on this in several of my books, but mention it now as a background for an account of the way in which Evelyn and I spent the summer.

Because we were interested in Greenland as a theocracy, I speak chiefly of the religious life of the country. The missionary priests were replaced by regular ones in a little more than half a century after its colonization, about A.D. 982. Around 1200 there were in Greenland 16 churches, a monastery and a nunnery, and 280 farms. Connections with the mainland of North America and with Iceland, Norway, and Britain were numerous, but they became rare after 1400. There are no records, but unrecorded contacts may have been made. Trade with North America, probably Labrador, in house and ship timbers is recorded as late as 1362. Numerous publications record this fact. The Roman Catholic Church was responsible for many of these.

With the coming of the Lutheran movement, however, the Roman Church lost control of all Scandinavian lands, including Iceland and Greenland. From about 1500 to 1721 there were no contacts with Europe. In the latter year there arrived in southwestern Greenland a group bent on saving the ten thousand or so Romanists whom the Lutherans supposed were still there. The Lutheran Church organized a rescue mission from Denmark under a Norwegian clergyman, Hans Egede, who became the national hero of Greenland. Egede's party seems to have expected to find in Greenland Europeans speaking Old Norse and behaving like Roman Catholics. They were naturally bewildered when they found, instead, New World natives dressed in skins and speaking scarcely a Scandinavian word. To account for this they invented the story, until recently believed by many, that some ten thousand Eskimos had killed off the ten thousand Vikings.

What probably really happened was first suggested by an Icelandic missionary, Eigil Thorhallason, who in 1776 published at Copenhagen a Danish work, *Rudera*. This, like earlier and less articulate attempts to be rational about the situation, was at first hushed up, and the belief in massacre by Eskimos prevailed until the Norwegian Fridtjof Nansen published his two-volume *In Northern Mists* in 1911.

We knew in advance that everybody in Greenland except a few newcomers spoke perfect, uncontaminated Eskimo. We knew, too, that, while we might without offense speak of Eskimo language and culture, we must always refer to the people themselves as Greenlanders. To do so would be doubly important now, for that very year the status of the inhabitants was being changed by an act of the Danish Parliament. This act converted the great island into a small political unit, the province of Greenland, represented in Parliament by two elected Greenlanders, one, if not both, of whom must be partly of Eskimo blood, though they would necessarily both speak perfect Danish.

Evelyn and I were not such important personages and showpieces on this Greeland trip as we had been in Iceland in 1949. We did not want to be, for we felt that the new trip was even more of an educational opportunity. We wanted to see rather than be seen, to hear and not be heard, to learn about European (Danish) points of view rather than brag about what we knew was being done in Alaska and Canada.

We sailed from New York to Copenhagen and found the government steamer *Umanak* awaiting us there. During part of our trip we were accompanied by the official head of our party, Prime Minister Eric Eriksen, and the senior representative of the government, Eske Brun. In conversations on the *Umanak* we found evidence to confirm what we had expected: that we were headed for a theocratically governed although democratic land. We knew that the Bishop, and not the King or the Prime Minister, was to the Greenlanders the head of their state. The people we were about to visit spoke primarily Eskimo and secondarily Danish, but in blood they were anything between pure Scandinavian and pure Eskimo, anything from typically Danish to typically Chinese in physique. By the time we returned to Copenhagen, we realized that a good proportion of the more than twenty thousand Greenlanders looked more Scandinavian than oriental.

This was not unnatural. Erik's Icelandic comrades had found no people in the tenth century when they reached Greenland, but they had found traces of human occupation, such as skin boats, stone cooking gear, and various articles that were identified some

twenty years later when Erik and his people began to associate with
Eskimos in Labrador. They fought Viking-style with some of those
whom they met and, also in Viking style, murdered some of those
whom they found sleeping. Nansen said, however, a Scandinavian
could not think so badly of his own ancestors that he could believe
that they had maintained such hostility for very long. Three hundred years after Erik the Red, when the Norsemen were wintering
as hunters north of Melville Bay and up along the Inglefield Gulf
coast, they no doubt had learned to live as comfortably and as safely
there in midwinter as any Eskimo did. As their culture became Eskimo, their speech did likewise, and their European ways began to
be neglected. By the fourteenth century they had enough commerce
with Europe to import the means of causing decay in teeth. Evidence of this has been found in the burials at and near Herjolfsnes,
a southern commercial center that, toward the last, was getting
European-style clothes, evidently from England, and with them
enough cereals to spoil some of their molars.

Up toward and beyond Melville Bay, the skeletons and arti-
facts alike, according to our 1953 informants, were a blend of Eskimo and Scandinavian. This was merely confirmation of what I
had long believed. When we reached the modern capital of Greenland, Godthaab, we confirmed from both monuments and local tradition that from 1500 on there had been little contact with Denmark
and Norway until 1721. Hans Egede never learned good Eskimo and
is therefore no doubt rightly blamed by his son Poul for spreading
much misinformation about contacts between Europeans and Eskimos from 1200 to 1600. Be that as it may, from 1750 to the present, the speech of both the Lutheran and the Moravian clergy has
been so authentically bilingual—Danish-Eskimo or German-Eskimo
—that unintentional misinformation has practically ceased to creep
in. However, while in Greenland, I learned about some intentional
misinformation in cases where Eskimo thinking conflicted with the
Lutheranism of the missionaries. I learned, for instance, about a little deliberate "improving" of the Eskimo language by the great
Samuel Kleinschmidt.

When we reached Godthaab, I was delighted to find a mon-
ument to Kleinschmidt overlooking the city. This seemed to me a
disproof of the saying that a prophet is not without honor save in
his own country. In Greenland this linguist and grammarian evidently stood among the Danes as Samuel Johnson stands in Eng-

land or Noah Webster in New England. The best linguist with whom
I talked, Dean Aage Bugge, knew that in Eskimo thinking a man
has two souls. He knew, too, that Kleinschmidt had tried to destroy
this belief and to establish, as if it were a fact, that there is only
one soul believed in by Eskimos just as by Lutherans. In this case
Kleinschmidt allowed his religion to outweigh his linguistic honesty.
Similarly, Kleinschmidt, for the sake of convenience, tried to get
Eskimos to ignore the fact that their nouns have singular, dual, and
plural forms, as in Greek, not just singular and plural as in Latin.
There are still other things about the Eskimo way of thinking and
speaking that Kleinschmidt must have known and which, if he did,
he consciously falsified in his grammar and dictionary.

The fact that I found things to criticize in the Greenlandic
handling of the Eskimo language did not, however, change my firm
opinion that the governing attitude toward the natives was vastly
better than that found in Alaska and Canada. The Danes, rather
than the English or French, attempt to live up to Paul's precept:
"Prove all things; hold fast that which is good." They have never
tried to Danishize the Eskimos the way we try to Americanize
them in Alaska or Canadianize them in Canada.

True, the Danes have never accepted the Eskimo idea of utiliz-
ing in clothes and houses the principle that cold air is heavy and
warm air light. There is some justification for the Danes in the fact
that the Eskimos did not themselves know and apply this principle
in Greenland as they originally did in northern Alaska and in arctic
Canada, from the Mackenzie River to King William Island. That
Nansen did not learn from the Eskimos to dress against the winter
cold as well as Amundsen did was, in my opinion, because Amundsen lived with the King William Islanders, who knew and practiced
an art that the Greenland Eskimos either never knew or had lost
from association with Europeans before Nansen came along.

The best way to show that the Danes are ahead of other Europeans in dealing with aboriginal Americans is to study what they,
and they alone, have done with that most important of Old World
inventions, the alphabet. Only in Greenland, or in regions influenced
by Greenland, has it been possible to prove that mankind is in-
herently intelligent—not just the European species, or the Chinese,
or any one race, but all mankind. In Canada, for instance, it was,
until recently, believed that it is advisable to destroy the Eskimo
language in order to make room for an English language in which

the Eskimos (and other natives) should be taught to do their think-ing and speaking. Kleinschmidt found that he himself could think better in Eskimo than in any of several languages he knew equally well—among them Danish, German, and Latin. He, as well as many others, tried to get the Eskimos to publish in Eskimo not only re-ligious books but all kinds.

One of the results has been that in Greenland they still publish a weekly Eskimo magazine that is as old as the *Atlantic Monthly*. That this could be done equally well in mainland North America has been testified to in English by Sir Wilfred Grenfell. I have a Victor Hugo novel in Greenlandic Eskimo that was translated by an Es-kimo at Godthaab and printed there—edited, set up, proofread, bound, and distributed. In Alaska or Canada, on the other hand, we are proud if an Eskimo, on a typewriter we have given him, can write us a letter in broken English. Grenfell found fifty years ago that the English in Labrador were getting Eskimos to write letters for them, and even to read English letters that had been written to them. Now, however, with the Moravians out of power and the gov-ernment doing the educating, the Eskimos are as illiterate as if they were English or French.

In Greenland during 1953, I was able to establish as fact, not merely as opinion, that when an Eskimo is allowed to use his own tongue he can do in it what can be done by Danes, English, French, and Russians in their languages. The Danes of today have demon-strated that Kleinschmidt was right in contending that Eskimo is a better language for expressing human thought than any of the African, Asiatic, or European languages he knew equally well.

Evelyn and I were fascinated by Greenland and its people. As we moved south from Greenland to Copenhagen and on to New York we felt an increasing admiration and respect for Denmark as the only nation of which Europeans may be proud because of its way of dealing with the natives of North America. It is interesting to speculate on what might have happened to the Greenland Es-kimos had William H. Seward, the United States Secretary of State who consummated the Alaska purchase in 1867, accepted the recom-mendations of a report made to him in 1868. This report, made at his request, urged that the United States negotiate for the purchase of both Greenland and Iceland.

47 *My New*
Stone Age

At the age of seventy-six, I entered the third Stone Age era of my life as far as diet was concerned. I am still in it as I approach my eighty-third year. Somewhere around my sixty-fifth birthday I began to notice a stiffening in my right knee. By the time I was seventy, the stiffness had begun to spread to other joints. Evidently the exclusively meat diet I had been on for twelve years between 1906 and 1918 and for a year around 1930 had not saved me from the deleterious effects of the carbohydrates I had eaten since 1931. I had been loudly proclaiming the bad effects of "sugar and spice and everything nice," but I had been somewhat lax in practice. I had been so healthy from the time I recovered from typhoid in 1918 that I paid no attention to nutritional rules, including my own, until I had a warning paralytic stroke in 1952.

As such things often do, the stroke came without preliminary warning. One morning I noticed a stiffening of my right cheek and a blurring of my speech. I looked in the mirror and found that the whole right side of my face was sagging. We had no family doctor then, so Evelyn called Dean Rolf C. Syvertsen, of the Dartmouth Medical School, and he called in Dr. Ralph W. Hunter, a practicing physician at the Mary Hitchcock Clinic in Hanover as well as a professor of neurology. Hunter found me overweight at 184 pounds, prescribed dieting, and gave me some drugs for a few days. My face was back to normal within a week; my right arm, which had also been affected, seemed nearly as good as ever for typing though not for handwriting.

Ralph, more a neurologist than nutritionist, pooh-poohed my idea that I ought to cut out carbohydrates in order to lose weight, and directed me to count my calories, as well as my blessings, in that the stroke had not been more serious. I cut down on eating and felt headachy and out of sorts, but I did lose weight until I was below 180. Then my will power broke down, and I began a seesaw of gains and losses. Meanwhile, Hunter sent me to Dr. Thomas P. Anderson of the Department of Physical Medicine in the Hitchcock Clinic. He had me lift sandbags for my stiff right knee, though my left was also stiffening, as were my fingers and other joints. In spite of some benefit from Tom Anderson's prescription of exercise and sandbag lifting, my stiff joints were far from well. My hip joints were so sore that at night the pain in either hip would wake me so that I had to turn and sleep on the other.

One day we were listening to radio bulletins from Denver about President Eisenhower's heart attack. We were especially interested in those which expressed the opinions of my friend Paul Dudley White, of the Harvard Medical School. Every now and then someone other than Dr. White would remark that the President was another victim of the deplorable modern habit of eating too much fat. Most to be avoided, the radio voices said, were animal fats, and especially the hard ones such as mutton. In spite of my sympathy for the President, I began to feel annoyed with this railing against fat mutton, my favorite of all domestic meats. Having lived my healthiest year on a diet that gave me 80 per cent of my calories from animal fats, I became the more restive the more the radio harped on this theme.

My annoyance finally spilled over, and as usual my wife suffered from the spilling. I reminded her that we had a freezer that was only half full, that she knew my favorite food was fat mutton, and that she had often said that in our market this was the cheapest meat. If she herself ate whatever she liked, would she mind if I lived for a few weeks as Charlie Andersen and I had in 1930, wholly on meat and chiefly on mutton? For one thing, I would then have no trouble, on this diet, losing the excess weight that continued to worry Dr. Hunter. I had not thus far succeeded in losing permanently more than five of my 184 pounds. With real or well-simulated cheer, Evelyn agreed.

I loved the fat mutton. As the English do, I like it boiled. We were alone on the farm just then and sometimes I did my own

cooking. When I did, I cooked mutton the way I like it best. I boiled
it the way the Eskimos boil caribou or mountain sheep, putting the
cold fresh meat into cold water, bringing it to a slow boil, and then
setting the pot aside to cool. Then, as Charlie Andersen and I used
to do during our Bellevue year, I would skim the fat off and drink
the broth.

As I have mentioned several times, I do not think it fattening
to take in added calories if they consist of fat meat, provided that
you do your best to avoid carbohydrates and too much lean meat.
As far as I know, the slimming effect of eating fat meat was first
explained by an accredited physician in print through a "Blue
Book," the British Admiralty's account of the first wintering of
Europeans on the north coast of Alaska. The author was naval sur-
geon John Simpson and the publication was an installment of the
British government's account of the search for Sir John Franklin.
That account I quote and paraphrase in my 1946 *Not by Bread
Alone.* When I republished this, slightly augmented, in 1956 as *The
Fat of the Land,* I received a flattering letter from Dr. Richard
Mackarness, a writer on nutrition for British publications who later
wrote a book called *Eat Fat and Grow Slim.* When an American edition was published later, my wife wrote an introduction to it. The
magazine *Coronet* liked this piece so well that they asked her for a
slight rewriting, which would adapt it to their audience. In the
Coronet article she told the story of my return to the eating regime
that had served me so well in the north and had been successfully
tested at Bellevue. Although she had not at first shared the diet, it
affected her as the provider of the household food. As she put it:

> To my astonishment and delight, the Stone Age diet not only
> proved effective in painlessly getting rid of Stef's overweight,
> but turned out to be cheaper, simpler and easier to prepare than
> our regular mixed diet! Far from requiring more time, it took
> much less. Instead of adding housekeeping burdens, it relieved
> me of several. Almost imperceptibly, Stef's diet began to be my
> diet. First through laziness, and then because I really enjoyed the
> food, I too began to eat like a Stone Age Eskimo.

Evelyn also reported on the results of my strict adherence to the
diet:

> At 75, Stef had been having increasing stiffness in one knee
> and soreness in both his hip and shoulder joints. As his knee stiff-
> ened, he began to go up and down stairs one step at a time. One

day, some months after the start of our meat diet, he found to his surprise that he could use both legs with equal facility in climbing the stairs. Astonished, he proceeded down. When he had reached the foot of the stairs, without pain or stiffness, he shouted for me to come and see.

I did indeed shout for Evelyn, because I had just discovered something that I had not forecast to her because I had not foreseen it. The recovery of not only my stiff right knee but of all my joints, blessedly including my typing fingers, had been "magical." It was almost certainly not an instantaneous magic but one that had been in process since I digested the first meal of my renewed Stone Age regimen. Of the several possible explanations for my delayed perception, the most logical is that I was so preoccupied with the step-by-step realization of the expected benefits that they obscured the ones that were not expected. Between 1906 and 1918, I had had no stiff joints from which I could have been relieved; nor had I had any during the Bellevue demonstration. Two or three years before we ceased spending our winters in New York, however, I used to require aisle seats in theaters in order to have a vacant space into which to extend my stiff leg.

In 1930 a good many Americans were afraid of lean meat, believing that animal protein caused hardening of the arteries and increased blood pressure. So highly did they regard fat meat in those days that some of those who feared protein accused Charlie Andersen and me of mitigating or escaping its deleterious effects by surreptitiously living on tallow, instead of on a real meat diet. Times have changed, and today many avoid dietetic fat while they praise rich lean meat. In view of this change in sentiment I no longer avoid milk, cream, and butter. Harmful as they are supposed to be, I indulge myself in them, intending to continue living dangerously and to brave whatever the next change in opinion may cause people to fear. Since 1955, I have aimed at a diet high in fat, medium in protein, low in carbohydrates. If I inadvertently gain two or three pounds, perhaps through inability to dodge a birthday cake at a party, I take them off by eating less lean meat, which I care less for, and more fat meat, which I enjoy most.

As I approach my eighty-third birthday, I work at my typewriter about twelve hours a day—perhaps half that on Sundays. As for my living schedule, I cultivate complete irregularity, going to sleep when I feel drowsy and back to work when I wake up, often sleeping an hour after lunch, five hours around midnight, and two or three hours just before breakfast.

At the original suggestion of Dr. White, samples of my blood have been taken by technical assistants of Dr. Frederick J. Stare, of the Department of Nutrition at the Harvard Medical School. Samples of blood have also been taken by Theodore V. Van Itallie, chief physician of St. Luke's Hospital, New York City. It is enough to say that the results have been contrary to the accepted theory. Blood pressure dropped when I transferred from a mixed diet to a diet high in fat. The cholesterol count also dropped with the long-continued use of a large intake of hard fats, chiefly mutton and some beef.

As to how it seemed to me when at seventy-six I changed from the helter-skelter mixed diet to the present one, it seemed that I became ten or twenty years younger. Except for the results of my stroke, noticeable chiefly in my right hand, my joints are still behaving about as I remember them twenty years ago. Pain disappeared from all joints after a few months of high-fat diet. It has not returned. My hip joints, which used to awaken me several times a night, have not disturbed me since 1955.

I recently had some correspondence with Ernest de Koven Leffingwell, with whose expedition I first went to the Arctic in 1906. Living in California, and then approaching ninety, Leffingwell assured me that he planned to live to be a hundred or die in the attempt. With my health good and my work in the Stefansson Collection and on such projects as this book, calling for all the effort I can give, it seems to me that I cannot do better than adopt Leffingwell's intention as my own.

Postscript

At this point—it is March, 1962—I have not much more to write about my life. There will, of course, be things that I shall, if I live long enough, be sorry I did not remember; and there is also the possibility, of which I am well aware, that, if I do not live long enough, my autobiography—like those of many men who have gone before me—may not appear in print exactly as I wrote it.

The death of an author is his last act and he cannot very well describe it in his autobiography. He can only hope that it will be seemly and perhaps pervaded by the odor of sanctity, which my Divinity School professor, George Foot Moore, the wisest man I ever knew, suggested might be the odor of unwashed linen.

I remember that in the Harvard Divinity School we used to try to be what William James described as "tough-minded." We were skeptics. It was fashionable at the time to say that if you could not find answers to your problems in your religion you could perhaps find them in atheism. We were brash enough to regard Ecclesiastes as the bible of atheism—in fact, some of us said that that book might have had as a subtitle "The Complete Atheist." We were fond of reciting those often-quoted but not always understood words:

I said in mine heart, God shall judge the righteous and the wicked: for *there is* a time there for every purpose and for every work.

I said in mine heart concerning the estate of the sons of men, that God might manifest them, and that they might see that they themselves are beasts.

387

For that which befalleth the sons of men befalleth beasts; even
one thing befalleth them: as the one dieth, so dieth the other;
yea, they have all one breath, so that a man hath no preeminence
above a beast: for all *is* vanity.

All go unto one place; all are of the dust, and all turn to dust
again.

Who knoweth the spirit of man that goeth upward, and the spirit
of the beast that goeth downward to the earth?

Yet, we were not entirely satisfied with the atheism of Ecclesiastes any more than we were satisfied with the religion of the
Bible's other books. We used to assuage our dissatisfaction by saying that the passage "Who knoweth the spirit of man that goeth
upward, and the spirit of the beast that goeth downward to the
earth?" must be a mistranslation, which perhaps should read,
"Who knoweth *whether* the spirit of man goeth upward . . ."

Today, rather than pretend to an atheism that can no more
be proved than can the existence of God, I prefer to think that
agnosticism is the only *modest* faith.

In Divinity School we argued, too, about the disposal of man's
remains, which is perhaps not within the province of the writer of
an autobiography, since it must, if managed with propriety, follow
his death. Yet, we did discuss this matter and I remember the discussion. Should a man be returned to earth in the form, though
without the spirit, in which he lived, or should he be cremated?
After all, man, we supposed from what we knew of science, has a
touch of fish in his ancestry, and have not fishes established the most
practical system of disposal of bodily remains? I do not mean the
sort of disposal that the Lord arranged for Jonah, for Jonah, as
perhaps befits a prophet, turned out to be indigestible. Real fish,
not designed for special purposes, must have very good digestions,
or they would not have lived long enough to become our ancestors.
As I recall it, we, being descendants of agriculturalists of the Near
and Middle East, as well as of fish, thought cremation a marked
waste of good fertilizer. Since we could not swallow each other
whole as fishes do, it seemed better to let the earth take care of
coming generations by swallowing us.

As theological students concerned with the problem of death,
we knew the Bible and we knew Shakespeare, but we did not know
the thoughts of a man like Darwin about his own life and death.

They had not been printed in 1904. Mark Twain had not published his thoughts on the same matter, for he was still alive. Now I know what those men thought, although I have no assurance that what they left in print has not been tampered with. I presume that I know what I think.

The only souvenir I ever kept from any expedition is an engraved silver platter presented to me in 1913. The face of the platter reads: "Presented by the Executive Council on behalf of the people of British Columbia to Vilhjalmur Stefansson Esq. Head of the Canadian Arctic Expedition on the occasion of the departure of the SS *Karluk* from Victoria, B.C. for the Arctic Ocean June 17th 1913." Under the rubric of "Scientific Staff" the reverse of the platter has fifteen names. As I type this at 5 :35 A.M. on the eleventh of March, 1962, I know that only five of these fifteen are still living: the cartographers Chipman and Cox, the anthropologist Jenness, the magnetician McKinley, and the geologist O'Neill. As we worked together in the north, we had our agreements and our differences, and as we look to the last chapter of our lives, we shall no doubt have similar differences and agreements.

Whatever others may think after reading these pages, I know what I have experienced, and I know what it has meant to me.

Wherefore I perceive that there is nothing better, than that a man should rejoice in his own works; for that is his portion: for who shall bring him to see what shall be after him?

Postlude

by Evelyn Stefansson

Stef's wish to achieve a seemly death was granted. On a hot day in late August, an old and distinguished friend of Greenland and Copenhagen days, Eske Brun, was our dinner guest, and we had invited all the Dartmouth polar and Scandinavian folk to come in afterward and greet him. During dinner Stef was in marvelous form, merry and witty, and, stimulated by Eske, a veteran of thirty Greenland years, he turned the conversation to medieval falconry (the best white falcons came from Greenland long before Columbus discovered America), to Greenland archaeology (Eske brought news of a churchyard discovery containing Leif Eriksson's skeleton), and to the infinite variety of Iceland's literary forms. Flushed with good wine and delight in each other's company, we moved to the living room for coffee. I poured into the old white ironstone egg cups we used for afterdinner coffee and passed them. Stef was about to take a sip when, with a trembling hand that splashed coffee, he painstakingly placed the cup back on the table. Then, in the silent language all well-married couples know, he sent a message, urgent as a cry, for help. Following unspoken directions, I rose quietly and, as I approached, discovered that he was silent because he was unable to speak. I offered my arm, and as we staggered out of the room to the hall, I called over my shoulder for Sven Gunderson, who heads our famous Hanover clinic. It was not news when he whispered seconds later, "He's had a shock," using the New England expression for a stroke. Since Stef had just suffered a massive stroke with its accompanying paralysis, it was theoretically impossible for him to have risen and staggered from the room. His enormous dignity, which would not permit him to ruin a perfect evening by collapsing in front of his guests, combined with a strong act of will, had powered his exit and enabled him to do at the close of his life what he had often done during it—the impossible! Blessedly, Stef struggled in a deep coma for less than a week, until the early morning of August 26, when he was what the doctors term dead. For me, the moment of his leave-taking was his poignant call for help, one of the few received in the last quarter-century for which I was unable to provide any aid whatever.

The seemliness of Stef's death was that on his last night with us, his wits were sharp, and he was able to amuse, instruct, delight, and draw each of us out, making the evening a memorable one. Many of our evenings were like that. Stef had the gift of making conversation go whether he held the floor or insisted that a visitor take it.

Perhaps Stef learned to love a party from the Eskimos. No formal affair was needed to make him happy; on the contrary, a small group of good conversationalists and a little drink and food (meat, of course, for Stef), neither of which had to be elegant or even very good, were sufficient. Any excuse would do, an out-of-town visitor was a favorite; so was good news of any sort, or even the *prospect* of good news. The philosophy behind celebrating the possibility of something good happening was that, if it didn't happen, you at least had the celebration. If a book contract was signed, if he received an advance from a publisher, if a royalty check fatter than expected arrived, if it was publication day of a new book, a celebration was called for. "Bookdays" were as important as birthdays in our family.

I first met Vilhjalmur Stefansson while I was studying art at Washington Irving High School in New York. A teacher who befriended me and a classmate who was a member of the famous Adler family of Yiddish actors, both lived in the Village not far from school, and it became my second home. Stef lived in Greenwich Village, and before we met I was already familiar with his tall figure and his distinctive walk, something like the rolling gait of a sailor walking the deck in a heavy sea. Hatless and coatless whatever the weather, his thick mane of white hair blowing in the wind, he was a person few failed to notice as they passed him on the street or, indeed, anywhere.

The year was 1930, the heyday of Romany Marie's. Marie, a gifted, handsome Rumanian gypsy with a musical, almost bass voice, had a genius for friendship and for bringing interesting people together. Painters, writers, actors, diplomats, dancers, musicians, and inventors flocked round her. Some were already famous, like Stef, Eugene O'Neill, or Fannie Hurst; others were to become so. Marie created an atmosphere so friendly and natural that with complete confidence a poet might read a new poem, a composer play a piano piece, a dancer work out some new choreography, with no response from Marie's customers except interest, admiration, and encouragement. It was here that I first found myself, to my own surprise, singing folk songs publicly to an audience of friends and strangers. It was here, too, that I met Stef.

In 1939, I was between jobs when we met by chance, and Stef obtained a position for me working on the Iceland Pavilion of the World's Fair. When that was finished, Stef suggested that I come and work for him. I protested that I was a puppeteer and display maker, used to working with my hands, not my brains. I knew nothing of the intellectual techniques I imagined necessary to be one of his staff members. Stef said that I had the two most important qualities needed in a good researcher, intellectual curiosity and enthusiasm. I admitted to owning these, but countered that I could not even type. Characteristically, Stef said, "If you will go to typing school, I will pay the tuition." Two weeks later, with a wobbly knowledge of touch typing and considerable trepidation, I arrived at the Stefansson Library. Olive Wilcox, Stef's gifted assistant, put me to work. I sniffed the atmosphere at 67 Morton Street and it smelled and tasted like champagne. As the newest member of the staff, I was assigned the most menial chores, but I considered it a privilege to do anything as long as I was part of this exciting new world. One of my duties was to prepare the staff lunches. My reward was conversation, good every day, but gorgeous when we had some distinguished explorer like Sir Hubert Wilkins, an anthropologist like Herbert Spinden, a scientist, or a military man as guest. They seemed to me then the most remarkable, interesting, and romantic people in the world, and they still do.

I lived near the library on St. Luke's Place and honestly enjoyed working overtime whenever there was need. Often I found myself working into the dinner hour, with other staff members gone and only Stef remaining. Sometimes we would dine at a nearby

Italian restaurant and go back to work until midnight. We drifted
into an easy arrangement whereby if neither of us had a date we
would dine together.

We were comfortable with each other, and for the first time I
learned the peculiar pleasure of being both attuned to and quiet
with another person. Apparently, Stef enjoyed it too. Later, when
he asked me to marry him, I was more shocked than thrilled. The
shock was composed of surprise (everybody *knew* Stef was a peren-
nial bachelor), knowledge of the difference in our ages, which then
seemed tremendous (although it bothered Stef not at all and me
less than expected), and Stef's stepping out of his assigned role.
Then I was shocked again, this time at myself, at the speed with
which I was able to shift gears and consider the strange idea first
with equanimity, then with excited interest. But I was cautious too.
I had been married before and soon divorced; I was determined not
to make another mistake. I think we were both astonished at how
quickly and permanently we engaged each other emotionally and
intellectually. Stef discovered my "intellect," such as it is, and it
would have been difficult to decide which of us had more fun as he
led me farther and deeper into his world of books and learning,
always graciously making me feel that I had something to contribute as well as take. He was a gifted teacher, and I had been
deprived. His need to teach, my need, first to learn and then to
pleasure myself by pleasing him, became inseparable. I can still
catch my breath remembering how thrilling the steady, cumulative unfolding of intellectual discovery became. In a kind of turn-
about I introduced Stef to the simple joys of having a home, of
sitting at a dinner table till midnight over pot after pot of espresso
coffee, and taking most of Sunday for breakfast in front of the fire
with the Sunday papers. For most of his life Stef had known work
for seven days a week; now he learned something about relaxation
and play. He learned to relax, but he never really enjoyed what
other people call play.

Despite dire predictions from almost every quarter, it was soon
obvious to all that we had a good marriage that was going to work.
I found happiness that I never dreamed existed, a purpose to my
life, an opportunity to grow and be needed, but above all, the
affection and devoted love of a remarkable man. There were trials
and frustrations, too, of course—no life is immune from them—but
they were by far the smaller fraction of the whole.

Part of Stef's teaching skill was anticipating the proper moment for me to absorb something new. He would design with cunning a problem calculated to simultaneously excite my imagination and take me one step farther into arctic lore. He constantly asked provocative questions that made me determined to discover the answers for myself. Later, when I directed the Arctic Seminar at Dartmouth, I was to remember the technique and make use of it, although I was unaware of its being a technique when I first encountered it.

By the late 1940s the Stefansson Library occupied four apartments and a ground-floor store in the Morton Street building. The staff numbered twenty—secretaries, researchers, writers, translators, librarians, and clerks. As library and staff had grown, Stef had simply taken one apartment after another. He would install bookshelves and office furniture and move new staff members in. When the apartment was full, the process was repeated. This unorthodox office arrangement was partly a result of wartime apartment shortages and was often awkward, since the apartments were on different floors. Eventually, we found on St. Luke's Place, right next door to where we lived, two floors of a beautiful old building with wonderfully tall ceilings. We lined the walls with bookshelves, and by judicious assignment the separate rooms provided private offices as well as a handsome, large reading room in the front parlor where half a dozen researchers could work in comfort. We were a polar-information factory, supplying both commercial and government agencies with reports ranging in length from a telephone call to a five-million word report.

When the Office of Naval Research withdrew its support of *Encyclopedia Arctica,* Stef decided to look for a permanent home for what had mushroomed into the largest polar library in the world and which cost a small fortune to house and keep up. After sounding out several universities in the United States and Canada, we chose Dartmouth, partly because it was only thirty-five miles from our farm. Stef had a long and happy relationship with the college which began in 1929 when he gave a series of extraordinarily popular lectures that each day had to be moved to a larger hall until he finished up in Webster Hall, the largest auditorium on the campus. In 1941, when we were newly married, we spent ten enchanting winter days in Hanover while Stef lectured, built snowhouses in the center of the green, and met with students and faculty. This was the first time I saw him in what was later to become a familiar setting, surrounded by a circle of students sitting on the floor and asking questions, with Stef, sparkling, unorthodox, humorous, making them laugh, but also making them learn. Dartmouth generously offered us free housing for our books in their famous Baker Library and working space for the two of us. So we became members of the Dartmouth College family.

Moving from New York to a beautiful but comparatively tiny New England town was probably the greatest single hurdle we had to clear in more than two decades of marriage. It was the equivalent of radical surgery for Stef to leave Olive Wilcox. He had dictated most of his books to her, and she was better informed than he was about his own affairs. A small comfort was that she would be in the neighborhood during summer vacation time. Parting with other staff members who had been with him for many years was also difficult. I was apprehensive about adjusting to small-town life after well-informed friends told me that Hanover was a "man's town" with few work or recreational opportunities for women. Fortunately for me, my friends were at least partially wrong. Hanover offered me many fascinating opportunities that the big city could not. Never having been to college, I had a lovely time auditing courses, studying Danish in preparation for our Greenland trip, brushing up on my Russian for a solitary trip to Siberia in 1959, singing madrigals and Bach cantatas, and acting in student productions of Shakespeare and Shaw. I *loved* Hanover!

It was in December, 1951, that we made the move. Once before we had moved the library from Morton Street's constellation of small apartments, around the corner to the single St. Luke's Place establishment. The experience had been gruesome but instructive. This time I decided to utilize the move to reorganize and rearrange the books. First, I made a plan on paper showing the revised arrangement we would follow at Dartmouth. Then two sets of identical numbered tags were made for every bookshelf in New York. The moving men were instructed to put books into their boxes in the exact order that they were on the shelf and to put only the contents of a single shelf in one box. A numbered tag was tied to the box. All duplicate tags were collected, and after great pondering a single tag was laid on a single shelf in the Dartmouth stacks, but in a new position. When the books arrived in Hanover, the tag on the box would be matched with the tag on the shelf and, theoretically at least, the library would be rearranged. It actually worked.

I supervised the loading of the first huge trailer truck and, when it was filled, went by train to Hanover. When the truck arrived, I was waiting at the freight entrance of the library with a pride of vigorous Dartmouth Outing Club volunteers who would unload and shelve the books to save costs. Each student had a mover's dolly. A box of books would be put on it, he would match tags, shelve the books, return to the loading platform for another box, and do it all over again and again. It was a wonderful introduction to Dartmouth for me, for these were a remarkable breed of young men who gaily made a party out of a hard job of work. When at last the enormous truck was empty, the exhausted men returned to their dormitories and I went back to New York on the train to repeat the process. It took three trailer trucks, each the size of a railway car, to move the entire library. By the time the books were shelved, odds and ends tidied, and Stef installed and working at his desk, I thought I had never been so tired in all my life. Stef, typing away with all ten long fingers, was framed by the window where he sat, and became a familiar sight to students changing classes for more than a decade. He was visible from early morning until dinnertime (he did not eat lunch) and, more often than not, in the evening too.

Now students and faculty began to visit and use the library. All were welcome. Stef could no more have refused anyone access to the library, even curiosity seekers, than he could help sharing food or money.

Within a year a Dartmouth alumnus, Albert Bradley, '15, bought the library and gave it to the college. We had the books alone (not the forty thousand pamphlets, the old and new maps or the card catalogue, the latter by far the most expensive single component) appraised by Charles Everitt, a famous New York Americana expert and book dealer. Stef had agreed that if Dartmouth could find someone to pay half of the appraised price we would give the other half. This was done and everyone was pleased, Mr. Bradley, the Stefanssons, Baker Library staff, and all the northern-minded students and faculty. I was given a half-time job looking after what became known officially as the Stefansson Collection. Later I became a full-fledged, full-time librarian, later still a member of the faculty.

Stef was a popular lecturer on the campus and loved to fill in for a professor who was ill or called out of town. He talked in the geography and anthropology departments, to medical school students about diet and cold-weather medicine and to the Outing and other club audiences about Eskimo hunting methods or the incredible intricacies of the Eskimo language. No matter how busy he was, Stef would always stop what he was doing to listen to a student or a young scientist in need of help. He honored them by listening with complete attention and sometimes overwhelmed them with the fullness of his answers. He must have given away a ton of his own books and those of others to men who could not afford to buy them and another ton to those he knew would be pleased to receive them. Stef's own wants were few, but a book he did not own, especially one he had searched for unsuccessfully, was something that made his eyes sparkle. He used to boast that he knew nothing about stocks or bonds (and how true that was!) but that he did know polar books. I never check a catalogue without being reminded that books he bought for one to ten dollars are now being sold for hundreds.

Stef was an inspiration to a generation of Dartmouth men. A surprising number made their careers in some aspect of northern work, and one, Jack Tuck, ended up in charge of the IGY Station at the South Pole. Stef was a conspicuous figure on the campus, still hatless and coatless, despite the bitter New Hampshire winter temperatures, and he was sometimes confused with his very old friend, Robert Frost. Both were big, white-haired, gentle, strong, and magnetic. Both were poets. By his own definition Stef qualified in that category, for he once wrote: "The explorer is the poet of action and exploring is the poetry of deeds."

Stef carried on a tremendous correspondence with a vast number of people. He never threw out a scrap of paper and carefully preserved carbon copies of all his letters, even those written from the Arctic. He would often have half a dozen carbon copies of a letter made and send them to as many people, involving the maximum number possible in an information quest, trying to create subsidiary search fires from the sparks he was sending out. If information eluded him, he remembered that it was missing and started up the search again the moment he met or heard of someone who might know the answer. It was this tenacity, combined with a concern for getting at the truth of any matter, plus his memory, which could sort and put together information from the unlikeliest sources, that was responsible for his success as a scholar. He was far prouder of having been the president of the History of Science Society than of all the gold medals he had received. Stef's correspondence dating from 1900 to 1962 fills well over a hundred vertical letter-file cabinet drawers. It contains exchanges with explorers like Fridtjof Nansen, Ernest Shackleton, and Dick Byrd; with literary figures like Sir James Barrie and Sir Arthur Conan Doyle; and political figures like Teddy Roosevelt, Sr., and Jr. This is a still largely untapped source of scientific and literary research, for it is uncatalogued and only through serendipity do we discover its most valuable items.

Not long after we moved to Hanover, the Canadian government, discovering through aerial surveys that the northeastern corner of Victoria Island in the Arctic was a sizable separate island, decided to name it Stefansson Island. It was a wonderful excuse for celebrating, and that we did, all week, with parties of several sizes and kinds. That Stef, who had named so many islands, bays, and straits after others, had never had a place in the north named after him (Wilkins named something for him in the Antarctic) was the result of several factors, the most important of which was Rudolph M. Anderson, second-in-command of the Canadian Arctic Expedition of 1913–1918. Anderson had started his career brilliantly at the University of Iowa and had done well on the Stefansson-Anderson expedition of 1908–1912. But after he married, his attitude toward Stef changed and eventually became extremely bitter and hostile, climaxing in a near-mutiny on the Canadian expedition. When it was over, Anderson remained in Canada instead of returning home to the United States. By working hard at the job, he managed to infect the Geological Survey and the majority of the Civil Service with his point of view, which was that Stef was a charlatan, spendthrift, and publicity hound whose scientific achievements, if any, were accidental digressions from his self-glorification. Stef's Canadian friends believed on the other hand that he was a great explorer, a man of vision, often too far ahead of his time to be understood by less gifted contemporaries, and therefore subject to attack. They thought him an articulate spokesman for the view favoring the development of the Canadian Arctic and tried to support and encourage him. Rifts developed and departments split, tempers got out of control and into the newspapers, some declared Stef was Canada's enemy number one for trying to deceive Canadians into believing that their northland had value when everyone knew it to be worthless.

Evidence of the bitter feeling against Stef was typified in the affair of the Rideau Club. He had been blackballed when first proposed for membership. Years later when a letter came offering him honorary membership in the club, I asked him if he would refuse the offer—after all, it was a bit tardy. The chances of Stef's using the club were nil, since he had suffered his second stroke and walked with difficulty, aided by a cane, but he replied, "Oh no, I will accept. It is a friendly gesture on their part. It would give me no pleasure to refuse and it will give pleasure to some members if I accept." This was typical of Stef's refusal to nurse a grievance and was perhaps a key to his success. In all the years I knew him, when the Anderson feud came up in conversation, he never attacked Anderson, and the fact that Anderson attacked him never blinded him to Anderson's good qualities. Although Anderson was the aggressor in the feud, Stef always felt sorry for Anderson rather than for himself, which doubtless further infuriated Anderson. Anderson spent much adrenaline and energy hating Stef, leaving that much less for work and for fulfilling his early promise. Stef never spent emotions wastefully and he husbanded his energies for his work.

During the early years of our marriage so many good things happened to me so often I wanted everyone to share my joy. We had heard from friends that it was really Anderson's wife who had stirred up trouble between him and Stef and that Anderson had been heard to say wistfully something about the possibility of making up with Stef. I saw Anderson at the first Alaska Science Conference. He was tall and lean and must have been handsome in his youth, but now he looked stooped and sad. I was touched by his appearance and said to Stef, "Suppose he wants to make up; wouldn't it be a pity if he had no opportunity? Help him, Stef, go over and say hello." Stef was reluctant, but he was in love and wanted to please me. He walked across the room to Anderson, I following in his wake, slightly exalted in my new role of peacemaker. Stef approached Anderson and held out his hand. Anderson turned on his heel and walked in the opposite direction. I wanted to die, and on the spot discarded forever the role of Pollyanna the glad girl. It was the only time I saw Anderson and the last time Stef did.

All this is by way of prelude to why we celebrated Stefansson Island Week. It was not just one more honor for Stef, who had received so many, but rather it symbolized the complete acceptance of Stef by a brand-new generation of young Canadians who did not care a twig about the old feud. They had discovered Stef for themselves and found that he had something to say to them and that he had been correct about a great many things that most Canadians had refused to believe at the time he said them. Stef had won a battle he thought lost. That's what we celebrated.

Comparing Stef's written words with my memory of his actual personality, I most miss two qualities that elude description: his personal warmth and his sense of humor. The former touched all who met him and, like radioactive carbon, was given off at a steady rate whether he was talking to our cleaning lady or the King of Denmark. It is impossible to describe, and had to be felt. To try to convey something of his humor may be equally impossible, but like cartographers who know they cannot *accurately* portray a spherical earth on a flat sheet of paper, they continue to try, and so will I.

Stef had a way of larding his conversation with one-line epigrams, which were delivered effortlessly. When he was in good form he could manage one per paragraph, and the cumulative effect would be to have us weeping helplessly with laughter. A few examples that come quickly to mind are: "False modesty is better than none," "A land may be said to be discovered the first time a European, preferably an Englishman, sets foot on it," and "Women knit in order to have something to occupy their minds while they are thinking."

He liked riddles and the last one he coined was: "What is the difference between unethical and ethical advertising? Unethical advertising uses falsehoods to deceive the public; ethical advertising uses truth to deceive the public."

Stef had an enormous store of the jokes and good lines of others. One of his favorites was that of Robert Ingersoll: "My brain may not be the best brain in the world, but it is so conveniently located for home use."

Stef was a skilled marksman, but he never hunted except for food. He took no pleasure in killing for sport and did not admire those who did. A well-known club composed chiefly of wealthy sportsmen, most of whom look down on what they call "pot hunters," often asked Stef to address them. Stef, knowing the difference in their points of view, refused, but once a close friend who was a member persisted and Stef agreed. After his talk the usual group remained to exchange hunting stories. The conversation turned to treachery among animals, and one member spoke up with,

"Now take the loon, *there's* a treacherous bird for you." Stef with rising irritation asked, "Just what do you mean by *treacherous?*" "I'll tell you," said the clubman with some passion. "I was out hunting and shot a loon, wounding but not killing him. As I closed in to finish him off that treacherous bird attacked me, right here on the cheek with his beak, why I might have lost an eye! That's what I mean by treacherous."

Once Stef and I went to a large dinner party at Gjon Mili's huge photographic studio in a loft on 23d Street in New York. Before dinner the famous Budapest String Quartet was to play. They did, superbly, a Mozart quartet, a Beethoven quartet, and finally a long one by Brahms. The appreciative audience applauded wildly and eventually prevailed on the group to play an encore. They chose another long Brahms quartet and, as the closing chords died away, Stef leaned over and asked the name of the piece. Charmed at his interest, for the only music he really liked was primitive and folk music, I told him. Closing his eyes with a look of relief on his face, he said he would remember it always. Delighted but puzzled, I asked why. "Because if ever I am condemned to death and have only an hour to live, as a last request I would ask to have this Brahms quartet played, then that hour would certainly seem endless."

All the scientists of Stef's earlier days, including the great Fridtjof Nansen and Robert E. Peary, believed that there was no life in the polar sea once you went some way out from shore. The Eskimos agreed with the scientists, but Stef persisted in his belief that there *had* to be animal life there. He said, "I have examined all the arguments in favor of no life in the Arctic Sea, and it seems to me that they are the kind of arguments that would appeal to a philosopher but would *not* appeal to a fish."

A long time ago a bright young man named Robert Lewis Taylor came to write a *New Yorker* profile about Stef. After supposedly reading all of Stef's books and interviewing his friends, he asked, "Tell me, Dr. Stefansson, have you ever been to the North Pole?" Stef, who thought the question a stupid one for someone who had been studying his works, replied, "NO, I'm a scientist, not a tourist." For about twenty years Stef standardized on this answer when anyone else asked him the same question, which they often, alas, did. In 1957, I went to Alaska to get material for a new edition of my *Here Is Alaska,* and flew by way of Copenhagen across the

North Pole to Anchorage on one of the first SAS North Pole flights. When I returned, Stef after greeting me said, ''Now at last I have a new answer when a newspaperman asks me, 'Tell me, Dr. Stefansson, have you ever been to the North Pole.' I can look him straight in the eye and say, 'No, but my wife has.' ''

Stef who loved to laugh and make others laugh would approve of our ending his book on a happy note. The rest of what I have to say about him must wait for another time and requires a volume to itself.

Evelyn Stefansson
Washington, D.C.

Index

Adams, Cyrus, 100, 101
Adamson, Hans C., 352–353
Adventure of Wrangel Island, The (Stefansson), 263
Agassiz, Alexander, 55
Akeley, Carl Ethan, 252, 296
Alaska (schooner), 155, 165, 188
Alaska Highway, 329
Alden, Henry Mills, 100
Alexander, Scott E., 346
Alexander (whaler), 75–76, 78, 105, 107, 110
Allen, Gertrude, 147, 222
American Aeronautical Society, 294
American Geographical Society, 59, 100, 101, 216
American Language, The (Mencken), 58
American Meat Institute, 286–287
American Museum of Natural History, 100, 101, 107, 110, 133, 134, 135, 145, 146
Amery, Leopold, S., 229, 260
Among Friends (Crothers), 41
Amundsen, Roald, 72, 73, 136–138, 140, 142, 143, 215–216, 239, 241, 380
Andersen, Karsten (Charlie), 200, 201, 288–292, 295, 368–369, 383, 384, 385
Anderson, John, 4–5, 46, 68, 69
Anderson, Mary, 46

Anderson, Rudolph Martin, 101, 102, 104, 106, 108, 109–110, 124–126, 131–132, 215, 216, 246, 398, 399
  Canadian Arctic Expedition, 146, 149, 150–152, 153, 154, 155, 157–162, 164–165, 188, 196
Anderson, Thomas P., 383
Anderson, William, 46
Andreasen, Ole, 163, 166, 167, 174, 179, 184, 185, 189, 191, 192, 220, 224, 346
Anglo–American Polar Expedition, 59–62, 65–76, 77–90, 91–98, 100
Archbold, Richard, 318
Arctic Institute of North America, 359
Arctic Manual (Stefansson), 325, 350
Arey, Ned, 92, 94
Arngrimsson, Friman, 10, 375–376
Arnold, H. H. (Hap), 316, 344, 350–351, 353, 356
Arnold, Milton W., 345
Asatsiak (Eskimo), 156

Baidukov (flier), 317
Baird, Bill, 334
Baird, Evelyn, 333–337
Baldwin, Evelyn Briggs, 59
Balestier, Beatty, 270, 271
Barnes, C. E., 346
Barrie, James, 398
Bartlett, Robert A., 150, 154–155, 187, 206, 216–217, 348

STACK
B
St322s

The Travels of
Vilhjalmur Stefansson
in Northwestern
North America

SCALE IN MILES